SUDDENLY SOMETHING CLICKED

Walter Murch has been editing film and designing soundtracks for sixty years. His work includes all three *Godfather* films, *THX-1138*, *American Graffiti*, *The Conversation*, *Julia*, *Apocalypse Now*, *The Unbearable Lightness of Being*, *The English Patient*, *The Talented Mr. Ripley*, *Cold Mountain* and *Jarhead*. He also co-wrote and directed the feature film *Return to Oz* (1985) for Disney, and has recently co-written and edited two feature documentaries: *Particle Fever* (2013) about the search for the Higgs Boson; and *Coup 53* (2019) about the 1953 MI6-CIA coup against the democratic government of Iran. He is the author of *In the Blink of an Eye* (1995), his previous book about film editing, and is the subject of two other books, Michael Ondaatje's *The Conversations* (2002) and Charles Koppelman's *Behind the Seen* (2005). He has been nominated for nine Academy Awards and nine BAFTAs, winning three of each. He has been married to Muriel 'Aggie' Murch for sixty years, and they have four children and three grandchildren.

WALTER MURCH

SUDDENLY SOMETHING CLICKED

The Languages of Film Editing and Sound Design

faber

First published in the UK and the USA in 2025
by Faber & Faber Ltd
The Bindery, 51 Hatton Garden,
London EC1N 8HN

Printed in Latvia

A CIP record for this book
is available from the British Library

ISBN 978–0–571–32885–7

Printed and bound in the EU on FSC® certified paper in line with our continuing
commitment to ethical business practices, sustainability and the environment.
For further information see faber.co.uk/environmental-policy

Our authorised representative in the EU for product safety is
Easy Access System Europe, Mustamäe tee 50, 10621 Tallinn, Estonia
gpsr.requests@easproject.com

2 4 6 8 10 9 7 5 3 1

Cinema is the only art whose birthday is known to us.
– Béla Balázs

———————————

To Aggie:

And all the time, my love: you too are there, beneath the word, above
the syllable to underscore and stress
the vital rhythm. One heard a woman's dress
rustle in days gone by. I've often caught
the sound and sense of your approaching thought.
And all in you is youth, and you make new
by quoting them, old things I made for you.

– Vladimir Nabokov, in dedication to his wife Véra,
for the novel *Pale Fire*

CONTENTS

PART TWO: SOUND DESIGN

INTRODUCTION

In late June of 1896 the Lumière brothers brought their *cinématographe* and reels of moving photographs to Nizhny Novgorod, 400 km east of Moscow. The city's only available venue was Aumont's café, an elegant brothel run by the French–Algerian impresario Charles Solomon. A bedsheet was strung up at one end of the central salon and the *cinématographe* installed at the other, while Nizhny's great and good (and not-so-great and not-so-good) crowded together to experience something they had never seen before: moving photography, projected onto a bedsheet in a brothel.

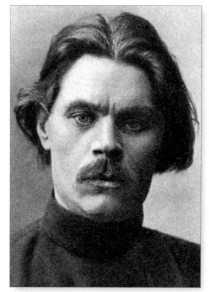

Maxim Gorky, then a twenty-eight-year-old reporter (later to become the novelist for whom the city of Nizhny would be renamed),[1] was in the audience taking notes. The *cinématographe*'s lamp ignited and a still image illuminated the sheet: 'A street scene in Paris,' Gorky wrote.[2] He was not impressed: 'I had seen this many times before.' But then the image fluttered into life: people, horses, carriages going about their end-of-the-nineteenth-century business. Despite the fact that he was seeing a photograph move for the first time, Gorky remained unimpressed: 'This is not life but its shadow, it is not motion but its soundless spectre.'

In his article, published a few days later, Gorky would describe the experience as 'A Kingdom of Shadows: before your eyes, life is surging, but it is a life deprived of words and shorn of the living spectrum of colours – a grey, soundless, bleak and dismal life.' Gorky's remarkable recoil from the miracle of moving photography was an early case of the *uncanny valley*: that queasy feeling inspired by an image that closely simulates reality

1. Under Stalin's dictatorship the name was changed to Gorky in 1932, and then reverted to Nizhny Novgorod in 1990, after the collapse of the USSR.

2. Gorky was wrong. It was a street scene in Lyon, home city of the Lumière brothers. Thanks to Denis Shiryaev, digital technology and AI, we can now see this shot in colour and with sound: https://vimeo.com/1010893555 (QR code on right).

but doesn't go quite far enough, as if the image were, zombie-like, alive and dead at the same time.

But there was something else, which Gorky mentioned only in passing: the instantaneous cut from one shot to the next. He had been watching the Lyonnaise street scene, when . . .

> . . . **suddenly something clicks**, everything vanishes and a train appears on the screen. It speeds straight at you – watch out! It seems as though it will plunge into the darkness in which you sit.

What he had heard – that *click* – and what he saw – *everything vanishes and a train appears* – was a splice in the film, jerking the audience instantly 350 km from the streets of Lyon to a station on the Côte d'Azur, where a train was just arriving.[3] This was the first time in history that anyone had written about the phenomenon of the cut from one moving image to another, yet this barely remarked-upon moment was the tiny seed that would grow, like a vigorously spreading, multi-trunked tree, into the only truly new art form of cinema: *montage*.

At the end of his article, Gorky wondered what this shadowy new medium would ever be used for. His conclusion: violence, pornography and domestic squabbles . . .

> For example, they might show a picture titled: *As She Undresses*, or *Madame at Her Bath*, or *A Woman in Stockings*. They could also depict a sordid squabble between a husband and wife . . . [or] impale a fashionable parasite upon a picket fence, as is the way of the Turks, photograph him, then show it.

If Gorky were alive today to survey all the films produced in our present century, would he be gratified or depressed to discover that his prediction had been proved largely correct?

> The full text of Gorky's article (in English) is at https://www.mcsweeneys.net/articles/contest-winner-36-black-and-white-and-in-color (QR code on left)

I suspect part of Gorky's initial disappointment, though he did not know it, was the absence of editing – montage – as a storytelling language. Even Louis Lumière famously (although perhaps apocryphally) said cinema was 'an invention without a future'. Why? I would guess because the energising, catalytic possibilities of montage

---

3. In pre-digital days, the extra thickness of the film at the point of the splice caused a loud *click* as it went through the projector.

had not yet been glimpsed, by him or hardly anyone else.[4] It was eventually to come, of course, along with Gorky's longed-for sound and colour, but the twelve-year infancy and childhood of motion pictures, between 1889 and 1901, were largely spent wandering through the world's brothels, music halls and fairground sideshows, amusing and astonishing audiences with single-shot events like *The Sneeze*, *The Kiss*, *Train Arriving at the Station*, *The Corbett–Fitzsimmons Fight*, *Peeping Tom at the Seaside* and, of course, at Gorky's suggestion, *Madame at Her Bath* – somewhat like the early cat-video years of YouTube. Motion pictures and cinema were not born simultaneously.[5]

Then, in around 1901, at the age of twelve, motion photography began to discover and exploit the intoxicating, virtually sexual power of montage. A character runs out of one shot and enters the next, photographed at a different location at a different time (perhaps even prior to the shot that preceded it), and the audience believes that the action is continuous. There was no guarantee that this trick would work: the human brain could have been wired in such a way that the sudden jump from one moving-reality space to another would trigger a disorienting nausea, even seizures. Instead, audiences not only quickly grasped the grammar of continuity, but came to enjoy, and then hunger for, those sudden and often delightfully surprising juxtapositions – visual chord changes, so to speak.[6]

As a result, Gorky's early disappointment turned to enthusiasm, and he permitted his 1906 novel *Mother* to be filmed by Vsevolod Pudovkin. The style and success of that film was, in turn, globally influential in the revolutionary way it established character and mood through dialectical montage – the Kuleshov effect – a technique at

---

4. The exception was William Dickson, the visionary inventor of motion pictures at Edison's Menlo Park laboratory. In his 1895 book on the history of the Kinetograph, Dickson – in spite of the limited evidence at the time – saw an unbounded future for cinema: sound, colour, naval battles, musicals, pageantry. He even accurately predicted that 'the latest doings on Mars, Saturn, and Venus will be recorded by enterprising kinetographic reporters'.

5. Georges Méliès, starting in 1896, made great use of the 'stop trick' – a jump cut that created the illusion of transformation, such as in *Vanishing Lady*, where Jehanne d'Alcy (later to be Méliès's wife) is turned into a skeleton and back again. He also made the single-shot *After the Ball* in 1897, whose subject matter is Jehanne undressing, as per Gorky's suggestion. But Méliès did not exploit continuity editing as such, preferring two-to-three-second dissolves between fixed tableaux, as in his *Cinderella* (1899) and *Joan of Arc* (1900).

6. There were exceptions, of course. Béla Balázs recounts the experience of a young Siberian woman on seeing her first film, a comedy: 'Oh it was horrible, horrible! Human beings were torn to pieces, and the heads thrown one way, and the bodies the other, and the hands somewhere else again!' She was reacting to the use of intercut close-ups of faces and hands.

variance with continuity montage, but an essential part of worldwide film grammar to this day. (There will be more about the tension between 'Hollywood' and 'Soviet' editing styles in the later pages of this book.)

Kuleshov effect: https://en.wikipedia.org/wiki/Kuleshov_effect (QR code on left)

What secret allows the alchemy of montage to work? Each film that we make clarifies and yet deepens the mystery, but I suspect, as others have, that montage has managed to tap into the archaic visual grammar of our dreams, a pre-existing 'language' we have been intimately familiar with for hundreds of thousands, maybe millions, of years. Perhaps even – for our non-human ancestors – hundreds of millions of years.

And, for both logistical and creative reasons, montage was what allowed cinema to grasp the future that Louis Lumière had denied it. Long, complex films could now be planned in advance, broken down into individual shots and scenes, photographed in the most efficient order (grouping exteriors together, making allowance for the schedules of busy actors, avoiding bad weather, etc.) and then reknitted into a convincing three-dimensional mosaic – two dimensions of space and one of time – that is able to represent, in symphonic or novelistic terms, the full breadth of *la comédie humaine*. Montage freed cinema from the binding gravitational pull of the single shot and allowed it to take off, in both a creative and a logistical sense. It is a poetic coincidence that those two miraculous symbols of the previous century, edited film (1901) and powered flight (1903), have almost simultaneous birthdays.

> The only thing that survives from any era is the art form it has created. This is how an art invented in the 19th century – cinema – brought into existence the 20th century, which by itself had not yet hardly existed.
>
> – Jean-Luc Godard, in *Histoire(s) du cinéma*

The words *montage, montaggio, montaje* and *монтаж* in the Romance and Slavic languages emphasise the architectural aspects of our work: a plumber will *monte* together the pipes of a house, just as a film editor will plumb together the shots of a film, and this construction – this montage – of a first assembly is the primary foundation of all the editor's subsequent work.

The English, German and Scandinavian words *editing, Schnitt* and *redigering* highlight instead the cutting-down and reorganisation of a pre-existing assembly. Our work as film-makers involves both aspects, of course, but as every film editor knows, we are *constructing* something, attempting to find the optimum balance points between content and length, story and emotion, density and clarity. It is for these reasons that I prefer *montage*, but I will use *editing* when necessary.

Combining the DNA of discontinuous, sometimes conflicting, sometimes harmonious images and sounds is the fertile paradox that lies at the heart of the equation MOTION PICTURES + MONTAGE = CINEMA.

I started compiling notes for this book about twelve years ago, and in 2015 Walter Donohue, who has been a friend for more than thirty years, reached out to ask if Faber could publish it once it was written. Of course I said yes – there would be nothing better than Faber's collective expertise and Walter's guidance. He asked me to write a few paragraphs outlining what I thought the final product might look like. The gist of my answer went something like this:

> A three-braided rope – theory, practice and history – intertwined to give each of them greater strength and flexibility. And some of the history will be short oddities from the coalface: strange cinematic predicaments where I found myself wondering if I would be able to Houdini myself out of a suddenly desperate situation. And there will be some unexpected discoveries.

Walter liked the sound of that, and contracts were signed. Except . . . the actual writing didn't truly begin until 2020, once I had finished the film I had been editing.[7] When Covid also came along that year, I had no excuses to delay diving into the inkwell.

What I did not foresee was the rope's final length. During those three and a half years of swimming around in the inkwell, I had not followed any preordained structure, letting the subject matter blow these pages – sometimes gently, sometimes with the force of a hurricane – across many cinematic latitudes and longitudes. Consequently, there were many surprising discoveries. After my wife Aggie had read each chapter and made her invaluable observations, I would send the manuscript over to Walter, and his encouraging responses kept me exploring. But how it was all going to come together was still a mystery.

When I finally reached shore and coiled everything together, in September 2023, it added up to over nine hundred manuscript pages. I was relieved (and surprised) to find that it cleaved, by topic, into three roughly equal-length parts – Post-Production, Production and Cinematic Philosophy – but it was too much to cram between the

---

7. This was the feature documentary *Coup 53*, directed by Taghi Amirani, for which I was co-author and editor.

covers of a single book. So what you have here is the first section: *Suddenly Something Clicked – Thoughts on Picture Editing and Sound Design for Cinema*. Subsequent sections, touching on Writing, Casting, Direction, Production, Cinema Aesthetics and Philosophy, are completed and will be published in due course.

It has been thirty-four years since the first edition of *In the Blink of an Eye*, my previous book on film, a span of time roughly equivalent to a quarter of the history of motion pictures. Much has happened in those years, but the most significant development was the two-decades-long (1990–2010) transformation of cinema from an analogue to a digital medium. As I suggested in *Blink*, it is a shift whose closest analogy in the history of European art might be when oil painting began to displace fresco in the fifteenth century. Digitisation has had, and will continue to have, equally revolutionary consequences for the creation and distribution of motion pictures.

In 1965 I began studying cinema as a graduate student at the University of Southern California and spent the next thirty years working (and studying, since work is another form of study) in a completely analogue world. I learned how to edit film on the American Moviola editing machine, but quickly (in 1969) moved to the German Steenbeck and KEM editing tables, with an occasional jump back to the Moviola (such as on Fred Zinnemann's *Julia* in 1976–7).

Then, in 1995, halfway through the shooting of *The English Patient* (1996), I switched from the sprockets of the KEM to the pixels of the Avid Media Composer (the details of that switch can be found in the later pages of *In the Blink of an Eye*). But for the last thirty years I have edited film and mixed sound digitally, using Avid's Media Composer, then Apple's Final Cut and, most recently, Adobe's Premiere Pro, as well as a whole variety of sound mixing desks – mostly the Euphonix and Pro Tools Icon. It has been a fascinating privilege to work in cinema during this revolutionary transition and to have those six decades split equally between analogue and digital.

In the Preface to *Blink*, I retold Ingmar Bergman's story about the vivid contrast between Stravinsky's theories of conducting (restraint!) and his actual performance (frenzied!), which was meant to alert readers to the dangers of blindly following advice from even unimpeachable sources, like Stravinsky. So I tried to be careful not to get too specific about my personal stylistic quirks, partly because I did not have a clear perspective on them when that book was written, but mainly because the more a suggestion is made specific, the more it can be rigidly interpreted

Make visible what, without you, might never have been seen

and become dogmatic. Rules are useful, but they should be broken at the right moment. Consequently I am going to break my own rules and be specific about some of my stylistic dos and don'ts, especially in Chapter 15, 'Elements of Style'. Let the reader beware!

But I *am* going to avoid keystroke-specific details about different non-linear editing systems. Software engineering is evolving so rapidly that anything I might write on the subject would be out of date in a few months; I hope my observations will apply to any editing system, digital or analogue. *Blink* was based on a lecture about picture editing and didn't venture into sound, but in this book I will dig into both, and the fruitful balance between the two.

I have written and directed only one feature film, *Return to Oz* (1985), but it was such an ambitious project – technically, artistically and even culturally – that 'lessons were learned', as the saying goes. Directors usually take their first plunge into the bracing and bloody, shark-infested waters of production in their mid-twenties, and there is much to be said in favour of that early immersion: the believed invincibility of youth carries many a soldier out of the trenches and into the storm of shrapnel, where some lucky and talented ones do survive and thrive (Orson Welles is eloquent on this subject).

I went 'over the top' at the age of forty and was perhaps overly conscious of all the buzzing bullets because of my age and my decade and a half of second-hand experience working with Francis Coppola, George Lucas and Fred Zinnemann, who had all survived their own close shaves. But second-hand is a pale shadow of first.

I will try not to duplicate any of the topics touched upon in *Blink*, or in Michael Ondaatje's *The Conversations* or Charles Koppelman's *Behind the Seen* – two other books that explore my approaches to editing and film-making. When there are topical overlaps, I will link to the relevant sections in those books.

There will be occasional QR codes dropped in alongside the text, as you have already seen, which will take the reader to examples or further explanations of the points I am making (most smartphones have a QR reader built into the camera). And as a chyron-like 'Greek chorus' of disparate, sometimes contradictory voices, there will be quotes running along the bottom of each even-numbered page, with the author's name on the facing odd-numbered page, as you see below. I have been gathering these 'fortunes' – they are sometimes as terse and oracular as the little papers you find inside Chinese fortune cookies – over the past forty-odd years, and they have given me the encouragement of knowing that other film-makers and artists have

Robert Bresson

travelled along similar twisting paths, facing related problems and uncertainties.[8]

Each of the 173 fortunes has been selected and calibrated either to amplify the text in the page above it, or to expressly contradict that text (following physicist Niels Bohr's dictum that 'every great truth is a truth whose opposite is also a great truth'). Sometimes the link between fortune and text is ambiguous, but ambiguity is often the point – the more obscure and paradoxical these fortunes seem, the truer they probably are, since much about cinema is still so mysterious. Rarely, but now and again, the page above the fortune is blank, which makes its own statement. Nonetheless, there is an overall intentional pattern to these fortunes, which are an integral part of the premise of the book. Readers are encouraged to interpret each fortune, with reference to the text above it, in their own way.

Blink was first published in 1991, when I was in the middle of my career. Now I am near the end of it, at the age of eighty-one. The two volumes of *Clicked* reflect that thirty-four-year difference: they cover more topics than *Blink* and are longer, more eclectic and speculative, looking back at the last six decades of my love affair with cinema and wondering about the future of the medium.

There are also some chapters that venture into the neurology of perception. All art is concerned, to some degree, with developing new ways of perceiving the world, and because of its multi-sensory temporality, none more so than cinema. Every adventuresome film is a kind of real-world laboratory, testing new modes of perception. A constant question during production, and especially in the editing and mixing rooms, is: 'This is really neat, but will audiences understand and accept it?' Think of Jean-Luc Godard in 1959, experimenting with his jump cuts in *Breathless*. Or us twenty years later, when we were cutting and mixing the sound for *Apocalypse Now* in the never-before-attempted split-surround LFE (low-frequency enhancement) format of what became 5.1 sound.

Cinema is so new in human culture, compared to the other arts, that I don't think we have yet grasped its full implications, nor how to plumb its depths – or even know how deep those depths might be. I wouldn't go so far as to say, as screenwriter William

---

8. Two French film-makers, Robert Bresson and Jean Cocteau, are widely represented in the selection of these fortunes. Bresson's are selected from his book *Notes sur le cinématographe*, originally published by Gallimard in 1975, but most recently as *Notes on Cinematography* in an English translation by Jonathan Griffin published by New York Review of Books (2016). Cocteau's fortunes, translated by me, come from *La Belle et la Bête: journal d'un Film*, published by Éditions du Rocher (1958).

Seek simplicity, but distrust it

Goldman wrote, that *nobody knows anything*,[9] but in spite of the technical wizardry that surrounds us in the twenty-first century, working on a film is the closest many of us will ever come to signing on with the crew of a sixteenth-century galleon, sailing halfway around the world across unmapped seas.

Thanks to the technology of the astrolabe, the crews of those ships would have had a rough notion of their latitude (their north–south position), but almost no idea of their longitude (their east–west position). They would know what was in the hold and would have a fervent hope of arriving at their destination, but little idea of how long it would take, nor what the market for their goods would be once they arrived, nor what they would eventually bring back home, for what profit. Menaced by storms and hidden reefs along still-unexplored shorelines, following charts whose vagueness and distortions were legendary – 'Here be monsters', the maps would warn – it was often doubtful that they would survive at all.

What guided those sailors was luck, combined with a sometimes improbable vision of their destination and an intuitive feel for the forces at work – supported by the word-of-mouth experience of previous generations, communicated through stories, examples and apprenticeship – trusting inspiration and the memory of painful failures to gauge how to set their sails in a storm and survive those long weeks when the wind had gone slack.

Our predicament as sailors on the sea of cinema is roughly equivalent. Each film worth making is a voyage of discovery, with hidden reefs, shifting shorelines and monsters to frighten us. The prize is hopefully the discovery of new cinematic continents – even hemispheres – which make the risk of sailing uncharted seas worthwhile. As André Gide observed, 'You do not discover new lands without losing sight of the shore for a very long time.' Robert Bresson sent Gide's metaphor into outer space: 'The film-maker is making a voyage of discovery on an unknown planet.'

No one has invented the cinematic chronometer to calculate artistic and commercial longitude, nor a Lloyd's of London to insure against filmwreck. The laws of physics are unchanging, and our GPS-guided maps of the physical world are now reliable to the millimetre, but the shorelines and currents of cinema are constantly in flux. Cinema is a kind of Schrödinger's world that we recreate in the process of discovery.

9. 'Nobody knows anything. Not one person in the entire motion picture field knows for a certainty what's going to work. Every time out it's a guess and, if you're lucky, an educated one.' From Goldman's book, *Adventures in the Screen Trade*.

Alfred North Whitehead

The subtitle of *In the Blink of an Eye* was *A Perspective on Film Editing*, and I would put extra emphasis on that first word, 'A'. There are many film editors and sound designers – more and more, in fact, thanks to digital technology – and there are many ways of editing many different types of media in our now image-saturated world. But I will be searching out a commonality underneath the variety, spinning a mixture of strategies, tactics, stories, examples and theories developed on my voyages to the film-planets I have visited and in the storms I have (so far) survived.

Some of the chapters get technical, which is inevitable when writing about film, but I have made every effort not to go too far 'into the weeds', as the expression goes. And certain other chapters propose hypotheses that are well grounded scientifically, but which undoubtedly require further study. I am thinking in particular of the chapters 'Saccadic Cinema', which offers a new explanation for why movies move, and 'The Spliceosome', which reveals procedural parallels between the post-production of films and the genetic processes involved in copying DNA to RNA, modifying the copy, and then making proteins from that modified RNA.

The ideas here have been influenced by the obsessions, deficiencies and tensile strengths of my own personality and the particular history I have been privileged to witness and participate in while serving alongside the crews and captains with whom I have sailed. So take from these pages what proves useful to you and set aside that which is not, or translate it into terms that fit your needs.

The excitement in our cinematic voyages – and this has certainly been the case for me – comes from the discoveries we make for ourselves, guided from time to time by the traces and trail-markings left by those who have gone before.

Walter Murch
London, August 2024

Inspiration comes, but she has to find you working

PART ONE
FILM EDITING

As you will discover, the chapters that follow are organised thematically, but the treatment of their subject matter is eclectic, as befits cinema, which itself is a many-sided mix of art, craft, technology and business. Some chapters focus on a single theme and develop it chronologically, but the order of the chapters themselves is not chronological. There are some chapters that are highly theoretical and speculative, others scientific, others historical, others practical. Practical advice can follow hard on the heels of metaphysics. And some are a quirky mixture, featuring odd behaviours and spooky coincidences, such as the first chapter, 'The Ghost of 47th Street'.

Pablo Picasso

You must believe in free will . . . you have no other choice

1: THE GHOST OF 47TH STREET

Senses Plus Mind Equals Reality – Leonard Mlodinow

16 June 1977

My seat companions on the flight from London to New York were two metal Goldberg film cans containing the preview print of the film *Julia*. Although we had shot, edited, scored and mixed the film in England, the proof of this cinematic pudding was in how an American audience would react to it. We – director Fred Zinnemann, producer Tom Pevsner and I – were going to preview the movie at three venues on the East Coast: Boston, New Haven and New York.

In those primeval days, we could not trust the print of a film to baggage handling, so an extra ticket was purchased in the name of Ms Julia Film, and I was able to keep my eye on her from the moment of leaving London until she was safely in my hotel room in New York. In her birthday suit, she weighed 56 pounds.

We arrived late that evening and decided to reconnoitre at lunch the next day, after we had recovered from jet lag. But my internal alarm buzzed me awake early, and Manhattan beckoned. I had been born on the Upper West Side, near Columbia University, and was curious to discover how many of my old neighbourhood signposts were still standing.

I didn't get far. In the hotel lobby, a familiar voice called out 'Walter!' – a voice I hadn't heard in a year and a half.

'George! What are you doing here?'

The tsunami-like success of *Star Wars*, released just three weeks earlier, had prompted 20th Century-Fox, the studio behind both *Julia* and *Star Wars*, to bring George Lucas and his then-wife Marcia – one of the film's three editors – to New York to do publicity and supervise doubling the number of theatres in which it would be shown. I hadn't seen George and Marcia since Christmas 1975, when they had left for England to start final preparations for the *Star Wars* shoot, which began in Tunisia on 22 March 1976. They didn't return home to San Francisco, where we all lived and

Isaac Bashevis Singer (paraphrased)

worked, until after Aggie and I and our four kids had in turn flown to England to prepare for the *Julia* shoot – coincidentally, at Elstree, the same studio where most of *Star Wars* had been shot. We had a lot of catching up to do.

But George was on a mission: he had to approve another theatre capable of showing the 70 mm six-track magnetic print of *Star Wars*. No time for coffee.

'Walk with me to Times Square, and we'll catch up as we go.'

He was simultaneously exhausted and exhilarated, trying to make sense of the unanticipated scale of the success of *Star Wars*. Back in 1969, when we were writing *THX 1138*, George and I had talked about his dream of combining the corny *Flash Gordon* Saturday-morning serials of the 1950s with the cutting-edge special effects developed by Stanley Kubrick for *2001: A Space Odyssey* (1968). Later on, in 1975, when Carroll Ballard and I were writing *The Black Stallion*, I had read an early draft of *Star Wars* but was embarrassed to say I couldn't make much sense of it.

My next contact with the film was a report from Fox executive Peter Beale, who spoke to me when we were at Rank Studios, just outside London, recording Georges Delerue's music for *Julia*. Once John Williams's score had been added to *Star Wars*, a preview showing had gone 'through the roof', smiled a happy Beale.

And then, in early May 1977, there was an advance screening at the huge Dominion theatre on London's Tottenham Court Road. Our entire family – Aggie, I and the four kids – attended and were gobsmacked, as the expression goes, by the experience: its vast and quirky ambition, the visual effects, the sound (in space they *can* hear you scream) and the music. But the scene I remember most vividly from that showing was the meditative shot of Luke looking out at the twin suns of Tatooine. This moment, deepened in colour by the music, captured the feeling of a young man, newly 'orphaned' after the death of his aunt and uncle, on the brink of a predestined but unknowable adventure. That was where, for me, the film thrust its roots deep into the nourishing collective unconscious, which would sustain it through all of the impressive surface bluster.

George and I turned left off Central Park South and started down Seventh Avenue, headed for the theatre on 46th Street. Listening to him on that twelve-block walk, George's situation reminded me of Luke staring out at those twin suns of an impending, unknown destiny. It was still early days, but the overwhelming cultural hurricane of *Star Wars* had already begun to gather: it wasn't just a successful movie, it was becoming a much larger cultural phenomenon. He was grappling with the fact that a film he had made 'for kids' was getting such broad acceptance by all age groups. His

What the public criticises in you, cultivate. It is you

Seventh Avenue analysis was that *Star Wars* had 'the right mixture of philosophy, action and goofiness' – *Flash Gordon* meets *2001*!

I reminded him of his pre-*Star Wars* attempts to get *Apocalypse Now* off the ground, and that what interested him about that story was that it grappled with the success of the 'rebel' Vietnamese against the overwhelming might of the American military empire.

George: '*Star Wars* is *Apocalypse Now* in a galaxy long ago and far away.'[1]

Me: 'Ironic that millions of Americans are now cheering for the Rebels to defeat the overwhelming might of the Empire.'

We paused to let this sink in as the 52nd Street cross-traffic grumbled by. George shook his head at the mystery of it all: 'People will see what they want to see. It almost doesn't matter what we film-makers think we are doing.'

I remembered Francis Coppola experiencing a similar shock when he sneaked into a commercial screening of *The Godfather* in Times Square, five years earlier, and the packed audience cheered in bloodlust at the revenge-fuelled assassinations of the heads of the Five Families. Francis (and all of us who had worked on the film) had intended this climactic scene, intercut with Michael soberly attending the baptism of his infant nephew, to be profoundly unsettling – the moment when Michael finally loses what is left of his soul. But many audiences, like the one in Times Square, took it completely differently. Francis emerged shaken from the experience.[2]

As we were considering these deep and somewhat chastening thoughts, I suddenly noticed a figure walking towards us.

'George! It's Carl Schultz!' I said.

Carl was about a block away. He had been the manager of American Zoetrope for eight months in 1972–3, during the production of *American Graffiti* and *The Conversation*. He was responsible for scheduling and the allocation of equipment, and thus incredibly important to us while we were working on those films. But then there had been a change: Carl was suddenly gone, replaced by a new manager, Ed Imparato. In the four years since, there had been little reason for George or me to think about

---

1. *Apocalypse Now* began shooting in the Philippines on 20 March 1976, two days before the first day of filming on *Star Wars*. But *Apocalypse* would not premiere until August 1979, two years and three months after *Star Wars*.

2. Former UK prime minister Boris Johnson has said that this sequence is among his favourite moments in all of cinema. It would be interesting to know which aspect appealed to him the most: the losing of the soul or the assassination of enemies. Or both equally . . .

Jean Cocteau

Carl, but there he was, walking towards us, easily identifiable by his beard, checked shirt and slightly duck-footed, ambling gait.

'Amazing! What are the chances of this?' I said. 'We've got to play a joke on him!'

As we approached each other, the 47th Street traffic lights turned red, and we stared at Carl through the passing cars. There was no recognition on his part, although he was looking straight in our direction.

'I've got an idea,' said George, as the lights turned green.

We walked towards Carl, who was, surprisingly, still oblivious. And then, just as George was about to spring his joke, Carl turned into . . . Not-Carl. There was still the checked shirt, the beard and the rolling gait, but he had morphed into someone different, an 'uncanny valley' version of the original Carl.

Both George and I had been absolutely convinced that we had seen Carl Schultz, until he was about eight feet away. What happened?

Greek Vision

The philosophers of ancient Greece developed a peculiar (to us today) idea of how vision worked, and it hung around as the official explanation for almost 2,000 years – from Empedocles through Plato, Euclid and Ptolemy (although Aristotle and Lucretius resisted it). Now called the *emission* theory, the idea was that the eye projected a beam of semi-divine light that would contact objects out there in the world and then bounce back into the eye, carrying with it a report of what it had seen.[3]

There are all kinds of scientific objections to this idea – if the eye emits light, for instance, why can't we see things in the dark? – but once the concept took hold, it had phenomenal staying power, largely because of the esteemed authorities backing it.

The first glimmer of our present theory of vision began to emerge in around AD 1000, in the writings of the Cairo-based scientist Ibn al-Haytham. His *Book of Optics*, known in Europe as *De Perspectiva*, was translated into Latin in around 1200 and printed in 1574, when Johannes Kepler was three.[4]

Haytham's theory, obvious to us now, was that some source (the Sun, a lamp, a candle) sends out a stream of light that bounces off objects within our field of vision,

---

3. This beaming–bouncing action is exactly how bats perceive the world – except that they emit high-pitched squeaks that bounce off surrounding objects and are reflected back into their ears, like sonar, to form a batty 'picture' of the world.

4. Kepler would go on to write *Dioptrice*, a foundational book on optics, in 1611. Much of it is based on the work of Ibn al-Haytham.

All you need for a movie is a girl and a gun

and this 'bounced' light[5] streams into our eye, releasing its energy in the retina, which triggers neuronal/chemical reactions that eventually reach the brain, where they are finally 'perceived' by our consciousness.

And there's the problem . . . consciousness.

Intense neurological research conducted in the second half of the twentieth century revealed that much of what we see is concocted internally, using fragmentary and sometimes contradictory trigger clues from the external world.[6] For example, only the images that are registered by the densely packed circle of cone cells in the centre of our retina, the *fovea*, are in focus. Hold your hand out at arm's length and look at the one-inch circle of your thumbnail: that area corresponds to the area seen by the two-degree diameter of the fovea. Our total field of vision, though, has an area of over 30,000 square degrees (210 degrees horizontal by 150 degrees vertical). The fovea sees only 0.0001 per cent of that area.

And yet . . . our *feeling* is that everything we see is in focus. This is the result of a furious amount of brain activity, busy 'behind the scenes' knitting together a quilt of convincing reality from the patches of focused images generated by our eyes as they saccade from focal point to focal point. And all of these fragments are then grouted together by our stored expectations of what reality must be like.

As physicist Leonard Mlodinow expressed it in *Subliminal*, his 2012 book on the neurology of the subconscious:

> Senses plus mind equals reality: The unconscious mind is a master at using limited data to construct a version of the world that *appears* to be realistic and complete to its serenely oblivious partner, the conscious mind.[7]

So, in a metaphorical sense, the ancient Greeks had it right. Except that the 'beaming' action is all contained within the 75 cubic inches of the human brain: triggered by the fragmentary signals from the retina, we concoct and beam 'outwards' a hypothetical version of what we expect to see, and this is adjusted in turn by the subsequent retinal signals.

Or not. The problem is that the amount of data sent by the retina is often tiny

---

5. Actually photons, absorbed and re-emitted by the surface of the object.

6. Approximately 30 per cent of all human brain activity is related to visual processing, ten times the amount for sound. In dolphins, this 10:1 proportion is reversed, which is probably also true for bats, since both dolphins and bats use sound to form a picture of the world.

7. Leonard Mlodinow, *Subliminal* (Vintage, 2012), p. 85.

D. W. Griffith

compared to the immense stream coming from our inbuilt reserves of stored expectations. An extreme example of this is the self-perception of people with anorexia: when they look in the mirror, they 'see' a fat person looking back, despite the evidence from their retinas, which register the skeletal figure that everyone else sees. Their 'inner beam' overwhelms any amount of retinal data.

It seems that George and I saw 'Carl' because the tiny amount of information (distant checked shirt, beard, gait) we were receiving was able to support, like an inverted pyramid, our stored idea of the actual Carl. In a sense, we clothed that perceptual figure with our expectations. As we moved closer, that balance of expectation versus data came under increasing tension, but we were able to maintain it until 'Carl' was about eight feet away. At that point, the detail coming from our eyes finally overwhelmed the image of Carl that we were projecting onto him – and 'Carl' suddenly morphed into who he really was, and passed by, oblivious to our amazement.[8]

Brief Encounter

As George and I were pondering these mysteries of perception, we reached the corner of 47th Street, turned right and bumped into . . . the actual Carl Schultz.

'Carl! We were just thinking of you!'

When coincidences are this shamelessly blatant, our logical mind collapses and we tend to roll over and accept them as inevitable ('Of course we would bump into the real Carl!'). The three of us exchanged pleasantries, Carl congratulated George on the success of *Star Wars*, we asked what he had been up to since his Zoetrope days, he wished me luck with the *Julia* previews, and we all shook hands and went on our way.

Still . . . if we had turned left instead of right, we would have missed the actual Carl, and I probably would not have remembered our encounter with 'false Carl'.

This raises an inevitable question: out of the hundreds of people in that two-block section of Times Square, why did George and I see 'Carl' walking towards us? He was among the most unlikely people to surge forward out of our shared memory: it had been more than four years since we last saw him, and much had happened in that space of time.

Putting my toe into a metaphysical tide pool, let's say that in the excitement of meeting each other after a year and a half, George and I unconsciously created a

8. An excellent article on the brain's interaction with vision: Denise Grady, 'The Vision Thing: Mainly in the Brain', *Discover* magazine, 1 June 1993: https://www.discovermagazine.com/mind/the-vision-thing-mainly-in-the-brain (QR code on left).

You are the ringmaster of a circus that is inventing itself

hypothetical ZAW (Zoetrope Awareness Wave)[9] and, like the Greek theory of vision, this wave energy somehow picked up – like a sonar blip of a hidden submarine – the actual Carl Schultz, who was approaching us, unseen, from around the corner of 47th Street. We registered this blip unconsciously, and our unconscious scanned the visual (retinal) field ahead of us on Seventh Avenue, looking for an explanation.

And it found someone: 'false Carl' (beard, checked shirt, duck-foot gait), who at a distance fitted enough of the parameters of our expectations of the actual Carl, and we latched onto him, the innocent victim, as the explanation for that metaphysical sonar blip. This is similar to the neurological phenomenon of 'blindsight' (discussed by Denise Grady in her *Discover* article), but it depends on an awareness beyond the usual senses. This will be touched on in a subsequent chapter, when I discuss the experience of watching a film in a theatre, surrounded by the 'awareness wave' of hundreds, perhaps thousands, of other people.

Of course, it could simply have been a coincidence . . .

George and I checked out the 1,700-seat Palace Theater on 47th Street. He approved it after a tweak to the low-frequency channels, and we went our separate ways, arranging to have dinner that evening. I was planning to begin work on *Apocalypse Now* in a couple of months, so I was glad to have this brief peek under the tent flap of a 70 mm magnetic multichannel film – in 1977 I had so far worked only on films with 35 mm monophonic optical sound. Lunch with Fred Zinnemann and Tom Pevsner followed, and I was briefly back in the world of *Julia*, planning for the upcoming preview in Boston.[10]

That evening, George, his wife Marcia and I had dinner at the Tavern on the Green in Central Park. My one vivid memory from that meal was Marcia, in happy/sad/confused/anguished tears at the sudden relief from the crushing amount of work and the months – years, really – of uncertainty that had now led to this incredible success. 'What does it all mean? What does it mean?' she kept repeating. 'We were just making a film for kids!'

Much of this book will be concerned with this concept of balancing expectation with fragmentary patches of reality and finding ways to apply it to cinema – or at least making sure that we take this balance into account. At any one moment, how can film-makers leverage what the audience expects to see versus what their retinas and eardrums are

9. Trust the wave, Luke . . .

10. Details of previewing *Julia* and other films will be found in the 'Pandemic of Desire' chapter of the subsequent volume of this book.

Francis Coppola (paraphrased)

registering, and use that difference to move them out of conventional ways of thinking and perceiving? Films, of course, need to supply a coherent vision, a structured way of seeing the world, but they mustn't be *too* coherent, too completely self-sufficient; they have to leave strategic openings for the audience to be able to project their own feelings and expectations onto that structure. Otherwise, the emotional connection will be lost.

This applies, as I hope to explain in subsequent chapters, at both the technical level – frame rate, multichannel sound, stereoscopy, etc. – and the creative – the script and what can safely be left out of plot structure, the nature of casting, the ambiguities of staging and editing, and so on. How much of a film is 'actually there' and how much of it is there because the audience expects it to be there? When our expectations are confirmed by the film, do we tend to esteem it all the more, or does it eventually bore us? When our expectations are challenged, do we reject it, or does it intrigue us further? When we expect sugar and instead taste salt, our reaction is all the more violent for the contrast between expectation and reality: the taste is 'uglier' than that of salt alone – the uncanny valley.[11]

I think that if film-makers are sensitised to this tension and can creatively manipulate and maintain it, this will (if we are lucky) produce a sustained déjà vu experience for the audience, where they cannot imagine what might happen next, but when it does, it feels inevitably right – like our meeting the actual Carl. It is a delicious feeling.

The tools for achieving this déja-vu-ness have to be rooted in the screenplay, of course, but they can be elaborated and amplified by directorial choices in terms of the

casting, the staging, costumes, production design, the choice of camera angles and the rhythm of those alternating points of view – the different camera set-ups – in the editorial structure of the film.

As director John Huston observed:

> The perfect film is as though it were unwinding behind your eyes and your eyes were projecting it themselves, so that you were seeing what you wished to see. It's like thought. Film is the closest to thought process of any art.[12]

11. Is there a 'canny valley'? Perhaps it is a Valley of the Barbie Dolls, where exaggeration of certain features makes us prefer distortion over reality. See discussion of Niko Tinbergen's *supernormal stimulus* in the 'Strange Attractor' chapter of the subsequent volume of this book.

12. Louise Sweeney, interview with John Huston, *Christian Science Monitor*, 26 July 1973: https://tinyurl.com/mr2c92z6.

Resign yourself to a life of divine dissatisfaction, of blessed unrest

2: THE DEVIL'S BLACK BOX
AND THE SNOWFLAKE

The Effect of Digitisation in Fiction and Documentary Films

I think if you travelled back in time to 1965 and whispered into my twenty-two-year-old film-student ear what the world of cinema would be like fifty-nine years later, two things that would most surprise – and please – me would be the resurrection of animation and documentary as vibrant artistic and commercial mediums.[1]

The common thread to both revivals is digitisation. This has empowered and transformed 3D animation (Pixar, etc.) and enabled more free-form, ambitious styles of documentary. The relative ease with which vast topics can be tackled, and hundreds of hours of material shot and edited, would be simply unthinkable if we were still using sprocketed film.

After leaving film school, my first creative jobs were editing educational films and several short documentaries. My first feature-film experience with documentary editing, though, was back in pre-digital 1987, for a seven-minute section in Philip Kaufman's film *The Unbearable Lightness of Being*. It's not strictly a documentary, of course, because *Unbearable* was based on Milan Kundera's novel of the same name, but the scene in question involved inserting our characters (Tomas and Tereza, played by Daniel Day-Lewis and Juliette Binoche) into actual documentary footage that was shot, mostly by Czech film students, during the Soviet invasion of Czechoslovakia back in August 1968. This event was almost simultaneous with the 1968 student protests in Paris and the political riots in Chicago, part of a world-wide upheaval. These were the first fully documented revolutions, filmed live by the participants, in our collective history.

This is something we are now completely familiar with; you might call them the cellphone revolutions – the Arab Spring and so on. But even back in 1968 there was a phrase chanted during the Chicago riots – 'The whole world is watching!' – that you could easily repeat today in Syria or Turkey or Gaza, or indeed in the marbled halls

---

1. George Lucas wanted to be an animator when he left film school in 1966, and he received a scholarship to go to Warner Brothers and study animation (Warner was the home of Bugs Bunny, Elmer Fudd and Daffy Duck). It was thanks to this scholarship that he met Francis Coppola, who was shooting a film (*Finian's Rainbow*) on the Warner Brothers lot.

Martha Graham (paraphrased)

of the US Capitol. Things that had previously happened in the dead of night or were never fully documented, like the MI6/CIA coup in Iran in 1953,[2] are now immediately uploaded into the world's consciousness via hundreds, sometimes thousands of cellphone cameras. There were none of these back in 1968, of course, but there *were* new, relatively inexpensive, portable 16 mm cameras, available to students enrolled in Prague's renowned FAMU film school. And dozens of them went out at three o'clock in the morning to record what was happening, with the encouragement of the school's director, Frank Daniel.

The material that they shot was immediately evacuated out of the country as undeveloped film and, like pieces of shrapnel from an explosion, these images and sounds landed in various cities in Europe and America, where they were quickly developed and put on the evening news. It was not the internet, but it was getting there. Fifteen years later, the exiled Czech author Milan Kundera published *The Unbearable Lightness of Being*, his novel about those days in August. And a few years after that, in 1986, Philip Kaufman and Jean-Claude Carrière wrote a screenplay based on the novel, and Phil, as director, hired me to edit the film.

Prior to shooting, it was my assignment to travel to television news stations around Europe and collect whatever invasion material they had in their archives. I felt like a bird collecting material for its nest, flying from Stockholm to Amsterdam to London to Brussels, and so on, collecting these pieces of cinematic shrapnel. The invasion had been photographed by so many cameras that many actions from Stockholm's archive – a tank ramming a bus, for instance – would be mirrored by a reverse angle from the one in Brussels. Ultimately, we gathered forty hours of archive material for that seven-minute section. There was a wonderful poetry to it all: fragments of film that had been scattered around the world by the political explosion of '68 were now, in '86, brought back into a single unified shell – an explosion in reverse.

Our technical and artistic challenge was to take Sven Nyqvist's original high-quality 35 mm material of Daniel and Juliette in the old-town section of Lyon, France (which was standing in for Prague), complete with Soviet-era tanks and period-costumed crowds, and integrate it with the decades-old documentary material, which was of highly variable quality, much of it many times duped, scratched or dirty, some of questionable origin, some in black and white, some in colour, some faded, some high-contrast. We loved the calico variety of those shots and didn't want to

2. This is the subject of the latest documentary that I edited, Taghi Amirani's *Coup 53* (2019).

A writer is someone for whom writing is more difficult than it is for others

homogenise them in any way. Instead, we wanted our new footage to have the same calico quality. Today, with digital, this would be pretty straightforward, but in 1987 we had to rely on the alchemical techniques of the laboratory. We made a workprint positive from Sven's negative, and I would edit it on the KEM flatbed, as usual, but at the same time allowing it to get progressively more scratched and dirty. When it was abused enough, I would send it to the lab in San Francisco (we were working in Berkeley), where we would make two 16 mm prints, one in black and white and the other in colour. Normally, this is forbidden. Never make copies directly from a work-print, otherwise terrible things happen![3]

But in this case we *wanted* those terrible things to happen, the same terrible things that had already happened to the documentary material itself over the previous twenty years – duping, scratches, dirt, etc. Then we double-exposed the black/white and colour reversal prints, depending on the result we wanted, by mixing different proportions (say, 70 per cent black/white and 30 per cent colour). And then we would fine-tune the correct degree of 'ageing'. Eventually, we became pretty good at estimating these proportions in advance.

This is now an arcane piece of cinematic lore, but we had to resort to it because there was no alternative. Today, we would make several mouse clicks and achieve all of this in a few minutes. It would certainly be easier, but would it be better? I'm happy to have dabbled in this ancient alchemy, but at the same time relieved that I don't have to do it any more.

In this way, forty hours of documentary material were eventually boiled down to seven minutes. That yielded a ratio of around 340:1, which is about the same as the two documentaries I have recently edited, *Particle Fever* (2013) and *Coup 53* (2019), both of which had over five hundred hours of raw material. How do you grab hold of five hundred hours and wrangle it into shape without a pre-existing script? I had worked on a few documentaries in the late 1960s, but none of them had anywhere near that much footage. Then, in 1969, I started working on scripted fiction films with Francis Coppola's *The Rain People*, and now, fifty years later, here I am, very happy to have cycled back to documentaries.

But in another sense I never left them, because Francis's direction of certain key scenes had been very much documentary-style. In *The Godfather*, *The Conversation* and *Apocalypse Now*, he would set up ten-minute-long chains of events – the wedding

---

3. If copies had to be made in the pre-digital years, the usual procedure would be to make what was called a fine-grain positive, and a new negative could be struck from that without too much degradation.

Thomas Mann

scene, or the secret conversation in Union Square, or the Kilgore 'Valkyries' attack. Not everything was planned, and it was all captured over multiple takes with four to six cameras. No one could ever predict exactly what we would get, which was the whole point – to yield a serendipitous realism and energy to the scenes.

So this approach influenced me, and I tend to apply it to other films that I am editing, even though they may not have been shot in this 'Coppola documentary' style. I approach the material *as if* it were a documentary – a found object, so to speak. 'Hmm, I wonder what we can do with this?' I am following the story in the script, of course, but a certain dash of this documentary way of thinking seems to open up the potential in the material, even (and especially) in the accidental parts.

Fiction and Documentary; Copernicus and Darwin

The different working methods of two revolutionary scientists, Copernicus and Darwin, highlight this contrast between fiction and documentary.

In 1543 Copernicus demonstrated that the Earth revolves around the Sun, but he didn't need to generate any new data to do this; he relied instead on the 1,500-year-old planetary records of Hipparchus (150 BC) and Ptolemy (AD 150). He had an idea – heliocentricity – and he tested it against the existing data to see if it worked.

In that sense, his approach is similar to the workings of a fiction film. The script is the pre-existing hypothesis, and the production is the experiment: *will this work?* – not just in terms of the schedule and budget, but the larger question of can the script's deepest intentions be translated into a finished film, which then rewards the audience with a satisfying (in the broadest sense of that word) emotional experience? The hypothesis is tested against the existing realities (weather, schedules, budgets, zeitgeist) that are out there in the world waiting to pounce. Some films pass the test, others don't.

On the other hand, there is Charles Darwin, the twenty-two-year-old naturalist who sailed around the world for five years (1831–6) on the British surveying ship HMS *Beagle*. He was 'shooting his documentary', so to speak – collecting data, but without knowing in advance exactly what story it was going to tell. When he returned home to England, he spent the next twenty-three years sifting through his discoveries, eventually publishing in 1859 the revolutionary book that made sense of the data: *On the Origin of Species by Means of Natural Selection.*

And Darwin's process is similar to how we make documentary films – certainly, the *Particle Fever* and *Coup 53* kinds of documentary – where we generate a lot of

If you want a happy ending, that depends, of course, on where you stop your story

data (the dailies), based on a series of observations, but we don't know yet what the story is going to be, what will be the hook, who will emerge as the main protagonists, and so on. The film-makers are midwives to the story as it evolves out of the material, rather than generating the material to conform to a preconceived story. The director Frederick Wiseman is eloquent on this point:

> For a fiction film, the story is written in advance of the shooting. In my documentaries the story is found in the editing. I have no idea before the shooting begins what the events, themes, ideas, or point of view of the film will be. This last statement is obvious, since before the six to twelve weeks of shooting I do not know what events will occur, what I will decide to shoot, or what words, gestures, emotions, and actions I will, by chance, find. If I knew all that, the film would not be worth making because there would be no surprises.[4]

As you might expect, the Darwin/Copernicus analogy is not as black and white as I have made it out to be. In 1834 Darwin *did* have some inkling of the 'script' that he might write on the *Beagle*, and Copernicus did undertake a few observations himself. But overstating the differences helps to make the general point.

Abundance and Limit

Once the initial assembly of a film has been completed, both documentary and fiction film-makers try to connect their subject matter with their audiences in the shortest (but not too short!), the clearest and most emotionally satisfying way possible. But *getting to* that assembly is where the difference lies. In scripted fiction, there is an abundance of interpretation and a limited number of scenes, whereas in a documentary there is the opposite: limited interpretation and an abundance of scenes.

In shooting a scripted fiction film, each action, every line of dialogue in every scene is delivered many times: perhaps seven takes from this angle, ten takes from that and two from this one, and so on. Each is slightly different: voice tone, body language, camera angle and lens. The challenge facing the editor and director is to find the best version of each particular moment, given what has happened previously and what will happen subsequently. Just as a colour will appear different depending on those adjacent to it, so it is with moments of action and lines of dialogue. We editors of scripted fiction attempt to thread our way through this vast diversity of

---

4. Frederick Wiseman, 'On Editing', *The Threepenny Review*, spring 2008: https://www.threepennyreview.com/samples/wiseman_sp08.html.

interpretive shadings, hopefully achieving the correct balance of colour and tone. But we have, as our resources, only the scenes that are in the screenplay. If an unanticipated structural problem emerges, we have to find a way to make things work with those resources, perhaps by restructuring some of the scenes or removing them. If that fails, then there is only the 'nuclear option' of writing and shooting new material to try to solve the problem.

In a documentary, however, *that* character says *those specific* words only once, and when they open *that* door, it is only from *that* angle and only once. So we have to find a way to make the best use of each singular moment. There is no fallback; find the best way to use that moment, or cut it out. On the other hand, we often have many more potential scenes than will ever wind up in the finished film, so the challenge will be to decide which we are going to eliminate from the surplus that we have, and then how best to organise what remains to tell the story. We must reveal the figure hidden in the block of marble, so to speak. In this sense, the editor of a documentary is participating in writing the film.

Fungible Film

History occasionally goes through sudden transformations, phase shifts where things that were once seen as separate become magically transmutable into each other. They have become *fungible*, and when this happens, social transformations are not far away. To take three phase shifts from the last few hundred years: credit, energy and information.

Credit and money became fungible around 1500, when people realised that you didn't have to physically transport five tons of gold coins from Florence to London; if there was trust on both sides (no small achievement), you could just declare on a piece of paper that this amount of 'gold value' is in deposit in someone's account in London. As can be imagined, this vastly sped up the exchange of wealth and fostered the growth of capitalism.

And then, in around 1900, energy sources became fungible. Thanks to the medium of electricity, you no longer had to have a steam engine or waterwheel in your factory, or coal delivered to heat your home. Steam, water and wind energy became fungible, converted into electrons that could then be sent hundreds of miles distant via transmission lines and retransformed into whatever form of energy you wanted to consume: light, heat, mechanical. It was a kind of energy-based banking system.

This is the alchemical essence of fungibility: we discover the wizardly means of

Only what is seen sideways sinks deep

transmuting something into something else, which can in turn be transmuted back again or into some third form.[5]

Towards the end of the twentieth century, digitisation allowed information to become fungible on an industrial, civilisational scale. We are still coming to terms with this transformation some twenty-five years later, trying to find different ways to take advantage of it and protect ourselves against its excesses, wondering where it is ultimately headed. Certainly, this digital fungibility has completely taken hold in both the creation (cameras, visual effects, sound recording, editing, etc.) and the distribution of cinema, resulting in convenience and crisis simultaneously. Almost all movie theatres have now installed digital projection, but that same technology allows the option of streaming films onto home screens with 5.1 sound,[6] or simply onto a tablet or smartphone. Sprocketed film lingers on life support thanks to directors like Christopher Nolan, Quentin Tarantino and Steven Spielberg, who still shoot with it. But the final projection will almost always be digital, since so few theatres now maintain the capability for 35 mm projection – IMAX being the notable exception.

This is me during the editing of *Apocalypse Now*, in 1978. I was throwing film around and plunging into the depths of the trim bin, trying to retrieve a clip of two frames that,

5. The same thing happens at the cellular level, where proton energy from respiration is transformed into ATP, the common currency of energy in cells, which depletes into ADP when used, ready to be recharged back to ATP by another burst of proton energy.

6. This crisis became existential in the face of the 2020 coronavirus pandemic, which shut down theatres all over the world. When the quarantines were lifted, previous patterns of behaviour did not fully resume, and streaming has become the new normal. Perhaps some unanticipated hybrid will eventually emerge.

Attributed to E. M. Forster

at that moment, was desperately important. A frame of 35 mm film weighs just over five-thousandths of an ounce, so a reel of film – eleven minutes of picture and sound – weighs 11 pounds; in other words, a pound a minute. There were 236 hours of workprint on *Apocalypse Now*, which works out at 14,000 pounds – seven tons of film that had to be broken down, boxed, catalogued, put in accessible racks, moved around from editor to editor (Richie Marks, Jerry Greenberg, Lisa Fruchtman and me), edited, and then the trims returned to their boxes in exactly the original frame order. There was a vast crew of assistants shepherding this material, totally focused on the correct location of every frame in every one of the 2,500 reels of workprint and sound. Their good work allowed us editors to chip a single frame out of that seven-ton block of cinematic marble.

The Lingering Death of Sprockets

The last film I edited mechanically, on sprocketed film, was Jerry Zucker's *First Knight* (1994). For the next twelve years, I edited digitally, using Avid's Media Composer or Apple's Final Cut, but the films themselves (*The English Patient*, *Touch of Evil*, *The Talented Mr. Ripley*, *Apocalypse Now Redux*, *K-19: The Widowmaker*, *Cold Mountain* and *Jarhead*) were shot on sprocketed film. Ever since, all the films I have edited, beginning with Francis Coppola's *Youth Without Youth* (2007), have been shot – and, of course, edited – digitally.

The size of the typical editing crew has shrunk since the days of *Apocalypse* about as far as it can go. The two documentaries I recently edited, *Particle Fever* and *Coup 53*, each had more than double the workprint of *Apocalypse*. And yet, on *Particle Fever*, the editing crew consisted of just me and the director, Mark Levinson, who also acted as my assistant, working with Apple's Final Cut 7 in a single room in New York. *Coup 53* was edited in London on Adobe's Premiere Pro from 532 hours of material, with an editorial crew consisting of director Taghi Amirani, associate editor Edie Franks and me. It is inconceivable that either of these challenging documentaries could have been made on sprocketed film.

So, with this implacable technical realignment, let's suppose it is inevitable that sprocketed film is going to disappear, even from the few sanctuaries to which it has fled for dear life. Most of the regret for the death of physical film will be about losing its characteristic 'look' and grain-structure, which Nolan, Tarantino and others feel is an irreplaceable part of the cinematic experience. I wouldn't want to minimise their regret, but as you might be able to tell, I don't particularly value the film look above any other, and I think it can be duplicated digitally, if that is what is required. The

---

I must say to my great regret: it is the cheapest tricks which have the greatest impact

most important things are the story that is being told and the characters on the screen who are helping to tell it.

Those who are nostalgic for 35 mm (or 70 mm) film, however, forget to mention one of the most fundamental qualities of the classic film experience that has been lost for a decade or so: the shutter.

Shutter Island

In 1982 I was asked by director Fred Zinnemann to check out a couple of theatres where he was planning to preview his latest film, *Five Days One Summer*. Exhibitors in those days were notorious for dimming the projector lamp in order to save money on electricity, so one of Fred's worries was that there would not be enough light on the screen. I was equipped with a spotmeter to make sure there was the recommended amount of illumination (14 foot-lamberts). The testing procedure was to ignite the lamp of the 35 mm projector, bathing the screen with pure white light, and point the spotmeter at the centre and then the four corners of the screen to make sure those photons were bright enough and evenly distributed. I was happy to see the needle registering 14 foot-lamberts, but I asked the projectionist to make a few adjustments to get a more even spread of light. Then, being thorough, I asked him to turn on the projector's mechanics, even though the film had not yet been threaded up. As soon as he did so, I was fascinated to see the needle of the spotmeter now jittering rapidly back and forth from maximum to minimum, even though the light on the screen appeared to be constant. What was happening?

The meter could see something that I could not: the effect of the projector's triple-bladed shutter, whirling between the lamp and the lens, blocking and then releasing the light seventy-two times a second (seventy-five in Europe), three times for each frame.[7] The retina of our eye, like the spotmeter, *does* register this alternation, sending it 'upstream' to the brain, but it is there, deep in the mystery of our thalamus, that an evaluation is made to eliminate the dark as irrelevant and pass along only the bright pulse to the visual cortex, after which the conscious mind is finally allowed

---

7. The purpose of the shutter, invented by William Dickson and Thomas Edison, was to obscure the blur that would occur when one frame is yanked away and replaced by the next. Edison's frame rate was forty per second, and it was subsequently found that a double blade moderated the distracting flicker that accompanies such a rate. The Lumière brothers' *cinématographe*, at sixteen frames per second, had a three-bladed shutter, which gave forty-eight pulses a second. A three-bladed shutter at 24 fps jolts the eye with seventy-two image pulses per second, which is above the human flicker-fusion point, and thus gives a flickerless experience.

Georges Méliès

to 'see' what appears to be on the screen. So the continuous beam of light in 35 mm projection is an illusion (so-called 'flicker fusion'), and is the result of highly sophisticated brain circuitry that is common to us all – indeed, in slightly different variations, common to all forms of life on Earth.

So every 35 mm projector assaults the retinas and brains of the audience with a strong and hypnotic pulse of seventy-two (or seventy-five) bursts of light and dark per second, bursts that the brain, engaged at this very primal level, has to filter out before it presents the results to our conscious attention. Digital projectors do not have this alternating shutter pulse: each frame is held for a twenty-fourth (or twenty-fifth) of a second and is then instantly replaced by the next one. The light hitting the audience's eyes is constant, even – I should emphasise – for those films originally shot on sprocketed film.

Every film you see now – in theatres, streaming at home, on your iPad or smartphone – has lost the primal intensity of that seventy-two-per-second shutter pulse. Does it make a difference in how the films are perceived? If you add up the time spent in 'shutter darkness' for a sprocketed film, it equals half the running time: for a two-hour film, you would spend one hour in darkness. How does that time in the darkness alter how you perceive the 'reality' of the film? Has some mysterious edge been lost that engaged the imagination of the audience at the primal level?

We are conducting a massive real-world experiment in perception and attention, so I imagine that sooner or later we will find out, if we haven't already.[8]

Sacramental Dailies

Beyond these questions of perceptual reality and the 'look and feel' of film, another inadvertent casualty of the transition to digital is the Ritual of Dailies (in the UK, the Ritual of Rushes).

When we shot sprocketed film, especially in the days before videotape playback (pre-1982), the heads of departments were required to assemble, usually in the evening or at lunchtime, and spend twenty minutes to three hours watching the dailies – the material that had been shot the previous day. The crew were tired, but there was no way around it: yesterday's film had been developed and printed overnight at the laboratory, and this was the revelation. There were always surprises, good and bad, like opening Christmas presents – a lovely orange or a lump of coal.

The last time I regularly screened dailies in this way was in 2005, on Sam Mendes's

---

8. There is technically no reason for preventing the shutter effect from being added electronically to digital projection.

History is a fact which sooner or later becomes a lie. Myth is a lie
which sooner or later becomes a fact

film *Jarhead*. In all films since then, the set has been scattered with plasma screens that are showing, live and in hi-def, what the camera is seeing. So, at the end of the day, everyone on the crew thinks, 'I've seen it. I don't have to look at it again.' And, on a certain level, they are right: they have seen it, and they need to conserve their energy, because shooting films is very tiring. But what has disappeared is the sacramental experience of watching the dailies, which had almost religious overtones: 'And now we're going to unveil the miracle of what we shot yesterday.'

Sometimes it was painful, because things hadn't turned out the way everyone hoped they would, or there were unforeseen technical problems in the lab, or the acting wasn't up to scratch, or the camera was slightly out of focus. Everyone had to just sit there and endure it because there was no fast-forward. But we learned from that discipline; we were all in the same room and we picked up on the director's feelings, even – and especially – unspoken ones. And vice versa: the director would absorb the feelings, spoken and unspoken, of everyone else on the crew.

When you're on the set, looking at a plasma screen showing what the camera is seeing, you're also wondering what the next shot is going to be, or thinking, 'We have to adjust the make-up for the next shot,' and so on. Not only are there dozens of simultaneous agendas, there are sometimes hours between set-ups. Whereas when you watched dailies in a screening room, the experience was continuous – one shot right after another, so differences between takes could be directly compared. There was no agenda other than to simply look at what was shot and absorb each other's thoughts and feelings. And this experience would, hopefully, create even greater crew unity, which would in turn influence how the shooting would go the next day.

Technically, there's no reason why we can't do this with digital, but the impetus is lost because there are so many alternatives: the shooting day is long, everyone is tired, and you can watch the dailies streamed to your laptop if you want to, but you probably won't. In any event, the communal, sacramental aspect has largely vanished.

Are there other changes in the creative process due to the shift to digital? Probably. But the loss of communal dailies is certainly the greatest unremarked change.

Stories in the Dark

Eighty years ago, almost the only way for people to experience cinema was in a movie theatre. With the rise of television in the late 1940s, things started to change. And now, in 2024, almost every week delivers a new way of looking at movies. Is this diversity good? What do we lose, what do we gain?

Attributed to Jean Cocteau

Now that we can watch a film at home in high-definition widescreen with 5.1 sound, will the theatrical experience become like the Ritual of Dailies: too much effort for not enough reward? Ever since the invention of language we have been assembling in the dark with other members of the tribe to tell each other stories around the campfire. This has been going on for perhaps 100,000 years or more, and it is deeply embedded in what it means to be human. Cinema is the latest iteration of that long history of storytelling in the dark. The difference is that with cinema, we assemble with (mostly) like-minded strangers in the dark cave of the theatre, and the flaming images themselves tell the story. For that fundamental reason, I don't think the theatrical experience of cinema will disappear. It may certainly change under the assault of new technology and societal shifts. The question is: how much?

When I started film school at USC Cinema in 1965, the loud message from our teachers was that the habit of going to theatres was dying. They had watched it get progressively weaker over the previous twenty years, under the assault of television. Consequently, the advice of Gene Peterson, the head of the camera department, was, 'Get out now. You can still get your money back. Hollywood is falling apart, and there are not enough jobs for all of you.' (In 1965 there were only 163 productions, the lowest number in Hollywood history, down from an average of 500 every year from 1930 to 1945.) About a quarter of the students took his advice and failed to show up the next day. Largely because we loved cinema and didn't believe there was any alternative, those of us who stayed were lucky enough to witness and participate in a regeneration during the 1970s. But now we are at another downturn in that cycle.[9]

Viewed from the wrong end of the telescope, cinema is 'just' a series of patterns of light on a screen, accompanied by sound vibrations from hidden speakers. Why would people, mostly strangers to each other, pay money to assemble in the dark at an appointed hour? And yet they do, and these moving shadows and vibrations can sometimes produce life-changing experiences.

Moviola Metaphysics

Cinema is a mass medium, and we try to get millions of people to see our movies, but at the same time we want each person in the audience to feel that the film is talking to them at a level that only they know – a paradoxical state I will call *mass intimacy*.

I think there are at least four things going on here.

9. As I was writing this in 2020, the situation was particularly bleak because of the coronavirus pandemic, which forced the closing of theatres around the world.

How things seem to seem is not enough. We must somehow
discover how things really seem

The first is that when a film really connects with its audience, it speaks to them on three levels – the heart, the head and what we might call the gut – and the better the film, the better those levels are expressed and integrated, a complex braiding of emotion, intellect and instinct. For reasons that I will try to explain, film is the only art that can do this as effectively as it does.

We can all think of times in our lives when our emotions have carried us away and left our intellect and instincts trailing along behind. And other times when our instincts have taken over and let our emotions and intellect follow. And then times when our intellect takes charge and holds emotion and instinct in check. It is all confusing and contradictory and part of what it means to be human. Much of the time we are out of kilter with ourselves and with the rest of the world. And we long not to be.

When a film is particularly well made, I think you can sense that each of these experiences – the intellectual, the emotional and the instinctual – is being directly addressed to that part of the brain that can 'understand' it. Then those three streams are integrated, woven together and, most importantly, rendered coherent by the story, the characters and the overall style of the film. The audience are being nourished with something that they don't experience, for the most part, in the normal course of their chaotic/boring lives. Cinema is especially powerful because it can communicate directly with those 'pre-linguistic' intelligences that lie within us. There is a one-to-one connection between certain powerful images and sounds and our instinctual, emotional reactions to those images and sounds. The question – and the responsibility for the creators of the film – is how to harness and channel that power for the good, because it can easily be misused.

I believe this could be a desirable goal for film-makers: to find a way to tell their story that speaks to these three levels of cognition and then harmonises them artistically; to supply the coherence that ordinary life does not. Such films would fulfil a unique social – almost a religious – function, helping people to align within themselves and with each other; helping them cope with, and maybe even make some sense of, the complexities and contradictions of life here on planet Earth.[10]

10. This approach is based on the theory of the *triune brain*, developed in the 1960s by Dr Paul MacLean of the US National Institutes of Health (NIH). This suggests that the human brain can be thought of as having three semi-independent 'operating systems', approximately located in the brain stem, limbic system and neocortex, which are respectively responsible for instinct, emotion and intellect. For more details, visit https://tinyurl.com/3a2z4ke9 (QR code on right). Also see the 'Cinematic Brain' chapter of the subsequent volume of this book.

Attributed to Bertrand Russell

The second factor relates to how this mass intimacy might be achieved, to know what and how much to leave out of the experience. If you show too much, as impressive as it might be, the audience has to just sit there and take it; they won't feel, individually, a strong personal, emotional bond with the film and the characters. But if you leave certain things incomplete, to just the right degree, most of the audience will complete those ideas for you. However, each member will complete them in their individual way, based on who they are and what their life experiences have been.

So everyone will have a slightly different impression of what it is that you've just shown them. They think they've seen the whole, up there on the screen, but some of the crucial elements bringing that whole to completion have come from them, not from the film, without them being aware of this process. In a sense, they are seeing themselves, or part of themselves, on the screen, but believing that it is the film-makers who are showing them this. This is what creates the intimacy. 'How does this film know my inner secrets so well?' It is because the film, through its judicious incompleteness, has drawn those secrets out of them and somehow put them up on the screen.

So the artistry in every department – script, direction, casting, acting, camera, production design, editing, sound, music, etc. – is to know what can be left out, so that this 'invisible emptiness' will encourage the audience to be the final collaborators in the creation of the film.

The third factor is what might be called the *cinematic gaze*. As we watch a film, we are allowed to look deeply into the eyes of beautiful/ugly/powerful/interesting people. We 'invade their space', so to speak. In daily life, this close access to beauty and power does not happen for 99.99 per cent of the population, and when it occurs in cinema, it is frequently intoxicating. Those beautiful/ugly/fascinating people seem not to know that we are watching them, which makes it even more exciting. All it would take would be for them to shift their eyes a few degrees and look into the lens, and we would be found out. But until then, we can watch with fascination as thoughts and emotions pass like shadows, storms and beams of sunlight across the faces of talented actors. Cinema is the only art form that can show and choreograph this theatre of thought with such power and intimacy. The intoxicating 'proximity to beauty and power' effect, mediated through eye contact, goes far back into our primate and mammalian past, and cinema is the one creative medium that has found a way to tap deeply into the wellsprings of this primitive and almost irresistible force of nature.

These three factors are available whether you watch a film at home on a 55-inch screen or an iPhone. The fourth factor, the theatrical experience itself, is only available

No artist ever sees things as they really are. If he did, he would cease to be an artist

while viewing a film in the dark, in the presence of like-minded strangers, in a remote location at an appointed time. If we forego this experience, in the name of convenience and economy, what are we losing?

Under the right circumstances, a theatrical screening can deeply enhance the experience. There is much to be said about this, and a lot of it veers into the mysticism of collective consciousness, which is hard to quantify but certainly exists in some intangible form. If we had the ability to visualise the emotions and thoughts of an audience under the sway of a well-made film, they would probably resemble the beautiful arcing loops that we see with large flocks of birds and schools of fish. Without doubt, the birds (starlings in the picture below) find the experience thrilling, in an avian sort of way. And the same, in human terms, could be said for the audience in the grip of a powerful film.

Starling murmuration (see https://www.youtube.com/
watch?v=V4f_1_r80RY; QR code on right)

Short of these mystical thoughts, there is simply the fact that when we displace ourselves from home, at some expense (babysitters, popcorn), with a little discomfort (parking) and risk (strangers! infection!), and we gather at a specific time, we are by those very actions of displacement, constraint and risk-taking primed to see the film in a more meaningfully expanded way than when we summon it into our house via Netflix. When we are in the dark, with many other people, we are alert to tiny sound signals from the audience that will trigger group laughter, screams or tears. When we are at home watching a film alone, or just with a few other people, these signals are

Oscar Wilde

proportionately reduced. The larger the audience, the more likely it is that someone will react first; they will get the joke before anyone else, and this first laugh will trigger everyone else. Similarly, at the end of a performance, there is a moment when the audience is ready to applaud, but uncertain whether now is the time. But as soon as someone claps, everyone else will follow along.[11]

The technical quality (the resolution of image and sound) of a film watched at home can now equal, or even exceed, one viewed in a multiplex. But what at-home viewing can never do, by definition, is provide that communal experience, at an appointed place and time, and to which we have to submit. In the best circumstances, that experience, involving an element of risk and inconvenience, can, paradoxically, sometimes expand our consciousness and awareness of our commonality, sharpening our senses in the mass intimacy of the darkened theatre.

The Devil's Black Box and the Snowflake

Where could this fungible digital juggernaut be heading?

The tension between control and spontaneity has always been at the heart of cinema, and probably of every art: how much control over your brushstroke or chisel, camera or keystrokes do you have? How much do you want? How much do you need?

What is happening in these early years of the third millennium is that digital technology, and now artificial intelligence (AI), are making this tension more overt: digital/AI holds out the promise of total control. I speculate that there is a Faustian bargain in our future, and one day Mephistopheles will slide up to the film-maker with an offer:

'I have something that might interest you; the price is trivial.'

Like all film-makers, he is always interested in what the Devil has to offer, and he encourages him to continue. The Devil produces a Black Box.

'This Black Box has the ability to read your thoughts and turn them into a film. You simply attach these electrodes to your temples, and there you have it. Just think your film into the box, push this button, and out it comes. No more bothersome coping with the frustrating limitations of reality.'

---

11. There is a phenomenon in physics where water (and other fluids) can be dropped below the point of freezing and remain liquid; in this state, it is *supercooled*. This happens when the water is extremely pure and the vessel containing it is very smooth. If an impurity is introduced or the vessel is agitated, the water will suddenly 'remember' that it should be frozen, and it will freeze instantly. The same effect happens above the boiling point. And it also happens with audiences.

It's not the note you play that's the wrong note – it's the note you play afterwards that makes it right or wrong

'How much will it cost?'

'Your immortal soul.'

'Hmm, very tempting . . . Can I change the film once I have thought it?'

'Just play it back and, when you find something you don't like, stop and think it differently. You have total control. Now, let's talk about that soul of yours.'

There are many film-makers who would jump at this, despite the cost. It represents something that all art has striven for: total realisation of a private vision, something never achieved in this world of compromises, schedules, temperamental actors and bad weather. But would actually achieving this goal be good? That's the question. Should we trade our immortal soul to achieve total control, and will it be coming to a screen near you very soon?

Well, we'll see. There are leaps and bounds in artificial intelligence happening every few months, powered by the innate fungibility of digital technology, which dissolves barriers as soon as they appear. Will cinema and the human mind eventually become inter-fungible? Will there be a Cinematic Singularity? Pixar is a way station on that path, reflected in its very name. Every pixel in a Pixar film has been blessed by someone.

At the other end of the spectrum from the Black Box, there is the snowflake, with its glorious variety and spontaneity. When the snowflake forms in nature, supercooled water vapour crystallises in an instant, faster than the water molecules can keep up with. If they had all the time they needed, they would form neat, flat, hexagonal crystals, arranged like bathroom tiles. But in the case of the snowflake they can't because of the speed of freezing. This imbalance of speed is what produces the lacy randomness of the snowflake, and that randomness is why no two snowflakes are the same. Which is why we love to look at them.

Digital media is a great enabler of spontaneity because you can now just grab an iPhone, or whatever digital camera happens to be at hand, and start filming. You can even make a short film in a day – writing, shooting, editing, sound mixing, everything. The software to do this, at least at an elementary level, is bundled for free with every laptop computer. In making a film this quickly, you will be organising your images faster than you might otherwise like, but this can yield an intoxicating spontaneity and freshness. It is a zero-sum game: to achieve this speedy spontaneity, you necessarily sacrifice some control; you will be at the mercy of the elements, the actors available, random passers-by. You can't control the weather during a revolution; it just *happens*, and you have to accept what comes. This is a hallmark of great art – the *feeling* (not necessarily the truth) that it is fresh, that it is happening right now in front of you, and that nobody is controlling it. And human beings love spontaneity: it is an essential spark of life. Nonetheless, the hexagonal nature of the H_2O molecule does impose itself underneath the variation; that's why all snowflakes, despite the filigreed randomness, have six points.

So the challenge for us film-makers now, in this digital/fungible age, is: where will you place your film on this spectrum, with Control at one end of the rainbow and Spontaneity at the other? The decision on how to achieve that balance will be different for every film-maker, and in fact, different for every film. But it is a choice that, from now on, and with increasing consequences, we are going to have to make.

Truth is stranger than fiction. Fiction has to make sense

3: RECUTTING ORSON WELLES'S *TOUCH OF EVIL*

'He Was Some Kind of a Man'

I delivered a short version of the following as a lecture at the School of Sound in London, on 17 April 1998, and it was subsequently published in the New York Times *on 6 September 1998. The text has been expanded for this chapter, and it contains some previously unpublished memos from Welles.*

```
ORSON WELLES
(as Hank Quinlan, drunk)
Read my future.

MARLENE DIETRICH
(as Tana)
You haven't got any.

WELLES
Huh?

DIETRICH
Your future's all used up. Why don't you go home?
```

– A scene from *Touch of Evil*

In the spring of 1958, Orson Welles's *Touch of Evil* was released by Universal Studios as a B-picture, the second half of a double bill. The top-billed A-picture was *The Female Animal*, a now-forgotten vehicle for Hedy Lamarr, directed by Harry Keller (about whom, more later). Neither picture attracted much attention, although some reviewers were intrigued by Welles's first Hollywood-studio work in ten years. Unfortunately, it turned out to be a commercial and critical disappointment, and Welles – only forty-three at the time – returned to Europe and never made another Hollywood feature. Thus, a chapter in Welles's life that had opened in 1941 with perhaps one of the biggest bangs in Hollywood history, *Citizen Kane*, ended seventeen years later with Marlene Dietrich's whispered 'Adios', the final word in *Touch of Evil*.

A couple of years previously, the executives at Universal had been very happy indeed with Welles's rewrite of a mediocre screenplay, *Badge of Evil*. It told the story of a cross-border battle of wills between an ageing, overweight, corrupt but charismatic American police captain, Hank Quinlan, who is haunted by the death of his wife thirty years earlier, and a young, idealistic police official in the Mexican government, Mike Vargas, who is newly married to a Philadelphia girl, Susan. Welles's version of the screenplay renamed the film *Touch of Evil*.

Charlton Heston, who was to play the lead, was the world's biggest movie star at the time; his role in *Touch of Evil* was bracketed by his portrayal of Moses in *The Ten Commandments* and his role as Ben-Hur the year after. Janet Leigh was to play Susan, and talks were under way to have Welles play Quinlan. It was apparently Heston's idea (he was a producer on the film) to have Welles direct as well, but the studio was suspicious of Welles's reputation for independence and offered only the fee he was getting as an actor. Welles accepted. Once production began, however, the executives were ecstatic after Welles managed to film 10 per cent of the script in the first two days. They celebrated by proposing that *Touch of Evil* be the first movie in a five-picture deal.

Shooting continued smoothly, despite the fact that Leigh had broken her left arm during a rehearsal in Venice. Russell Metty was hired as the director of photography (he worked with Kubrick on *Spartacus* a few years later), and many veterans of *Citizen Kane* joined the cast. Joseph Calleia played Pete Menzies, Quinlan's sidekick; Marlene Dietrich was Tana,[1] the gypsy madam of a Mexican brothel; and a young Dennis Weaver (Chester in the TV series *Gunsmoke*) was inspired casting as the befuddled 'night man' of the motel where Leigh is presumably gang-raped. Actors and crew alike loved Welles, and vice versa, and principal photography was finished on schedule and under budget, despite Leigh's broken arm.[2]

Trouble began during editing, which was not an unusual situation for Welles ('The only picture I've ever been allowed to complete to my satisfaction was *Citizen Kane*,' he once said). As far as the executives at Universal were concerned, he was taking too long to put the film together, and when by some subterfuge they sneaked a look at the work-in-progress assembly in late spring of 1957 – while Welles was in New York, appearing on *The Steve Allen Show* – they were horrified. What they saw committed perhaps the worst sin in the Hollywood Ten Commandments: it was a decade

---

1. In the printed screenplay, her name was Tanya, but in shooting it was changed to Tana. In Italian, *tana* means 'lair' or 'burrow', a place of safety for an animal.

2. Throughout the film, Leigh's left arm is usually draped with a sweater, concealing the plaster cast. In the rape scene, a body double was used.

It is later than you think, but earlier than you fear

ahead of its time. Somehow, despite all evidence to the contrary, the executives had been expecting a conventional picture, and they were upset and confused by the film's innovative editing and camerawork, its use of real locations, its unorthodox use of sound and, most especially, the boldness of its reversals of stereotypes and routine acceptance of human degradation.

Harsh words were spoken on both sides. Welles, his feelings hurt, went off to Mexico to work on his *Don Quixote*, a strategic mistake that gratified the studio, and in the remaining six months while the film was completed he was not allowed back into the editing room. Universal hired Harry Keller (the director of *The Female Animal*) to write and shoot four new explanatory scenes and substantially recut the remainder of the film. From Mexico, Welles sent a telegram to Heston, counselling discretion and minimal co-operation during these 'unjust' reshoots:

> There's this character – (known and loved by all) – he might be called
> Cooperative Chuck . . . he is not merely well-disciplined in his work, but
> positively eager – even wildly eager – to make things easy for his fellows on
> the set and for all the executives in their offices . . . In a word, he's the Eagle
> Scout of the Screen Actors' Guild. The purpose of this communiqué is to beg
> him to leave his uniform and flag in the dressing room . . . On the set, in the
> commissary and elsewhere, do not permit yourself for a moment to grant **any
> element of justice to any part of this operation**, since all such expressions
> from you are treasured up and will most certainly be used – as they've been
> used before. There's nothing I can do about meeting the excitations of the
> close-up lens, but I can implore you to curb your peace-making instincts and to
> maintain an aloof and non-committal silence. That goes for Janet, too, dammit.
> In a word, keep your yap shut. Much love Orson.[3]

Universal were contractually obliged to show Welles the results of all this, and they did so reluctantly, letting him view the film only once, at a screening in late November 1957.

Welles quickly typed up fifty-eight pages of comments – astute, insightful, boiling with passion under the surface, but tactfully restrained since he was addressing the heads of the studio (particularly the head of production, Ed Muhl), who were his declared enemies. It is heartbreaking to read, both for the obvious waste of talent and

---

3. *Orson Welles: One-Man Band* by Simon Callow (London: Jonathan Cape, 2015), p. 270. It is a remarkable telegram, considering that in 1957 Heston was the biggest star in the firmament and Welles was thought to be a has-been.

---

insight of one of the twentieth century's great film-makers, and because, with hind-sight, we know *Touch of Evil* was to be Welles's last film within the Hollywood system.

But it is inspiring as well as heartbreaking. The memo is a unique document that gives us precious insights into Welles's creative process, insights that we wouldn't pos-sess if Universal hadn't taken *Touch of Evil* away from him. This is the silver lining in an otherwise rather dark cloud that closed around the film in late 1957.

Welles, who died in 1985, claimed never to have seen the film again, which is per-haps a good thing, since an additional fifteen minutes were cut from the November 1957 version after an unsuccessful preview screening in early 1958. Consequently, Welles's memo was forgotten, and subsequently believed to have been lost.

Complete fifty-eight-page memo with annotations:
http://wellesnet.com/touch_memo1.htm (QR code on left)

Then, one afternoon about forty years later, my phone rang. This call out of the blue was from Rick Schmidlin, someone I didn't know at the time. He introduced himself as a Welles aficionado and told me that a couple of years earlier, he had come across some tantalising fragments of the long-lost memo Welles had written. And from that moment on, Rick had made it his mission to locate the entire memo – which, amazingly, he eventually did – and then, equally improbably, to convince Universal Studios to let him start moving ahead with a recut and remix of *Touch of Evil*, using the memo as a bible. This would be for the fortieth anniversary of the film's release, in 1998. Rick was looking for someone to take on the interpretive aspects of the project, and he thought of me because he felt I had the necessary expertise in pic-ture editing and sound mixing: Welles's notes required changes in both areas in equal measure.

What you see on the screen is, in part, determined by what you hear, and how you hear something is partly determined by what you see. So, even though, techni-cally, they are separate departments, the mutual influence of sound and picture is inextricable. Even for me, who works in both areas, they are sometimes completely mysterious in their chemistry.

I had three questions: can you send me the memo? Is the negative in good shape? And is there a magnetic three-track master of the final sound mix?

Rick sent me a copy of the memo and explained that Universal, who still controlled the rights to the film, had discovered that the negative for the 1958 version was in good shape, although everything else (the out-takes) had been destroyed long ago;

that there was a preview print, found in the mid-1970s, which had the missing fifteen minutes in it;[4] and that the original magnetic mix of the film had been located, conveniently split into three channels (one for dialogue, one for music, one for sound effects), which would allow us to separate one track from the others, raise its level, eliminate it or shift it in time. Many of Welles's notes concerned sound, and if there had been no way to separate the dialogue from the music from the sound effects, it would have been impossible to proceed. The fact that the master was on magnetic film also meant that the frequency response of the finished recut could approach digital standards.[5]

I was more than intrigued by Rick's proposal and accepted his offer, so Rick drew up a budget, which was low for this sort of thing, and Universal agreed to go ahead. Using Avid's Media Composer, we started work upstairs in the barn in Bolinas, California, in January 1998 and finished three months later, in April.

Rick and I were constantly aware of the sacred ground that we were treading in tackling something like this. *Touch of Evil* is an almost holy object for many people, from the members of the French New Wave on. Jean-Luc Godard and François Truffaut awarded it the grand prize at the Brussels World's Fair of 1958, and it has influenced several generations of young people to pick up their cameras and microphones and become film-makers.

In the course of an interview for the *LA Times*, I mentioned that each decade sees another interpretation of *Touch of Evil*, and the version that was in the theatres at the time of the piece was Curtis Hanson's *L.A. Confidential*. Shortly afterwards, I received the following note from Curtis: 'Thanks for the mention. There's no work whose name I'd like paired with *L.A. Confidential* any more than *Touch of Evil*. I have the original poster; when I walk up to my office, I see it every day and I bow down before it.'

So when I told friends what I had been up to, they got this shocked and slightly despairing look in their eyes; one of them even said, 'You know, this is like hearing that God just phoned and wants changes in the Bible.' But the truth is that Welles was deeply disappointed with the final version of the film (he never saw it again after that one sad screening in November 1957). The whole thing was a particularly traumatic experience for him because he was reliving the nightmares of *The Magnificent Ambersons* (1942),

---

4. This was probably the version of the film that Welles saw in November 1957.

5. The release prints of *Touch of Evil* had optical track sound, deficient in high frequencies.

Robert Bresson

The Lady from Shanghai (1947) and other films of his, where the post-production had gone wrong and he'd lost control of the final phase of their completion.

This memo-guided 1998 version of *Touch of Evil* has a different structure to the 1958 release, particularly in the first forty-five minutes, with some deletions (notably, one of the explanatory scenes added by the studio), different uses of music, and many subtle trims and repositionings that serve to emphasise and clarify the story. The laboratory team at Universal, led by Bob O'Neil, was able to repair, digitally, some scratched and torn shots in the otherwise superb master negative, and to make a high-quality inter-negative off the 1976 preview print that contained the missing footage. The sound team, led by Bill Varney, was able to digitally process the forty-year-old soundtrack to a new level of clarity. In the end, we made fifty changes.

Those changes did not transform the film into something completely different. We did not find the equivalent of the missing last reel of Welles's *Magnificent Ambersons*, for instance. This *Touch of Evil* is simply a better version of the same film, which is to say, more in line with the director's vision, more self-consistent, more resonant, more confidently modulated, clearer. In other words, more as it should have been in the first place. Whether the film is now the way Welles would have wanted it had he been given a free hand, we will never know. This version follows Welles's memo scrupulously, but the memo itself deftly acknowledges the studio's hammerlock:

> The purpose of this memo, is not to discuss every change I think should be made in the final version. I am passing on to you a reaction based not on my conviction as to what my picture ought to be, but only what here strikes me as significantly mistaken in your picture.

Whether that last phrase should be taken at face value or read as an astute political gesture, I don't know. It certainly indicates how deeply Welles's pride was hurt.

As it turns out, one of the changes with the biggest impact occurs in the film's famous opening shot, a three-minute-twenty-second tour de force that has become a kind of Rosetta Stone for film students over the last sixty years. The length of this shot has not been changed by a single frame. It still begins with a close-up of the clock of a time bomb being set at three minutes and twenty seconds, the bomb's insertion into the boot of a car by a shadowy figure, the arrival of a laughing man and woman who get into the convertible and drive away, then the introduction of the two visiting honeymooners (Heston and Leigh), walking blithely through the fictional town of Los Robles, occasionally

Style is a simple way of expressing complicated things

walking beside the car as it winds its way through traffic, in and out of frame, and the final explosion of the bomb at exactly the moment that was predicted at the beginning of the shot (three minutes and twenty seconds later). Two significant things have been changed, however: the main titles have been removed, and Henry Mancini's well-known title music has been replaced by a complex montage of source music.

Bob O'Neil luckily discovered a short piece of negative that turned out to be the original opening shot without the titles. It was damaged and incomplete, but it gave us what we needed to digitally reweave the opening without any credits.

Welles had wanted the shot to run without any credits and sought something very different on the soundtrack, as he describes at the beginning of his memo:

> I assume that the music now backing the opening sequence is temporary [Welles was referring to the Mancini score]. As the camera moves through the streets of the Mexican border town, the plan was to feature a succession of different and contrasting Latin American musical numbers, the effect, that is, of our passing one cabaret orchestra after another. In honky-tonk districts on the border loudspeakers are all over the entrance of every joint, large or small, each blasting out its own tune, by way of a come-on or pitch for the tourists.
>
> The fact that the streets are invariably loud with this music was planned as a basic device throughout the entire picture. The special use of contrasting mambotype rhythm numbers with rock 'n' roll will be developed in some detail at the end of this memo, when I'll take up details of the beat and also specifics of musical colour and the instrumentation on a scene-by-scene and transition-by-transition basis. In the version I was shown yesterday, it's not clear where you've decided to place the credits.

Later on, he writes about the music coming from the nightclubs and through the doors of the smallest bars and cantinas:

> It is very important that the usual ranchero and mariachi numbers should be avoided and the emphasis should go on Afro-Cuban rhythm numbers. Those few places where traditional Mexican music is wanted will be indicated by special notes. Also, a great deal of rock 'n' roll is called for. Because these numbers invariably back dialogue scenes, there should never at any time be any vocals. The rock 'n' roll comes from radio loudspeakers, juke boxes and, in particular the radio in the motel. All of the above music, of course, is 'realistic' in the sense that it is literally playing during the action.

Jean Cocteau

To fulfil Welles's wishes, we needed to create a multilevel montage of seven or eight pieces of source music, yet we didn't want to bring anything new and 'foreign' into the film. So we plundered fragments of source music from later in the film to weave together at the beginning, like an overture.

One of the by-products of having the magnetic masters was that when we removed the Mancini title music, something was revealed that had been hidden for forty years: the sound effects track for this opening scene. It was a complete surprise to us that it even existed, buried as it was under the score. It has been restored to its original balance in the film, allowing the audience to hear the town, the voices of the pedestrians, their footsteps, the laughter of the crowds, the sirens – even the bleating of a pack of goats stuck in the middle of the road.

When we raised the level of the effects track, a lot of analogue tape hiss came along with it, so we had to suppress the noise digitally. But that was something we were doing to the entire soundtrack – the dialogue and music, as well as the effects. Just a bit more in this case, because we were raising the level of those opening effects by ten decibels or so, which is considerable. And because we were able to remix the whole film in digital, the soundtrack now has full-frequency range and, I guess, what might be called 'appropriate' dynamics. It is still monophonic: the film was originally conceived in mono and finished in mono. If *Touch of Evil* had been made twenty years later, Welles would almost certainly have used stereo, but since he was no longer around to guide us, we kept it monophonic.

There's a perennial cat-and-dog fight between the music and sound effects departments on almost every film. And unless the ground rules have been made clear, and everyone keeps up to date with what everyone else is doing, there are inevitably going to be moments when the sound effects and the music want to hold centre stage at the same time. The decision usually goes to the music, for various artistic, political and economic reasons. Welles was keenly aware of all this, given his own background in live theatre and radio and his twenty years of experience in making films, and so he writes about how certain things in the music will have to be underplayed in order to give the sound effects room to breathe. The memo allows us to listen in on him orchestrating all this; he knows not only what should be done, but how to achieve the final effect that he's after.

Also, significantly, there is now music coming from the radio of the convertible that has the bomb in it. Notice how the car will veer out of frame while the camera will go somewhere else, and then the car will come back into frame again. That happens three times, and on each occasion, in the new version, the re-entry of the car is preceded by the tune that was on the radio when the ignition was started – American rock'n'roll, in contrast to the Afro-Cuban music in the town – which allows the audience to track the progress of the car with the ticking bomb in it as it drives closely alongside our two stars, Heston and Leigh.

When the opening shot had titles and music on it, the audience would 'know' subconsciously that the bomb will not explode until the titles are over. In the new version, there is the possibility that the bomb could go off at any time, which adds an extra element of danger when you hear the rock'n'roll music approaching and the car passing by.

Film-makers spend a disproportionate amount of time getting the beginnings of their films right, primarily because two things have to be accomplished simultaneously: the story has to be started in an interesting way, and operating instructions have to be given, implicitly, on how to understand the film as a whole. If these contain a mistake, it can cast a long, baleful shadow over everything that follows.

Universal's decision to run titles and music over the opening shot of *Touch of Evil* kept viewers at a distance from the action, and the title music told them that this was a *certain kind* of detective story. Later in 1958, Mancini used an almost identical theme for *Peter Gunn*, a television show starring Craig Stevens as a debonaire detective. *Touch of Evil* is actually a kind of anti-*Gunn*: Welles's Quinlan is the opposite of debonaire, eventually plunging to an ignominious death in a trash-choked open sewer.

All this is in retrospect, of course. There was nothing particularly wrong with the use of superimposed titles; it was a conventional and adequate solution, as was Mancini's music. But in comparison with Welles's original intentions, now that we can see them realised and appreciate how much source music he used throughout the entire film, the studio's approach in 1957 started things off on the wrong foot.

Of all the notes that he gave in his memo, the one to which Welles dedicated the most space (eight of the fifty-eight pages) was his plea to restore the intercutting of the stories of the separated honeymooners, Susan (Leigh) and Mike Vargas (Heston): 'No point concerning anything in the picture is made with such urgency and confidence as this. Do please – please – give it a fair try.'

The studio had flattened out Welles's original pattern of editing, presumably believing that an audience for a B-picture could not maintain two storylines simultaneously.

Scandinavian saying, attributed to Jean Sibelius

Consequently, when the newlyweds are separated right after the bomb goes off, the studio's version stayed with Vargas for the entire sequence at the site of the explosion. Only later do we return to Susan's story and learn that she was picked up in the street and menaced by the crime boss, Grandi (Akim Tamiroff). What Welles had intended instead was to cut back and forth between the two stories:

> What's vital is that both stories be kept equally and continuously alive; each scene should play at roughly equal lengths until the lovers meet again at the hotel. We should never stay away from either story long enough to lose their separate but relating threads of interest.

This argument did not hold water with the studio at the time, but now that we can see what Welles had in mind, his solution is obviously superior. The whole film is about the separation of the newlyweds, who are briefly reunited, only to be separated again and again, crossing the border multiple times and not finally coming together until the end.[6] By intercutting the two stories from the beginning, the film lets the viewer know that the stories are equally important, and that their interrelationships are as important as the stories themselves. Since the Vargas thread comes first in the studio version, the audience is encouraged to believe that his story, not Susan's, is the significant one.

Specifically where these scenes were to be intercut was not indicated in Welles's memo. He gives several options, some of them slightly contradictory, so it is clear that this was an area that had not been fully worked out before he was dismissed. Much of the memo, in fact, has a certain ambiguity to it; there are few editorial instructions that do not require a degree of interpretation. That extra amount of responsibility made the work exciting for me, but I should say that the tone of the memo is so pungent with Welles's presence and thought processes that you can pick up what he would have preferred almost by osmosis. There were several times during the editing when I felt that he had given me these notes shortly before going into the next room to take a nap, and that I was trying to finish them all to his satisfaction before he woke up.

One of the smaller changes we made, but one with the largest repercussions, was the removal of a close-up of Menzies, Quinlan's sidekick, in the police archives room, where Vargas is looking over the records. It is particularly interesting that Welles,

---

6. On the subject of border crossings, it is interesting to contrast the recent disputes over the porousness of the US/Mexico border with Mike Vargas's praise for the openness that existed in 1958.

The soundtrack invented silence

in asking for this change, phrased his request in technical terms: he wanted the shot removed, he wrote . . .

> . . . because of a mistaken use of the wide angle lens which distorts Menzies's face grotesquely. There is no use upsetting the audience this way. The scene played all right without this weird close-up.

At first, this note appeared to me to be out of character for Welles, because there are many other 'weird close-ups' in the film that use the same lens, and he never talks in such solicitous terms anywhere else about upsetting the audience. Initially, I resisted this note. Welles's reason for cutting the shot did not convince me, and actually making the lift was technically difficult because of the lack of coverage for that scene (remember that all the out-takes for the film had been destroyed long ago). I tried it anyway, and the result was awkward – it looked like something had been crudely removed – so I restored it to the way it was and moved on.

However, Rick didn't want to leave any note undone and kept insisting, diplomatically, that we try again. I had other notes to do and thought it was a lost cause, but eventually I went back and found a way to more or less solve the awkwardness of the resulting lift, much to Rick's gratification. I still thought it was the only one of Welles's notes that didn't make sense, but when we finally sat down to view the film as a whole, with all of the changes done, I saw the real reason for it, which Welles carefully avoided telling the studio. He masked his intentions by blaming himself, hoping that this would soften up Ed Muhl, but the removal of the close-up had much greater implications than the size of the lens: it was to adjust a significant character point, and the cutting of that shot resonates throughout the final reels of *Touch of Evil*.

The 'weird close-up' occurs when Vargas has confronted Menzies with evidence of Quinlan's criminality. Menzies collapses onto the table, and the agony of acknowledging the truth about his boss is revealed in this close-up: Quinlan must be guilty. Almost instantly, though, he jumps back to his feet and defends Quinlan, but the damage has been done: Vargas has seen him acknowledge the truth, and more to the point, Menzies has seen Vargas see this. As a result, everything that Menzies does in the 1958 version's last half-hour is done under duress: not authentically, because the character believes it to be best, but because he must, having revealed his knowledge of the truth to Vargas. Menzies has a metaphorical leash around his neck.

By cutting this close-up, it also cut the leash. He never collapses in the scene with

Robert Bresson

Vargas, continuing to defend his boss. It is only later on that we – not Vargas – see the doubt and anguish on his face, during the scene on the porch, when Menzies agrees to carry the wire and participate in entrapping Quinlan. (Vargas does not see this expression because of the staging of the scene.) Welles clearly must have felt that the moment of Menzies's weakness in the police archives came too soon in the story and wanted to delay it until the porch scene, but didn't want to say as much to the studio executives. He described *Touch of Evil* as a story of love and betrayal between two men, Pete Menzies and Hank Quinlan. The removal of Menzies's 'weird close-up' plays a significant part in realising this vision for the film.

There are frequently moments like these in the making of films, when issues of character and story are decided by the inclusion – or not – of a single shot that will reverberate throughout the film. By firing Welles, the studio prevented him from having a hand in this fine-tuning of his own work, ensuring a certain level of dissonance in the finished product. A dissonance that has now been eased away.

> The effect should be just that, exactly as bad as that . . .
>
> – Orson Welles

During the course of our work together, Rick did not cease his detective work. Universal had told him that there were no living survivors from *Touch of Evil*'s post-production crew, but he was not convinced and combed through the LA phone book for various names, particularly that of Ernie Nims, who was head of post-production at Universal back in the late 1950s. Significantly, Nims had edited Welles's *The Stranger* back in 1946, the only film of Welles to have been a financial success immediately upon release.

Rick located an E. Nims in Century City and rang the number. It turned out to be *the* Ernie Nims, who was, at the age of eighty-nine, going out for a round of golf but had time to tell us that 'Orson was a great film-maker, but his trouble was that he was twenty years ahead of his time.' Rick explained what we were up to and asked if Ernie had any documentation from *Touch of Evil*. 'Yeah, two file boxes in the attic. Tell you what, I'll leave them out on the porch, and you can come by and pick them up. Love to meet you, but I can't stay – got to tee off.'

Rick explained, slightly panicked, that we were in a barn in Bolinas, 400 miles to the north, and that he would have a messenger service come by and pick them up. Ernie thought that was a great idea and hung up. We were astonished at our luck and the blithe and trusting cheerfulness of Mr Nims.

A film can be so realistic that you don't believe a moment of it

Three days later, the two boxes arrived: production details, telegrams from Welles to Nims and, among many other things, a copy of Welles's extensive notes on the music for the film, written months before he was fired, when things were still going well. The following excerpt from that music memo may give you some idea of what Universal was dealing with. Welles is writing about the treatment of the music in the scenes where Susan is talking to Grandi:

> The music should have a low insistent beat with a lot of bass in it. This music is at its loudest in the street and once she enters the tiny lobby of The Ritz Hotel, it fades to extreme background. However, it does not disappear but continues and, eventually, there will be a segue to a Latin-type rhythm number, also very low in pitch, dark, and with a strong, even exaggerated, emphasis on the bass.

Then his typewriter breaks into capital letters, and he centres the next paragraph right in the middle of the page:

IT IS VERY IMPORTANT TO NOTE THAT IN THE RECORDING OF ALL THESE NUMBERS, WHICH ARE SUPPOSED TO BE HEARD THROUGH STREET LOUDSPEAKERS, THAT THE EFFECT SHOULD BE JUST THAT, JUST EXACTLY AS BAD AS THAT.

He continues:

> The music itself should be skilfully played but it will not be enough, in doing the final sound mixing, to run this track through an echo chamber with a certain amount of filter. To get the effect we're looking for, it is absolutely vital that this music be played back through a cheap horn in the alley outside the sound building. After this is recorded, it can then be loused up even further in the process of re-recording. But a tinny exterior horn is absolutely necessary, and since it does not represent very much in the way of money, I feel justified in insisting upon this, as the result will be really worth it.

In that paragraph, if you are a Universal executive in 1957, are two completely incompatible concepts: after the music is recorded 'it can then be loused up even further' and 'the result will be really worth it'.

Put yourself in the shoes of Ed Muhl, who was head of production at Universal. Here is a director saying that he wants to take a well-recorded music track and louse it up by re-recording it through a tinny speaker in an alleyway, and then louse it up even further in the final mix; to top it all off, 'the result will be really worth it'. It wouldn't take much more to make you question everything that Welles was doing. And if he was taking a long time doing it, you might feel justified in removing the film from his control.

Rick also discovered that Muhl himself was still alive, ninety years old and living in the San Fernando Valley, so we called him up to tell him what we were doing and see if he had anything to suggest (our rewarding experience with Ernie Nims had gone to our heads). Muhl, however, was an acerbic and unrepentant enemy of Welles; he felt that Welles had been a conceited poseur and an alcoholic who never directed a film that made any money, and of course Universal were justified in taking *Touch of Evil* away from him. He thought what we were doing was misguided, and he slammed the phone down.

Well, we now know exactly what Welles was up to with his alleyway recording. It was the analogue forerunner of all the digital reverberation techniques that have blossomed over the last forty years, allowing us to colour a sound with an infinite variety of acoustic ambiences. Welles's description of his technique had a particularly strong impact on me because this is something – what I then called *worldising* – that I developed on my own in the late 1960s. Or at least I thought I had, until I read this part of the memo. Having screened *Touch of Evil* at film school, I was probably subconsciously influenced by what Welles had done, though I had always – even when I was playing with my first tape recorder in the early 1950s – been fascinated by the peculiar emotion that a spatial treatment of sound can give and was frustrated with the limited technical resources available to do that at the time.

There is also a practical reason for adding spatial colouring: you can put acoustically treated sound – music, let's say – in the background of a scene, and it will tend not to interfere with the intelligibility of the foreground dialogue because its sonic 'edges' have been softened and diffused by a kind of acoustic *sfumato*. This is very much the equivalent of a shallow depth of field in photography. If you were taking a photo portrait of somebody, you would typically choose a long (75 mm) lens and a wide aperture to give a shallow depth of field. Then you focus on your subject's eyes, and consequently the rose hedge in the background is thrown out of focus. When somebody sees the resulting photograph, they know immediately, without thinking, what they're supposed to be looking at, because that's the part in focus; the rose hedge is just an attractive blur in the background.

Dismantle and put together again until you get intensity

So my technique would be to take a soundtrack out of the studio and into the world, along with another tape recorder and a speaker, and position the two so that the second machine recorded the other playing back with a nice envelope of reverberant sound around it – say, an abandoned subway station for some of the voices in *THX 1138*. In the final mix, I would lay this new track alongside the original, so that I could fade from one to the other, going from a dry, clean sound to a diffuse, atmospheric, 'dirty' one, depending on the needs of the scene. As far as I can tell, this 'double-track' technique is the difference from Welles's approach; he just used the single 'dirty' track recorded in the alleyway. Nonetheless, I feel that I owe a debt of gratitude to him for pioneering the way.

Many of the soundtracks I have mixed are full of this: Coppola's *Rain People* and *The Godfather*, as well as Lucas's *THX 1138*. The most extreme is probably the latter's *American Graffiti*, where the music runs throughout the whole film, alternating between the out-of-focus diffuse background and the in-focus sharp foreground. I should mention that *Graffiti* was also distributed by Universal, fourteen years after *Touch of Evil*, and our sound mix was initially evaluated by the studio as 'one of the worst soundtracks we have ever heard. An embarrassment to Universal Studios.'

Here are Welles's comments from the music memo about the sound outside the Ritz strip club, where Zsa Zsa Gabor makes an appearance as the manager:

> This music should have a highly casual, low, almost improvised feeling, and the colour should be dark and rather menacing. This continues faintly throughout the acid-throwing business, with the percussive part of it building. The actual drumming should be extremely muted, however, in the original recording, so that there is no conflict between this throbbing rhythmic effect and the sudden sizzling, frying effect of the acid landing on the poster of the girl.

He's addressing the thorny issue of music conflicting with sound effects and asking the music to suppress something in its normal development, so that, at the right moment, the sound effect of acid being thrown and hitting a poster on the wall can be shockingly sizzling.

I have never before read director's music notes that were so extensive and have such a deep and precisely articulated understanding of the complexity of the soundtrack and how it interacts with the image. (You can read this unpublished memo at https://archive.org/details/orson-welles-music-memo/mode/2up; QR code on right.)

Robert Bresson

As Rick and I progressed through the film, chipping away at Welles's fifty suggested changes, we also had the time to appreciate his work, even (perhaps especially) in areas where he had given few notes.

In the final reel, I admired the beautiful editing of this sequence, where Pete Menzies is carrying the wire transmitting back to Vargas, and Vargas is clambering through the oil-saturated landscape, trying to keep within range of Menzies's radio. It is put together with an absolute understanding of the audience's focus of attention and the motion within the frame, and of exactly how long each shot should last.

Welles was able to create these long, continuous, complicated shots, like the famous opening sequence or the Sanchez interrogation, but also to come up with the most amazing editorial constructions. Usually, directors are good at one, less so at the other. Welles was excellent at both. He knew when a sequence needed to be shot in one continuous take for dramatic reasons, as well as when it had to be constructed editorially in a dynamic way.

I also loved the interplay of the actual voices of Quinlan and Menzies with those on the tape recorder Vargas is carrying. Inevitably, it reminded me of the opening scenes of *The Conversation*, where the couple, Ann and Mark, are walking through the lunchtime crowd in Union Square, with Harry and Stan crouched in the parked van, listening to their recording. Are Ann and Mark going to say something incriminating? Will they discover that they are being bugged?

Here, the same questions: will Quinlan say something incriminating? Will he discover he is being bugged? Welles manages, masterfully, to resolve these two questions almost simultaneously. Just after the moment when Quinlan admits to strangling Grandi and planting the dynamite in the Sanchez case, the sound of his voice acquires an echo . . .

QUINLAN
Don't you think Sanchez is guilty? He's guilty. He'll confess . . .
(echoing)
Hey! Listen to that . . .
(water sloshing)
Hear that?

MENZIES
Hear what?

QUINLAN
Like an echo . . .

To achieve greatness, you need two things: a plan; and not quite enough time

(after a pause)
Vargas . . . Maybe he's tailing me with a bug. Recording. Hey! Are you carrying a bug for him? A microphone?

MENZIES
Hank, I . . .

QUINLAN
Don't lie to me!

Vargas had been forced to wade under one of the arches of the bridge Quinlan and Menzies are crossing, and the sound of his recorder had ricocheted off the archway. This makes Quinlan suspicious, and he figures it out: Pete must be carrying a wire. A struggle ensues, a gun is drawn, and Quinlan shoots his old buddy Pete. The denouement is not far away.

The fact that the quality of the sound changed when Vargas was forced to go underneath the arches was in the screenplay, and is the pin around which the resolution of the whole story turns. Welles had written, directed and acted in theatre, radio drama, film, television. He knew all the tricks and was particularly sensitive to the potential meaning of something as insignificant as a slight echo (for the use of silence in Welles's *War of the Worlds* radio broadcast from 1938, see https://vimeo.com/424374539; QR code on right). This use of a subtle shift in quality is an outstanding example of how sound can be pulled deep into the fabric of a screenplay and then used at the right moment to yank the plot to its conclusion.

Quinlan's last words come from the tape, as his dead body floats away in the trash-strewn river . . .

QUINLAN
Pete . . . That's the second bullet I . . . I stopped for you . . .

. . . before the recorder's lid snaps shut and his friend Tana delivers her famous final valediction for him.

So here we are, back at the first meeting between Tana and Quinlan in many years, and the source music accompanying the scene, written by Henry Mancini, is from a pianola. When Quinlan leads the others out the back way from Zsa Zsa Gabor's nightclub, he stops, hearing the sound of the pianola wafting in the air.

Leonard Bernstein

This music should not be playing at the start of the scene but should begin just a beat before Quinlan notices it. That is to say, it does not fade in but has a straightforward musical commencement, as though the player piano had been started at this point. Tana's is some distance away and the player piano should be distant in this shot, particularly since we want to get a rather startling contrast on the next cut, where we go directly to a close shot of the player piano in full operation. In this cut, of course, the piano should be loudest.

When Quinlan enters Tana's, the music itself reaches a definitively slower and more romantic section, and this continues through the dialogue scene between Tana and Quinlan. The music itself should be subdued enough and slow enough so that by monitoring it well down, we can have the needed colour for this scene without any confusion or difficulty in making out the words.

Again, Welles is taking everything into consideration . . .

The music itself comes to a complete finish just before Quinlan says *That Pianola* . . .

In the 1958 release, the studio didn't do any of these things. The pianola was playing right from the beginning of the alleyway sequence, and it continued, barrelling on through the whole scene between Tana and Quinlan. When you do what Welles wants, however, it has three positive effects. First of all, the music acquires more personality, because it isn't simply playing irrespective of who is in the alleyway; it is waiting for Quinlan to show up. As soon as he appears, there's a second's pause, and then you hear the first notes. The music is now purposeful: it pounces as soon as it sees its prey, dragging him into Tana's.

Secondly, by shifting the starting point, one of the wonderful, serendipitous things we found is that the music itself has an internal pause that occurs just before Dietrich, as Tana, has her first line. So at exactly the moment the music comes to this brief stop, she says, 'We're closed,' and then it starts up again for its coda. As a mixer, you pray for this kind of thing, and sure enough, there it was as soon as we did what Welles wanted and shifted the starting point of the music.

And thirdly, at the halfway point in the scene, the piano roll comes to a stop. You now notice that the scene is articulated. The first part, which has musical backing, is all atmosphere.

QUINLAN
Do you know who I am?

> TANA
>
> We're closed.

> QUINLAN
>
> I'm Hank Quinlan.

> TANA
>
> I didn't recognise you. You should lay off those candy bars.

. . . all smoky innuendo about what may or may not have passed between them in previous years. But then the music stops, Quinlan makes a brief comment about the pianola, and Tana gets down to business:

> TANA
>
> What can I offer you?

> QUINLAN
>
> Do you know anything about the bomb?

> TANA
>
> That happened on your side of the border.

> QUINLAN
>
> Yeah, I know, but in a place like this, you hear things.

> TANA
>
> (*after a pause*)
>
> I heard the explosion.

She's not going to tell Quinlan whether she knows anything about the bomb. The second half of the scene is all plot. First half: atmosphere with musical backing. Second half: plot with no music. This was Welles's original plan. When there is music all the way through, as in the 1958 version, there is a blurring and lack of dramatic articulation; the music is telling you, subconsciously, *This is all atmospheric. They're just saying things to hear themselves talk; don't bother yourself with the words.* Now, when the music stops, it's like a switch goes on in the audience's heads that says, *OK, pay attention now. Listen to what they're saying, because it's about the story.*

One of the fascinating things I learned during this recut is that Tana is a creation of the shooting; she's not in the original script. About a week or two into production,

Marcel Proust

Welles must have felt, *I need Marlene, I need something that only she can give to a film like this*, so he called her up and said (hypothetically):

'Darling, can you help me? I want you to play the madam of a whorehouse, and I'm shooting your scene in three days.'

'Marvellous. What should I look like?'

'Well, you're supposed to be Mexican.'

'Darling, I can't do Mexican.'

'It doesn't matter. Remember that Gypsy outfit you wore a couple of years ago? And I think we've got one of Elizabeth Taylor's wigs.'

'I can do Gypsy. I'll be there. Delightful.'

Marlene Dietrich as Tana

Despite the haste, this was not a frivolous decision. Welles was, I believe, worried about the final assessment of Quinlan's character in the script. The epitaph 'He was a great detective but a lousy cop' was, in the original, to have been delivered by Vargas over Quinlan's dead body. After a couple of weeks of filming, Welles must have felt uncomfortable about giving this crucial line to Vargas, so he rewrote the scene, reuniting Vargas with his wife Susan and getting him out of the way, and left the final assessment of Quinlan to his long-time friend Tana (as Dietrich was a long-time friend of Welles). Detective Schwartz now feeds her the line . . .

'Hank was a great detective all right . . .'

And Tana counters with . . .

. . . and a lousy cop.

Often the hands will solve a mystery that the intellect has struggled with in vain

SCHWARTZ

Is that all you have to say for him?

TANA

He was some kind of a man . . . What does it matter what you say about people?

In later years Dietrich referred to this as the best line and best delivery of her entire career. She was fifty-six years old at the time of filming.

The point is that Welles created, while shooting, a character who seems irrevocably part of the film, who had a past – probably a romantic one – with Quinlan, and who could consequently assess his character with more depth and humanity than the slightly tin-horn Vargas. In fact, the final image of the film is Tana, walking away into the night, saying, 'Adios.' It doesn't hurt that there was probably a romantic link between Welles and Dietrich back in the 1940s, which gives an added frisson.

That paradoxical contradiction, 'Great detective, lousy cop,' also has, in hindsight, a spooky resonance with Welles's career. He was a great director – one of the greatest – but, at the same time, I suspect that there was something else about him that was deeply flawed, 'lousy' from the point of view of how to successfully make the system, almost despite itself, yield the results he was after.

Charlton Heston, Janet Leigh, Dennis Weaver and a number of other actors came to the cast and crew screening in 1998, after we finished the recut and remix. The restored version reminded them of the film that Welles had described during rehearsals in 1957, and the good times and hopes they all had during the shooting.

From my conversations with Heston after the screening, I gathered he had told Welles, 'You can charm us actors, you can make us melt in your hands . . . Well, just use that same charm with the studio guys, and you'll get what you want.' But Welles found this difficult to do, for unknown personal reasons – I suppose because he felt threatened by their power over him – and his reaction was to either turn combative or run away.

Which is strange, when you recall that as an actor he specialised in playing blustering, devious, authoritarian figures similar to Ed Muhl and his other enemies at Universal: Citizen Kane, Harry Lime, Gregory Arkadin, Hank Quinlan, Will Varner, Cardinal Wolsey and so on, all 'studio guys' in a sense. His last role before he died was J. P. Morgan, the powerful banker who foreclosed Nikola Tesla's dreams for a world powered by clean, inexpensive electrical energy. You might think that Welles's ability,

Carl Jung

as an actor, to psychologically inhabit these authority figures would make it possible for him to understand and outwit their real-life counterparts through charm, flattery or subtle craft. But, for some reason, this was not possible.

Touch of Evil is a highly designed film. Welles wrote it, directed it, starred in it. As can be seen in the fifty-eight pages of notes and the music memo, he was concerned about the minutiae of music, sound and picture editing, character and motivation, and style. So when the film was taken away from him and given to someone else, things just began to get fuzzy. What I think we accomplished in this 1998 recut and remix is a reduction in that conceptual fuzziness. The examples I have given here are just a few of the fifty changes that Welles requested – we were able to provide solutions to all of them – but they are representative of what Welles was asking for.

Obviously, the damaged 1958 version is still a great film – great enough to inspire many people to go into film-making. The changes we made are subtle; they certainly don't turn the film inside out, but they give it more tensile strength. The organisation and emphases of the new version are more consistent with the film as a whole. *Touch of Evil* is now more itself.

It is both wonderful and sad that Welles's memo exists. Wonderful because it gives us insights into the mind of one of the greatest film-makers of the twentieth century, fighting for the soul of his film. And also because the memo's rediscovery has allowed us to finally restore, as far as is possible, a film of great historical importance. Sad because, clearly, the memo should not have had to be written in the first place. Whatever the disagreements, Welles should have been allowed to finish his film, and of course, had he finished it to his satisfaction, he never would have had to write the memo. And most of all, he would have gone on to complete his five-picture deal and then make many more films after that.

But life frequently offers up these ambiguous bargains.

Is the new version exactly what Welles had in mind? It is closer, but certainly not definitive. If Welles had woken up from his nap, and Rick and I had shown him this 'memo' version, it would have become the basis for another round of ideas and changes inspired by the new juxtapositions – that is just the kind of director Welles was. But he has left us, and there will be no final version of *Touch of Evil*.

But I hope that when Orson wakes from his nap, he will be reasonably happy with what he sees and hears.

Ask for forgiveness rather than permission

4: NODALITY

A Defence of Film Editing as Poetry

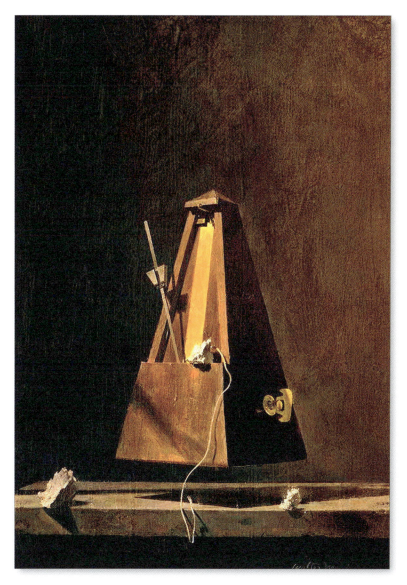

Levitating Metronome (Walter Tandy Murch)

Werner Herzog

Another thing bothers me about Tavares: he comes to dinner and he has a pile of potatoes and nothing else, or he has a lot of meat and nothing else. A man with taste like that *can't* make a good film editor.

– Producer Mack Sennett to editor Bill Hornbeck, 1922[1]

Arthur Tavares, the editor Mack Sennett was disparaging for his monochromatic taste in food, was an actor in early silent films (mainly Sennett's own *Keystone Kops* series) who, despite Sennett's reservations about his diet, went on to have a successful international career as a film editor in the 1920s and '30s.

But Sennett may have a point with his meat and potatoes. When we compare the five fundamental commandments of cuisine and cinema, they seem to be in fairly close agreement: (1) use fresh ingredients as much as possible; (2) in distinctive combinations; (3) with a mix of contrasting but complementary textures, colours, tastes and 'smells'; (4) sizzly or steamy where appropriate; and (5) presented attractively, with an eye to the nourishment, health and enjoyment of the customer ;-)

Lying atop those cornerstones of cuisine are the many regional varieties: French, Chinese, Mexican, Indian, Egyptian, Italian and so on. But this colourful diversity is the fruit of tens of thousands, perhaps hundreds of thousands of years of development since humans invented cooking. In fact, there is a case to be made that cooking our food, thereby partially 'digesting' it with heat before we eat it, is responsible for the exponential growth of the human brain itself.[2]

Cinema, by contrast, is barely a hundred years old. Are there different 'cuisines' of cinema? Or is it the truly universal language, becoming even more homogenous with time?

As cinema began waking up from the infancy of the single shot in the early 1900s, two schools of how to 'cook' (i.e. edit) the images began to develop: the *Invisible* and the *Soviet*. The Invisible school, in America and Europe, sought to minimise the impact of the cut by whatever means available: short four-frame dissolves instead of cuts in Edwin Porter's *Life of an American Fireman* in 1903, the trick of cutting on matching action in his *The Great Train Robbery* in 1903, and so on. Editing was viewed by this school as a slightly shameful prosthesis, a necessary crutch that shouldn't call attention to itself. The goal was the appearance of smooth continuity, telling a story through an *apparently* continuous stream of reality, with few sudden jolts to disturb the life-like illusion.

---

1. From Kevin Brownlow, *The Parade's Gone By* (London: Columbus, 1989).
2. Richard Wrangham, *Catching Fire* (London: Profile Books, 2009).

Translate the invisible wind by the water it sculpts in passing

> **What is cutting on matching action?** An actor initiates an action in one shot – getting up from behind a desk, for instance – and halfway through that action a cut is made. The first frame of the next shot picks up that same action at the halfway point, and then carries it through to its conclusion.

The goal of the Soviet school was: *the more jolts the better!* To wake the audience up with the clash of contrasting shots brought into sparking proximity through montage, and to get them to participate in deriving C from the juxtaposition of A and B. It is the metaphysical mathematics of creativity, where the whole is greater than the sum of its parts.[3]

The Soviets disparaged Invisible editing as bourgeois, and the advocates of invisibility called the Soviet school 'Bolshevik'. Inevitably, these two seemingly opposed but complementary approaches to film editing could not be kept apart, and they finally surged together, yin/yang tributaries flowing into the cascading river of cinema, during the first decades of the twentieth century.

Hollywood meets Moscow (1929): directors Grigori Aleksandrov,
Sergei Eisenstein, Walt Disney and cameraman Eduard Tisse

3. More properly, the Soviet school should be named after Lev Kuleshov, who first theorised it, and directors Sergei Eisenstein and Vsevolod Pudovkin, who popularised it.

Robert Bresson

Soviet director Sergei Eisenstein was inspired by D. W. Griffith, who in turn was inspired by Charles Dickens. ('Dickens has been stolen by Marxists, by Catholics and, above all, by Conservatives,' as George Orwell observed.[4]) And the style of Eisenstein's films *Battleship Potemkin* (1925) and *October* (1927) subsequently had a huge impact on film-making in Europe and Hollywood. Now, almost a hundred years later, we are free to be as bourgeois or as Bolshevik, as yin or as yang as we wish, using whichever method is appropriate to the material at hand; we might call it *Bourgevik* or *Bolshois cinema.*

By 1972 I had edited an educational film, a few commercials, a documentary for the United States Information Agency and, of course, a number of student films. I had also watched the editing of *THX 1138* (by George Lucas) and *The Godfather* (by Bill Reynolds and Peter Zinner). I had sound-edited and mixed *The Rain People* and *THX 1138*, too, and been the sound effects supervisor on *The Godfather.*

So when Francis Coppola asked me to edit picture on *The Conversation* in the summer of 1972, I jumped at the chance. But having accepted the offer, I was quickly sobered by the challenge of taking on not only my first feature film, but the next movie by the man who had just directed *The Godfather.* Expectations would be high, to say the least; if the film did not succeed, then surely that would be blamed on such an inexperienced editor!

I was mixing *American Graffiti* while Francis was shooting *Conversation*, and associate editor Richard Chew was shouldering half of the latter's assembly.[5] But consequently I was falling behind with my half, so I asked assistant editor Pat Jackson to put together the 'Tape Assembly' scene, based on a paper edit that I had sketched out.

Paper edits are sketchy things, with many details to be filled in and leapt over once you start putting the actual images together, and Pat thankfully made a number of inspired infills and leaps that I had not specified – one of which was a cut from a close-up of surveillance expert Harry Caul (played by Gene Hackman), realising that he had missed a crucial line of dialogue, to the click and release of his tape recorder's pinch wheel. Pat bypassed the logical 'action match' sequence, which would have been for Harry to push the stop button; instead, she cut instantly from Harry's look to the

---

4. Orwell's magnificent essay on Dickens is available at the Internet Archive: https://archive.org/details/dickensdaliother0000orwe/page/n9/mode/2up.

5. Richard would go on to edit *One Flew Over the Cuckoo's Nest* and *Star Wars*.

If there's anything worse than not being taken seriously, it's being taken too seriously

'click' of realisation, symbolised by the sudden release of the pinch wheel. As soon as I saw this, and the grammar of it, I knew that it would be key to the editorial style of *The Conversation*. It was a literal *click* and a metaphorical click at the same time (*Suddenly something clicks!*). Whenever I screen *The Conversation*, I salute this moment as the key that unlocked a treasure chest. So here is a thank you to Pat, and by extension to all the assistants and collaborators with whom I have worked over the years, who have made such essential contributions to the films I have been involved with.

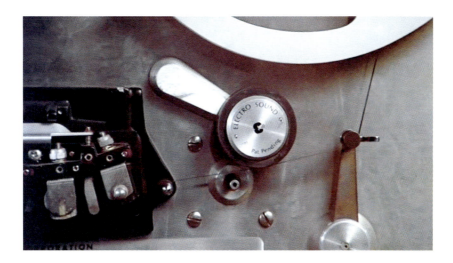

I can think of no cut that better captures the essence of cinema editing, its ability to compress time, its storytelling efficiency, its metaphorical poetry. It is also a great example of a 'Soviet' cut, essentially identical to the classic Kuleshov experiment of cutting from the face of a man (A) to a bowl of soup (B), and then back to the man (A), whose juxtaposed logic (A+B+A) equals C, *hunger*.

In the case of *Conversation*, the bowl was replaced by the clicking pinch wheel, and C became *sudden realisation* – that Harry had just heard the first clue to the missing line of dialogue: '*He'd kill us if he got the chance.*' But then, instead of cutting

Billy Wilder

back to Harry, we cut to the close-up of his finger pressing the rewind button – the reaction to his realisation – skipping the pace along even further.

To see this sequence, go to Vimeo: https://vimeo.com/519903008 (QR code on left)

In the dailies of this scene, there was ample material to create a chain of 'invisible' matching action (Harry reaching out to press the stop button, etc.), but the fact that I was not at all interested in pursuing that path gave an indication of the kind of stylistic choices that would emerge more clearly as work on *Conversation* progressed. As is usually the case, there was also a practical reason behind these decisions. The script for *Conversation* was 157 pages long (about forty pages longer than a 'normal' screen-play), and during filming Francis had added to that by exploring many additional plot and character options, resulting in a first assembly that would eventually reach four and a half hours. So any stylistic choices that would help to skip the story forward would also help reduce the running time.

This pressure to shorten the film made me wary of cuts on matching action, which inevitably tie the pacing to the action at the time of filming (how many steps to get from here to there, etc.), so wherever there was an alternative, I would take advantage

To see these clips in motion, go to Vimeo: https://vimeo.com/553000469
(QR code on left)

Children are innocent and naturally love justice, while the rest of us
are wicked and naturally prefer mercy

of it. A simple example is Harry walking to work after the Union Square recording. (The dotted red lines in the image above indicate a cut, and the red circles represent the audience's probable focus of attention.)

Harry crosses the railroad tracks in a wide shot, and when he is on the far right, at *a certain point* I made a skip/cut to a medium close-up of him in the elevator. In the first frame of that shot he is on the left, the opposite side from where we left him in the wide shot, but I chose an opening frame where his face was covered in shadow, so the audience's focus of attention has time to shift from the bright slats on the right to Harry's face on the left (arrow), when his features are wiped into brightness as the elevator rises. When the elevator reaches the second floor, the shot dollies to the right as Harry lifts the gate, revealing his large, empty work space for the first time. He walks deep into the shot, directly away from the camera, and at a certain point I made another skip/cut to Harry taking off his raincoat and wishing his assistant Stan good morning. The circle of attention remains in the same place on either side of that cut.

> I am using the term *skip/cut* rather than *jump cut* because these are not jump cuts in the usual sense, where there is a jump forward in time *within the same shot*. We *are* making leaps forward in time with each cut, but skipping from set-up to set-up, while still taking into account the audience's focus of attention. For those readers familiar with my *rule of six*, this example abandons number six (three-dimensional continuity), while respecting number four (eye-trace, which is another term for 'focus of attention'). The question is: how to determine that *certain point*? It has primarily to do with rhythm, but . . . rhythm of what? Harry's walking pace? That is one element, but the main rhythm in these three shots will be something more intangible: the *rhythm of the audience's thoughts* as they watch the images unfold.[6]

We editors usually say, 'I just cut where I felt it was right' – and that is true, as far as it goes. But I believe that much of the time, what we are really doing is predicting, as closely as we can, what the audience will be thinking and feeling. And the key here is that thinking has a structure and takes a certain amount of time. Each shot is a vessel of thought, and when that vessel is empty – when the shot has nothing new to say or

---

6. There is music accompanying these three shots, but they were cut this way before it was written. David Shire fit the music to the pre-existing rhythm of the shots.

G. K. Chesterton

is about to deliver something that we don't want the audience to think about – then we cut to the next shot.

Of course, technically, you can choose any frame you want – there are twenty-four options every second – but out of those twenty-four, there are better and worse places to graft a new branch, which is to say, a new shot. If you select the right frame, then the grafting will 'take' – the vital sap of the audience's thoughts and emotions will flow easily from the trunk into the branch. If you select the wrong one, you might be interrupting the audience in the middle of a thought, forcing them to switch to thinking about the subject of the new shot you have just given them before they are ready. Those successful grafting points are *nodes* – like the knots in the structure of a tree where it 'decides' to send a branch out from the trunk. If the grafting point is in the wrong place, the 'sap' of the audience's thoughts and emotions cannot flow freely into the new 'branch', which is to say, the new shot. I was feeling my way as I was assembling *Conversation*, but I became more and more aware that for this film, cutting on matching action was not the best option. I didn't know why this was, but I continued to follow my instincts, avoiding match action wherever possible. I was aware, too, that an overtly 'Soviet' style of editing can be useful, but it can also become desiccated through overuse.

So what I would like to propose – and explore for the balance of this chapter – is a third 'cuisine' of editing, a fusion of the Invisible and the Soviet, which I am going to call *nodal*. I hope to explain how it can help determine when and where you decide to make a cut, which is a more organic process than the name implies. It is really a *graft*, in the arboreal sense of that word, and many of the analogies that follow are biologic and organic.

And poetic! But to explain that word, a digression . . .

In every art there is a diabolical principle which acts against it and tries to demolish it

Film as Translation

In 1997 I was interviewed by the poetry journal *Parnassus* on the subject of literary adaptation and *The English Patient*, and in the course of my conversation with the interviewer, Joy Katz, I offered an analogy – that film-makers adapting a novel are performing a kind of multilevel translation from the *language of text* to the *language of moving images and sound* – and that the old Italian adage '*traduttore, traditore*' ('the translator is a traitor') particularly applies: an attempt to be overly faithful to the text often results in a damming-up of the deeper currents of the project, so that an artful betrayal of the original work seems to serve an adaptation best, something along the lines of Picasso's dictum 'Art is a lie that tells the truth.'[7]

Driving home after the interview, however, I was struck by the fact that I didn't really know what I was talking about, as far as language translation was concerned. So I decided to give it a try.

Ten years earlier, when Phil Kaufman was shooting *The Unbearable Lightness of Being* in Lyon, I flew to France to help direct second unit for the film's invasion sequence, when the Soviet tanks overrun Czechoslovakia. I wound up staying for a month, two weeks longer than planned, and consequently ran out of things to read at night. A bookshop down the street from the hotel introduced me to the Italian writer Curzio Malaparte, and I fell under his spell.[8]

At that time, only a few of his books had been translated into English, and since I had studied Italian at Johns Hopkins University and the University of Perugia in 1963, and had just been working in Italy on *The English Patient*, I decided that translating Malaparte would be a test case.

Thankfully, I discovered that my intuition had been right. The mental space and internal chatter of translating turned out to be identical to my frame of mind when editing film, despite the fact that my hands were doing very different things. 'Should I use this shot or that one? This word or that one? Well, if I use the first choice, it may be literally accurate (it follows the script), but it's not particularly strong. Perhaps I can find something that achieves the same result, but in a more concise, poetic way? Yes? But if I do *that*, then I have to compensate by doing *this*' – and so on, a long chain of if/then decisions.

7. The full interview can be found at https://www.filmsound.org/murch/parnassus.
8. Curzio Malaparte on Wikipedia: https://en.wikipedia.org/wiki/Curzio_Malaparte.

Robert Bresson

Each language has different efficiencies and awkwardnesses – in Italian there's no word for 'shallow', and in English there's no word for 'the day before yesterday' (as there is in Polish) – and the translator has to navigate those differences. It's the same in translating from script to film, where a picture may be worth a thousand words, but often a word is worth a thousand pictures. What surprised me, however, was discovering that even though Malaparte's stories were written in prose, some of my translations insisted on being arranged in free verse. This was particularly mysterious to me because I am what might charitably be called 'poetically challenged'. I love poetry in the abstract but don't care for most poems in particular, somewhat like those unfortunate people who love humanity but have a hard time with human beings. Although there were some exceptions – Rilke, Dickinson, Masters and Frost, for instance – my poetic 'tone deafness' bothered me, and so free verse it would be. I was curious to see where this road might lead.

Giving more space on the page seemed to aerate the density of Malaparte's text, allowing it to breathe and permitting his startling images to be appreciated in a more measured way. And since Italian – particularly Malaparte's Italian – is a more sonorous language than English, the poetic form helped to restore some of the musicality and rhythm lost in a prose translation. In the process, I also realised what should have been obvious to me, which is that the ragged structure of free verse emphasises the internal rhythms and tensions of each line and puts an added, if subliminal, emphasis on the last word of each line – an emphasis that is often *independent of the grammatical construction of the sentence*. That final word acquires a kind of glow from the whiteness of the page, which it would not have if it were lodged within the densely woven nest of a prose paragraph.

An original Malaparte paragraph, part of a longer piece titled *Sleepwalking*:

Era quella la mia terra nativa, dove avevo sofferto la solitudine del diverso, la solitudine della speranza e del futuro, e l'angoscia prima dell'uomo. Era quello il paese dove ero morto la prima volta, e avevo percorso con Edo le strade del altro paese, del paese dei morti, e alzando gli occhi avevo veduto scorrere i fiumi nel cielo, e le radici degli alberi, che sopra il tetto eran foresta, pendere brune nel vuoto, sopra la mia testa.

My free verse translation into English:

So this is my native country,
the land where I was born a foreigner,

---

the home where I came to know the loneliness
of the outsider, the solitude of hope,
the struggles of becoming a man.

And it was here I died,
that first time, and descended
to wander with Edo the streets of that other country,
the country of the dead,
and lifting my eyes I saw rivers
flowing through the sky, and the roots of trees
hanging like brown forests
in the vaulted ground above my head.

Here is this same English translation as a prose paragraph, highlighting the final words of each of the above lines.

So this is my native **country**, the land where I was born a **foreigner**, the home where I came to know the **loneliness** of the outsider, the solitude of **hope**, the struggles of becoming a **man**. And it was here I **died**, that first time, and **descended** to wander with Edo the streets of that other **country**, the country of the **dead**, and lifting my eyes I saw **rivers** flowing through the sky, and the roots of **trees** hanging like brown **forests** in the vaulted ground above my **head**.[9]

Rhythm, both internal to the shot (or line) and then within the overall sequence of shots (or lines), is as essential to film editing as it is to poetry. Once a shot is selected, and the opening frame identified, the crucial question follows: *at what precise moment* to bring it to an end? Just as the end of a line in free verse is often independent of the grammatical structure of the sentence but dependent on the rhythm of the words, the ending frame of a shot is often independent of the overt dramatic structure of a scene. But in both cases, the decision of where to end a line or shot is a secretly architectural/musical way to shape the poem or scene, largely by emphasising the contrast or 'rhyme' between – in editing – the final image of the outgoing shot and the first image of the next, or – in poetry – by the comparison of the final word of a line with those of the previous and subsequent lines. If you were to scoop out those final words on

9. An animated version of this can be seen at https://vimeo.com/553775587 (QR code on right).

Rebecca Solnit

the previous page, you would get a strong sense of the poem itself: *country, foreigner, loneliness, hope, man, died, descended, country, dead, rivers, trees, forests, head.* These words are both a summary and a commentary on the rest of the poem. So it should be in film, with the final images of each shot.

But what is the cinematic equivalent of the 'glow' cast by the white page? I'd like to suggest it is the cut itself – the violence of it, when one image is instantaneously snatched away and replaced by another, and the effect this violence has on our visual cortex.

At the moment of the cut, the previous smooth flow of incremental frame-to-frame motion vanishes, and a wholly new image appears. This is a shock, and there is a moment, measured in milliseconds, when that outgoing image is 'tabulated' – memorised by the visual cortex – so that it can be compared with the first image of the next shot. So, rather than the glow of the white page, there is a mental 'flashbulb' that goes off at the moment of the cut, preserving both the outgoing and the incoming images in our visual cortex. The more interesting and relevant those images are to the themes and the aesthetic of the film, the more powerful and poetic the film will be. A classic example of 'nodality' is the cut in *Lawrence of Arabia* from Lawrence blowing out the match to the desert horizon just before the rising of the Sun – a transition that was intended to be a dissolve in the script.[10]

We marked a dissolve, but when we watched the footage in the theatre, we saw it as a direct cut. David and I both thought, 'Wow, that's really interesting.' David said, 'That is a fabulous cut. It's not quite perfect – take it away and make it perfect,' and I literally took two frames off, and that's the way it is today.

– Interview with Anne Coates, *Washington Post*[11]

10. See this cut and Anne Coates's explanation on Vimeo: https://vimeo.com/384952832 (QR code on left).

11. Travis Andrews, 'How Anne V. Coates Created One of the Most Famous Cuts in Movie History', *Washington Post*, 9 May 2018: https://www.washingtonpost.com/news/arts-and-entertainment/ wp/2018/05/09/how-anne-v-coates-created-one-of-the-most-famous-cuts-in-movie-history.

Editor Anne Coates has said that she prepared this moment as a dissolve, following the script (right) by Robert Bolt. In those days (1961) a dissolve was indicated by a diagonal line of grease pencil (aka china marker) covering the length of the intended dissolve between two workprint shots, A and B. At the exact mid-point of that diagonal would be a cut from shot A to B. But when Coates and Lean screened the first assembly of the film, what struck them forcefully was the power of the cut itself.[12]

That cut is the opposite of matching action or a dissolve, whose implicit goal is to blur the moment of the transition. Neither frame on either side of an action match or a dissolve is memorable, precisely because the goal is to obscure the moment of the transition – to imagine that it didn't happen.[13]

Matching action is prose, nodal is poetry.

On that point, I was astonished to read a quote from editor William Hornbeck (1901–83)[14] disparaging matching action. I say 'astonished' only because I assumed that he would have been a champion of the technique, given that the five decades in which he was working at his prime (1920s to 1960s) were the high-water mark of traditional Hollywood editing. Instead, he calls out matching action for being guilty of the very thing that it was trying to avoid: visibility.

```
DRYDEN is irritably tapping a black Russian cigar-
ette for himself.

LAWRENCE steps forward, takes a box of matches and
lights it for him.

                   LAWRENCE
                 (very quietly)
            No, Dryden, it's going to
            be fun.

The set intensity of his expression is in utter
contradiction to his words.

50 CLOSE UP. DRYDEN. He looks from the burning
match in Lawrence's finger to Lawrences's face.

                   DRYDEN
                 (rather sourly)
            It is recognized that you
            have a funny sense of fun.

51 CLOSE UP. LAWRENCE. He smiles and raises the
flame to his lips. He blows it out in the normal
matter.

                                      DISSOLVE TO

52 SUNRISE IN THE DESERT:

A series of shot taken with an under-cranked camera
so that the change from grey dawn to brilliant sun-
light is speeded…
```

12. I interviewed Anne Coates in 2000. She had just finished *Erin Brockovich*, and I had recently completed *Apocalypse Now Redux*: https://filmsound.org/murch/coates.htm.

13. This is not to say that dissolves cannot achieve another kind of diffuse poetry, such as the three-level dissolves in the opening minutes of *Apocalypse Now*.

14. William Hornbeck's career spanned sixty years, from editing around two hundred Mack Sennett shorts in the 1920s to working in England for Alexander Korda in the 1930s (*Four Feathers*, *The Thief of Baghdad*), editing the *Why We Fight* series in the 1940s and then working with Frank Capra and George Stevens in the 1950s (*It's a Wonderful Life*, *Shane*, *Giant*, etc.). He was supervising editor of Universal Studios from 1960 until his retirement in 1976, and was almost assigned by Universal to recut George Lucas's *American Graffiti*. In 1977 ACE members voted him the best film editor the industry had produced.

I detest where someone starts to turn in a shot, and they pick it up from another angle – I detest that. I've done it because there was no other place to do it, but I would guard against that, because now I notice the cut, and I'd much rather change on a spot where you wouldn't be consciously aware of the film being cut.

– William Hornbeck, interviewed by Kristin Thompson and David Bordwell[15]

With hindsight, Hornbeck's aversion to matching action could probably be explained by the twelve years he spent editing Mack Sennett's two-reel comedies. From 1922, at the age of twenty-one, he became the supervising editor responsible for 'punching up', as he put it, the work of five other editors, working with gag writers like Frank Capra. The jokes in Sennett's slapsticks demanded fresh and 'punchy' timing, the collision of thrust, parry and pratfall, which is antithetical to the prosaic nature of matching action.

But if the goal of matching action was invisibility, and Hornbeck is calling it out for achieving the opposite, what is going on? Hornbeck doesn't elaborate, but I will attempt to channel his spirit regarding matching action, which I think is pretty close to mine. As soon as an action is initiated, a new thought begins, like a new phrase in music, but a match cut interrupts this thought after only a few frames (a third of a second or less), replacing it with a new shot, which our visual cortex must then figure out while also following the action through to its conclusion. As a result, there is a 'stutter' of three things happening within less than a second of time: the initiation of an action; the cut to a new shot; and the completion of the action. It is this stutter that Hornbeck was objecting to, I think, and which made the match cut annoyingly noticeable to him.

To call in an airstrike on my own position, however, here are a couple of illustrations of matching-action cuts from *The Conversation*. These are from the 'Tape Assembly' scene, just after Harry arrives at his workshop in the morning. It is four minutes long, with thirty-five cuts. Only two of those are matching action; the first one in the Vimeo example is not even technically a match action, but it is close.[16]

Harry's hands can be seen moving in his close-up, then they pass out of the bottom of the frame, there is the cut, and next we see his hands manipulating the reels of tape.

15. Kristin Thompson and David Bordwell interview William Hornbeck: https://tinyurl.com/2jm9d62n.

16. See this example on Vimeo: https://vimeo.com/554269480 (QR code on left).

If you are too careful, if you leave no door unlatched, poetry will be scared off.
It's hard enough to trap as it is

If I had cut a few frames earlier, before his hands moved out of the frame, it *would* be a match action.

But . . . that's not where I made the cut.

The second example is a real match action, and I wince slightly when I see it, because I remember struggling with this in 1973, and the only way I thought it would work was to make it a match action.

Harry's hands start to move from the motion controller in the first shot, and then after twelve frames I cut to the down angle, at the point when his hands are half-way through the move to the mixing knobs, where, after another twelve frames, they come to rest. The reason I made the cut this way was because the down angle is a cheat: Harry's hands were moving not from the motion controller, but from a resting position on the edge of his bench, and at the time I felt it was important to link the controller and the mixer. To quote Hornbeck, 'I've done it because there was no other place to do it.' And so the cut became a match action. But its virtue today is that it is a good illustration of the stutter effect I mentioned earlier.

At the end of the Vimeo is a revision of this cut, showing how it might have been done 'nodally' – cutting away from Harry's hands right after he hits the stop command, and then cutting to the down angle, with the hands moving to the mixer. It is not perfect, but you don't really notice that his hands are in a different position relative to the motion controller because you are busy trying to figure out this new down angle. If I had the trims from fifty years ago, I would probably add a few frames at the start of the down angle. But as it is, this is sufficient to give you an idea of what I mean by a nodal cut as opposed to a match action.

What is a *nodal* cut?

A *node* refers to a point in a network, diagram or organism where 'pathways' of some kind intersect and branch out. In my terminology, an editing node is that moment in a shot when the potential for branching out is inevitable *but not yet realised*. If a cut is made at a node, the realisation of the potential in the previous shot begins with the first frame of the next, where the potential of the previous one begins to unfold, like a plant flowering or a branch budding off from the trunk.

In *matching action*, however, the action has already begun to unfold in the final frames of the first shot, is interrupted by the cut, and then continues in the second.

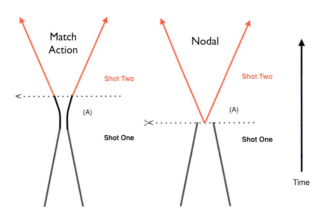

As Shot One progresses, at a certain point (A) a new action is introduced, changing direction.

A *match-action* cut will allow that new action to start changing in Shot One, and will then cut to Shot Two *midway through the action*, making sure that there is a match at the cut point to Shot Two.

But a *nodal* cut will occur *before* A, at a point where action is inevitable *but not yet initiated*.

An actor says his line, a cloud moves, the sun hits his hand, and everything is different

Shot Two will then initiate the action with its first frame, allowing it to unfold organically from the beginning of the shot, without interruption.[17]

Does this mean I never use matching action? Or that I would always advise against it? No – the eighteen-minute party scene at Harry Caul's warehouse in *Conversation* has four or five match-action cuts out of a total of just under a hundred – but I do not use matching action as a default method, and I would advise against using it unthinkingly. It has become a 'rule' of editing simply by convention.

Action scenes, which are typically a swirl of continuous, balletic movement, are places where I would make greater use of matching action, or its opposite, contrapuntal (aggressively *non*-matching) action (movement in the opposite direction). Also, you might find yourself working with a director who prefers matching action, as I did with Brad Bird on *Tomorrowland*. I think this was because of his background in animation, where shots are generally conceived with matching action in mind.

One of the reasons for the widespread normalisation of matching action is its pervasive use as a teaching tool, since the cut point is unambiguous and easy to understand. The editor, in a sense, is 'only following orders' that have been laid down by the director, the actors and the camerawork. But if we are *not* 'following orders', then how do we determine the moment to cut away from a shot, to bring the line of poetry to an end – what I have referred to as *that certain point* where the *precise moment* of the cut is inevitable *but not yet realised*?

So this is my native country,
the land where I was born a foreigner,
the home where I came to know the loneliness
of the outsider, the solitude
of hope, the struggles
of becoming a man.

And it was here I died,
that first time, and descended
to the streets of that other country,
the country of the dead,
and lifting my eyes I saw rivers
flowing through the sky, and the roots of trees
hanging like brown forests
in the vaulted ground above my head.

17. Animation of these images can be found on Vimeo: https://vimeo.com/555385317 (QR code on right).

Attributed to Orson Welles

The ragged structure of free verse shows this graphically. Each line has its own blend of content and rhythm, which means that the lines will vary in length . . .

. . . and so it appears when comparing shot lengths in a film scene.

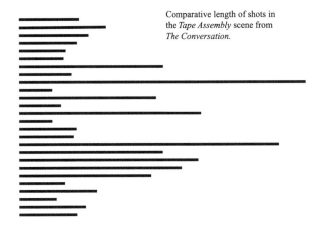

Comparative length of shots in the *Tape Assembly* scene from *The Conversation*.

I am encouraging a comparison between film and poetry because I believe cinema is an inherently poetic medium, and poetry is the well from which the greatest moments of cinema draw their nourishment, as we saw with *Lawrence*. Of course, I am expressing a personal preference. And I could just as easily make a comparison between cinema and music (I have written elsewhere that cinematic montage is *visual music*), because the structural rules of poetry and music are so closely aligned. The difference is that music and film are temporal – the pace is determined by the creators of the work – whereas poetry can be read and reread at a speed determined by the reader.

How, then, to locate a potential node, where the grafting of a new branch – a new shot – can be most successful? This is a particular problem if the shot doesn't have much action or dialogue in it.

I have just made an analogy with music, and it might be helpful to think of the film editor as part of a jazz quartet, with the other three members being (1) the actors, (2) the camera and (3) the imagined thoughts of the audience. I say *the actors*, but really that encompasses whatever it is that the camera has focused on – a tree, a tornado, a tarantula or Tom Cruise.

It is that third member of the quartet – *the imagined thoughts of the audience* – which is the slipperiest, because these thoughts are in the future, but they have to be imagined by the editor in the course of their work. If I had to put my finger on one of the most essential talents of a film editor, it would be this ability to more or less correctly imagine what the audience will be thinking and feeling as they watch the film. Of course, the audience is really a million-headed creature with many different attitudes and assumptions, so the editor is making educated guesses, for a film that they are in the process of creating – talk about floating variables! But that is what an editor has to do. And, of course, they are thinking their *own* thoughts, but interleaving them with the assumptions that an audience might make when seeing these images for the first time, trying best to avoid the errors that come from the editor's own overfamiliarity with the material.

The key idea is that thinking and feeling *take time*; they have their own rhythms of origin, development, confusion, sudden realisation, contemplation, wonder, tension and so on. And it is those *rhythms of thought* that will most frequently determine where the cut points – the nodes – are located.

As an example, consider the shot from *The Conversation* of Harry arriving at his warehouse workshop. It begins with Harry in the elevator as it rises to the second floor, follows him as he exits, revealing the size of the warehouse space, and then remains static as Harry walks away, towards his caged-in laboratory. As originally shot, he continued walking all the way to the door of the laboratory, taking another twenty seconds longer than the shot as it currently exists.

This is a fairly straightforward example, but it does impose some conditions on the editor: (1) Harry simply walks away from camera – there is no further development or dialogue; and (2) the camera comes to rest once its movement out of the elevator stops. So it seems we will have to rely on number 3, the imagined thoughts of the audience, to determine where to cut.

Starting in the confined space of the elevator, the main revelation of the shot, as it dollies to the right, is the first sight of Harry's huge warehouse. Once the move comes to a stop, we (the audience) are simply left to absorb the stark utilitarian beauty of this space, and then perhaps to wonder why it is so empty and where Harry is headed.[18]

18. You can see this shot, which I referenced earlier, on Vimeo: https://vimeo.com/553000469.

Robert Bresson

Given these conditions, how can we determine *the exact frame* out of the half-thousand on which to cut?

Dynamic Trimming

The tool that came to my aid in 1973 was the mechanical frame counter attached to the KEM editing machine. Today we would use the *time-code* readout of whatever program we are using. This time code is going to allow us to lasso the intangible thoughts of an audience that does not yet exist! I have called the method I am about to explain *dynamic trimming*, which is a way to determine the cut point at film speed – twenty-four frames a second.

Start with Harry in the elevator, raising the gate, and run the shot, imagining what someone would perhaps think and feel, never having seen this before: *How big the room is . . . how starkly beautiful . . . Why is it so empty? . . . Where is Harry headed?* Four thoughts, probably wordless, but which nonetheless take time to emerge and be considered, revealed by the now-immobile camera and accompanied by Harry's rhythmic step, step, step . . . And then . . . *Cut!* . . . you stop the shot with a press of the space bar, brake or button.

Now look at the time-code readout; note the number of the frame on which you have landed. Let's say the last four digits are 13:08 (thirteen seconds and eight frames). How did that moment of *Cut!* feel? Satisfying, in a musical sense? Or perhaps not . . . Perhaps it felt a beat too late? Or too early?

Run the shot again, consider those 'audience' thoughts as you watch Harry walk away into that space. Imagine that you are standing at the back of a theatre and watching the finished film, with 350 people sitting between you and the screen . . . *Cut!* Now look again at the time-code readout: perhaps it says 13:03 – five frames shorter than previously. How did it feel this time? Better?

You have just measured, in musical terms, what five frames feels like *for this shot, in this scene, at this point in the film.*

Do it again. And maybe again. Each time, you will sensitise yourself to the rhythms of the shot and the thoughts that go with it. One of those times you will probably land on the same frame again, 13:03. It is not just chance that allows you to do this; you are responding with greater and greater accuracy to the interplay of the shot and the previously mentioned jazz quartet that you are performing with.

The cut point, the node, is the moment the instrument *you* are playing adds its voice to the ensemble. But here's the curious thing: what you will be adding is itself

---

The great battles are always waged where the maps overlap

another phrase, but one performed by the three other players – the *actor*, the *camera* and the *thoughts and emotions of the audience* – while you fall silent until the next cut. There is a highly recursive, Escherian quality to this.

And so on it goes, shot after shot, as you build the scene, and then the next, and the next, and ultimately the whole film.[19]

There will be times when you can't get a consistent time-code reading – the numbers from the different tries at a *Cut!* come out wildly different. This is probably because the node you are after is an illusory one, and you need to find a better, more organic cut point either earlier in the shot or later. Or maybe try an alternative take, or even a completely different shot. This gets back to that discussion about the internal debate accompanying editing and translation: which shot or word should I use?

But when dynamic trimming works, it is amazing that out of perhaps six hundred frames or so, you will be able to land on the same frame two or three times in a row. It's as if you were at a funfair shooting gallery, with twenty-four metal ducks zipping by every second, and you are able to shoot the same bird twice. This is *impossible* to do through any kind of rational thinking; it is achievable only because you have tuned yourself to the visual 'musical' rhythms of the shot and the thoughts that accompany it, and so you hit the right note, or node, at exactly the right moment, to bring a new branch into being. If you can hit the same frame two or three times, this is about as powerful a validation as that decision is ever going to get.

When his organ-playing was admired by a pupil, Bach said, 'It's just a matter of striking the right notes at exactly the right moment. The organ does the rest.'

I have gone into some detail about dynamic trimming simply to expose its inner workings. Do I really perform this repetitive process with every cut? During the first weeks at the start of a film, yes, I do, because I am trying to get a sense of the film's unique *rhythmic structure*. Once I have begun to internalise that rhythm, the need for

19. You can view this sequence of shots, with an audience added, on Vimeo: https://vimeo.com/558249046 (QR code on right). Imagine what those people are thinking as they watch the film.

Napoleon Bonaparte

those repetitions gradually drops away. But it can resurface again when I encounter a difficult scene or problematical moment. What I will never do is try to identify a nodal frame by scrubbing the film back and forth, identifying, for example, the exact frame where a door is fully closed. I will always make that selection in real time, because that is how the audience will be seeing it.

But this relates to one of the essential functions of the film editor, which is to discover/uncover the film's rhythmic structure, learning from the decisions of the director in staging the scenes, the actors in performing it and the camera in capturing it. And then taking that rhythmic structure, refining it and extending it into other areas, modifying it as necessary according to the requirements of each scene. You are simultaneously discovering and participating in the creation of the *metronomic signature* of the film. Anne Coates said something similar in my interview with her:

> I find when I start on a new film, it usually takes me a scene or two to get into the film and find the particular style or feeling for that film. I usually cut two or three scenes and I think, 'Oh, God, I've lost my touch,' and then I cut a scene and think, 'Wow!' That gives you the confidence, and you go back to the others, and you've got the line, you've got the feel for the film.[20]

By *metronomic signature* I don't mean that the cuts come at regular intervals. A good analogy would be with how a conductor will determine the overall temporal signature of a performance: is it largo or prestissimo, or somewhere in between? This does not mean a uniform interval between notes.

Every film will have its own DNA, determining the pattern of rhythmic branching from shot to shot, just as the DNA of the oak produces different branching patterns from the beech, which is different from the ash. You have to discover what kind of 'tree' your film is.

OAK   ASH   BEECH

20. https://filmsound.org/murch/coates.htm (QR code on left).

With each brush-stroke you risk your life

Practical and Philosophical Considerations

One of the practical advantages of nodal editing is its greater modularity – the ease with which you can rearrange shots into a different order when recutting a scene. Each node is like an attachment in a Lego kit: it can be easily un-snapped and linked quickly to many other potential shots. A match-action cut, on the other hand, is custom-designed to sew together two specific shots, so it has to be carefully 'disentangled' when recutting.

Nodality also has the potential to free you from the rhythms that were established at the time of shooting. After his final line of dialogue, how long did the actor pause before getting up? You can maintain the length of that pause if you wish, but if the scene has been moved to a different location, it may require a different rhythm, and nodal editing accommodates itself easily to this.

Are these considerations really important? Aren't there bigger issues than nodality and action matching? Of course, there are always large-scale editorial questions about structure, character and length, but these are concerns that the editor shares with the director and the producer. The 'smaller' issues we have been discussing in this chapter – these micro-rhythms – are largely the domain of the editor's craft. They are the equivalent of bowing techniques for the violin or the fingering and pedal techniques of pianists and guitarists, which are vitally important to the interpretive style of the individual artists. It is how we distinguish Eric Clapton from Jimi Hendrix, Jascha Heifetz from Fritz Kreisler, Simon Barere from Grigory Sokolov.

Switching analogies from music to motoring: no single shot (no single automotive gear) can work efficiently for long, under a variety of circumstances, particularly in a story with (hopefully) lots of interesting curves and hills, so to speak. Just as you have to shift gears up or down when driving, in film you have to cut to another shot that continues the story more effectively. But which shot you use and *where* you make the transition is critical to smooth and effective, impactful storytelling. If the cut point is right, there is a pleasurable shift of energy, and the changes of g-force in the 'ride' that you are taking the audience on are enjoyable and exciting. It's the same with shifting from one gear to another on a winding, hilly landscape: if the change happens at the wrong time, the ride becomes jerky and unpleasant – and there is even the danger of losing traction and spinning out of control.

Intangible, but even more helpful than the practical advantages, is the frame of mind that accompanies the concept of nodality: the appreciation of cinema's structural and

Paul Cézanne

metaphorical links with biology, poetry, music – and even driving an automobile;[21] the realisation that cinema is – or can appear to be – a living entity, like Mary Shelley's creature, conjured up out of pixels (or, in the old days, out of celluloid, silver nitrate and magnetised iron), then animated by electricity into a powerful modern Adam capable, if treated with respect, of teaching us, by reflecting our nature, something about the mystery of ourselves and the world.

If abused, like Shelley's monster it has the power to wreak havoc.

Coda: Translation as Occupational Therapy

I've found that the directness and immediacy of language translation helped to solve – for me, anyway – a persistent practical dilemma in the life of every film editor, which is that there is usually no way to edit, in a fully creative sense, without actually *working on a film*. It is as if a musician found they could perform only in official full-dress concerts, without the ability to practise on their own or in smaller groups. The resonances between film editing and translation have provided me with an alternative, inexpensive, immediate and risk-free 'cross-training' that is so important to the lives of artists and athletes, but which is generally denied to most film-makers because of the technical, expensive nature of our particular crafts. Translation has been particularly helpful for me, a kind of methadone treatment right after the completion of a film, when there are weeks of disorientation; the lodestar of your professional life for the past year or so has just been eclipsed and your compass is spinning. Translating has helped me to settle down slowly rather than crashing, before eventually finding another lodestar and embarking on a new voyage.[22]

21. See Chapter 13, 'The Spliceosome', for further links to biology.

22. Those Malaparte translations were collected and published in *The Bird That Swallowed Its Cage* (Berkeley: Counterpoint Press, 2012).

Not just beautiful photography, not just beautiful images,
but necessary images and photography

5: THE DROID OLYMPICS

When Film Editing Was a Competitive Sport

This essay was written by my fellow editor Paul Hirsch for Cinemontage, *the journal of the Motion Picture Editors Guild, in March 2005. Paul graciously allowed me to reprint it here, to give a flavour of the times before digits replaced sprockets.*

And they're off! The opening heat in the 1982 Worst Hand Anyway competition

The Droid Olympics could only have happened at the time and the place that they did.

When I heard the announcement in December that Francis Ford Coppola's American Zoetrope Productions was closing after 35 years of operation in San Francisco, I thought back to a couple of special days I spent in the Bay Area over 20 years ago. Although I was based in New York at that time, and had never lived and worked anywhere else, I edited three pictures in Marin County, California.

In 1969, Coppola and fellow producer/director George Lucas had set up editing facilities in Northern California in order to get away from the massive gravitational forces exerted by Hollywood and the studios. They were surrounded by a small community of like-minded film-makers, among them Walter Murch, Matthew Robbins, Hal Barwood, Carroll Ballard, John Korty, Phil Kaufman, Michael Ritchie, Robert Dalva,

Thelma Schoonmaker, Richard Chew and Marcia Lucas. There was a connection to New York, too, partly due to the fact that Coppola, Murch, Robbins and Dalva came from there, and partly due to the natural sympathy that these two regional outposts of the film industry shared, as communities of independent-minded cinema enthusiasts.

I was brought to Marin County in Fall 1976 to help out on a picture that had fallen behind schedule. It was entitled *Star Wars*. I arrived from New York, and immediately was beguiled by the physical beauty of the place with its rolling golden hills, and by the friendly and inclusive atmosphere that existed among these various film people. My wife Jane was pregnant with our first child, and we couldn't have been greeted more warmly by the families there.

Marcia Lucas competes in the Speed-Splice in the 1982 Games as Duwayne Dunham
(red hat), Richard Hymns and Dale Strumpell look on

This was, after all, the late '70s. Watergate was only a couple of years behind us. The last chopper had left Saigon only 18 months earlier, and the counter-culture was alive and well in Marin at that time. San Francisco had been the locus of the Flower Power movement, and Marin was a centre of Zen studies, hot tubs and alternative lifestyles. Although it is easy to make fun of all that now, there was a sweet and innocent aspect to much of this.

There should be nothing in the unexpected that is not secretly expected by you

The friendly spirit of camaraderie and community, combined with an excitement about the art and craft of film, reached its epitome for me in the event known as the Droid Olympics. There were actually four of them: one in 1978, one in 1980, one in 1982, and the last in 1987. I missed the first and last of these, but was lucky enough to be there for the middle two, and they were among the most enjoyable memories I have of my days there.

The notion for these Olympics came from Murch, who was editing *Apocalypse Now* for Coppola in 1978, when the first event was held. According to him, 'There was a lot of film – 1,250,000 feet of workprint – with so much robotic reconstituting of trims, that the half-dozen assistants on the film started calling themselves "droids" in honour of the robots in *Star Wars*, which had come out the year before.

'In June of '78, my wife Aggie had put on a horse show for the local kids in Bolinas,' Murch continued. 'And I was eyeing the ribbons and trophies when the idea came to me to throw a similar event for the assistant editors on *Apocalypse*, to celebrate their skills.'

These are all arcane abilities today, largely forgotten in the wake of the now 10-year-old digital revolution in the professional cutting room. The games were staged at times when there were enough feature films cutting in the area to supply teams to compete, usually four or five. There never was much of a film industry in San Francisco, and the activity ebbed and flowed. But when there were enough pictures working at the same time, the 'Games' were held. In those days, editing crews ran from three or four assistants up to eight or more.

The site for the events was the Murch residence at Blackberry Farm in Bolinas, up the coast from the Golden Gate Bridge. The events were staged outdoors, in front of the house and on the porch, and there was a potluck lunch served. There were Moviolas, editing benches, synchronizers, splicers, racks and trim bins. Families came in groups to cheer the contestants on, and the day was spent outdoors (amazing for editors!) in a festive atmosphere of good-natured competition, with children and dogs running around in the glorious weather peculiar to that part of the world.

The idea was a Decathlon of editing skills, some were head to head competition, some were against the clock. The events were:

Speed Splicing
The challenge was to splice 10 eight-frame pieces of leader together, front and back, against the clock. The resulting single spliced piece of leader had to be able to run through a Moviola without tearing.

Robert Bresson

Paul Hirsch tries his hand at Speed Splicing back in '82 under the
watchful eye of Matthew Robbins

Demolition Rewinding

Starting with a 1,000-foot roll of picture and a 1,000-foot roll of track, you had to
thread up the film onto take-up reels, put the start marks in a synchronizer, wind
down as fast as possible to sync marks at the end, stop on that given frame and lock
the synchronizer – all against the clock. One of the difficulties faced by contestants
(which they never faced in their professional lives) was the wind, which made the
very first step difficult.

Art Repola demolition rewinding

Tell the truth as you see it. Let the beauty take care of itself

Putting the Sync (Putting as in Shotput)

This was the game that bored assistants always played during slow times on the job, spinning the synchronizer as hard as they could to see how high a number they could reach. At the 1982 games, the sync block had been worked on by some machinists at Industrial Light and Magic, and was so finely balanced and tuned that it would spin (seemingly) forever. Scores of more than 1,000 were not uncommon.

Brad Bird timing the counter on a Moviola. Carrie Angland
makes sure he doesn't peek

Veeder-Root Sharp Shoot

This event, named after a maker of counters, had contestants sitting blindfolded in front of a Moviola. The counter was set to zero, the motor was engaged and the competitors had a hand on the brake. The idea was to let go, count to yourself for 30 seconds, and hit the brake as close to 45 feet as you could. (In 1982, Dalva hit 45 feet and 3 frames and lost!)

The Cornel Wilde Memorial Footage Guess

This was akin to guessing how many marbles in a jar. There was a roll of film, and you had to guess how long it was just by looking at it. (I won this one, and still have my Blue Ribbon.) According to Murch, 'The event was named for Mr. Wilde because, when he was interviewing editors for his documentary about the making of *Beach Red*, he would quickly pull a reel of film out of the drawer of his desk, flash it before the startled interviewees (Robbins and Lucas among them) and ask how much film it contained.'

Fred Zinnemann

Bobbing for Smitchies

Against the clock, you had to find a two-frame 'smitchie' in a trim bin, filled to overflowing, without dislodging the hanging strips of film. Some of the times were phenomenal: under one second. The reason was that the trims were rubber-banded to the pins, and people would simply reach in and grab the entire ball of film, throw it up in the air, and if you were lucky, the smitchie, the two-frame trim, would be lying at the bottom of the bin.

Worst Hand Anyway

This required winding 50 feet of yellow leader onto a three-inch plastic core, using only one hand, against the clock. If you were a righty, you used your left hand, if you were a lefty, you used your right hand, hence the name of the event. (If you lost, you could say, 'Well, it was my worst hand, anyway.') This was an exciting spectator event. The participants would line up on the porch, and the 50-foot yellow leaders would be extended out onto the grass in front of them. There were heats, since you could only do about eight people at a time. At the start, people would start furiously twisting their wrists, winding the film, and spectators lining the playing field could watch the film moving toward the porch, like runners in their respective lanes. Lots of cheering and rooting went on.

Trims and Outs Dash

In this one, you were loaded up with full trim boxes higher than your eyes, with your arms extended below, and then in groups of four, you had to run as fast as possible down the 50-yard gravel driveway without spilling any of the boxes. One producer, Tom Sternberg, with hubristic visions of victory dancing before his eyes, took a particularly spectacular fall.

Flanging

You had to wind handfuls of trims into rolls using the plate on the left side of a Moviola, without ripping or bending the film. This was a timed event and the clock didn't stop until you got the roll off the Moviola. The frequent difficulty for the enthusiastically inexperienced was that the film would get so tightly wound it would be almost impossible to get it off the flange.

Rack Arranging

This was a team event – the only one – although individual events were counted toward team totals. Four people on a team had to alphanumerically sort about 100 trim boxes jumbled in a heap, and put them on a rack in correct order against the clock.

Murch's team winning the Rack Arranging

All these skills are being slowly forgotten, and it's unlikely there will ever be another Droid Olympics. But those days back then, out in the sun with fellow film-makers competing and cheering and eating hotdogs and salads, were among the most enjoyable I have ever spent.

———————————————

Walter Comments:

In the summer of 1978, as I was editing the Sampan Massacre scene in *Apocalypse Now*, I heard a strange noise from the bench, where my assistant, Steve Semel, was working. Instead of film, he had attached wires to the hubs of the two reels positioned

Oscar Wilde

left and right (see picture on page 88) and tied the ends of the wires to the hands and feet of a plastic/rubber 1970s superhero named Stretch Armstrong. Stretch's particular talent was the ability to – as you might imagine – stretch his body to apprehend malefactors or escape from confining predicaments. Steve had then locked Stretch's body into the sprocketed gate of his synchroniser and was torturing Stretch on the rack of this machine, winding his elongated rubber body back and forth through the pointed teeth of the sprocket wheel.

Me: What are you doing?

Steve: Stretch has to suffer.

It was at that moment the idea was born to stage an Editorial Olympics, to celebrate the skill and dedicated patience of the platoon of assistants who were, day after day, doing the routine but exacting drudge work of reconforming the shrapnel of all the trims that we editors generated carelessly during our daily work. Within a day or two, Editorial Olympics became Droid Olympics.

Reading Paul's essay now, twenty years after it was written, thirty years on from the digital revolution of 1995 and forty-seven years after the first Droid Olympics, it is clear that the skills we had then are as recondite – even more so – as the adze and

Sound supervisor Richard 'Twiggy' Hymns in 2005, proudly
wearing the Droid Olympics ribbon he won in 1982

To what is dense, add clarity. To what is clear, add density awl in carpentry. So much depended on an ecosystem of suppliers, equipment and maintenance procedures that have now almost entirely disappeared.

What is curious, however, is that the symbols we still use for cinema – the reel, sprocketed film, the clapboard or the old Mitchell camera – have not faded away, even though none of that equipment is used today.[1] There is simply no compelling visual replacement for these icons in the surging waves of 1s and 0s we are now surfing. I guess it is similar to the situation with lumberjacks: the double-bladed axe and the two-man saw are instantly recognisable, even though hardly anyone uses them now in the chainsaw world of the present.

1. Except for the clapboard occasionally, though its main function, establishing sync between picture and sound, is now handled digitally. Some directors (Christopher Nolan, Quentin Tarantino) still shoot on film, but they quickly digitise it onto hard drives for editing and finishing, colour correction, etc. Michael Kahn (Spielberg's editor) held on to his scissors and Moviola for a long time, but now edits digitally as well.

Walter Murch

6: SACCADIC CINEMA

The Uncanny Persistence of the Persistence of Vision

I begin this chapter with three outrageous facts:

(1) You are blind every time you move your eyeballs.

(2) You experience reality approximately 120 milliseconds (three film frames) after it has happened.

(3) You are not aware of either of these facts.

I will use these strange but scientifically well-established phenomena to urge the final abandonment of the so-called *retinal persistence of vision*, which is often used (still!), two hundred years after it was first proposed, as an explanation for why we see motion when we watch a motion picture – which is, after all, just a series of still images.

Using the attributes of the *saccade* – the jump of the eyeball from one focal point to another – I hope to provide a satisfying replacement for retinal persistence. Cutting to the chase, it will amount to this:

> The neurology of saccades, which evolved over hundreds of millions of years of vertebrate sight to smooth out the shifts of attention that happen during the sudden movement of eyeballs, was hijacked and put to use when motion pictures were invented.

2033 will mark the two-hundredth birthday of motion pictures. In 1833 Belgian physicist and mathematician Joseph Plateau invented a device he called the *phénakistiscope*, a word derived from the Greek words *phenakistes*, meaning 'imposter', and *skopein*, meaning 'to look'. It consisted of a rotating disc with slits around its circumference, like the hours of a clock, and a series of drawings on the opposite side from the viewer – usually of a human being in action (walking, jumping, etc.) – each image lining up with one of the slits. To operate it, you would hold the disc between your eye and a mirror and then spin it while looking through the slits. Amazingly, the images – if they were drawn correctly in sequence – would animate in a repeating loop, exactly like today's GIFs.[1]

1. See YouTube – https://tinyurl.com/48aeespw – for a visual tribute to the *phénakistiscope* (QR code on left).

The public does not know what it wants. Impose on it your decisions, your delights

The *phénakistiscope* was an instant popular success, releasing a surge of dammed-up creativity, both in the fabulous nature of the drawings created for it – rats or snakes surging from the centre of the disc to the circumference! – as well as an improved technology, the *zoetrope*, invented in 1834 by British mathematician William Horner.

Phénakistiscope   Zoetrope

Plateau's feelings about his 1833 invention of the *phénakistiscope* can be guessed at from his name for it: Greek for *imposter viewer*. There is still something uncanny about the fact that these images spring to life when we spin the disc, so imagine how it must have seemed 190 years ago. What was making this happen? When Plateau was asked his opinion, he referred to a lecture given in 1824 at the Royal Society in London. This presentation, by Dr Peter M. Roget, a Fellow of the Royal Society, was dauntingly titled 'Explanation of an Optical Deception in the Appearance of the Spokes of a Wheel Seen Through Vertical Apertures'.[2]

Roget was referring to an illusion that he (and many others) had noticed in those days of spoke-wheeled carriages and picket fences. When a carriage drove by on the

2. Dr Roget, a Swiss citizen living in London, was also the author of *Roget's Thesaurus*, a crucial development in linguistic knowledge.

Robert Bresson

other side of a picket fence, at just the right speed, the spokes of its wheels would seem to become static and grotesquely deformed. Roget's conclusion was that vertically sliced images of the rotating wheel, seen through the slats of the picket fence, impressed themselves as a succession of still images on the retina, and then this cascade of 'still' images was re-formed in our minds as a frozen, distorted 'deception', as Roget called it.[3]

Here is Roget's illustration of a distorted wheel and his conclusions as to its origin. Notice that he ties his explanation together with the illusion of a circle of light formed by a swirling torch:

The true principle, then, on which this phenomenon depends, is the same as [. . .] the illusion that occurs when a bright object is wheeled rapidly round in a circle [like a torch], giving rise to the appearance of a line of light throughout the whole circumference: namely, that an impression made by a pencil of rays on the retina, if sufficiently vivid, will remain for a certain time after the cause has ceased.[4]

Roget, Plateau and their audiences at the time would have been familiar with eighteenth- and nineteenth-century magic-lantern shows, where the lantern would be fitted with two lenses and two slides so that the operator could make a dissolve between one image and the other. It was inferred that on the lantern-show screen, as on the retina, there was a *persistence of vision* from one image to the next, and that this dissolve between two slightly different images was interpreted by the observer as motion from one frame to the next. This illusion of motion, alternating quickly between two slightly different slides, was performed in many of the magic-lantern shows, as early as the eighteenth century, to great audience-pleasing effect.

Roget's interpretation of retinal persistence was accepted throughout the nineteenth century as the explanation for the illusion of motion in animation devices, and then motion photography when it was perfected in the early 1890s. Amazingly, it is often mentioned even now and can be found on current websites, such as Adobe's:

As with other motion simulation inventions, the illusions created by the zoetrope rely *on the human retina* [my italics] retaining an image for roughly

3. An excellent presentation by Michael Bach of the distorted-wheel deception can be found at https://michaelbach.de/ot/mot-Roget.

4. Roget's original presentation: https://royalsocietypublishing.org/doi/pdf/10.1098/rstl.1825.0007.

a tenth of a second. If a new image appears in that time, the brain merges them and the sequence appears continuous.[5]

Of course, there *is* such a thing as retinal persistence of vision: when the photoreceptors in your retina are over-stimulated with a sudden flash of bright light, they will continue to generate a current for a few seconds even after you close your eyes, just as your ears will continue to ring after a sudden loud gunshot. But as we all know, it is an imprecise, 'fuzzy' image, whose length of persistence depends on the intensity of the original flash.

When we watch a film, we do not see a cascade of fuzzy, overlapping images piling on top of each other in a visual smear, which is what retinal persistence would imply – something like Marcel Duchamp's 1912 painting *Nude Descending a Staircase, No. 2* or Étienne-Jules Marey's chronographs. Instead, the frames are individually distinct, the motion between them is precise and the illusion of motion is not dependent upon the intensity of the projector's light.

Nude Descending a Staircase, No. 2, Marcel Duchamp, 1912

Chronograph by Étienne-Jules Marey, 1886

5. Adobe's website explaining the principles of animation: https://tinyurl.com/4zdj4v4e.

André Gide

Enter the Beta Effect

In 1912 (the same year that Duchamp first exhibited his *Nude Descending a Staircase, No. 2*) Max Wertheimer, one of the founders of the Gestalt school of psychology, published 'Experimental Studies on the Seeing of Motion'. He proposed a new name for the illusion of apparent motion, which he called the *beta effect*, moving its origin out of the retina and deeper into the neurological circuitry of the brain. He did not explain what was going on in the brain nor where.[6]

> It is not sufficient to draw upon pure peripheral [i.e. retinal] processes in relation to a single eye: we must have recourse to processes which lie behind the retina [i.e. in the processing brain].

The beta effect is similar to the *phi effect* (also proposed by Wertheimer; see https://tinyurl.com/3zuvwwwb; QR code on left), which involves the illusion of a ghostly moving shape created by the rapid appearance and disappearance of objects separated in space, such as flashing light bulbs on a theatre marquee.

Harvard professor Hugo Münsterberg (1863–1916), a colleague of William James (the father of American psychology), amplified these ideas in his book *The Photoplay: A Psychological Study*, published four years after Wertheimer's article.

> It is not necessary to go further into details in order to demonstrate that the apparent movement [of motion pictures] is in no way the mere result of [a retinal] afterimage . . . The movement is in these cases not really seen from without, but is superadded, by the action of the mind, to motionless pictures.[7]

As for the cause of this *superaddition*, Münsterberg was optimistic that its origin would soon be discovered:

> The statement that our impression of movement includes a higher mental act is in itself not really an explanation. We have not settled the nature of that higher central process.[8]

6. See https://tinyurl.com/mwjt775z (QR code on left).
7. Hugo Münsterberg, *The Photoplay: A Psychological Study* (New York: D. Appleton and Co., 1916), p. 69.
8. Münsterberg, *The Photoplay*, p. 69.

Münsterberg intended to dig into this and proposed to 'settle the nature of the higher central processes' through experimentation in his laboratory. Unfortunately, he died in 1916, the year *The Photoplay* was published, and both the book and his proposal were ignored.[9]

Despite the surge in cinema's popularity in the years following the 1918 Armistice and nominal acceptance of Wertheimer's phi and beta effects, retinal persistence continued to be used in the popular press and even by certain twentieth-century film scholars (Arthur Knight, André Bazin, James Monaco, among others) as an explanation for the motion in motion pictures. Forty-six years ago, this situation prompted Joseph and Barbara Anderson to publish 'The Myth of Persistence of Vision' in the *Journal of the University Film Association*, where they mused about the uncanny longevity of the idea of retinal persistence. Fifteen years later, their frustration boiled over in 'The Myth of Persistence Revisited' (1993):

> The damned thing is a myth! It won't die. It still functions as a myth today. Those engaged in film study cling to persistence of vision because they need it. Just as the story of Adam and Eve explains not only the mechanism by which people originated and reproduced but also specifies the relationship of human beings to God, the myth of creation for the motion picture contains not only the mechanism for the origin of motion, but implies the relationship of the film to the (passive) viewer, upon whose sluggish retina images pile up.

The Andersons concluded their article with two suggestions:

> First 'persistence of vision', the term, the concept, the myth, must be given a place in the history of film scholarship, but can no longer be given currency in film theory . . . Second, and more important, the concept of the passive viewer implied by the myth, the one upon whose sluggish retina (or brain) the images pile up, must be replaced by an enlightened understanding of how viewers

---

9. Why was his book ignored? Münsterberg had been brought (by William James) from Germany in the early 1890s to head Harvard's psychology department. He was a tireless advocate for better German–American relations, and when World War I broke out, he supported the German side against the British. Although the US did not enter the war until April 1917, the year after his death, Münsterberg had been suspected of being a German spy, shunned by his colleagues and even received death threats, which may have contributed to the cerebral haemorrhage that killed him at the young age of fifty-three. His excellent book on film can be read, searched and downloaded at the Internet Archive: https://archive.org/details/photoplayapsycho005300mbp/page/n3/mode/2up.

Attributed to Jim Hightower

actually interface with motion pictures . . . These are elements to ponder in a
new theory of the motion picture.[10]

Turning Point: *Renaissance de Persistence*

Two years before the Andersons published the first of their commentaries, an article
titled 'The Resources of Binocular Perception' by John Ross (professor of psychology
at the University of Western Australia) appeared in the March 1976 issue of *Scientific
American*. If the Andersons had read Ross's work, it would have handed them a powerful tool to help put retinal persistence out of its misery, but not persistence of vision
itself, which in Ross's experiments staged a dramatic and mysterious rebirth.[11]

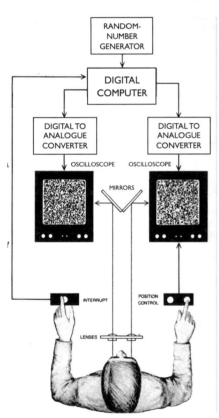

I was told about Ross's paper by my colleague Mark
Berger back in 1976, when it was published. I read it
with interest, and it had (and still has) a great influence
on my thinking about the neurology and psychology
of what goes on when we watch a film. Ross employed
stereograms to reveal that our perceptual system
extracts information about depth and motion from our
visual input even before we are conscious of what we see.

Ross and his team performed an ingenious series of
experiments using random-dot video displays (similar to the visual white-noise 'snow' seen between
broadcast television channels). But these displays had,
hidden within them, three-dimensional shapes that
would only be revealed when viewed stereoptically.
Subjects would be shown two apparently identical
video screens, arranged so that each of their eyes saw
only one of the screens – a set-up similar to nineteenth-
century stereopticons or those View-Masters from the
1940s and '50s. Looking with only one eye at a time, the
scene was flat-screen chaos: thousands of swirling dots

---

10. The Andersons' article is a complete survey of all the various interpretations of the illusion
of motion from 1824 until 1993. https://archives.evergreen.edu/webpages/curricular/2005-2006/
emergingorder/seminar/Week_1_Anderson.pdf.

11. John Ross, 'The Resources of Binocular Perception', *Scientific American*, March 1976: https://
www.scientificamerican.com/article/the-resources-of-binocular-percepti.

---

in a mad 'ant-hill' scramble, 30,000 pairs of dots arriving every second. But when viewed with both eyes, the subject would see either a square three-dimensional 'hole' punched in the screen or a panel floating over its surface. This was achieved by displacing a square section of the right-hand screen by a certain number of pixels relative to its partner screen on the left. Ross could turn the displacement on and off, and the hole would appear and disappear. Or he could shift the pixel displacement in the opposite direction, and the hole would become a square panel floating above the display, closer to the viewer. To be able to extract such information out of visual chaos is amazing, but it is a fairly standard demonstration of the power of our visual system.

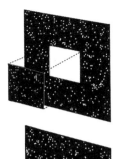

But what Ross did next was to progressively time-shift the right-hand screen's displacement, delaying it by ten milliseconds at a time. The depth illusion still appeared, even though there was a 10, 20 or 30 ms delay between the left and right screens. Intrigued, Ross pushed further, delaying the right-hand screen by 40, 50, 60 and 70 ms. The depth illusion still occurred with delays of 40 and 50 ms, but when they were greater than 50 ms, it disappeared.

Let's take a moment to assess what is going on here. To see the illusion of the hole in the screen, our visual system must analyse the positions of thousands of swirling dots on one screen and correlate them with their twin-sister dots on the other. If the correlation is identical, each dot lining up exactly with its sister on the other screen, no hole will be perceived. But when the dots that form Ross's virtual square in the right-hand screen are all shifted in the same direction by an equal number of pixels, our visual system recognises that despite their displacement, they are sisters to the dots on the left-hand screen, and the illusion will suddenly appear. The greater the displacement, the greater the height of the panel

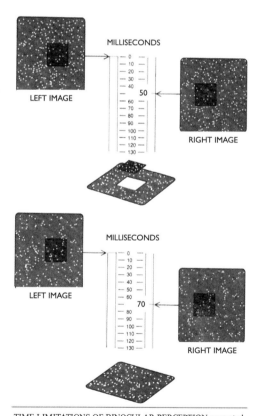

TIME LIMITATIONS OF BINOCULAR PERCEPTION were studied by immediately presenting the stream of points to the left eye and delaying the stream to the right eye. When the delay is less than 50ms (top) the targets are seen in depth. When the delay exceeds 50 ms, the impression of depth collapses (bottom).

Robert Bresson

off the plane of the screen. But with a delay introduced into the right-hand screen, the achievement becomes even more remarkable, because by the time dot A appears on the right-hand screen, the corresponding sister dot has already disappeared from the one on the left. And yet the depth illusion is seen! What does this mean? It means that an exact, precise memory-image of the swirling dots is kept somewhere, for a certain amount of time, in our visual cortex, readily available in case there is a need to compare it with something that is seen at a later moment. And, sure enough, 10, 20, 30, 40, 50 ms later, along comes something that is worth comparing, and we suddenly see a floating panel or hole in the screen.

Here is Ross commenting on this development:

> It would be impossible to match pairs of points *unless a record of the thousands of points seen is stored in some way* [my italics]. What is more, the record must be extremely accurate if it is to be utilised to find the exact disparity between pairs of points.[12]

The retention of such a large amount of data to give an exact memory-image of the previous 50 ms is expensive, neurologically speaking, so there is understandably a time limit beyond which the oldest images have to be deleted to make room for new ones coming in. Accordingly, when Ross increased the delay of the right-hand image beyond 50 ms, the floating panel would no longer appear because the information from the left-hand screen was no longer available.

> We found that binocular perception can tolerate a delay of about 50 ms (a 20th of a second) but not a longer one. It varies a little above or below 50 ms for different observers, but it is quite constant for a given observer.[13]

What can we conclude from this? That there must be the equivalent of a RAM cache somewhere in the brain – probably in the visual cortex, located in the occipital lobe at the back of the brain – which preserves a pixel-accurate record of everything we have seen over the previous 50 ms. This cache is readily available when there is a need to compare those stored images with something currently being seen. In the interests of brevity, clarity and authorship I am going to call this hypothesised cache the *Ross cache*.

---

12. Ross, 'The Resources of Binocular Perception'.
13. Ross, 'The Resources of Binocular Perception'.

This is literally persistence of vision. But it is not retinal persistence; it is something lying much deeper in the brain, as both Wertheimer and Münsterberg intuited. Much deeper and much, much more accurate than retinal persistence, and limited to a storage capacity of 50 ms. That is one twentieth of a second, and the mathematically inclined reader will have already compared this to the twenty-four- or twenty-five-frame-per-second speed of cinema. Each frame of a film is accordingly held for 41.67 ms (at 24 fps in the US) or 40 ms (at 25 fps in Europe), a shorter time than the hypothesised 50 ms Ross cache.[14]

This means that a frame of film *and the previous one* can be in this cache at the same time, ready to be compared with each other and for the fruits of that comparison to be sent to our conscious awareness. Just as in Ross's experiment, where the fruitful comparison between two images separated in space resulted in *depth*, in this case the comparison of two images separated in time yields *movement*. Both the depth and the movement are *apparent*; both are creations of the mind.

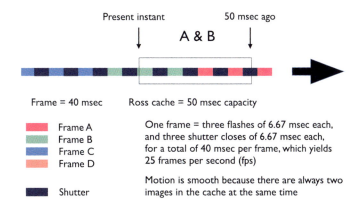

**Film projection at 25 frames per second
three-bladed shutter**

To see an animation of this drawing, go to https://vimeo.com/862354349.
Analysis of mechanical projection: http://tinyurl.com/2s3a64mk (QR codes on right)

14. This is related to, but different from, the visual phenomenon of *iconic memory*. Iconic memory lasts for several hundred milliseconds, instead of a definite 50 ms for the Ross cache (https://en.wikipedia.org/wiki/Iconic_memory). Both caches are probably located in the occipital lobe, particularly the primary visual cortex, which is heavily involved in the initial processing and temporary storage of visual information.

Robert Bresson

Ross's conclusion:

> It appears that there are records of visual input that can be consulted before anything at all is seen in order to determine the proper framework for perception. What these records are, how many separate repositories there are and what their physical basis is we do not know.

And here he ties his observations about binocular perception together with the subject of this chapter: the illusion of apparent motion.

> A number of puzzling visual effects such as apparent motion can be brought together by the assumption that perception must wait on the analysis of independent visual records before we are able to perceive.[15]

At twenty frames per second, each image is held on screen for 50 ms, which is at the limit of the Ross cache. This means that at frame rates slower than 20 fps, with a longer duration for each frame, there will be many moments when there is only one image in the cache, and consequently no ability to compare it with a subsequent frame in order to synthesise motion between them. As a result, perceived motion begins to stagger at frame rates slower than 20 fps.

Comparison with Sound

Just as images begin to stagger below 20 fps, we also begin to lose the ability to hear tonality in music below 20 hertz (cycles per second). We still 'hear' sounds below this frequency, but we feel each pulse as a separate impact rather than the tonality we hear above 20 Hz. The parallels between the lack of smooth motion below twenty frames per second and the lack of tonality below twenty cycles per second are intriguing.

You might say that tonality is to sound as motion is to image.

A further comparison can be made between the 50 ms Ross cache for vision and the 50 ms Haas effect for sound. The Haas effect[16] (also known as the precedence effect) says that if two nearly identical sounds are played in quick succession, with less than 50 ms between the leading edge of each

---

15. Both quotes on this page from Ross, 'The Resources of Binocular Perception'.
16. Haas effect on Wikipedia: https://tinyurl.com/23kwhusj (QR code on left).

It's those extra shots, the ones you discover at the last second, which nourish and enrich your film

> one, the listener will hear a single sound with a slightly 'off-mic' quality. If the separation between leading edges is greater than 50 ms, the listener will hear two separate sounds, in a distinct echo effect.

But why and how does the synthesis between two still images yield motion? I believe the explanation lies in the sudden movements of the eye known as *saccades*.

Saccades

These sudden, mostly involuntary movements of the eyeball are quick (20–200 ms) and common: we experience on average three saccades every second, for a daily total of well over 150,000.[17] They are particularly frequent when we are reading, with our attention jumping from phrase to phrase, but they are happening all the time, almost always below our conscious awareness.[18]

It is in exploring saccades that we encounter the first of the 'outrages' listed at the beginning of this chapter: *When you move your eyeballs, you are blind.* The reason for this is that the motion of saccades is so rapid (around 1,800 arc seconds per millisecond) that it far outstrips the response time of even the fastest photoreceptor cells.[19] This is a remarkable fact, so I will repeat: the moment our eyes start to move in a saccade, the degraded signals coming from the retina are blocked until our eyes come to rest again, perhaps 120 ms (three film frames) later. Consequently, we do not see these blurred images, nor do we see any evidence of their removal.

---

17. The actual number, for sixteen waking hours, would be 172,800. In an uncanny convergence, this is exactly the number of frames in a two-hour film. Saccades of a sort persist when we are asleep, but now they are called REMs (Rapid Eye Movements). REMs occur during periods of intense dreaming, and it is natural to assume that they are saccades freed from the constraints of external reality. The images of dreams are constructed by us, and we can freely 'pan and scan' those images, like shifting our attention across the various parts of the film frame (see footnote 20 on next page).

18. A fascinating animation of all the saccades recorded during a small-audience screening of a scene from Paul T. Anderson's *There Will Be Blood* can be seen at the Film Cognition website: https://www.cinelabresearch.com/film-cognition. View under 'Demo Videos' (QR code on right).

19. It takes cones 20 ms to respond to light: https://tinyurl.com/mrsndwpr. But the 'dwell time' of a point of light on the average photoreceptor during the sweep of a saccade is around 20 microseconds, a thousand times slower than the response time of the fastest cone cells. If we could see what the retina 'sees' during a saccade, it would be a horizontal smear of different tonal values and colours from the scene in front of us, but with no detail of any kind – like a *swish pan* in cinema.

Jean Cocteau

> A vivid demonstration of this is as close as your nearest mirror. Stand about five inches in front of it and ask a friend to watch the goings-on, perhaps making a video at the same time. Now look at your left eye for three seconds, and then suddenly, without moving your head, look at your right eye. What you will experience is . . . nothing, no change. Now look back at your left eye. You will also experience no change. It just seems to you that you have been looking at yourself for six seconds or so, with no movement of your eyeballs. What your friend sees, and what the video will show, however, are your eyeballs moving from left to right and back again. Your visual system has sneakily edited out the movement of your eyeballs and concealed the fact of that edit. This process has a name: saccadic masking.[20]

So you are effectively blind for the 120 ms that you moved your eyes. This fact is of great use to magicians and masters of three-card monte, whose con artistry is to get you to move your eyeballs at the exact same moment that they quickly perform their tricks, which consequently are invisible to you.

We may be effectively blind, but we do see *something* during a saccade. What is it? And how does our visual system perform the magic of providing us with vision during a saccade? It accomplishes this by taking the last clear image before the start of the saccade, comparing it to first clear image after the saccade, constructing a plausible connection between the two, and then editing that construct into the gap created by saccadic masking.[21] This is exactly Münsterberg's and Wertheimer's intuition about the origin of motion between still frames of a movie. As Münsterberg wrote, 'The movement is not really seen from without, but is *superadded*, by the action of the mind, to motionless pictures.'

The mirror experiment is dramatic, but there is not much movement in it. So here's another one, this time with movement:

> Sit down and hold your hands out, palms upwards, about a foot away from your eyes and separated by about fifteen inches. Stare straight ahead, wiggle

20. Saccadic masking on Wikipedia: https://en.wikipedia.org/wiki/Saccadic_masking. Also: Akash Peshin, 'What Is Saccadic Masking?' *Science ABC*, 18 January 2018: https://www.scienceabc.com/humans/what-is-saccadic-masking.html.

21. Mlodinow, *Subliminal*, pp. 46–7. Also: Peshin, 'What Is Saccadic Masking?'

The purpose of life is to be defeated by greater and greater things

the fingers of both hands and now look at your left hand without moving your head. You see your left fingers wiggling, but you can also see, peripherally, your right fingers wiggling. Now saccade your eyes to look at your right hand, also without moving your head. You see your right hand's fingers wiggling and, peripherally, you can still see your left hand's fingers wiggling.

The saccade you just performed lasted around 200 ms (five film frames), during which you were blind, but nonetheless you saw your fingers continuing to wiggle perfectly naturally. Those five frames of wiggling motion were created by your visual cortex, which compared information captured from just before and just after the saccade, and then made best guesses about what would most probably link the two.

This is the result of extremely sophisticated brain software, to say the least, similar but superior to the digital cinema applications that can expand old films shot at 16 fps to 48 fps by making best guesses, using artificial intelligence, about how to interpolate the missing two frames between every one of the original frames.[22]

A reasonable question from the reader: But this mental software you are describing can only construct the missing information *after* it has registered the first clear image at the end of the saccade. And yet our experience of reality is that it moves continuously forwards. This seems to cycle backwards – to add information retrospectively.

An answer: Our experience of reality is forwards, as you say. But recall the second 'outrage' at the beginning of the chapter: *We are living in the past.* More exactly: our experience of reality is of something that has already happened approximately 120 ms previously.[23]

Yes, We Live in the Past . . . but Only the Slightly Past

Snap your fingers and you experience a satisfying synchronicity of image, sound and touch. You see, hear and feel the snap at the same moment. And those three things *do*

22. Peter Jackson's film *They Shall Not Grow Old* (2018) is a vivid example of the artistic possibilities of this technology: https://www.youtube.com/watch?v=wWIJLAe2pEI.
23. The length of this delay will depend on the complexity of the sensory processing involved.

Rainer Maria Rilke

happen together, but by the time you feel/see/hear the snap, it has already occurred some time earlier.[24] What causes this?

The signals of sight, sound and touch arrive at different times to our central sensory processing unit, the thalamus, located near the centre of our brains. Hearing arrives first, as it is the quickest of our senses; then touch; then sight, which is the slowest because it is the most complex and requires the most processing. The thalamus waits for them all to arrive, puts them in sync, after which they are processed further, and only then finally delivered to our awareness.[25] All of this processing takes time – about 120 ms on average. And this is approximately how much lag there is between reality and our perception of it.[26] The three senses have been put in sync with each other, but they are no longer in sync with the events that triggered them.[27]

David Eagleman, professor of neuroscience at Baylor University, has this to say about our predicament:

> The strange consequence of all this is that you live in the past. By the time you think the moment occurs, it's already long gone. To synchronise the incoming information from the senses, the cost is that our conscious awareness lags behind the physical world. That's the unbridgeable gap between an event occurring and your experience of it.[28]

This lag gives our visual system the time to generate the interpolated images that will replace the blurred ones suppressed by saccadic masking, supplying them to our awareness just before our lagging consciousness arrives at the first moment of suppression.

---

24. Explanation from David Eagleman, 'Motion Signals Bias Localization Judgments: A Unified Explanation for the Flash-Lag, Flash-Drag, Flash-Jump, and Frohlich Illusions', *Journal of Vision*, March 2007. https://jov.arvojournals.org/article.aspx?articleid=2192987&resultClick=1#87872220.

25. This process integrates various parts of our visual processing, and it is called the *binding window*. See Mark T. Wallace and Ryan A. Stevenson, 'The Construct of the Multisensory Temporal Binding Window and Its Dysregulation in Developmental Disabilities', *Neuropsychologia*, November 2014, pp. 105–23: https://www.ncbi.nlm.nih.gov/pmc/articles/PMC4326640.

26. https://theconversation.com/what-youre-seeing-right-now-is-the-past-so-your-brain-is-predicting-the-present-131913.

27. Alcohol levels slow down the speed of this processing considerably: the more alcohol we consume, the slower the speed. This is the main reason why it is dangerous to drink and drive, and it explains the characteristic stumbling of the drunk.

28. David Eagleman, *The Brain* (Edinburgh: Canongate Books, 2015), p. 50.

Shudderings of images awakening . . .

Another reader's reasonable question: Ross proposed a time limit to his cache of 50 ms. But, on page 105, you wrote that saccades last up to 200 ms. How do you reconcile a 50 ms cache with a saccade that lasts four times longer? Won't the information in the cache have evaporated by the time the longest saccade is over?

A probable answer: The *capacity* of the cache is 50 ms, but that does not necessarily affect its *duration*. Under normal, constant, non-saccadic vision, as in the Ross experiment, the 50 ms cache is constantly filling up with new information at one end, so to speak, and deleting it from the other, like a fountain bowl of a certain capacity overflowing thanks to the water streaming in from below. But the inflow of images suddenly *stops* when a saccade begins (saccadic blindness), so the Ross cache freezes, holding that last 50 ms of good data in readiness for the moment when the saccade ends and good data starts to flow again. It makes no difference whether the saccade is 20 ms or 200 ms.

Fast Reaction Times

You can easily imagine the difficulty that sensory latency creates for athletes who play tennis, baseball, cricket, football and other 'fast-ball' sports. Pitching and bowling speeds in professional baseball and cricket can exceed 100 miles an hour, and aggressively fast serves in tennis can attain 150 mph. At that speed, a tennis ball travels approximately 18 feet in 80 ms, so by the time the receiver 'sees' it consciously, the ball is no longer where it appears to be.

One of the solutions to this problem is that athletes can apparently learn to bypass sophisticated consciousness and rely on instinctual 'knee jerk' *reflex arc* responses processed in the spinal cord, which are many times faster than 'conscious' perception routed through the brain – think of how we instinctively yank our hand away from unexpected contact with a hot stove before we are even aware of its heat. Also, after years of experience, athletes become expert at making predictions about where the ball might be, even

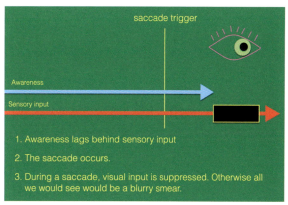

To view an animation explaining saccades and saccadic masking, and how they relate to motion pictures, go to https://vimeo.com/960915799 (QR code on right)

Robert Bresson

though they may not be able to 'see' it in the normal sense of the word.[29] As tennis player Ben Shelton said at the 2023 US Open, 'Sometimes you just have to shut off the brain, close your eyes, and swing.'

Musicians also go through similar 'bypassing of consciousness' training, and it is essential in Formula One racing, as well as other activities where reaction times need to be as short and 'predictive' as possible.

Digital Cinema

A frame of digital cinema (at 25 fps) is held for 40 ms and then immediately switches to the next. This switch, without a 'shutter moment' of black separating two adjacent frames, as there is in mechanical projection, does not seem to bother us.[30] A frame duration of 40 ms does not 'overshoot' the 50 ms Ross cache and will share memory space with the subsequent frame, enabling our visual system to create the apparent motion needed to link the two still images.

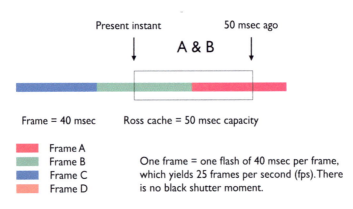

Digital projection at 25 frames per second

To see an animation of this, go to https://vimeo.com/861785668 (QR code on left)

29. How to outwit the illusion of saccadic blindness in fast-ball sports like tennis and cricket: https://faulttoleranttennis.com/why-you-cant-return-a-kick-serve-saccadic-blindness.

30. In fact, when a digital projector switches from one frame to the next, there is a very brief pause in the light output as the data for the new frame is processed. This moment of darkness lasts around 300 microseconds, but as brief as that is, it can be noticed as a slight flicker, especially in white areas. The counterintuitive solution is to repeat the frame three times in 1/25th of a second. This ensures that there are seventy-five of these slight dimmings every second, well above the sixty per second *flicker fusion* rate for humans. As a result, they are no longer noticed.

Your film: let people feel the soul and the heart there,
but let it be made like a work of hands

Conclusion: Cinema Is Saccadic

The analogy between cinema and saccades was especially precise in cinema's first mechanical super-century (1894–2004). Every camera and projector had to have a shutter to mask the blurring that would occur when the film was rapidly jerked from one frame to the next. And this shutter performed the same job that saccadic masking does when it prevents us from seeing the blurry result of the rapid jerking of the eyeball during a saccade.[31]

This 'behind the curtain' operation of the saccade is so extremely close to what happens when we watch a film that a saccadic explanation for why we see motion in motion pictures seems inescapable, circling us back to the objective expressed at the beginning of this chapter:

The intricate neurology of vertebrate sight, which evolved over hundreds of millions of years to deal, in part, with the rapid eye motion of saccades, was simply hijacked and immediately put to use when motion pictures were invented 190 years ago.

So persistence of vision has persisted, after all, but in a much more sophisticated form than *retinal* persistence: sophisticated both in its pinpoint accuracy, as Ross has demonstrated, as well as in its crucial role in enabling our visual system to create the illusion of movement, which is how the brain resolves the differences between one image and the next. Whether it is the intermittent nature of the movement of our eye during saccades or the intermittent nature of the modern motion picture film, the process is the same.[32]

31. Birds are an interesting example of vertebrates whose eyes do not move in their sockets, so they do not have saccades in the human sense. But they compensate by moving their heads in quick 'saccade-like' jerks, familiarly stereotyped as being characteristically 'bird-like'. See https://academic.oup.com/book/10639/chapter-abstract/158654053?redirectedFrom=fulltext.

32. What I have called the 'Ross cache' for simplicity's sake is actually a multilayered part of the visual cortex known as *extrastriate visual areas V1 to V5*. Specific neurons in regions like V5 are tuned to detect motion. These neurons specialise in comparing changes in position between adjacent frames, effectively 'stitching' together the differences between still images to create the perception of motion. While there isn't a literal 'frame storehouse', as implied by the term 'Ross cache', the visual cortex and interconnected areas do maintain a dynamic, continuously updated sequence of visual 'snapshots' of everything that has been seen in the last 50 ms. See R. T. Born and D. C. Bradley, 'Structure and Function of Visual Area V5/MT', *Annual Review of Neuroscience*, vol. 28 (2005), pp. 157–89.

Robert Bresson

7: TETRIS I

Timing and Dosage in Editing *The Conversation*

Shooting of Francis Coppola's *The Conversation* began the Monday after Thanksgiving 1972, eight months after the release of *The Godfather*. Haskell Wexler was the cinematographer, as he had been on *American Graffiti*, and Dean Tavoularis was production designer, as he had been on *The Godfather* and would be on *The Godfather: Part II*. *The Conversation* was released in April 1974, nine months before the Christmas release of *The Godfather: Part II*. George Lucas's *American Graffiti* – another Zoetrope production – had started twenty-eight days of shooting in the summer of 1972 and was ready to be mixed in January 1973. It was released in August of that year.

Murch aboard his Sausalito houseboat

I was the sound effects supervisor on all four of those films, lead re-recording mixer on three of them[1] and, although I had never previously edited a feature, film editor on *The Conversation*. It was an intense couple of years, marked also by the premature birth of our daughter Beatrice in May 1973 and, a month later, moving from the $7,000 Sausalito houseboat we had bought in 1969 to the farmhouse in Bolinas where we still live today.

Despite the intensity of all that overlapping work, *The Conversation* is a quiet and at times meditative study of an anonymous character, Harry Caul (Gene Hackman), who is a professional recorder of secret conversations. Francis began work on the screenplay in 1967, influenced by a 1966 discussion on surveillance he had with director Irvin Kershner, Michelangelo Antonioni's film *Blow-Up*, and a *Life* magazine article entitled 'Snooping Electronic Invasion of Privacy'. This led to a connection with fellow San Franciscan Hal Lipset, a real-life Harry Caul who became

---

1. *The Godfather* was mixed by Richard Portman (lead mixer – dialogue), Bud Grenzbach (music) and Curly Thirlwell (sound effects).

In order to work, poetry has to be a little bit stupid

an adviser on the film and was subsequently chief investigator for the US Senate's Watergate committee.[2]

Another tangential influence was Noël Coward and David Lean's 1945 film *Brief Encounter* and the shadowy character of Stephen Lynn (Valentine Dyall), who makes his apartment available for the potentially adulterous, but never consummated, encounter between Laura (Celia Johnson) and Alec (Trevor Howard). Francis told me that he wanted to take a walk-on part like Lynn's and, in *Conversation*, flip the telescope around to concentrate the entire film on a conventionally marginal character – in this case, Harry Caul. What does this anonymous person do, how does he do it, and what crises will afflict him that we would never suspect?

To deepen the challenge further, Francis decided to style his character study on Hermann Hesse's novel *Steppenwolf*, whose protagonist is a Middle European 'cipher' (as Francis described him), but then alloy it with a tense, Hitchcockian murder mystery, like *The Wrong Man*: two elements that aren't naturally disposed to fusion; in fact, each one is a direct challenge to the other.[3]

But *challenge* was the whole point. Francis had not wanted to make *The Godfather*, but out of financial necessity he threw himself into that studio production wholeheartedly. Now he had agreed to do *The Godfather: Part II*, but on condition that he be allowed to make a small, personal film in between – *The Conversation* – staking out his own turf to keep himself from being swallowed alive by the studio system.

> The Godfather was an accident. I was broke and we needed the money. We had no way to keep American Zoetrope going. I had no idea it was going to be that successful. It was awful to work on, and then my career took off and I didn't get to be what I wanted to be. I wanted to be a guy who made films like The Rain People and The Conversation. I didn't want to be a big Hollywood movie director.[4]

The Conversation is told exclusively from Caul's point of view: he is either in every shot or the shot is something he is looking at. As a result, we (the audience) know

2. *Life* magazine: https://tinyurl.com/yftj7ayc. The character of William P. 'Bernie' Moran in *Conversation* is modelled in part on Bernie Spindel, a close associate of Jimmy Hoffa who is featured in the *Life* article. It was Spindel who bragged about bugging the pay phone in his tenement when he was twelve years old, a line of dialogue that is given to Moran (Allen Garfield).

3. The protagonist in *Steppenwolf* is named Harry Haller. In early drafts of *The Conversation*, Harry Caul was named Harry Caller, later changed to Harry Call, then finally Harry Caul.

4. Anisse Gross interview with Coppola for *The Rumpus* (2012): https://therumpus.net/2012/08/17/the-rumpus-interview-with-francis-ford-coppola-2.

only what he knows. This intense first-person subjectivity, shared by *The Talented Mr. Ripley* (1999), *Chinatown* (1974) and others, is a particularly useful device when the main character – like Harry Caul, Tom Ripley or Jake Gittes – is conventionally unsympathetic for some reason. As a result, there is no escape – we never go off with other characters to get a perspective on Harry from 'outside' – so we either have to accept the premise of the movie or get up and leave. In a sense, the film takes us hostage and forces us to identify with a character whom, under other circumstances, we would reject: a sort of cinematic Stockholm syndrome.

Another device to prevent the alloy from breaking apart was Francis's decision to keep himself intentionally ignorant about the other characters and their motivations. What is the relationship between the Director (Robert Duvall) and Ann (Cindy Williams)? Is she his young wife? And what power does she wield relative to Mark (Fred Forrest) or Martin Stett (Harrison Ford)? We just don't know.

'If I knew these things,' Francis told me, 'the natural tendency would be for me to elaborate them, to make more of them, because things like that are catnip to an audience. The discipline of *not knowing* put a brake on my tendencies to embellish, and to keep things strictly from Harry's point of view. He didn't know, so why should I? And why should the audience?'

> I was afraid that the character of Harry was so essentially boring that it would be easy to cross over into a thing where the audience was really more interested in the couple and their story than in him. And since that wasn't the point, I did whatever I could to make it seem like a citadel of power with almost Henry VIIIth types of relationships, without ever giving you a hint that you were meant to go into that story. I was frankly scared that if I was any more specific, then everyone would be irritated that I was not making the movie about Ann and Mark, the couple.[5]

The Watergate burglary was discovered in June 1972, and that political drama unravelled in parallel with the production of *Conversation*: the film's release in April 1974 was coincidentally just a month after the indictment of the so-called 'Watergate Seven' and a week before the subpoena of sixty-four White House tapes. Inevitably, this raised expectations for *The Conversation* because many of the Watergate burglars (Liddy, Hunt, etc.) were cousins, so to speak, of Harry Caul. But

5. Interview with Coppola by Brian De Palma: *Filmmakers Newsletter*, May 1974: http://tinyurl.com/c49657ps (QR code on left).

Any Universe simple enough to be understood is too simple to produce
a mind capable of understanding it

Francis's desire for personal expression kept him faithful to his original screenplay, hatched years earlier.

> When Watergate happened, I was really frightened that people would expect *The Conversation* to be about spies and tapes and that sort of thing, and then be very angry that it wasn't. Well, right from the beginning, I wanted it to be something personal, not political, because somehow that is even more terrible to me.[6]

Nonetheless, there was a feeling among certain members of the crew, particularly the politically active director of photography Haskell Wexler, that Francis's screenplay wasn't up to the task, given the developing Watergate scandal. Haskell's simmering reservations boiled over after three weeks of shooting,[7] and a technical argument about backlighting the location of Robert Duvall's office was the trigger for Francis to fire him.[8] Production was shut down for several weeks over Christmas while Francis searched for another cinematographer.

Complicating things further, Harry Caul was a difficult role for Hackman because of the continuous verbal and physical restraint required, which was very different

from the actor's own easy-going and voluble personality. There are only four short moments of release in Hackman's entire performance: the throwing of a wastepaper basket and the snapping of a pen recorder during the warehouse party; Harry's brief struggle to get past security when trying to see the Director; and the smashing of a plastic statue of the Virgin Mary. Arguments between Coppola and Hackman about interpretation consequently flared up on a regular basis.[9]

6. Anisse Gross interview with Coppola for *The Rumpus* (2012): https://therumpus.net/2012/08/17/the-rumpus-interview-with-francis-ford-coppola-2.

7. Haskell had told me that Harry Caul had to either 'shit or get off the pot'.

8. It was a difficult situation, since Wexler, a personal friend of George Lucas, had rescued the cinematography of *American Graffiti* earlier in 1972, when serious focus and lighting problems persisted after the first week of production.

9. See *Close-Up on* The Conversation: https://www.youtube.com/watch?v=JuQ9-lolwxc.

John Barrow

Luckily, cinematographer Bill Butler, who had photographed *The Rain People* for Francis four years earlier, was willing and available to take over from Haskell.[10] With him on board, the mood lightened and the pace of shooting quickened, but Harry was still a struggle for Hackman, time had been lost that would never be made up and *Godfather II* was looming, implacably.

While all this was happening, my 'day job' was sound-designing and mixing *American Graffiti*. The mix schedule had been extended into February because the releasing studio, Universal, had demanded the deletion of a number of scenes after we had completed the final mix in January. Consequently, I was not available to work on *Conversation* full-time until the *Graffiti* mix was finished. Under the circumstances, associate editor Richard Chew began assembling scenes as they were shot, helped by first assistant Julie Zale. But thanks to Butler's multiple-camera coverage, the amount

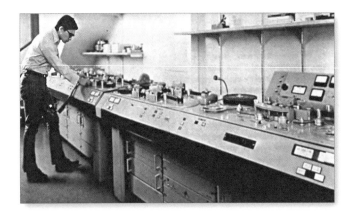

Peter More threading the KEM mixing transports used on every Zoetrope
film, from 1969's *The Rain People* to 1979's *Apocalypse Now*

of film printed each day was close to overwhelming us, so I asked second assistant Pat Jackson to start assembling some of the scenes I was supposed to edit, guided by 'paper cuts' I had sketched out using script supervisor Nancy Tonery's line script.[11]

The last day of shooting on *Conversation* was scheduled for 28 February, but on the 20th, the final day of the Alta Plaza 'foggy park' scene between Harry and Ann, troubles with the noisy fog machine (which used a pungent oil-based fluid that settled onto parked cars and gardens) riled the surrounding neighbourhood, and the police

10. In 1974, Butler would shoot *Jaws* for Spielberg, and in 1975, *One Flew Over the Cuckoo's Nest* for Miloš Forman.

11. See the 'clicked' moment described in Chapter 4, p. 64–6.

Once projected, the scene begins to live in a vacuum where the smallest mistake appears monstrous

were called. Arguments broke out, and in frustration Francis shut the whole production down completely, with seventy-eight scenes left unshot.[12]

> The shooting script of *The Conversation* can be viewed at https://tinyurl.com/yrxzntzz (QR code on right). This is Francis's final draft, issued on 22 November 1972, five days before the start of principal photography. It is 157 pages long and consists of 397 scenes.

There were multiple reasons for this radical decision, but underlying all of them was the imminent collision between shooting *The Conversation* and pre-production on *The Godfather: Part II*. *Conversation* was already sixteen days over schedule, and another six days would have perhaps ripped the edge of the envelope. I can only imagine what kind of pressure Francis was under, but Paramount certainly considered *Godfather II* more important than *Conversation*.

Nineteen of those seventy-eight unshot scenes were relatively minor 'connective tissue' that had already been judged superfluous. But the other fifty-nine were split between two major sequences: Harry pursuing Ann through a fog-shrouded San Francisco (thirty-five scenes, nos. 282–316); and Harry returning to his warehouse to find it being ransacked by shadowy agents of the Director (twenty-four scenes, 332–55).

The first sequence, involving a slow-motion pursuit between two electric trolley-buses, was intended to be the lead-up to Harry's personal 'confession' to Ann in the foggy park. Without the pursuit, it was not clear how to explain the scene in the park. The second sequence, crucially, provided the clues to the hidden meaning behind the Union Square conversation itself, showing that the presumed victims, Ann and Mark, were actually the culprits – it was they who ordered their own conversation to be recorded – and that the victim was the Director, whom Harry had assumed to be the culprit.

Without these two sequences, it was not obvious how to resolve the plot of the film, but as Francis left to start work on the pre-production of *Godfather II*, his advice was to cut the film together the best way I could, and if anything was required to fill the holes left by the unshot scenes, which would almost certainly be the case, he would ask Paramount to release some money for a few days of reshoots.

12. See interview with Coppola by Brian De Palma: http://tinyurl.com/c49657ps (QR code on right).

Jean Cocteau

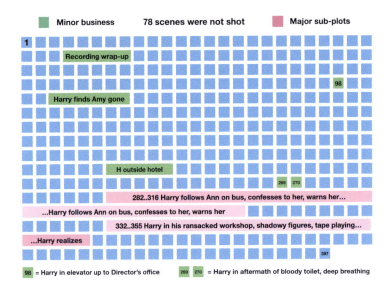

A graphic of the seventy-eight unshot scenes (in green and magenta) – 20 per cent of the original 397 – and their location within the remaining 319 scenes of the screenplay, represented in blue. An animated version can be seen on Vimeo: https://vimeo.com/701393493 (QR code on left)

Richard and I were naturally somewhat spooked by this sudden development – neither of us had edited a feature motion picture before, and now two crucial sequences remained unshot – but we gathered some reassurance from Francis's relaxed attitude. He seemed to be taking all this in his stride, and given what he had gone through on *Godfather*, who were we to second-guess the situation?

Once the *Graffiti* mix was finished, right around the last day of shooting on *Conversation*, I was finally able to join Richard full-time. Francis had printed over 400,000 feet of 35 mm film, around seventy-five hours of material, and the main item on my plate was the opening of the film: Harry's secret recording of the conversation itself. Haskell had shot this sequence over five days as if it were a documentary, with four hidden cameras and radio microphones. Each take lasted ten minutes (a full load of 35 mm film for each camera), and Haskell repositioned the cameras in different hidden locations for each of the seven takes, which yielded 4 × 7 = 28 different camera set-ups. As a result, the workprint for the whole sequence totalled over 40,000 feet (seven and a half hours, 10 per cent of the total for the whole film) and almost all of it was in intentionally *vérité* style, as if grabbed surreptitiously. Fred Forrest and Cindy Williams (playing Mark and Ann) had walked in circles around Union Square, frequently lost among a surging crowd of San Franciscans who didn't know they

Certain kinds of mistakes don't matter much. They help to put things in relief

were being photographed, and the camera operators had been happy to occasionally be able to get the actors in focus and speaking in sync. As a result, there were no detailed script notes accompanying each take, other than a general description of each camera location and which lenses were being used, but the cameras caught many serendipitous moments that could not have been achieved in any other way. Because of microwave interference, approximately a third of the sound was unusable. To get a handle onto this semi-chaotic situation, I drew a grid with all the lines of dialogue for the scene on the X-axis and each camera take on the Y-axis, and then filled in the relevant squares when a line of dialogue was on camera – coloured red if it was a particularly good capture.

The grid helped, and the KEM horizontal editing desks we were using were state-of-the-art editing machines in those pre-digital years, but it was a fascinating, holding-on-by-my-fingernails challenge to put this sequence together, especially given the length of those ten-minute takes and their often random nature.[13] But I can still recall the thrilling moment when I allowed the dialogue of the conversation to spill over into the shot of Harry walking to his van, where all of the recording equipment was humming away under the supervision of his assistant, Stan (John Cazale). Suddenly, everything that we had been looking at, and listening to, began to make some kind of sense.

Because of these inherent difficulties, the seventy-five hours of material and – it needs to be said – our inexperience, it took us eight weeks after the end of shooting to put together a four-and-a-half-hour first assembly of the film.

While this was going on, Aggie was in and out of hospital with complications from her pregnancy – kidney problems and high blood pressure – and some of her doctors were worried that she and the baby might not survive childbirth. We were still living aboard the Sausalito houseboat with our four-year old son Walter, but preparing to move to the Bolinas farmhouse after the baby was born. It was an intense and nerve-racking time.

Fortunately, both 'babies' were born successfully: we screened the first assembly of *The Conversation* for Francis on Saturday 12 May, and ten days later Beatrice was delivered, a month early, by Caesarean section. She was, as with all preemies, underweight, at four and a half pounds. *Conversation*, as with all first assemblies,

---

13. Francis used this same multi-camera documentary technique to film Connie's wedding-party scene for the opening of *The Godfather* and for many sequences in *Apocalypse Now*, notably Kilgore's 'Valkyries' Air Cavalry helicopter attack on the village of Vin Din Drop.

Jean Cocteau

was overlong, at four and a half hours (much longer than the usual first assembly). Beatrice needed to put on weight, which she did, rapidly, and the film needed to lose time, which it did – but slowly.

An assembly of this length is like a wildly overgrown garden, where the location of the pathways is not clear or even where the stems of intertwined plants are located. So editing has to proceed carefully, and it can take a few weeks of trimming and pruning before the underlying structure is glimpsed. Only then may it be safe to try lifting whole bushes (which is to say, scenes), while being careful to avoid damaging the intertwined roots of adjacent plants. It is somewhat similar to the problems encountered when remodelling a house.

Both problems – overgrown garden and house remodelling – confronted us, literally, when we moved from Sausalito to Bolinas in June 1973, a month after the birth of Beatrice and the completion of the first assembly of *Conversation*.

The 1880 farmhouse that we had bought in Bolinas, on the Pacific coast, just north of San Francisco, had survived (mostly) the 1906 earthquake and was surrounded by four acres of couch grass, blackberry brambles and mattress vine. It had been a dairy until the late 1960s, and the house needed heavy-duty repairs. It was still resting on a redwood log perimeter that had been in place since it was knocked sideways in the earthquake, and we had to jack it up several feet into the air to pour in new concrete foundations. Basic work

Left: black-and-white photograph of our house in Bolinas, taken by G. K. Gilbert of the United States Geological Survey in 1906, a few days after the great San Francisco earthquake. Above: colour panoramic of Blackberry Farm, taken at the same time of day in 2019, exactly 113 years later (notice the angle of the shadows). Aggie and I and our family have lived here for over fifty years

In silence, images drop their masks and look at us with wide-open eyes

like this was completed during the time between buying the house, in June
1972, and moving in a year later, but more – much more – remained to be
done. Writing this, I am shaking my head in appalled/amused amazement,
thinking about all the work involved, but we were in our late twenties and
game for these kinds of challenges.

After the first-assembly screening, Francis was cautiously optimistic, but it was clear
that the film was much too long and that the unshot scenes had left jagged plot
holes that would somehow have to be filled. Francis, Richard and I spent a couple of
days discussing strategies for how to improve certain scenes, plus how to get the film
under three hours, and those sessions generated half a dozen pages of notes. Francis
also let us know that because of his *Godfather II* workload, he would not be in the
cutting rooms on a regular basis, and that Richard and I should just proceed on our
own, following those notes, and see where that got us. And if we had any other ideas,
to try them out without consulting him: 'Surprise me when I come back' – which, he
said, would be in about a month.

It was an unusual situation. The director who had just triumphed with *The
Godfather* had left the editing of this intensely personal film to two young editors
who had not previously edited a feature. But much of what had already happened at
Zoetrope over the last five years was unusual. In fact, the whole purpose of Zoetrope
was to be unusual, to break the mould of how films were made.

That first meeting set the pace for the next four months. Richard and I would work
on our own for several weeks, Francis would return and there would be a screening – usually with five or six guests, often people who had nothing to do with the
film business. A discussion, spread out over a couple of days, would follow, new
notes would be written up, and then Francis would return to *Godfather II* for the
next three weeks.

Taking out our gardening tools, the first 'bushes' we tried uprooting were scenes
relating to Harry's relationship with his neighbours in the apartment block where he
lived. It was a risky idea, because doing so would seem to undermine Francis's goal
of blending a character study with a murder mystery – and here we were chipping
away at the character part of the formula. But there didn't seem to be any other way to
quickly get the film under three hours.

The neighbours subplot involved the other residents of the building complaining
about the utilities – water, heat, electricity – which were being neglected by an absentee

Béla Balázs

landlord (scenes 42–4). Harry is esteemed by his neighbours as an upstanding busi-
nessman, although no one has any idea what his business is, and so he is elected to go
to the offices of the lawyer, McNaught (Abe Vigoda), where the rent cheques are sent,
and file a complaint against the anonymous landlord.

Coppola, Hackman and Abe Vigoda (as McNaught)

The scenes in McNaught's offices (93–5) reveal that Harry himself is the landlord, and that he was holding off on any major repairs because the building was in
a redevelopment zone, soon to be bought by the city. Harry decides to do nothing
except pump out the basement and asks McNaught to send a form letter to the ten-
ants, with the bland assurance that the 'landlord will take positive action'.

He prepares to leave, but McNaught has a surprise: Harry's thirteen-year-old
niece Tony (played by Mackenzie Phillips) is in the next room, having run away
from home in California's Central Valley. McNaught leaves them alone, and Tony
awkwardly explains the reason for her visit: ashamed of a drunken sexual encounter with a schoolboy friend and afraid of her mother's reaction, she hopes that her
Uncle Harry can somehow help calm things down. Harry reassures Tony with a
story of his own pre-teen escapade with a girl cousin, discovered by his outraged,
religious mother, and how *his* uncle, the cousin's father, consoled him. He offers to
put Tony on a bus back home, 'and maybe in a week or two I can come up and visit
on the weekend'.

This three-and-a-half-page scene 95 was the only clue in the film that Harry had
relatives near by and that he was emotionally capable of such a personal and heartfelt

A thing that has failed can succeed, if you change its place

outpouring – a full page of dialogue – in sharp contrast with his usual constricted (Hackman called them 'constipated') speech patterns and secrecy.

Perhaps it was the contrast itself that motivated Francis to write this scene, but Tony's story was never developed any further in the screenplay, and so scene 95 was the first major plant that we uprooted.

> 'If in doubt, cut it out' was the mantra we learned at the knee of Professor Dave Johnson at USC's cinema school. The only way you will really discover a questionable scene's importance is by cutting it out and seeing what happens. If it is secretly vital to the health of a film, it will find its way back in, no matter what. If it is an unnecessary appendix, it will disappear without a trace, which is what happened with scene 95.

The final episode involving Harry and his neighbours occurs near the end of the film (scenes 377–8). Two of the residents angrily confront Harry, who has just learned about the death of the Director in a supposed car accident, with their suspicion that Harry owns the apartment building. Harry explodes, threatening to evict them – in fact, to evict everybody and 'tear the building down!' He returns to his apartment and starts playing the saxophone to calm himself.

As Harry is playing his sax, the phone rings: it is Mark, telling Harry not to get involved any further, that his apartment is bugged and that 'we know that you know'. This menace triggers Harry's attempt to find the bug, tearing up his apartment in the process. Twenty scenes later, the screenplay ends with Harry, bug still undiscovered, in despair.[14]

```
397   HIGH FULL ANGLE                                    397

      Harry stands helplessly in his stripped down room.
      He gets on his hands and knees, prying the base-
      board apart from the wall, using a screwdriver.

      At each phase, he realizes that something better
      must have been used, and he becomes more and more
      desperate until, in the privacy of his room, he
      begins to weep.

                                             FADE OUT:

            - THE END -
```

14. In the film, the last shot is of Harry playing his saxophone in the ruined apartment.

Robert Bresson

Encouraged by the lifting of scene 95, Richard and I went further and removed the entire subplot of the neighbours, along with the revelation that Harry was the owner of the apartment building. All of it disappeared without a ripple, and the film was suddenly thirty-five minutes shorter. How would this affect the balance of character and mystery, of Hesse and Hitchcock? We would know only when we screened the whole film on Francis's return.

It became clear when we held that screening, in mid-June, that the film had to get as quickly as possible to the scene of Harry mixing his Union Square recordings (scenes 56–91, eleven pages of script). Francis consequently approved the lift of the neighbours subplot, but only as an expedient to get the film substantially shorter, leaving the possibility open, later on, to fit parts of it back in.

In the following weeks and months, we continued to trim, to experiment with lifting other scenes and to begin some restructuring. We transplanted Harry's church confession, for instance (scenes 230–1), so that it now followed immediately after his mixing of the tapes. It was an eighty-page leap forward from the scene's original place, late in the screenplay. Our reasons for doing this were to give the audience, as early as possible, an insight into Harry's thoughts about what he had just discovered. With the film's single point of view, and Harry's reticent nature, a confession scene was a rare and powerful resource.

A transplant like this was possible because Francis had kept Harry's costume – his plastic raincoat, grey sports jacket, white shirt, dark monochrome tie and crepe-soled shoes – virtually the same throughout the entire film, which takes place over five days. 'In reality, people don't change their look that often, particularly people like Harry,' Francis observed when I asked him about this. 'The film itself will be under two hours long and covers five days in Harry's life, so keeping the same clothes seems reasonable. Costume departments are always anxious to show what they can do, and so they will naturally take advantage of any pretext to change a character's costume. But from the audience's point of view, a costume is like the feather display of a bird – part of the identity of the character. And if the costume keeps changing, it makes it hard to restructure.'

The two big plot holes remained – until we had the idea of plugging one of them by transforming Harry's 'foggy Alta Plaza park' scene into a dream. The trigger for that idea was a brief image in the screenplay (scene 185), where Harry dreams of Ann, after having slept with Moran's assistant, Meredith (Elizabeth MacRae).

I thought that the existence of this image might give us permission to replace it with the entire foggy-park sequence (317–31), where Harry attempts to explain

Combine a belief in your own infallibility with the power to learn
from your past mistakes

```
184   HARRY ASLEEP                                    184

      Although we know that he is dreaming.  We begin to
      hear a distant electrical hum, that continues and
      grows louder from this spot.
                                              SUPERIMPOSE:

185   EXT.  UNION SQUARE - DAY                        185

      PANNING VIEW ON ANN

      Speaking thought we cannot hear.  She seems terrified.
      The hum grows louder.
```

something of himself to Ann and warn her of the danger he thinks she is in. Since we had lifted scene 95, in which Harry revealed some personal information to his niece, this would be the only other chance to hear details about his early life – that as a child he had polio and almost died; that he felt responsible for the death of a friend of his father – plus his fears for Ann's safety. As he says to her, 'I'm not afraid of death, but I am afraid of murder.'

Alta Plaza park, scenes 317–31

Over the next twelve weeks we continued to trim, lift and restructure, punctuated by screenings for small groups every two or three weeks to gauge our progress. Our audiences were intrigued and frustrated by the film in equal measure, not knowing whether it was a murder mystery or a character study, neither one being wholly

George Orwell

satisfying.[15] At one point we tried accelerating the beginning – giving it an injection of editorial steroids – but that just made the problem worse, and we quickly restored its methodical and mysterious unfolding.

The scenes we lifted were all 'Hessian' character scenes: Harry shopping and picking up his laundry; Harry confronting his assistant Stan with fears that Stan was giving away secrets; Harry travelling around San Francisco by electric bus, etc. Tellingly, no 'Hitchcockian' scenes were removed.

At the beginning of September 1973 the length of the film had shortened considerably: we had cut out almost two hours. But by that time Francis was almost ready to start production on *Godfather II*, and his monthly visits to the cutting room stopped abruptly. In September and October Richard and I would fly to the *Godfather*'s filming location at Lake Tahoe every week or so to show Francis the film's progress. The scenes involving Harry's neighbours remained lifted, along with another two dozen, for a total of thirty-nine. Added to the seventy-eight that had not been shot, the number of 'unseen' scenes totalled 117.

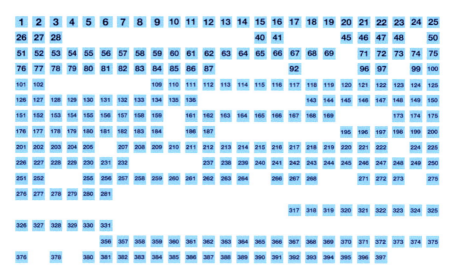

A graphic representation of the tattered fabric of the film, showing the gaps left by these unshot or deleted scenes. An animated version, giving the identity of the lifted scenes, can be viewed on Vimeo: https://vimeo.com/705325760 (QR code on left)

Our work over the summer was considerably less deliberate and straightforward than suggested by the graphic above. Lifting a scene affects the chemistry of the

15. At the time, I kept thinking of Haskell Wexler's criticism: 'Shit or get off the pot.'

It is not enough to refuse the Légion d'honneur . . . the important thing is not to have deserved it in the first place

ones formerly surrounding it, which are now brought into direct contact with each other, and we experimented with many structures that either didn't succeed or raised questions about their viability. But some were promising: moving Harry's church confession, for instance, put his morally anguished moments after collecting his fee next to checking in at the Jack Tar Hotel, where the murder will take place. But turning the Alta Plaza scene into a dream meant that Ann never sees or speaks to Harry other than near the end of the film, when she is sitting in her Mercedes and the two characters exchange a moment of silent eye contact. And we still hadn't found a way to fill the plot hole left by the twenty-four unshot scenes (332–55), where Harry comes to realise how wrong his assumptions were, and who the real culprits are.

Despite all our efforts, the hoped-for alloy of character study and murder mystery was still not fusing. The character study of a 'cipher' did not alone hold enough interest to sustain a feature film; and the dynastic power struggle between the Director and the triumvirate of Ann/Mark/Martin did not have enough psychological detail and intrigue to stand on its own. The answer, if one existed, was to discover ways to balance the two elements – Hesse and Hitchcock – so that they leaned against each other, like the sides of a triangle in dynamic tension. But we had not found that balance, and the film seemed, to some of those who had been invited to our work-in-progress screenings, self-indulgent and pretentious.

Aggie offered us words of advice from her training as a nurse: *timing* and *dosage*. 'Give the right amount of the right medicine at the right time.' Too little of the right medicine at the wrong time can be as bad as too much of the wrong medicine at the right time. But what was the medicine, how much should we give, and when? None of our prescriptions so far had cured the patient. It was understandable, then – with *Godfather II* two weeks into production – that Francis decided to shut down the editing of *Conversation* until shooting on *Godfather* was complete. That would be in June 1974, at the earliest – eight months into the future.

Erik Satie

I went for an eight-mile run in Point Reyes, out to Pelican Lake and beyond, to try and clear my head and come to terms with this existential crisis for the film. What would be the best approach? Acceptance?

Or resistance . . .

Pelican Lake, Point Reyes, California. The ocean can be seen in the distance

Pretend you are building a table. Let the audience decide whether to eat at it, appreciate it, or make a fire with it

8: TETRIS II

Restructuring *The Conversation*

By the time I turned around and started for home, I had decided on resistance, and as soon as I got back, I phoned Francis. 'Let's keep on schedule. I have a few ideas we haven't tried yet. Give me a week, and I'll put something together to show you.'

I was thinking of the health of the film and the danger that it might not emerge from such a deep freeze, but also, selfishly, of my budding career as a film editor, which was now threatened with an early frost. Francis had taken a huge risk in giving this job to me – someone who had never edited a feature before – and stopping at this point would inevitably be blamed, in the eyes of the film-making community, on my fumbling inexperience. With *Godfather*, Francis had been helped by two of the best editors in the business, so why would he hire this novice for *Conversation*? And although *Conversation* was a modest project compared to *Godfather*, the latter's success had raised the profile of whatever film Francis decided to do next, particularly one close to his heart, from his original screenplay.

'OK,' was Francis's response. 'See you in a week.'

There was great relief on my part – Francis didn't even ask what I had in mind – but also anxiety because I didn't really know what I was going to do, other than some vague ideas about restructuring. We had a week: would I be able to solve something that had so far eluded us? Asking for this extra time was audacious, but nothing is achieved without audacity.

> After all, we approve of a toddler of three who decides that he will fight a giant.
> – Astronomer Johannes Kepler, 1597

Overwhelmed, I turned the decisions over to my Hands, in the way that musical improvisation will sometimes free the unconscious mind from the bars and staffs of the score. Perhaps something that had hidden in the shadows until now would emerge spontaneously.

> **Wisdom of the Hands**: my catchphrase for letting the unconscious take control, a spontaneous 'automatic writing' reaction to the material, with

minimal conscious intervention. The feeling is that 'someone else' is making
the decisions. This mode is particularly useful when you have reached
an impasse, as we had in October 1973. To give an example of the split
between conscious and unconscious thinking: you may be able to touch-
type quickly and accurately, but try to quickly populate a drawing of an
'empty' keyboard with the correct keys and you will see how difficult it is.

The Hands responded enthusiastically to their new-found freedom by lifting the
sequence of Harry visiting his secret girlfriend Amy (scenes 45–7) and setting it aside
for the time being. This further shortened the distance between the Union Square
tape-recording and Harry's next-day mixing of the tapes. In the screenplay, those two
'Hitchcockian' sequences were separated by seventeen pages of 'Hessian' character
material. We had already shrunk this separation to eight pages by lifting the neighbours subplot, and now it was reduced to two.

In those two pages (covering scenes 40, 41 and 48) we learn that Harry lives
alone in a modest apartment, that it is his forty-fourth birthday, that he is obsessive
about his privacy (multiple locks on his alarm-equipped front door), that when he
is home he takes off his trousers, and at night he plays solo 'karaoke' saxophone to a
monophonic jazz record from the 1950s. Was this enough 'Hesse'? Was the timing
and dosage right? It amounted to four minutes of screen time, but at this point I
was just following what my Hands were doing and not worrying about these questions until later.

After Harry's karaoke sax – a night scene that fades to black at the end of the story's
first day – the next morning dawns in the Hitchcockian atmosphere of his warehouse,
a large, empty space, of which he occupies only a small fenced-in corner. Harry says
good morning to Stan, threads up the three Union Square tapes, synchronises them,
and then re-records them onto a master tape, selecting lines of dialogue from whichever tape had captured the 'fattest', least distorted sound.

As written, the sequence covered eleven pages of screenplay (scenes 49–91) and as
edited together was twelve minutes long. The Hands decided otherwise, preferring to
dissolve away early, at the five-minute mark, before any of the scene's later complications had time to develop. The feeling of this shortened sequence might be described as
'business as usual' – what Harry would do when everything was working smoothly –
and I tried to make his technical manoeuvres as simple and clear as possible. The
scene ends with him still happily mixing his tapes, and the final shot – what the Hands

Truth never comes into the world but as a bastard – to the eternal ignominy
of the one who brought her forth

selected to bring this scene to a close – is an extreme wide angle of Harry's warehouse space, with the voices of the conversation reverberating off the rough brick walls.

The Hands left the next scene undisturbed: Harry calling from a payphone to let the Director know he has completed his assignment. It is a short scene – a single shot with a slow move-in on Harry in the phone booth. The secretary on the other end of the line tells Harry to deliver the tapes at '2.30 this afternoon'.

The next scene was intended to be Harry's visit to McNaught's law offices, but we had already lifted this months earlier, so following the logic of the screenplay, it should have been Harry delivering the tapes. But such a close and logical juxtaposition seemed wrong to the Hands, who now retrieved the sidelined Amy scene and inserted it here. I made a note to have the secretary's dialogue changed to '2.30 *tomorrow* afternoon'.

The seven-minute length of this 'Hessian' character scene between Amy and Harry, showing Harry's reluctance to reveal anything about himself, even to his girlfriend, was now in proportion with the previous 'Hitchcockian' six minutes of Harry mixing his tapes. The Amy scene concludes with her decision to end the relationship, so to soften the blow the Hands inserted a moody fragment of Harry alone on a night-time city bus, dissolving to a tender 'memory' moment of Ann kissing Mark (Harry is beginning to dream about Ann), and then returning to Harry in silhouette. A fade-out brought the story's second day to a close.

The third day starts with Harry delivering the tapes, a three-minute 'Hitchcockian' scene introducing the oddly menacing Martin Stett. Martin seems too anxious to get hold of the tapes, which upsets Harry: he was supposed to deliver them to Martin's boss, the Director. After a brief struggle, Harry yanks back the tapes, but is warned not to get involved because 'Those tapes are dangerous. You've heard them. You know what I mean.'

In fact, Harry does *not* know what Martin means; what he (and we) heard of the Union Square conversation seemed neutral, even boring. But when he leaves Martin's office, he is unsettled to see Mark, in conversation with a few other executives. And once aboard the down elevator, Harry is unsettled further by Ann herself, who gets on at one of the intermediate floors. Harry finds himself red-faced, alone with her, speechless. The plot thickens. What was on that tape that made Martin say it was dangerous? And who was in danger?

The Hands thought the answer to these questions was to cut directly from the mounting tension in the elevator to the rapidly spinning reels of tape. We are back at Harry's warehouse – only in this case it is the second part of the original twelve-minute scene. For a minute or so, Harry scrolls impatiently through the tape, at random, trying to find a clue he might have missed, but nothing shows up. His frustrated assistant Stan asks (in an added line), 'I thought you turned those tapes in,' and Harry tells him (also an added line) to keep quiet. An argument boils over as a result of Stan's simmering resentment that Harry never tells him anything about the work they are doing:

> STAN
> It wouldn't hurt if you filled me in a little bit once in a while, did you ever
> think of that? It's curiosity, you ever hear of that? It's just God-damned human
> nature!

Harry's awkward non-answer comes to a sputtering stop . . .

> HARRY
> Listen . . . If there's one sure-fire rule that I have learned in this business, it's
> that I don't know anything about human nature. I don't know anything about
> curiosity. That's not a part of what . . . what I do . . . What I . . . This is my
> business, and when I'm . . .

. . . and it is too much for Stan. Disgruntled, he goes off to lunch.

It is only now that Harry focuses on a section of loud bongo drums that might conceal something. He plugs in a self-made, cobbled-together filter, tweaks it, and the bongos thin out like a receding tide, leaving behind an uncovered line of dialogue. A dangerous line . . .

> MARK
> He'd kill us if he got the chance.

In the screenplay, an unnerved Harry unplugs the filter and raises the bongos back up to their original level, re-obscuring the dialogue. The Hands decide instead to leave the dangerous line on tape, exposed.

Harry turns off the machines, perturbed, and the next scene, as previously decided, is the church confession, where we eavesdrop on Harry's thoughts. After recounting

The cinematographer is making a voyage of discovery on an unknown planet

some trivial sins (taking newspapers without paying for them, impure thoughts, etc.), he admits that he is worried about 'two young people' and what might happen to them because of his work. But he tells God, through His priestly representative, that 'I was in no way responsible. I'm not responsible.'

The Hands had done their work – it had taken three days for them to restructure the first forty minutes of the film – and I was grateful. Below is a graphic representation of the scene order of the 'Old' (pre-Pelican Lake) and 'New' (three days later) structures. Blue represents 'Hitchcock' and yellow stands for 'Hesse'.

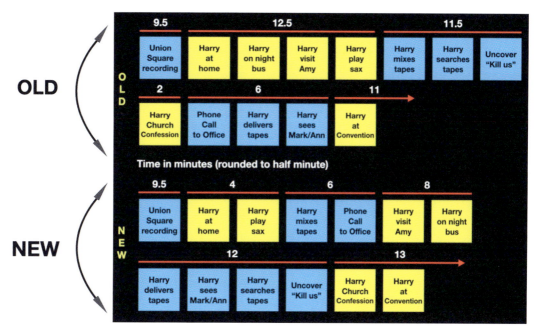

An animated version of this graphic can be found on Vimeo: https://vimeo.com/707371530 (QR code on right)

Looking at this graphic in the light of day, it is clear what the Hands were after: a quicker alternation of character and mystery. Too long spent in the stream of character stems the flow of the mystery, and vice versa. This increased pace was especially important in the first thirty minutes, and alternating blue and yellow sections were now in single digits (9.5 – 4 – 6 – 8 minutes), while those in the previous structure (9.5 – 12.5 – 11.5 minutes) were twice as long. Also, splitting the tape-mixing sequence into two sections, separated by a day, gives the audience the chance to focus exclusively on Harry's technical routine with the tapes – mixing the best sounds from each of the three recordings – before Martin complicates the plot by telling Harry that the tapes are dangerous.

Harry's subsequent research, back at his warehouse, looking for what he might have missed, now has an added, specific urgency: we know what he is looking for. Even his petty argument with Stan has more resonance, because the reasons for his heightened anxiety have been established: breaking up with Amy the night before and serious problems with his work. Now that the line 'He'd kill us if he got the chance' has been uncovered, will Harry hand over the tape and collect his fee? A moral dilemma that was previously not so pointed.

Was this structure ready to be shown to Francis? Perhaps not: the plot hole at the end of the film remained unfilled, and there was still something unfocused around the two-thirds mark, after Harry sleeps with Meredith, Moran's assistant.

When Harry wakes up in the middle of the night, Meredith has gone, and in the screenplay he finds circumstantial evidence that she has rifled through his files and cabinets before leaving. Not unsurprisingly, he believes that she has been working undercover for Moran, sent to discover Harry's secrets.

As a general rule, it is good – especially in a film like *Conversation* – if there is a feeling, around the two-thirds point, that the plot lines are gathering and tightening. But instead, with Meredith and Moran's treachery, those lines were opening up into another subplot: Harry's secrets being stolen by a professional rival. It was while mulling over this problem that the conscious, analytic part of my mind, no doubt jealous of what the subconscious Hands had achieved, came up with the idea to weave Meredith more tightly into the central story. What if we changed things to show that she *stole the tapes* instead of just going through Harry's files, and thus imply that she was working for Martin Stett, twisting two plot threads together? To make this work, we would need to pick up a shot of Harry finding that the tapes were missing. There was already a useful close-up of him reacting to Meredith's treachery, which would work perfectly as a reaction to the disappearance of the tapes:

```
187   CONTINUED:                                                        187

                             HARRY
                    (realizing that he's been had)
              Bitch!

                                              FADE OUT:
```

Chance is destiny in disguise

Richard Chew and I brainstormed about the implications. To help cement the idea, it seemed that we could advance two phone calls between Harry and Martin (scenes 378 and 379) and put them right after the stolen tapes (187). Also, we would have to deeply revise the sequence of Harry delivering the tapes and collecting his $15,000 (scenes 195–222), to show instead that Martin and the Director already *had* the tapes and were in the middle of playing them when Harry arrived to collect his fee. Difficult to pull off, but much creepier, and better. There was an existing shot of Harry approaching the office door, supposedly listening (per the script) to 'a strange thumping sound', which now would work perfectly as him hearing the sound of his tapes being played from behind the office door.

I started rearranging the two phone calls, and Richard took over the sequence of Harry at the Director's office. The first call didn't need any internal revisions; it showed Harry urgently trying to contact Martin, with no success. When Martin did return the call, in the next scene, it required new dialogue about his involvement in stealing the tapes, and him telling Harry to come to the office and pick up his money. I wrote a first draft of this dialogue and recorded myself as Martin to help pace it out.

What made this repositioning of the phone call easier was Francis's decision to film Hackman with his back to the camera, giving us the freedom to reinvent the conversation. In his new dialogue, Martin would admit stealing the tapes because Harry was acting 'disturbed' and . . .

STETT

I couldn't take the chance that you might destroy our tapes. You understand, don't you, Mr Caul? Why don't you come over now? The Director is here and he's prepared to pay you in full.

Richard had a harder time reworking the Director's office scene. We see Harry moving through the corridors of the office building with a blue plastic envelope, which actually has the tapes inside, but the plastic was opaque, so we were safe. There was also some business with a guard dog in the corridor that had to be largely eliminated, but getting Harry into the office with the tape already playing, and Stett and the Director present from the beginning, was particularly tricky. Richard eventually found an out-take: a wide angle of the office with Martin in full figure on the left, which was the key that unlocked time and space.[1] As mentioned earlier, in this version Harry had

1. It is worth reading the screenplay, scenes 195–229 (pp. 112–22), and comparing them to the sequence in the film in order to get a sense of the complex reconfiguration involved.

left the line 'He'd kill us if he got the chance' on the tape after he uncovered it, and it was chilling to be able to sync up that line, playing in the background of the scene, as a virtual 'answer' to Harry's question to the Director, 'What will you do to her?'

By the end of the week we had still not solved the plot hole left by the missing scenes 322–55, but so much else was different in this version that we thought it was time to show Francis. For this screening, when Harry discovers that Meredith has stolen his tapes – something that would have to be shot – we would use the time-

honoured 'Scene Missing' leader, which has a long pedigree in film editing, going back to the 1920s.

The call was made, and Richard and I flew up to Lake Tahoe at the end of October to screen the film for Francis, producer Fred Roos and associate producer Mona Skager. All of them were enthusiastic about what had been achieved, and Francis, risk-taker that he is, decided to perform a U-turn and go ahead with finishing *Conversation* in time for release on his thirty-fifth birthday: 7 April 1974. He was particularly happy with the idea of Meredith stealing the tapes and said this new structure had given him some ideas about how to solve the plot hole at the end. In the meantime, he called a friend in Los Angeles who was shooting a film at Paramount to ask if we could borrow a corner of one of his stages to build a little set reproducing Harry's workbench, and the plan for shooting Harry discovering the empty tape boxes was set in motion.

Of course, it was a great relief. Our 'medical procedures' had succeeded, and it seemed the patient had just woken up from a deep freeze. But would these vital restructurings have been achieved without the existential crises of a shut-down? Perhaps . . . but sometimes shock therapy can achieve what nothing else can.

The little set of Harry's workbench was built in the corner of a stage at Paramount by Alex Tavoularis, Dean Tavoularis's brother (Dean himself being busy on *Godfather II*).[2] Gene Hackman was also unavailable, so his brother was hired – it would be an over-the-shoulder shot. Francis was also busy on *Godfather II*, so I became the designated director. Fortunately, cinematographer Bill Butler was available to recreate the

2. Dean Tavoularis was production designer/art director on all of Coppola's films from 1972 to 1999.

Planning is everything. Plans are nothing

lighting, and he operated the Arriflex 'B' camera that we borrowed from the production whose set we had invaded under friendly terms.

The action of the shot was simple: a sudden reaction from Harry after he yanks the take-up reel apart and finds it empty, and then Harry discovering that the boxes of the three original Union Square tapes were also empty.

When we were finished with the third of three takes, the director and the star of our host film came over to see how it was going: they wanted the 'B' camera back for their next set-up. It was Roman Polanski and Jack Nicholson – Jack with his nose bandaged up – and, of course, the film was *Chinatown*. If we had kept the camera running and panned over to Roman and Jack, we would have linked *Conversation* with *Chinatown*. A lost opportunity![3]

Francis's solution for repairing the plot hole was to take the scene of the reporters swarming around Ann, Mark and Martin after the news of the Director's death in an 'auto accident', intercut it with material of the hotel murder scene – the indelible image of the bloody hand on the translucent glass is now explained in a reverse shot – and then intercut it further with telling phrases from the Union Square conversation – among them, 'He'd kill us if he got the chance' – in a short version of the assassination montage in *Godfather*. And then to follow this with an expanded phone call to Harry, who, seeking emotional refuge in music, has been playing a jazz riff on his saxophone. When the phone rings, he picks up the receiver, and a recording of that same saxophone riff is played back over the phone, accompanied by a warning from Martin:

3. This section of *The Conversation*, from Harry waking up and finding the tapes gone through to the two repurposed phone calls and the conclusion of playing the tape for the Director, is available on Vimeo: https://vimeo.com/710663256 (QR code on right).

Dwight D. Eisenhower

MARTIN
We know that you know, Mr Caul. For your own sake, don't get involved any
further. We'll be listening to you.

Harry hangs up, existentially shaken. The next sequence is the final montage
of him searching, without success, for the bug and tearing his apartment to pieces
in the process.

I screened this new version, including the 'missing tapes' shot, for Haskell Wexler
in late November 1973, to find out if he wanted a co-credit for cinematography.
Disappointingly, Haskell declined: he told me that he thought the story problems had
still not been solved and didn't want his name on the film.

Nevertheless, we moved forward with the finishing. Howard Beales, whom I had
worked with on *Godfather*, prepared the footstep soundtracks, Pat Jackson recorded
and cut the supplementary sound effects, David Shire recorded a final version of the
piano music, final voice replacement (ADR) was recorded and opticals – dissolves,
fades, enlargements, etc. – were ordered from the lab. By January we were ready for
the final mix and preparing to cut the negative.

It took me two weeks to mix the sound for *The Conversation*, on the same KEM
equipment we used for *American Graffiti*, *THX 1138* and *The Rain People*, and which
we were shortly to use again on *The Godfather: Part II*. The mixing desk did not have
automation (that was to come on *Apocalypse Now*), but it did have pick-up recording, which made it feasible for one person to mix an entire film. The plan was to
record a first draft of the mix and fly to New York to show it to Francis, who was four
months down the road of the eight-month shoot of *Godfather II*, and then return to
San Francisco for any final revisions.

Late one night, as I was mixing the last reel, including the final repetition of the
line 'He'd kill us if he got the chance,' I suddenly recalled an alternative reading from
the recording I had made a year earlier with Fred Forrest and Cindy Williams. On the
fourth of four takes, Fred had put the emphasis on the word 'us' rather than 'kill'. The
implication being: *we should kill him, because if we don't, he will kill us*. My thinking
was that this reading of 'He'd kill *us* if he got the chance' would tie the ribbon of guilt
around Mark and Ann for anyone in the audience who might still be confused. I dug
around in the library, located that reading, lifted it out and re-recorded it into this
mix of the film.

It is to you, not to the public, that your actors give those things which the public
perhaps would not see. You then make them visible. This is a secret and sacred trust

Two days later, Aggie and I, along with our nine-month-old daughter Beatrice, were in New York to screen the film for Francis. I warned him in advance about the different line reading, and he said he was interested to hear it in context, with the final music and everything else that would be new to him.

After the screening, Francis said he liked the whole approach of the mix, and even the new line reading, despite the fact that it went against his original intention, which was to have the conversation exactly the same for every repetition. He added that it raised an interesting question about the filters that we have in our heads, whereby we often distort reality to match our expectations and desires. In this sense, Harry had used his technical filters to remove the bongo music that had obscured the line, but because he perceived Ann as a victim, the final distortion – the one in his head that put the emphasis on 'kill' – was only removed once he had to face the fact that she was a murderer, and now he was hearing it as it really was.

On one level it is a cheat, of course, but a 'creative' cheat of the same nature as the images of Ann and Mark that reoccur throughout the film – images that are imagined by Harry to accompany the sound. The same can be said of those imagined scenes of the murder itself.

Beyond these semi-philosophical questions, however, lies the practical reality that for six months or so, Francis, Richard and I had been trying to find whatever it was that would help the audience grasp that the supposed victims were the murderers, and vice versa. Since the film was told exclusively from Harry's point of view, there was no way for us to levitate to another dimension where the 'truth' could be clearly explained, as would happen at the end of every episode of the *Perry Mason* TV show. Instead, we had to keep everything from Harry's point of view. This shifting of the line reading was simply one final attempt to nudge the bolt into the lock.

The negative was cut, the film's images were colour-balanced, and release prints went out into the world on 7 April 1974. The reviews were very good, the business less so – probably for reasons related to the expectations of the audience. They were imagining a film by the director of *The Godfather*, starring the man who had just been Popeye Doyle in *The French Connection*, with a story that resonated with the unfolding Watergate scandal – expectations that were not met by the cool, deliberate, intensely personal nature of *The Conversation*, whose repressed protagonist was anguished by guilt that his work might result in the death of the innocent subjects of his surreptitious recordings. In *Godfather* and *French Connection*, deaths are abundant and

Robert Bresson

considered as business, not personal. In *The Conversation*, Harry's conscience makes those deaths personal, to the point that it destroys him.

The next time I saw Haskell, he laughingly threatened me with a clenched fist, saying, 'You tricked me!' He thought I had showed him a version of the film that was intentionally worse than what was released so as to keep him from putting his name to the film. But it was an identical version, with the exception that I had not yet done the final mix, with the final music, sound effects and that different reading of 'He'd kill us if he got the chance.'

The Conversation was entered in competition at the Cannes Film Festival in May 1974, where it won the Palme d'Or. It was nominated for Best Picture, Best Screenplay and Best Sound at the Academy Awards, losing to *The Godfather: Part II* in the first two categories and *Earthquake* in the third. At the BAFTAs in London, *Conversation* was nominated for Best Direction, Screenplay, Actor, Editing and Sound. It lost the first three of those categories to *Chinatown* but did win for Best Editing and Best Sound.

Coda

The finished version of *The Conversation* is significantly different from the screenplay (see the images on facing page), but to quote Francis's well-known aphorism, 'The director is the ringmaster of a circus that is inventing itself.' That was certainly the case on *The Conversation* – more so, in fact, than on any other film I have worked on. And yet the finished film, different as it is, remains true to the impulses that motivated Francis to write the screenplay in the first place.

116 scenes out of 397 - 30% - were not in the final version of The Conversation

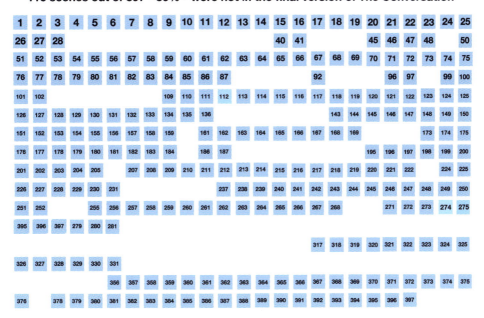

The Conversation Final Version · 281 Scenes

A New material - a single shot of Harry discovering that his tapes had been stolen by Meredith

◼ Continuous scene development

◼ Leap of less than five scene numbers

◼ Leap of greater than five scene numbers

Three things made it possible to achieve the results that we did:

· We had in Francis a director–ringmaster who allowed us circus performers the freedom to develop our editorial trapeze act.

· We had enough time to try a whole range of solutions to the issues raised by the missing scenes.

· We had a screenplay whose DNA rendered it capable of the flexibility necessary to achieve these recombinations without breaking.

That last point – flexibility – needs to be emphasised, as it applies, more or less, to every screenplay. Compared to a play written for the theatre, a film's screenplay is vulnerably exposed to the chaos of the world – it's rough out there! The realistic locations, the relatively great expense, the weather, the casting, current events, the tight schedules, the sometimes conflicting personalities of cast and crew, the complex, technical nature of all the crafts involved, travel between locations, the inevitable surprises and disappointments, the whims of the producers and so on – including noisy oil-based fog machines – all can batter the best of intentions. The screenplay must be capable of surviving those batterings, and even thrive on them, somehow, without losing the essence of what motivated the writer in the first place. In a sense, it must be like a hologram, which can suffer the loss of sizeable chunks of its matrix and yet still be capable of reproducing the entire image. Think of the difficulties that Spielberg had with 'Bruce', the mechanical shark in *Jaws*. In the end, there was very little of the actual Bruce and much more was left to the imagination of the audience, and the film was all the better for it.

How to achieve the resilience that gives a film the ability to absorb punches from the world and remain standing is one of the most mysterious and darkest aspects of screenwriting and directing. It has something to do with what could be called the *tensile strength* of the screenplay (and the director), and also what might be termed *creative redundancy*: with no foreknowledge of what will happen during shooting, having the skill/intuition to write scenes that do not seem superfluous upon reading, but which have the potential to be selectively and carefully recombined, restructured or jettisoned once the film is assembled and evaluated as an organic, rhythmic whole, in all its specificity and complexity.

In each of us lies an unborn Mozart, assassinated

A complete seven-minute, scene-by-scene 'Tetris' animation of the restructuring of *Conversation* is available on Vimeo: https://vimeo.com/710004860 (QR code on right). This animation shows in detail the movement of each sequence, from its original position in the screenplay to its final place in the film. The actual working-out of this scene order was much less linear than implied by this Tetris-like animation – there were many blind alleyways and somersaults – but it does give an approximation of the work involved.

9: N-VIS-O SPLICING

And the Breezy Darkness

Every cut is a commitment!

– USC Professor Dave Johnson

The cement splice – the technique of joining two pieces of celluloid by chemically melting them together – had been an essential part of film-making from the very beginning. For many years it was the *only* way of attaching one shot to another: the workprint for every film was edited with cement splices until the middle of the twentieth century. But cement began losing ground to mylar tape in the mid-1950s, and by 1965, my first year at USC's cinema school, the battle was almost over.

16 mm Griswold splicer

Dave Johnson

Not for Dave Johnson, though, our editing teacher during the first year. He insisted that we learn how to do the cement splice, of which there were two types: cold and hot. *Cold* was used to cut workprint using hand-operated Griswold splicers; *hot* was reserved for cutting negative with more precise and expensive pedal-operated machinery.[1]

---

1. Hot splicing was so called because the splicer was electrically heated to make the glue – the 'cement' – congeal faster and more securely. This was used for cutting film negative until the early years of the twenty-first century, when digital scanning techniques superseded it. The Griswold cold splicer pictured above would have cost over $450 in today's dollars. A good demo of how to make a cold splice: https://www.youtube.com/watch?v=9ikpCMcAyfo (QR code on left).

The same image brought in by ten different routes will be a different image ten times

Both hot and cold systems had the same brutal characteristic of destroying the frame adjacent to the cut point – a kind of celluloid auto-cannibalism. This was necessary to provide an overlap for the cement – a toxic brew of aromatic solvents, nasty acetone and even nastier dichloromethane – to chemically dissolve one piece of film into the other.

But the main virtue, from Dave's point of view, was the very brutality of cement splicing, which he hoped would force us students to *think about the cut* before doing it. Once you made a cement splice, there was no going back, unless you were able to afford reprinting the whole shot, which we certainly were not.

With tape splicing, however, no frames were harmed; the blade cut cleanly along the frame line. The flip side of this undoubted virtue, at least in the minds of Dave and the other teachers at USC, was that it opened up a Pandora's box of student indecision and fiddling: add a couple of extra frames, take them away again, cut deeper, switch to a new take and so on, until the film became a sorry patchwork.

Dave had a point about commitment, and he made it frequently enough to drill it into our heads. Was he right? Yes. But can't we also learn by experimentation, by fiddling around to find out what does and doesn't work? Also, yes. There were grains of truth in both arguments, and which was right depended on the situation and the personality of the film-maker. We all went along with Dave's instructions – we had no alternative! – but our hearts were with tape splicing. It was the future!

The previous generation – like Bill Reynolds, who edited the first half of *The Godfather* in 1971 – had usually delegated the messy, delicate, health-endangering task of cement splicing to their assistants. No self-respecting film editor would ever make a splice personally! I watched in amazement as Bill would mark the cut, scissor through the adjacent frame and then

1964 ad for splicers, from *American Cinematographer* magazine

Robert Bresson

paper-clip one shot to the next – and so on and on, until all his choices were rolled into a reel that he would hand to his assistant, Jack Wheeler. Bill would then start making choices for the next scene, while Jack was splicing the previous one. (Concerned about his health, Jack had switched to tape splices many years previously.)

'Tape or cement, I don't want to think about making splices,' Bill told me. 'It's too mechanical and it stops the flow. When I'm done marking up this scene, Jack will have finished splicing the last one, and then I can look at it with fresh eyes.'

True enough, though most of our generation enjoyed the ritual of tape splicing and we prided ourselves on how fast we could perform it. There was the gratifying whack of the blade and the rip of the sprocketed tape, along with the knowledge that it was a non-destructive way of editing. We could retrace our steps if necessary, leaving a 'breadcrumb' trail of mylar tape as evidence of the paths we had explored. The one defect of tape splicing compared to cement: during screenings, we could always see the margins of the tape fluttering past at the moment of the splice.

In 1976, four years after *The Godfather*, I found myself in London editing Fred Zinnemann's *Julia*. The director of photography was Douglas (Dougie) Slocombe, then sixty-four years old to Zinnemann's sixty-nine. I was half their age, having just turned thirty-three.[2] Zinnemann had been impressed by my work on *The Conversation* and wanted to have as many Americans on the crew of *Julia* as possible, since it was a story about two American women, Lillian and Julia (Jane Fonda and Vanessa Redgrave), but it was being made in England and France.

Dougie had begun his career in 1939, aged twenty-seven, as a documentary cameraman. He was filming in Poland when World War II broke out, barely escaping to Latvia after the train he was on was strafed and bombed by the Luftwaffe.[3] After the war he became the main cameraman at Ealing Studios, shooting many of the classic comedies for which Ealing became famous, among them *Kind Hearts and Coronets*, *The Lavender Hill Mob* and *The Man in the White Suit*. In all, he shot eighty-three films in forty-seven years; among his last before retiring in 1989 were Spielberg's first

2. Coincidentally, 1976 was the year that the Griswold cement splicer factory in Port Jefferson, New York, finally went out of business after fifty-six years. There was a lovely short film about the last days of the Griswold factory, but it has now been taken down from YouTube.

3. There is only one surviving print of the film Dougie was working on, Herbert Kline's *Lights Out in Europe*, which is preserved at the Museum of Modern Art in New York. More information can be found at: https://www.moma.org/calendar/events/7708.

The superfluous: a very necessary thing

three *Indiana Jones* films. He accumulated ten BAFTA and three AMPAS nominations, with three BAFTA wins – including one for *Julia*. He died in 2016 at the age of 103, six weeks after a fall.[4]

The first day's shooting was along the Norfolk coast, on the set that reproduced Lillian Hellman and Dashiell Hammett's house in Martha's Vineyard. As the new kid, I had been invited to go on location and absorb the mood, and vice versa, the production team would get to know this stranger.

On the morning of the second day I was having breakfast with Dougie at the hotel, when he suddenly dived from the shallow end of the usual morning pleasantries into the deep end of the pool: 'When I was your age, starting out after the war, I was nervous about being able to do the job, and so I would try to think of the styles of previous films I could imitate. I was frightened of the emptiness of a dark sound stage. But after a while I learned to love the emptiness, that it was, in fact, my best friend. I would go into that darkness and just stand there, as long as I could, with the breeze blowing through my brain. Out of that breezy darkness, ideas would eventually come to me that were original and not directly influenced by other films.'

Dougie Slocombe, aged thirty-three

Just then, Dougie's camera operator, Chick Waterson, came over with an urgent problem, and the two of them went off to solve it, leaving me to ponder the mysteries of *breezy darkness*.

Later, instead of *good morning*, the provocative two-word phrase *breezy darkness* became the preferred salutation between Dougie and me. And as a code word for the creative process, *breezy darkness* has remained a part of my vocabulary ever since: that meditative silence out of which original ideas will eventually emerge, if you let them.

The photographic sensitivity of the fine-grain Kodak film stock Dougie had chosen for *Julia* was low, at 100 ASA, which meant that at night the practical lamps in the Hellman–Hammett house had to be augmented with theatrical lighting. I watched

4. I was privileged to have tea with Dougie a couple of months before his death. He was alert and full of memories, particularly his escapades in pre-war Poland, one of which involved interrupting a speech by Goebbels with the sound of his noisy Eyemo camera and barely escaping arrest.

with curious interest as Jane Fonda, as Lillian, turned off the house lights, while assistant director Tony Waye counted out loud in order to get Jane and the lighting gaffer in sync; her finger would have to click off the 60 watt lamp switch at the same moment as the gaffer extinguished the 600 watt lamp lighting the scene. It took three tries before they succeeded – although there was still something not quite right which I couldn't identify at the time.

When I was back in London looking at the dailies for this scene, the unidentified problem revealed itself: it took the 600 watt lamp a third of a second – eight frames – to fade completely, whereas Jane's 60 watt bulb blinked off instantly. To my eye, this gave the scene a theatrical rather than a naturalistic feel. On a whim, I wondered what would happen if I cut out those eight frames. Jane was moving as the lights went out, but in the spirit of experimentation, I tried it anyway. Amazingly, it worked, even though Lillian was in a different position on either side of the cut. Why was this? The instantaneous shift in brightness was so extreme, I believe, that it overwhelmed the eye, and in effect erased the visual memory of where Jane was just prior to the jump cut. It was a piece of prestidigitation. Hey presto!

But there was still a problem: the edges of the tape I was using to make the splice were visible across the top and bottom of the 1.85 aspect ratio frame, resulting in a slight flutter that revealed there had been a cut (see example A in the drawing on the next page; blue represents the mylar splicing tape, which was two sprockets wide). Nonetheless, I wanted to prove to myself that my idea would work once the final negative had been cut. One solution would have been to use a longer stretch of mylar tape that covered all eight perforations of both frames, so that the edge of the tape fell invisibly on the frame lines (see example B in the drawing on the next page). There were two difficulties with that, however: the tape inevitably trapped air bubbles and dirt, which distorted the images underneath; but more serious than that were the dreaded 'greenies'.

> **Greenies:** there was a problem throughout the 1970s and '80s with the binding of the photographic emulsion of Kodak stock. When the splicing tape had fully bedded in place, after about a week, it was dangerous to remove it because now the magenta layer of the emulsion would come off with the tape, leaving the image a sickly cyan/yellow-green.

The length of a shot is a breath. The moment of the cut is a blink.

My solution was to go in the opposite direction and trim the tape down to the width of one sprocket, so that it would fall outside (above and below) the 1.85 aperture used on *Julia* (see example C in the drawing below).

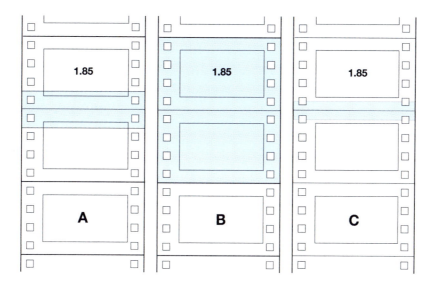

It worked! There was no visible trace of the splice when I ran it through the Moviola. Lillian turned off her light, and it extinguished instantly, matching our experience when we turn off a lamp in our own homes. And the mismatch with regard to her position remained remarkably unnoticeable.

But . . . one-sprocket width of transparent mylar tape does not give enough adhesive strength to withstand the abuse that 35 mm workprint is subjected to over many months of editing and projection. Even the standard two-sprocket width was fragile. My answer was to use the super-adhesive opaque white tape used for editing sound.[5] Since this splice lay outside the aperture for a 1.85 film, it didn't have to be transparent. And it was that transparency, produced by chemical agents, that weakened the adhesive qualities of the tape used for splicing picture.

To do all this routinely, my Rivas splicer eventually had to be modified in a machine shop, grinding down the arm that held the tape-trimming razor blade and slicing a compensatory groove through the left-hand registration pins – a slot into which the blade would now fit to trim the tape to a one-sprocket width (see drawing on the next page). I dubbed this modification *N-VIS-O*, and spread the word around

5. The latex adhesive used for editing sound film was a natural Sumatran latex, without any of the chemical additives that make the adhesive transparent but also weaken its grip.

Walter Murch

the editing community. We now had the ability to edit 35 mm workprint without leaving any physical trace that it had been cut in any other way than as presented; there was no fluttering and jittering of visible tape. And without destroying the adjacent frame, as the Griswold would have done! Over the following years, other editors began adopting the N-VIS-O. It encouraged experimentation and made the experience of watching projected cut workprint very close to that of seeing a final answer print. In a convincing way, it anticipated by several decades the look of digital editing that became widespread in the twenty-first century.

GROOVED REGISTRATION PIN
INTO WHICH RAZOR BLADE FITS

Beyond the technical aspects of the N-VIS-O splice, the aesthetic lesson I learned from Lillian and her light bulb was that if there is a big shift in luminance – light to dark, or vice versa – or even a sudden loud noise, a jump cut will be invisible, or at least not appreciated *as such*. This would be the case whatever system was being used. A version of this technique can be useful to spike moments of violence – when somebody is shot, for instance – by judiciously lifting out a couple of frames at the moment of impact, accompanied by the sound of the gun.

Liberated by the N-VIS-O's invisibility, I experimented with many other cuts, among them using end-of-camera-roll flash frames to visually augment the sudden passing of a train in the opposite direction, startling Lillian awake (examples of these jump cuts from *Julia* can be seen on Vimeo at https://vimeo.com/1002027634; QR code on left).

Unfortunately, I was not able to use the N-VIS-O on *Apocalypse Now*, the next film I edited, since it had been shot in 2.39 anamorphic Technovision, an aspect ratio that used every part of the frame, from top to bottom. But I was able to N-VIS-O splice all the other films I worked on over the next twenty years, from 1985 to 2005.

In 2005 there was a final improvement to N-VIS-O on Sam Mendes's *Jarhead*, when I discovered polyester/silicone powder-coating tape, an industrial product that has nothing to do with the film industry. It is designed to withstand very high kiln temperatures, so it was ideal for standing up to the heat of the projector lamp.

Sadly – or not – all things come to an end, and *Jarhead* was the final film I worked on where we projected 35 mm workprint, so it was the last to benefit from N-VIS-O. After 2005 the resolution quality of digital editing systems had become high enough that we were able to preview using a Quicktime or H.264 digital output.

From a wider perspective, what was finally coming to an end was the century-long intersection of creativity with easily accessible, materials-based crafts: from concocting the pungent chemistry of film cement in the 1890s; to Frederick Griswold, a modest Long Island theatre-owner, designing a better cement splicer in 1920; to Carlos Rivas's design of his tape splicer in the early 1950s; to Leo Cattozzo (Fellini's editor)[6] and his invention of the CIR guillotine splicer in 1957; to my N-VIS-O modification in 1976; to the repurposing of powder-coating tape to film editing in 2005, using Cattozzo's splicer. And you could multiply this list many times over for each of the film-making crafts. In our now digital-dominated age, of course, almost all innovation is software-based. The same thing has happened in the automobile business and many others. Grease-smeared teenagers tinkering with the engines of their cars is now a distant memory of the twentieth century.

The Griswold, Cattozzo and Rivas 35 mm film splicers, each one
named after the person who invented it

Although I am certain that the clean presentation of N-VIS-O-spliced films made favourable, subconscious impressions on preview audiences, only one person ever commented to me about it. We had a workprint preview screening of Anthony Minghella's *Cold Mountain* late in 2003, and Sydney Pollack, one of the producers of

6. Leo Cattozzo was the editor of Fellini's *La Strada* (1954), *Nights of Cabiria* (1957), *La Dolce Vita* (1960) and *8½* (1963), as well as many other films.

Bette Davis (her advice on how to get ahead in Hollywood)

the film, came up afterwards and wondered, 'I didn't know we had already made an answer print!' At that point, I had to let him in on the secret.

Hats off to you, Mr Pollack, wherever you may be.

Daffy Duck in Hollywood (Warner Brothers, 1938)

10: HER NAME WAS MOVIOLA

The First Editing Machine

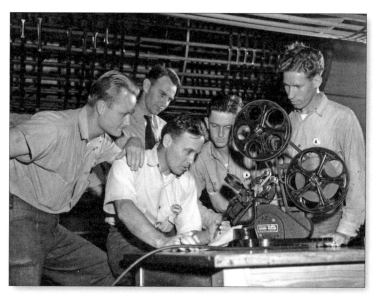

Servicemen at the US Navy School of Photography, Pensacola,
gather around a 'bull's eye' Moviola, *c.*1948

Almost every film made in Hollywood from the mid-1920s until the late 1990s – the seven-decade-long simmering summer of the studio system, encompassing the arrival of sound, Technicolor, 3D, Cinemascope and Smell-O-Rama – was edited on a Moviola.

We edit on very different machines now. You would even hesitate to call them 'machines': Avid Media Composer, Apple Final Cut, Adobe Premiere, DaVinci Resolve and perhaps a half-dozen others. This 'de-mechanisation' of the tools of cinema has now almost completed its work – *all that is solid melts into air* – and we consequently treasure those few mechanical islands which have managed to resist being submerged under the rising sea of pixels.

Fred Zinnemann's *Julia* was the last film that I edited entirely on a Moviola. We were working – shooting, editing and mixing – at the EMI–Elstree Studios just north of London, forty-seven years ago. Twelve years earlier, in 1965, I had been starting out as a film student at USC Cinema in Los Angeles, newly married to Aggie. Neither of us

Robert Bresson

had any background in film: Aggie was a nurse, and I had just graduated from Johns Hopkins University with a liberal arts degree in History of Art. Luckily, I had received a fellowship to go to USC, and Aggie had landed a job as a nurse at the USC medical clinic, where she dealt mostly with football injuries – scrapes, breaks and concussions.

I received my own concussion, of sorts, from my first encounter with one of the dozen or so Moviolas that populated the 'bear pit', a large room helter-skelter with editing equipment: benches, rewinds, bins, Moviolas – some of them the old 'Black

Maria' models, which must have been manufactured in the 1930s. It was love at first embrace. And it *was* an embrace: you had to dance with the Moviola, a clattery sewing machine on caster-wheeled stilts, and she responded most lovingly when you had one hand on her brake, the other on her warm, whir-ring flywheel. And a foot on her pedal.

After a couple of weeks of late nights in the bear pit, I came home to a frosty Aggie, who threw invisible daggers at me. 'What's up?' I asked, afraid of the answer.

'You have a mistress!'

'That's right,' I said, getting ready to duck.

'I knew it!'

'Her name is Moviola.'

The Moviola was born in Hollywood more than a hundred years ago, the invention of Dutch immigrant Iwan Serrurier. He had made a comfortable fortune in Pasadena real estate and was looking around for something else to do in the early years of the twentieth century. Victrolas were spinning 78 rpm records, pianolas were tinkling to the tune of perforated piano rolls, and Iwan must have put three and four together to come up with the *Moviola*: a machine to play films in the home!

The original 1917 Moviola was encased in a bespoke mahogany cabinet and cost $600 – almost $14,000 in today's money. You could run ten minutes of silent film at a time, before you had to change reels. And those reels were made of flammable cellulose nitrate. Understandably, Iwan did not have many takers: few would want a $14,000 machine in their living room that was ready to explode at any minute. The threat of flaming death and destruction took most of the pleasure out of the home-movie experience.

Good editing makes a film look well directed. Great editing makes a film look like it wasn't directed at all

Seven years later, Iwan was visiting an editor friend at United Artists on Santa Monica Boulevard, and the subject of the rejected Moviola came up. The friend wondered if Iwan could give him just the guts of the machine, without the mahogany: an intermittent Maltese-cross sprocketed and shuttered mechanism, with a bull's-eye magnifying glass to enlarge the image.

'Just as a test.'

It caused a sensation in the cutting rooms of United Artists. Douglas Fairbanks, the heart-throb, swashbuckling founder of UA (along with his wife Mary Pickford, Charlie Chaplin and director D. W. Griffith), came over to see what the commotion was all about. You could see the film move *in your cutting room*! Editors didn't have to try to book time in a busy projection room and hope there was a slot available. Fairbanks ordered half a dozen Moviolas on the spot. And then a dozen more the following month. The Moviola quickly spread from UA to all the other studios.

Model C or Cutting Room Model

For viewing short lengths of standard (35mm.) film before being assembled. Machines of this model may be used for viewing film on reels with the aid of a set of rewinders, which should be operated by hand so as to give sufficient slack for the film before and after passing through the machine.

Moviola editing was highly *external*: every aspect of the process was a broad, sometimes brutal physical gesture in space and time. A trim bin is physically *a bin*, a splice is physically *a splice*, you have to rewind using muscle power to get from the end of a reel back to the beginning, and so on.

By 1965 the Moviola was entering its fifth decade. A few things had been added to the essential core: a sound reader, a chassis of sorts, take-up arms and a cloth bin attached to the rear of the chassis to keep film from spilling onto the floor. But it was still a no-nonsense industrial product, like the cars of the 1930s or a sewing-machine on stilts. If you had a screwdriver and some common sense, you could work out what was wrong and fix it. But very little ever went wrong. It was not cheap – the simplest model cost $2,800 in 1965 ($27,000 in today's money) – but it had a monopoly. There was simply no competition, at least in Hollywood: if you wanted to edit film, you had to get your hands on a Moviola.

Nothing lasts forever. In 1969 the assault of the German editing desks began: first Steenbecks and then KEMs. They were horizontal, compared to the Moviola's verticality, sleek, silent, prismatic, even more expensive than the Moviola, capable of hurtling film through uncomplainingly at 240 frames a second and, like Iwan's original dream, able to deal smoothly with an entire ten-minute reel of film (non-explosive this time) without scratching it.[1]

Thus began twenty-five years of jousting between European horizontality and American verticality, with passionate advocates in both trenches. *Apocalypse Now* was edited in 1978 on two Moviolas and two KEM Universals. Legendary editors Dede Allen and Anne Coates stuck with Moviolas. Thelma Schoonmaker gravitated to the KEM. *Star Wars* was edited on two KEMs and a Moviola. Richard Chew and I edited Coppola's *The Conversation* on two KEM Universals.

---

1. Flammable celluloid had been replaced by plastic acetate in the late 1940s.

First: engage in battle. Second: see what happens

Waiting in the wings, however, were the emulsifiers: silicon and pixels, in the form of Avid, Lightworks, Apple's Final Cut Pro, Adobe's Premiere and a 'Burgess Shale' explosion of other computerised editing programs. By 1995 the editing landscape began to tilt irrevocably towards digital non-linear systems. There were a few holdouts: Michael Kahn and Steven Spielberg kept the faith and only abandoned the Moviola with their 2011 film *The Adventures of Tintin*. I switched to the Avid in 1995 with *The English Patient* and have not gone back to editing sprocketed film in the three decades since.

You will occasionally see a Moviola in the lobby of post-production companies, a curious sculpture symbolic of the past, like a metallic Winged Victory. But no one uses them any more. The whole infrastructure that went along with the Moviola has also scattered, Gone (almost) with the Wind. But there are some of us editors still around who cut our teeth on the Moviola and retain (perhaps!) the muscle memory of how to assemble a film with that century-old machinery. Our number has dwindled down to perhaps a hundred. I am one of them.

Strange to say, there has never been a documentary that explains all the details of Moviola editing. The necessity of making such a film occurred to me around fifteen years ago, but it simmered on the back burner until 2020, when I mentioned it to Howard Berry, head of post-production at the University of Hertfordshire School of Creative Arts, just north of London. Being an educator as well as a producer, he instantly saw the historical necessity of the film, and was just as enthusiastic about it as I. We shot a short video, demonstrating the concept and the necessity, created a crowd-funding website to raise the £30,000 budget, and we were off and running.[2] The goal was a one-hour documentary demonstrating all the processes, both technical and creative, that went into editing a film on a Moviola, from the printing of 35 mm picture and sound, through synchronisation, screening of dailies, numbering, breakdown and cataloguing, to the first assembly of the film and the restoration of trimmed material.

There would be two people on screen: me and Dan Farrell, the assistant editor responsible for all administrative duties, including the synchronisation, coding, cataloguing and refiling of trims.[3] In the Moviola days, editor and assistant worked much

---

2. The video can be seen at https://moviolathemovie.com (QR code on right).

3. Dan was an assistant on *Return to Oz*, forty years ago, and worked with me subsequently on *The English Patient*, *First Knight*, *The Talented Mr. Ripley* and, most recently, on *Coup 53*. He was an assistant to Michael Kahn on Spielberg's *Empire of the Sun* (1987) and recently edited two films for Richard Eyre: *The Children Act* (2017) and *King Lear* (2018).

Napoleon Bonaparte

more in harness, complementing each other like runners in a three-legged race. Both of us would keep up an on-screen commentary of what we were doing and why, with anecdotes from our experiences of editing on 35 mm film.

The major difference between 1972 and today is the sheer physicality of the process. Each step is overtly visible: the splicer really does cleave the film in half, the trim bin really is a metal bin, overflowing with film. There is constant motion – of the editor, the flapping of film, the spinning of rewind wheels, the *whack* of the splicer. A generation has grown up since 1996 with no direct experience of any of this, and we wanted to demonstrate the physical origins of so much of the terminology that is used to describe the computerised editing process today.

Thanks to Howard's contacts in the industry and sharp eye for bargains on eBay, he was – miraculously – able to gather all the necessary support equipment for the Moviola. The most difficult acquisitions were, as you might expect, the most ephemeral: heat-sensitive printing tape for the Acmade numbering machine (sourced, ironically, from that epitome of digits, Pixar) and 35 mm magnetic-stripe sound film (sourced from Christie's in Los Angeles; we grabbed the very last ten reels they had in storage). Had Howard not been able to find those last two items, the whole project would have been stillborn. *For want of a nail, the shoe is lost . . .*

Of course, the most important ingredient of all was 35 mm film of uncut rushes. Fortunately, Howard and I were able to convince director Mike Leigh to loan us the original files of all the material for two scenes from his 2014 film *Mr. Turner* (which he had shot digitally), and then find a laboratory in Kent that was able to 'reverse engineer' the process and print them in 35 mm. Locating someone who could transfer the sound files to 35 mm magnetic film was even more difficult, but Howard solved that problem as well.

Howard Berry with the assembled equipment

Then, in August 2022, we shot for ten days at BBC Elstree (just across the street from where I had edited *Julia*), with Howard producing and directing, and Dan and I doing our bits as assistant and editor. We went meticulously through each of the processes involved: syncing, coding, wrapping, labelling, logging, boxing and finally editing eighty minutes of rushes, condensing them down to two scenes lasting eight minutes. Photographed by two cameras operated by students from Howard's school, and with Taghi Amirani shooting on his iPhone using the Filmic Pro app, Dan and I gave a running 'golf commentary' about each phase of the process.

At one point, after watching Dan go through all of the steps required to synchronise sound and picture, the student sound recordist leaned in to ask Dan, confidentially, 'Did you do this on *every* film?'

Dan's answer: '*Every* take for *every* film!'

Once the scenes were edited, we needed to show them to Mike, but it turned out that there were no longer any theatres in London that could run double-system 35 mm picture and magnetic sound, so through Howard's contacts we were able to venture out to Stanley Kubrick's estate in nearby St Albans and use the Steenbeck bought for *The Shining* (1980). It was tucked in a corner of Kubrick's archive, among the crates of 35 mm prints of all his films.

Jean Cocteau

Mike Leigh and Walter Murch at Stanley Kubrick's Steenbeck

Mike arrived, and we screened the assembled scenes, which he approved, with some reservations, and I reminisced with him about the days of mechanical film-making. Mike and I then watched those scenes in a streamed version of the original *Mr. Turner* on a laptop perched on top of the Steenbeck. Talk about universes colliding! It was fascinating to discover the differences and similarities between the two versions. Those two scenes I edited will probably – almost certainly – be the last ever to be edited on a Moviola, one hundred years after its invention.

Interestingly, all of the jiu-jitsu moves required to work with the Moviola came back instantly, as if I had just finished editing *Julia*. Dan's last dance with the Moviola was co-editing Kenneth Branagh's *Love's Labour's Lost* (1999), and he felt the same. Perhaps our instinctive responses came from the complex muscle memory the Moviola required of our arms, feet, hands and fingers, as well as the considerable differences that exist between making a cut with a guillotine splicer, rewinding a reel, syncing picture and track, hitting the brake, and finding a trim hanging in the luxuriant forest of the bin. And each of these tasks is accompanied by different sounds and feelings: the whack of the splicer, the clanging of the reels during rewinding, the thud of the brake, and so on. Even the smells: fresh workprint from the lab, acetone for cleaning that workprint, the fumes from the Acmade numbering machine. Today, Moviola editing rooms would be shut down by workplace health-and-safety agencies. Luckily, we were operating under the radar.

But with digital systems, all the different commands – cutting, scrolling, 'rewinding', searching for a trim, etc. – are accomplished just by pressing a slightly different combination of letters on a keyboard. And there is no distinction between the sounds of those keystrokes. Perhaps this explains why if we editors have been away from a digital editing system for only a couple of months, there is always an awkward week of finding our fingers, so to speak. From a muscle-memory point of view, each command closely resembles the others, so it gets more easily washed from our minds with the passage of time.

Would I ever work with a Moviola again? It was fascinating, but . . . no. After its century-long run, the era of Moviola editing is over. There are many reasons why books are no longer typeset using hot-lead Linotype machines, and the same applies to film editing. We showed that Moviola editing can still be done, here in the third decade of the twenty-first century, but it is expensive in terms of money, time and energy – not to mention all the acetate involved!

And it *was* physically exhausting, more like blacksmithing than anything else. At the end of our daily twelve hours, Dan and I went home and collapsed onto our respective sofas. When you are younger and there is no alternative, of course you rise to the challenge.

Editing with the Moviola was a love affair of its time, and that precious album is now closed and part of history.

Farrell and Murch at the Moviola

Robert Bresson

Her Name Was Moviola had its world premiere at Sheffield DocFest in June 2024,[4] followed in August by its North American premiere at the Telluride International Film Festival. Written by Walter Murch, from his original idea. Produced, directed and edited by Howard Berry. With Walter Murch, Dan Farrell, Mike Leigh and Howard Berry. Further information can be found at https://moviolathemovie.com (QR code on left).

Farrell and Murch at the Kubrick estate

4. *Guardian* review of *Her Name Was Moviola*: https://tinyurl.com/yc5jxvdt.

The axe forgets. The tree remembers

11: TAKING NOTE

Making Comments on Screenplays and Screenings

Fred Zinnemann was famous for always screening the first assembly of his films alone, armed with a yellow notepad and his thoughts. And so it was with *Julia*, when I had finished fitting it together, in late January 1977.

'There is reason not to be pessimistic,' he said with a wry smile, emerging from the projection room at Elstree. Nonetheless, every page of his yellow pad appeared to be full of notes. 'Don't worry, I only write one idea on each page. That way I keep myself from writing on top of a previous note.'

Fred Zinnemann

He went on to say that he never took his eyes from the screen, writing legibly on the pad in the dark without looking down at it. He was understandably proud of this talent.

'It's a method I adapted from Darryl Zanuck. He had an assistant sitting next to him, but since I want to be alone when I watch the film for the first time, I have to be my own assistant.'

Zanuck had created 20th Century Pictures in 1933, after a decade at Warner Bros. Following two hugely successful years, in 1935 he took over the bankrupt Fox Studios to create 20th Century-Fox. Just like Zinnemann, Zanuck never took his eyes off the screen, but as the head of a studio he did not like the encumbrance of yellow pads. Instead, he had an assistant sitting next to him, armed with a stopwatch. At the beginning of the screening, the watch would click into motion, and when Zanuck had an idea, he would tap his assistant's arm, and the assistant would write down the time of the tap. No words were spoken. Afterwards, the assistant, with the help of the film's editor, would figure out what was happening at the time of each tap. This would then be typed up and sent to Zanuck. Triggered by these descriptions, Zanuck's ideas would come back to him.

Darryl Zanuck

'If they didn't, then the ideas probably weren't important,' Zinnemann said. 'He didn't want his thoughts to get in the way of the screening.'

Ugandan proverb

What kind of notes film-makers take and how they do it, and whether they even take notes at all, depends on the individual. Brad Bird, in screenings of various versions of *Tomorrowland*, would write many pages of notes on his yellow pad, head down, only occasionally looking up to glance at the screen.

I am temperamentally on the Zinnemann/Zanuck end of the note-taking spectrum. Instead of a yellow pad, I used 5 × 7 index cards, until silent electronic typewriters came along in the mid-1980s. Then I switched to a notes database I created in Filemaker Pro, which – improved over the years – I still use to this day. It is a computerised version of the Zanuck system. The moment a screening starts, I set the program running, with its internal clock silently ticking away. Then, when a thought occurs, I tap a control key and a new record is created with a unique time stamp on it. Following Zanuck, I never take my eyes off the screen, touch-typing in the dark with the screen dimmed. *Not* following Zanuck, I will sometimes write down the germ of an idea associated with the time stamp.

Taking Notes When Reading a Screenplay

What about taking notes when reading a screenplay? It is a very different creature from a film; in some respects it is like a series of X-rays of the film that it will become. Some 'bones' are very visible: the dialogue, for instance, running like a spine down the centre of the page. Other hugely important aspects, though, are not yet apparent: the

Audrey Hepburn as
Sabrina

fleshly substance of actors, for instance.

When we were making *Cold Mountain*, producer Sydney Pollack told me the following story. In the early 1990s he and David Rayfiel were working on the screenplay for a remake of *Sabrina*, the 1954 film directed by Billy Wilder and starring Humphrey Bogart, Audrey Hepburn and William Holden. Sydney and David were struggling with the logic of why the wealthy, upper-class character David Larrabee would fall in love with Sabrina, who was the poor daughter of the family's chauffeur. After going round in circles for a while, Sydney had a brainwave: they should go and talk to Billy Wilder himself, who was still alive, aged eighty-eight. Billy agreed to see them, and they earnestly explained their problem to him. He looked at them in wonder with his owlish eyes and beckoned them to come closer:

Put this giant dream machine in motion! Struggle with the angel of light, the angel of machines, the angels of space and time!

'He falls in love with her because she is . . . *Aud . . . rey . . . Hep . . . burn!*'

So, in reading a screenplay, you have to give many things the benefit of the doubt: *it will be like this, somehow, and it will work.* Much of the subtle craft of screenwriting is aimed at inspiring the reader to visualise possibilities that are not yet even on the horizon. So allow yourself to be slightly hypnotised as you read.

Another difference is that a film exists in time; once the projector starts rolling, it doesn't stop until the end. The reader of a screenplay, though, can put it down, walk away, pick it up again, read a page twice, start again the next day, and so on. For that crucial first reading, therefore, I suggest invoking a phantom projector: start reading at two o'clock and don't stop until you finish the last page at 4 p.m. To keep the momentum going, follow the Zanuck method: if you have a thought, good or bad, put a check mark in the margin, but don't stop to write down what that thought is. If it is important, it will come back to you when you review those marks later. Another suggestion is to circle the name of each character when they make their first appearance, to help cement their identity in your mind. Usually – but not always – their name will appear entirely in CAPS in the screenplay.

The important thing is to keep moving forward and, as Zinnemann said of Zanuck, not to allow your thoughts to get in the way. You don't yet know how the story is going to develop or end, so let yourself be carried along. Reflection will come later.

Later . . .

Perhaps a day or so later, read the screenplay again and review those check marks, fleshing them out with your thoughts, which are now informed by knowing how the story ended. Things you initially thought were problems might have turned out not to be and, vice versa, things that you thought were fine at the time might have turned out to be troublesome. Or so it seems to you, the reader, who is not yet privy to the director's intentions or the imponderables of casting.

Now take a sheet of paper and draw a horizontal line dividing it in half. Populate this sheet with the names of the characters, with the protagonists (in blue) above and the antagonists (in red) below. Then draw lines connecting the characters, indicating their relationships. Who is in love with whom? Who is whose enemy or rival? What characters crossed the line from antagonist to protagonist, or vice versa? Be creative with the lines: make them arrows, dotted, coloured, wavy, thick, thin and so on. But don't become obsessive – this is just a sketch to help cement the characters and their relationships in your mind.

Jean Cocteau

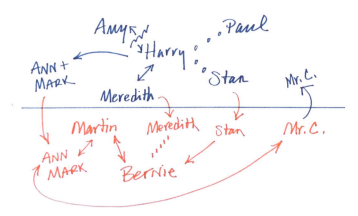

Character map for *The Conversation*

Type up your thoughts, organising them into central and secondary ideas. What did you feel was particularly good? Where were you moved? Where were you confused? Where did you have an idea that might help the story? How can a character's traits be intensified? Where did you get lost? If you have been asked to do so, send these thoughts to the director. Fred Zinnemann requested that I type up my thoughts on the screenplay of *Julia* a month or so before shooting; since we had never worked together before, it was a quick way for him to get to know me better.

I would also suggest giving these notes to the director even if you haven't been asked to do so. It is risky, of course, and you should season the notes with praise for what you liked and as many *perhaps* or *it seemed to me* condiments as necessary. I do this on every film that I am considering, and it mostly works out fine. But even in those cases where it didn't and the job fell through as a result, it was good to become aware of this incompatibility in advance, rather than signing on and discovering it later.

Dailies, aka Rushes

The first time you see any shot, the feeling that comes with that experience is the closest you, as an editor, are going to get to what an audience will feel when they see that shot in the finished film. You should write down that feeling, particularly because you will see that shot hundreds, if not thousands, of times over the course of the many months of post-production, and such overfamiliarity will inevitably dim the fresh impression of that first viewing. It doesn't matter how you express that feeling; any word will do, including even the most absurd – in fact, the more absurd and spontaneous the better. If, for some reason, you start thinking of bananas, write that down;

A script goes through three stages: a musical one, where it is composed;
an architectural one, where it is constructed; and a textile one, where it is woven

the shot will become the 'banana' shot in your memory, which will allow you to recall it more quickly.[1] It is a peculiar fact that in dailies, different takes of the same set-up will appear almost indistinguishable. Months later, they will appear as different as chalk and cheese.

I know that there are many talented editors who do not take notes, other than jotting down the director's preferred shots. This 'bareback' approach is particularly feasible now with non-linear digital editing, where accessibility to hundreds of hours of material is as easy as a few mouse clicks. But when I started out, fifty years ago, notes were a form of self-defence against the overwhelming weight of hundreds of thousands, and sometimes millions, of feet of 35 mm film. It is a habit that I formed early, when it was a necessity, and it fitted my personality.

Another determining factor in my case was that the first feature I edited, *The Conversation*, had a great amount of film, from a script that was forty pages longer than normal, while at the end of production seventy-eight of the 397 scenes had not been shot (and never would be). Consequently, there had to be a considerable restructuring of the story, and the notes that I had taken became essential supports in that process.[2]

On top of that, Francis Coppola's method of shooting certain scenes was quasi-documentary: the Union Square sequence in *The Conversation*, for example, was covered in multiple takes by four cameras simultaneously. The goal was to capture authentic, spontaneous moments that could only be created by the chance synergy of cameras and actors.[3] But this meant that the script supervisor's notes, written at the time of shooting, were only superficial summaries and had to be supplemented by the notes that I took while going over the shots themselves when they came back from the lab.

Even the briefing scene in *Apocalypse Now*, where Willard gets his assignment, was shot this way. Although Francis did not use multiple cameras here, he instructed the Italian camera operator, who did not speak English, to pan from one actor to another whenever he felt like it. The intention was to simulate Willard's hungover state of mind and also to keep the three other actors – G. D. Spradlin, Harrison Ford

---

1. A trick that actors sometimes use in 'cattle calls', in which many of them compete for a part at the same time, is to wear something slightly absurd or quirky, and this later becomes a hook for the producers to remember them by.

2. For a detailed account of that restructuring, see Chapters 7 and 8.

3. Francis used very a similar technique when shooting the wedding scene in *The Godfather* and the 'Valkyries' attack in *Apocalypse Now*.

Robert Benjamin

and Jerry Ziesmer – on edge, nervous, not knowing when they would suddenly be on or off camera.

These experiences with Francis's documentary style led indirectly to my invention of another form of 'note-taking': the selection of a number of representative frames from each set-up, and then mounting those photos on boards corresponding to each scene. My goal was to answer, in visual terms, the questions: why did the director shoot this set-up? What emotional or compositional moments were they attempting to capture? And can I represent those moments 'hieroglyphically' in a single frame? It is sort of a Cartier-Bresson *decisive moment* approach. I first started doing this during preparatory work for Phil Kaufman's *The Right Stuff* in 1981 and have continued to do so on every film since.[4]

Detail of photoboard and frame capture of Philip Seymour Hoffman in *Cold Mountain*

Anthony Minghella and Murch editing *Cold Mountain*,
with photoboards mounted in the background

4. I have written in more detail about these photoboards in *In the Blink of an Eye*, in Michael Ondaatje's *The Conversations* and in Charles Koppelman's *Behind the Seen*.

Let nothing be changed and all be different

Secondary Notes

When I am ready to start assembling a scene, I review the material and make a second series of notes. The first screening had been at the dailies, where we watch everything that was shot the previous day, but these viewings can typically consist of a salad of material from several unrelated scenes, perhaps with pick-ups for a scene that might have been shot weeks earlier. This second review, however, is focused solely on the material for the scene in question. These notes, as you will see, have more of a dispassionate, 'medical' feel to them – strengths and weaknesses, abrasions and elegances – all linked to a time code so that I can locate things quickly. I am a surgeon, wondering where to put the knife in, figuring out where the joints and arteries of this strange new organism are.[5]

I try never to write simply 'NG' (no good), but always to say *why* a moment might be NG; frequently, what is wrong in one context can be exactly what is needed in another. I will then print those notes out and review them, highlighting in orange things that I think are particularly good and/or useful, and using green for moments that are questionable and perhaps not so useful.

These secondary notes become crucial when I am putting together the first assembly of a film. Each highlighted moment is similar to what is called a *key frame* in animation, and my challenge, editorially speaking, is to get from highlighted moment

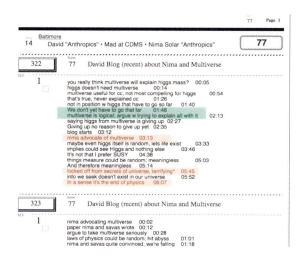

Secondary notes for Mark Levinson's *Particle Fever*

5. See Chapter 16.

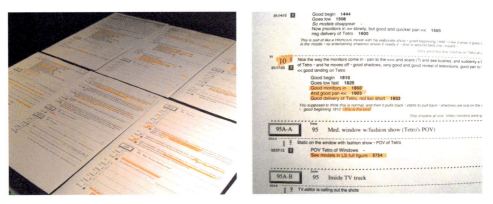

Secondary notes for Coppola's *Tetro*

to highlighted moment in the most interesting way – what in animation is called *in-betweening* the action from one key frame to the next. Photoboards become especially useful here, because many of the images represent these key moments visually, kind of like reverse storyboards. They also serve as a constant reminder of everything that was shot, so I don't accidentally forget something. I want to squeeze all the juice I can out of the orange!

Also, because the images on those boards are laid down in shooting order, there is a certain randomness to their organisation. Letting chance determine which ones happen to be next to each other, both horizontally and vertically, helps me to become subconsciously aware of unexpected but interesting and provocative juxtapositions.

As I mentioned earlier, there are some editors who don't take notes at all, or very few, and yet produce wonderful work. I look upon these prodigies with awe; I am simply not capable of doing what they do. I need my 'backpack' of notes to carry with me into the jungle – paradoxically, so that I can get lost. Or rather, so that I will have the confidence to explore off the beaten track, knowing that I will be able to find my way back if I do get lost. I may not even refer to them after a certain point, but it helps to know that they are there.

There are certainly practical advantages to be gained from making detailed notes, as I hope I have been able to explain. If there is major restructuring to be done, as there was on *The Conversation*, *Apocalypse Now* and *The English Patient*, then the notes are a tremendous resource, because they help to reveal the exact location of the 'tectonic plates', so to speak, of the film. But it is always a judgement call in terms of how much time and energy you spend making them and how detailed they should be. There needs to be a balance; you don't want the note-taking to drain the life out of the film-making.

But having said that, I think there is more going on with note-taking than simply leaving a trail of breadcrumbs in the jungle. Even if there is no major restructuring, the process of writing notes itself helps by sending more of those ideas deeper into the subconscious, where mysterious things can happen. There, they intermingle profligately and produce offspring, new ideas that will often – in the middle of the night or in the shower the next morning – burst into the living room of consciousness from the basement of the subconscious, or wherever they have been hiding.

And sometimes they don't burst in; they creep about and speak in whispers, and you have to listen carefully, ignoring the racket of everything else that is going on and paying attention to what they have to say. If you do, they will reward you generously.

Happy listening!

Curzio Malaparte

12: *STANDFLEISCH*

Your Chair Is Your Enemy

Editing *Coup 53*

The word 'editor' in the job description *film editor* inevitably compares us to our colleagues, the editors of books, newspapers, online publications, etc. This implies that our task, like theirs, is to cut down and rearrange a work created by someone else, an author, who has submitted a manuscript to an editor, who then reads it and suggests changes. The author considers these ideas and writes a second draft, which is resubmitted to the editor for further evaluation, and so on.

In cinema, it's the reverse: it is the *editor* (in Spanish, the *montador*, the 'assembler') who produces the first version, painstakingly constructing it over many weeks (or months!) from thousands of shots, guided by the screenplay and the director's notes. This is shown to the director, who suggests changes. And then it is the film editor who makes those changes, producing a second version, which is shown to the director, who suggests further amendments, and so on.

I have simplified the process in order to make a point, which is that the editor/director collaboration is very different from the editor/author relationship. It more closely resembles actor/director or composer/director relationships, and we film editors are, in that sense, interpretive performers, offering our version of the film for the director to evaluate. Like the work of actors or composers – and unlike the work of authors – our work is temporal: it exists in time, following a choreography of cinematic rhythms. To be modified, of course, as the actor's or the composer's work is modified. None of us are the final arbiters, except the director, who has ultimate responsibility for the film.[1]

That distinction between text and film was brought home to me when I made the transition, in the early 1970s, from the vertical Moviola editing machine to the horizontal eight-plate KEM Universal. As I have written elsewhere, you had to be on your feet and dance with the Moviola – I would be constantly in motion, manually rewinding, swirling long trims into the bin, hitting the brake handle, going back and forth to the film racks to retrieve rolled-up shots from their cardboard boxes, wrapping up and rubber-banding the shot that I had just looked at, and so on. Under these circumstances, being on my feet was a necessity.

In contrast, although I loved the fast, silent operation of the KEM and the fact that its modular arrangement could handle ten minutes of film at a time, with three separate picture screens if needed, or three sound readers and one picture screen (or any combination thereof), and that its smooth rotating-prism action did not damage the film, I was forced to sit down at it, becoming a sedentary editor at a desk! Francis Coppola had banished the Moviola from the American Zoetrope studios because it was the past and the KEM was the future, so in 1973 I edited *The Conversation* sitting at a KEM.

The Moviola and the KEM

1. That is, if the director has 'final cut'. Otherwise, the opinions of the producers and the financing studio must also be taken into account.

Curzio Malaparte

With the KEM (and its cousin, the Steenbeck), almost all you ever needed to do was move your wrist and push a few buttons. So it was not long before I developed what I called *Steenbeck neck*: knotted tension in the neck and shoulders, which never happened with the Moviola because of all that dancing and those broad arm movements.

In the following decade I bounced back and forth between systems. *Julia* was edited on a Moviola, *Apocalypse Now* on a KEM (although Richie Marks and Jerry Greenberg, two of my co-editors on the movie, used Moviolas). *Return to Oz* was a Moviola film. Finally, on *The Unbearable Lightness of Being* in 1986, I had a revelation: looking at the KEM one day, I realised it was simply a rewind bench, but one where the reels of film ran horizontally rather than vertically. If that's all it is, then let's raise it up fifteen inches to the height of a rewind bench!

Chris Boyes – later to win Oscars for sound mixing *Titanic*, *Pearl Harbor*, *Lord of the Rings* and *King Kong* – was at that time working as a young jack-of-all-trades at Fantasy Films in Berkeley, where we were editing *Unbearable*, and I asked him to build two heavy-duty wooden cubes out of thick plywood. Job done, four of us lifted the 600-pound KEM onto those boxes, and I was standing again. And I have been standing to edit ever since.

 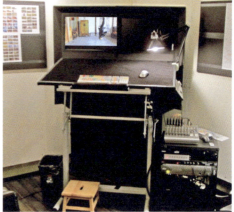

Left: the standing KEM on its plywood boxes: editing Jerry Zucker's *First Knight*
Right: the architect's drafting table: editing Brad Bird's *Tomorrowland*

Nine years after *Unbearable*, in 1995 I made the transition to electronic editing on the Avid for *The English Patient* and bought an architect's drafting table (at my assistant Sean Cullen's suggestion), and I have been standing at that same table, creating my cinematic 'architecture', for the last twenty-seven years.

Do not seek greatness in life. Instead, put greatness into it

A couple of pages earlier, I offered a comparison between film editors and composers, and elsewhere I have compared us to brain surgeons, conductors and short-order cooks. What unifies all these different occupations is the time factor, which is crucial to surgery, music, cooking . . . and film editing. Why do surgeons, conductors and cooks all stand to do their jobs? I think it is because when they are on their feet, they have a more 'full-body' sense of the flow of time, they can better feel the rhythm of what they are doing and they have an easier command of the space in which they are working.[2] In fact, I think you will find that for any occupation where time is an important element, its practitioners will be on their feet. Of course, the prime example of the relationship between body and rhythmic time is dancing, and film editing can be thought of as a kind of dance, a choreography of images and sounds in the flow of time, forged in movement, eventually crystallising into permanence.

So, if all this is true, why don't all film editors stand to edit? I proselytise about the benefits of standing, but the vast majority of film editors remain seated at their consoles – and make wonderfully edited films! I even include myself in that sedentary group, since I edited both *The Conversation* and *Apocalypse Now* sitting at a KEM.

Habit and personal preference are certainly reasons to remain seated, and editing desks are normally built for sitting, even though some of them now have a standing option. Also, there is the fear that standing would increase fatigue in a job that already has long hours and a great deal of pressure, and medical reasons for why sitting is preferable – bad backs, foot problems, etc., although sitting all day is something that can *give* you a bad back. A sensitivity to power relationships is another reason to remain seated: someone who is standing can be seen as more threatening, and directors usually take a seat when they come into the editing room. Editors don't want to loom over the director.[3]

I should add that I don't stand all day. I sit when I am reviewing material or doing what now passes for 'paperwork' – reading and writing memos, file management, working out schedules, etc. But when I am actively editing, I will be on my feet, standing at the architect's desk, for perhaps seven hours out of twelve. I also have help from a small footstool (visible in the photo on p. 174), which keeps my lower back from 'dishing' inwards; I alternately put one foot or the other on it, which rotates my

2. This sense of the body in space and time is called *kinaesthesia*.

3. Jerry Zucker, however, loved the standing KEM, and would 'sidle up to the bar' as he put it, standing next to me as I was editing *Ghost* and *First Knight*.

Friedrich Schiller

pelvis into a more vertical position.[4] And I have a cushioned wrist rest attached to the leading edge of desk, against which I can lean occasionally to relieve the pressure on my feet.

Since good editing can be accomplished either sitting or standing, is there any reason to stand, other than these theoretical musings, my personal history and my quirky preferences?

There does seem to be something that has recently been discovered . . .

Redraw the Anatomy Textbooks!

We mammals have two circulatory systems: the heart–lung system, which delivers oxygen throughout our body, and the lymphatic system, part of our immune response, which flushes out intercellular waste products.

The heart is the dedicated muscle-pump that ensures almost immediate delivery of oxygen throughout the body; we die in a few minutes if that delivery fails. But although the lymphatic system is ultimately just as important as the heart–lung system, it is not so critically time-dependent. Its operation is measured in days rather than minutes, so there is no need for a single dedicated pump. Instead, it is the flexing of the body's large muscles that does the job, and since the biggest ones are in our legs, it is they that provide much of the power for lymphatic circulation. When we are on our feet, even if we appear to be standing still, the muscles in our legs are constantly tensing and relaxing, maintaining our balance, and it is this flexing that energises the lymphatic system. When we sit for long periods of time, however, lymphatic circulation slows down, leading to an accumulation of intercellular debris. Can you offset the damage caused by prolonged sitting by going for a daily jog? Medical opinion seems to say no.[5] But I still walk three miles a day, do calisthenics and go for eight-mile runs on weekends. Those kinds of exercise are important for other reasons.

This has all been known for many decades and should be reason enough to consider getting a standing desk. However, in 2015 an article was published in *Nature*, the pre-eminent scientific journal, that detailed a startling discovery about the link between the brain, the lymphatic system and the rest of the body. It was entrenched medical opinion

---

4. I learned this footstool trick from watching the ladies who sell perfume and cosmetics on the ground floor of most department stores. They stand all day long, and many of them have one of these footstools under their display counters to help relieve back problems.

5. Olivia Judson, 'Stand Up While You Read This!', *New York Times*, 23 February 2010: https://archive.nytimes.com/opinionator.blogs.nytimes.com/2010/02/23/stand-up-while-you-read-this/

When a truth becomes a fact, it loses its intellectual value

until a few years ago that the brain had its own immune system, but in 2014 Dr Antoine Louveau and researchers at the University of Virginia Medical School established that there is, after all, a connection between the brain and the body's lymphatic system. This astonishing and unexpected discovery means that the anatomy textbooks, which medicine had declared complete sometime around 1950, would now have to be redrawn.

A lymphatic vessel, cunningly hidden behind a major artery in our necks, acts as a drain to get rid of intercellular debris that accumulates in the brain. It has been there forever, hiding in not-so-plain sight, and it was only entrenched medical opinion that prevented anatomists from looking for it. Louveau first detected the connection in mice, and a short while later discovered it in human beings.[6] That this connection could have escaped detection when the lymphatic system has been so thoroughly mapped throughout the body is surprising on its own, but the true sig-

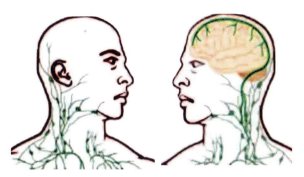

Lymphatic connection to brain

nificance of the discovery lies in the effects it could have on the study and treatment of neurological diseases such as Alzheimer's and multiple sclerosis.[7]

So, if standing rather than sitting provides better lymphatic circulation, it is good for not only your body, but your brain as well![8]

Except for three years when I was sitting at the KEM, I have been standing to edit on various machines for over fifty-five years. I am now eighty-one and still doing so, taking my inspiration from orchestra conductors well into their eighties who stand to conduct. At this point I cannot confidently and comfortably edit in any other way.

6. See *Science Daily:* https://www.sciencedaily.com/releases/2015/06/150601122445.htm.

7. Josh Barney, 'UVA Identifies Brain's Lymphatic Vessels as New Avenue to Treat Multiple Sclerosis', *UVA Today*, 17 September 2018: https://news.virginia.edu/content/uva-identifies-brains-lymphatic-vessels-new-avenue-treat-multiple-sclerosis; 'UVA Brain Discovery Could Block Aging's Terrible Toll on the Mind', *UVA Today*, 25 July 2018: https://news.virginia.edu/content/uva-brain-discovery-could-block-agings-terrible-toll-mind; National Institutes of Health, 'Brain Cleaning System Uses Lymphatic Vessels': https://www.nih.gov/news-events/nih-research-matters/brain-cleaning-system-uses-lymphatic-vessels.

8. For further discussion of health practices for film editors, see *Fitness in Post*: https://www.youtube.com/watch?v=Vn_9Wt4ea-o.

Oscar Wilde

I am also inspired by writers who worked standing up, such as Ernest Hemingway, Virginia Woolf, Winston Churchill, Charles Dickens, Lewis Carroll and Thomas Wolfe.[9] And when he was on set, director Fred Zinnemann would never sit down; he had a special inclined 'leaning board' against which he could rest between takes. The German word for persistence in any task is *Sitzfleisch*, so I guess we would have to coin the new word *Standfleisch*.

To my shame, however, I confess I am writing this book sitting down. There's no accounting for taste! For me, it is better to stand when I am editing, to sit when I am writing and to lie down when I am attempting to think up original ideas.[10]

Virginia Woolf's desk had a slanted surface; mine is adjustable for both angle and overall height. This, along with its large surface area, makes it convenient for displaying all my notes for a scene. As you can see in the picture below, I have covered the surface of the desk with black flocking fabric, which has the advantages of being easy on the

eyes, holding the sheets of notepaper in place and functioning as a giant 'mouse pad' (the nap of the fabric is luckily such that a tiny shift of the mouse equals one pixel on the screen!). I also construct foam-core masking around the two screens, which 'de-clutters' the visual surroundings. To either side are two white paper-doll cut-outs that serve to remind me how big the film's image will actually be when it is projected in a theatre.

All film editors spend time arranging the space of their room to accommodate the particular way they work and so that it is inviting to other people when they visit to see how the film is progressing. The Chinese concept of *feng shui* is useful here, not perhaps in any strict sense, but as a general recognition that a sensitivity to the arrangement of the working environment will positively influence the work that is done there and how it is received.[11]

9. Standing writers: https://www.writingroutines.com/famous-writers-standing-desks.

10. See the 'Wrestling with the Daemon' chapter of the subsequent volume of this book for more detail about my writing process.

11. *Feng shui* translates literally as 'wind water' but is generally understood to mean 'good fortune'. In Chinese tradition, there are many precise rules for the arrangement of objects in a room, and for the room itself in relation to the compass.

Your camera catches certain states of the soul which it alone can reveal

Coppola's *Tetro* (2009), with paper cut-outs to give a sense of scale

So, ultimately, whether you sit or stand, whether you work at a studio, in an office or from home, the important thing is that your work environment agrees with you and reflects who you are. So take my suggestions about standing for what they are worth and see if they coincide with your own personality and interests. If, after reading this, you are intrigued by the idea of standing to edit, my advice is to give it a try; there are many creative options now available for elevating your desk's work surface. Your lymphatic system will thank you!

Robert Bresson

13: THE SPLICEOSOME
Our Lives Depend on Editing

We think of film editing as a quintessentially modern development, and in a narrow sense this is true. As Béla Balázs observed, 'Cinema is the only art whose birthday is known to us.' But as we have so often discovered, biology has an uncanny way of anticipating our inventions. Or rather, we have a way of eventually coming to the late realisation of something that biology developed long ago. In the case of the subject of this chapter, long, *long* ago.

It turns out that 'film editing' is going on inside every cell in your body – in fact, in every cell of every complex life form on Earth – and has been for perhaps two billion years.

The double-helix structure of DNA (full name: DeoxyriboNucleic Acid) was discovered by Watson and Crick in 1953 and has had a grip on our popular and scientific imagination ever since. It is routinely invoked to explain our behaviour, our strengths and our deficiencies and to impeach presidents, establish ancestry and criminality and fatefully absolve us of responsibility ('It was in my DNA!'). And now that biologists have decoded the six billion 'letters' in the human genome, it offers the tantalising prospect of miracle cures for intractable diseases and even the Faustian lure of creating super-humans by combining our DNA with that of other creatures, or even with artificial DNA concocted in laboratories.

> DNA uses a language whose alphabet consists of the four molecular 'letters' A, C, G and T (adenine, cytosine, guanine and thymine). Sixty-four 'words' (called *codons* in biology) can be created out of any three of those letters (ATG, GAC, TTC, etc.), and sixty of those three-letter codons neatly correspond to amino acids – the building blocks out of which proteins are made. A 'sentence' made of these codons corresponds to a gene, which is the instruction package for making a single protein. A gene is typically from fifty to 2,000 codons long, but can reach up to 12,000.

As befits its importance, DNA lives in splendid isolation in the nucleus, a sort of walled citadel within the cell, where it is protected from the storm of activity in the

---

main body of the cell (the cytoplasm) – the 'factory floor', so to speak. This is where millions of tiny ribosomes, furiously active biological machines, make proteins using instructions from DNA data. But how does information get transferred from DNA to those millions of ribosomes, from citadel to factory floor?

The carrier of that data is another molecule, RNA (RiboNucleic Acid), which copies a section of a single strand of DNA and then, with its thread-like structure, wiggles through openings in the tightly meshed membrane of the nucleus.[1] Now there can be a marriage of sorts between a thread of RNA and a ribosome, wherein the RNA's information, copied from the DNA, is used by the ribosome to manufacture the protein described by that information. The image of an information-rich ticker tape clicking along, guiding the action of a compliant machine, is almost exactly true in this case.

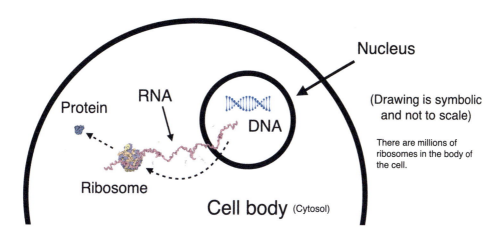

This activity is going on in every cell in every organism on the planet, from fungi to ferns to fish, including bacteria and baseball players. Having allowed the copying of some of its data to RNA, DNA remains serenely above the fray in its nucleic citadel.

DNA is a dead molecule, among the most nonreactive, chemically inert molecules in the living world. That is why it can be recovered in good enough

1. A typical RNA molecule is 2 nanometres (2 billionths of a metre) in diameter and 300 nm long, almost exactly the same proportion as a strand of spaghetti (2 mm by 300 mm). A ribosome, on the other hand, is a lumpy ball, typically 30 nm in diameter. If RNA were spaghetti, the ribosome would be a meatball. But, at 30 nm, a ribosome is too large to penetrate the fine-mesh double membrane of the nucleus. Something to ponder the next time you are dining at the Old Spaghetti Factory.

Jean Cocteau

shape to determine its sequence from mummies, from mastodons frozen tens
of thousands of years ago, and even, under the right circumstances, from
twenty-million-year-old fossil plants . . . DNA has no power to reproduce itself.
Not only is DNA incapable of making copies of itself, aided or unaided, but it is
incapable of 'making' anything else.

– Richard Lewontin, Harvard geneticist

But, in 2001, DNA received another knock to its popular image when biologists
successfully completed the decoding of the information in human DNA: more than
90 per cent of that DNA was 'junk' or, more politely, 'non-coding'. Humans are not
uniquely cursed: *all* complex life – vegetable, animal or fungal – has a high proportion
of non-coding information in its DNA. The lowly onion has five times as much DNA
as a human being, and 90 per cent of *its* DNA is non-coding.

The problem posed by this peculiar discovery is that the presence of non-coding
DNA should mean a failure to produce valid proteins, which is the whole purpose of
the DNA » RNA » ribosome sequence. But, nonetheless, we, algae, onions and mush-
rooms – all complex life forms on Earth – are able to produce valid proteins despite
the presence of non-coding 'junk' in our DNA! What is going on?

Enter the Spliceosome

Hiding in plain sight was the responsible party: tiny, previously undiscovered protein
complexes – up to 100,000 of them – that live in the nucleus of every cell.[2] They were
first glimpsed through their effects in 1977 by biologists Phillip Sharp and Richard
Roberts, who in 1993 won the Nobel Prize for this research. They discovered that
something was making the RNA code 'discontinuous' compared to the DNA of which
it was supposedly an exact copy. By the mid-1990s an explanation for this discon-
tinuity was beginning to emerge, and after the human genome was sequenced in
2001, that explanation became increasingly clear. Our current understanding now
runs as follows: the DNA of complex organisms does indeed contain a very high number of non-coding sections, officially called *introns*. RNA accurately copies a section
of DNA, including that non-coding material, but then it is immediately seized by a
spliceosome, which proceeds to remove those introns. The remaining good material,
termed *exons*, is then spliced together. But sometimes the spliceosome skips some of

2. There may be a hundred thousand of them, but they are so small that they take up only about 1
per cent of the volume of the nucleus.

The world that is looked at deeply wants to flourish in love

the exons, or it unexpectedly leaves an intron in the mix, or it rearranges the exons in a 'better' order than in the original DNA.[3] This process is called 'alternative splicing', and the RNA from 90 per cent of human genes gets this treatment, according to Reinhard Lührmann, a director at the Max Planck Institute for Biophysical Chemistry in Germany.[4] How the spliceosome determines what is 'better' remains a matter of much investigation, but it seems to be responding to the organism's needs at particular developmental stages.

On average, every strand of human RNA has about three alternative splicing sites, but the RNA from some human genes gets spliced into thousands of different arrangements. The fruit fly has RNA from one gene that gets alternatively spliced some 33,000 distinct ways.[5]

It is this cleaned-up and re-edited version of RNA – now called *messenger RNA* – that goes happily on its way, wiggling through tiny openings in the membrane of the nucleus and out onto the factory floor of the cell. (I have animated a schematic of this process, which can be found on Vimeo: https://vimeo.com/360517366. There is also Drew Berry's scientific animation: http://tinyurl.com/2xc73hjc; QR codes on right).

I have skipped over many of the finer points of this fascinating sequence to make a broader point as clear as possible: there are 100,000 film editors alive and well inside the nucleus of every cell in your body, as well as those of all the complex organisms on Earth![6] The exceptions are bacteria and archaea, single-celled organisms that do not have a nucleus.[7] Their RNA does not need editing because the DNA is being continuously pruned back to 'fighting weight', ridding it of introns as soon as possible. Biochemist Nick Lane,

---

3. Sarah Everts, 'Uncovering the Spliceosome's Secrets', *Chemical and Engineering News*, vol. 93, issue 39, 5 October 2015: https://cen.acs.org/articles/93/i39/Uncovering-Spliceosomes-Secrets.html.

4. Another not too technical article on the spliceosome: Sarah Everts, 'Divining the Spliceosome', *Chemical and Engineering News*, vol. 87, issue 18, 4 May 2009: https://cen.acs.org/articles/87/i18/ Divining-Spliceosome.html (QR code on right).

5. Everts, 'Divining the Spliceosome'.

6. See the boxed appendix at the end of the chapter for more detail.

7. Life on Earth is divided into two domains: prokaryotes and eukaryotes. Prokaryotes are split into bacteria and archaea and do not have nuclei. (Archaea are very similar to bacteria, but can survive in environments of extreme temperature and pressure.) All other life forms on Earth, including us humans, are *eukaryotes*, whose cells do have nuclei – and spliceosomes!

Rainer Maria Rilke

in his book *The Vital Question* (2015),[8] has compared bacteria to lean fighter jets and the cells in all other life forms (eukaryotes) to bulky aircraft carriers.[9]

As film editors well know, there is a great deal of 'non-coding' material in the dailies (the rushes) of a film. The proportion of everything that is shot to what gets used is called the *shooting ratio*. During Hollywood's 'golden age' (1930–60) that averaged 10:1, which is just under the junk/good DNA ratio of 12:1. Many of Alfred Hitchcock's films had an amazingly low ratio of 3:1. On Zinnemann's *Julia*, which I edited in 1977, it was 34:1, ten times Hitchcock's proportion. On *Apocalypse Now* the ratio ballooned to 95:1, *Mad Max: Fury Road* (2015) was 240:1, while on *Coup 53* it was 266:1, almost a hundred times that of Hitchcock.[10]

Why is there so much non-coding material in our gigantic 'aircraft carrier' cells? We still don't fully understand the answer to that question, but according to Lane, some of it seems to be a residue from ancient DNA that once belonged to the mitochondria in our cells when they were free-living bacteria. But it helps to know that there is a further distinction to be made between *junk* and *garbage*. *Garbage* DNA is truly bad, you might even say rotten – the equivalent of day-old banana peels. Lane has called garbage DNA 'decayed parasitic corpses'. They have been corrupted by something – a stray X-ray perhaps – and are incapable of making a valid protein. *Junk* DNA, on the other hand, is more like an old CD player that you used to love and can't bear to throw out, so you put it away in a box in the attic, with the thought: 'Who knows, I may need it someday.' It still works, and in the right circumstances might be useful again, even if only to ransack for parts.

> Eyeless fish, for instance, living in pitch-dark caves for millions of years, have
> similarly kept the 'junk' instructions for constructing eyes just in case they

8. It was in reading Lane's excellent *The Vital Question* that I first encountered the name *spliceosome*. See https://www.amazon.com/Vital-Question-Why-life-way/dp/1781250375. Although the name *spliceosome* does not appear, its activity is examined in Denis Noble's superb short book on systems biology, *The Music of Life* (2006).

9. The volume of a cell in a eukaryote (a human being, for instance) is from four thousand to a hundred thousand times greater than an average bacterium. An aircraft carrier has around ten thousand times the volume of a typical fighter jet.

10. Vashi Nedomansky, 'Shooting Ratios of Feature Films', 6 February 2016: https://vashivisuals.com/shooting-ratios-of-feature-films.

Provoke the unexpected. Expect it

> are required in future. If those fish are hybridised with blind fish from another, distant cave, the eyes will return after a couple of generations because the spliceosome now somehow believes that eyes, like that old CD player, might be useful again. The 'junk' label is removed and the eyes pop back into action.[11]

An analogous situation frequently arises in film-making when a scene becomes redundant: it is cut out of the film, but carefully set aside. Months later, it may be brought back into the movie because something else has changed that has made the rejected scene useful under these new circumstances. The 'director's cut' of a film will often give examples of this.

So our DNA retains this 'junk' information because it is never certain, in the long sweep of evolutionary history, when it may become useful again. Or it may be ransacked for spare parts. It is difficult and 'expensive' to remove information from code, as software engineers know: it is much easier, and less risky, simply to block and patch a section of software rather than trying to uproot it – an action that would potentially cause hard-to-predict collateral damage.

In the floppy-disc days (1980s) of personal computers, memory was so precious that software was relentlessly pared down to 'fighting weight' (I am recalling the WriteNow word-processing program from the primitive 'bacterial' days of personal computing). Once computer memory became orders of magnitude less expensive, we moved into the present 'eukaryotic' computer world, where software bloat is accepted as normal. In complex life forms like us (and onions!), DNA has a similar case of software bloat, so to speak, and therefore requires an editing agent – the spliceosome – to keep things under control.

And, as in genetics, we film editors also distinguish between *junk* and *garbage*. Nick Lane's 'decayed corpses' would produce zombie proteins if they were allowed to enter a ribosome. The equivalent in cinema would range from damaged film (dirt, scratches, lack of focus, dead pixels, scrambled code) to the clapsticks at the beginning of every shot and the flash frames at the end – although, as I wrote in an earlier chapter, I found a way to make use of those flash frames in *Julia*, to simulate the close-up of a train passing by. And Bill Morrison's *Decasia* (2002) is a powerfully emotional film

11. New York University, 'Progeny of Blind Cavefish Can "Regain" Their Sight', *Science Daily*, 8 January 2008: https://www.sciencedaily.com/releases/2008/01/080107120911.htm.

Robert Bresson

made out of literal cinematic garbage, the 'decayed corpses' of nitrate film in advanced stages of disintegration.[12]

Cinematic junk (a harsh word) is a different matter: it refers to something that might have been useful but for various reasons has been rejected. But beautiful films have been made entirely out of this material: Carl Dreyer's classic *The Passion of Joan of Arc* (1928) was reassembled out of initially rejected takes after the original cut negative was destroyed by fire at a laboratory in Germany.[13]

As I wrote in *Blink of an Eye*, the popular idea of what we film editors do is 'cut out the bad bits', and it is spooky to discover that this is exactly what is going on at a furious rate in the trillions of cells of the human body, and that our lives and health depend on the correct decisions being made by those tiny spliceosomes. Of course, in cinema, the artistry lies in discovering what is a 'bad bit'. Many are obvious, but most are not; they even sometimes masquerade as good bits, and it takes courage and artistic intuition to identify all of them, or at least as many as possible. As Miles Davis said of music:

> It's not the note you play that's the wrong note – it's the note you play next that makes it right or wrong.

After the audience previews of *Julia* in 1977, one of the 'bad bits' removed was a perfectly valid scene about the years of McCarthyism in America. In fact, it was the very scene in the screenplay that had convinced Zinnemann to dedicate a couple of years to making the film, but it finally proved to be an awkward fit in the time-telescoped structure of the opening minutes, so it was removed.

The Equivalence Between Cinema and Biology

The camera negative can be seen as the equivalent of DNA: it is the master 'encyclopaedia' from which everything will subsequently be derived, but it is riddled with extraneous material, some of it garbage and some of it junk.

The positive workprint, which is a direct copy from a section of the negative, is the equivalent of what is called 'pre-messenger RNA', which is a faithful copy of a section of DNA, 'junk' and all, but with every base pair switched in 'polarity' (A for T, C for G), just as the film workprint is a positive copy of a negative.[14] The spliceosome is the film

12. *Decasia* trailer: https://www.youtube.com/watch?v=hDa-mmSldDg (QR code on left).

13. *The Passion of Joan of Arc*, release and different versions, on Wikipedia: https://en.wikipedia.org/wiki/The_Passion_of_Joan_of_Arc#Release_and_different_versions.

14. See the boxed material in the appendix to this chapter for more detail of this amazing process.

Art is the constant darner, who mends the fabric of reality which language, history and every other ill-conceived human cleverness has left in shreds

editor, who cuts out the 'bad bits' (the introns) from the workprint and alternatively splices the 'good bits' (the exons) into a better order than they were in the negative.

When this editing is done, the cut workprint (the messenger RNA) leaves the sanctuary of the editing room (the nucleus) and goes out to the laboratory (the main body of the cell), where the ribosome makes the internegative (called *transfer RNA*) from the cut workprint, switching the polarity of the base pairs back to what they were in the original DNA, although now cleaned up and 'de-junked' by the spliceosome. Then an answer print (the protein built from the transfer RNA's instructions) is quickly made.

I have framed this comparison using terms from the days of physical film because

```
Camera negative . . . . . . . . . . . . . . . . . . . . . . . . . . . . . . . . . . . . . DNA
Positive workprint . . . . . . . . . . . . . . . . . . . . . Pre-messenger RNA
Film editor . . . . . . . . . . . . . . . . . . . . . . . . . . . . . . . . . Spliceosome
Bad bits . . . . . . . . . . . . . . . . . . . . . . . . . . . . . . . . . . . . . . Introns
Good bits . . . . . . . . . . . . . . . . . . . . . . . . . . . . . . . . . . . . . Exons
Cut workprint . . . . . . . . . . . . . . . . . . . . . . . . . Messenger RNA
Editing room . . . . . . . . . . . . . . . . . . . . . . . . . . . . . . Nucleus
Laboratory . . . . . . . . . . . . . . . . . . . . . . . . . . . . . . . Ribosome
Internegative . . . . . . . . . . . . . . . . . . . . . . . . . . . . Transfer RNA
Answer/release print . . . . . . . . . . . . . . . . . . . . . . . . . . Protein
```

the negative/positive analogy is so clear with DNA/RNA, but there are equivalents in digital film-making.

In his book *The Vital Question*, Nick Lane makes the point that spliceosomes take much longer to edit RNA than ribosomes need to make proteins from it. So if there were no nucleus, or if its membrane were more permeable, ribosomes would barge in and grab unedited RNA and consequently make jumbled, incoherent proteins. The death of the organism would soon follow. The nucleus itself, and the tight mesh of its membrane, is a cautionary protection (a prophylactic!) to prevent 'the studio' (the ribosome) from making release prints before they have been properly edited.

So, as we film-makers are working away on our next projects, we should take inspiration from the fact that our bodies are made of thirty-seven trillion cells, each one hosting 100,000 spliceosomes, all busy editing RNA and recombining the good bits into a better order so that we can continue our work doing the same thing!

Anonymous, 454 West 23rd Street

A final thought: how is it that we humans seem to have reinvented a system of data storage and processing that is billions of years old, but of which we were almost completely ignorant until just a few decades ago? It is most likely a case of *convergent evolution*, in which the demands of the 'environment' are so similar that resemblances between the systems designed to deal with those demands are almost inevitable. Nobel laureate Phillip Sharp's comments are illuminating in this regard: 'The spliceosome makes errors, and it's very complicated, but there is beauty in the fact that splicing is so arduous,' he says. With so many players and such a complicated sequence of steps required to properly splice RNA, it may seem incredible that the spliceosome ever works at all.

Sharp suggests evolution may have found some advantage in going with a system so complex that it is doomed to fail with some regularity. 'The ability to excise introns in different patterns and to shuffle exons is integral to the evolution of all complex, multicellular organisms'; in other words, by having an enormous, error-prone strategy for creating complexity, evolution has a platform to experiment.[15] There is beauty in the fact that splicing is so arduous. A system so complex that it is doomed to fail with some regularity. An enormous, error-prone strategy that provides a platform to experiment.

Sounds familiar, doesn't it? We could make very similar observations about film-making!

Appendix

The famous double helix of DNA is composed of two intertwined, connected strands, the code letters 'shaking hands' with their partners on the opposite strand of the helix. Those molecules (called *bases* in biology) are geometrically shaped in such a way that A pairs with T and C pairs with G,

15. Sarah Everts, 'Uncovering the Spliceosome's Secrets'.

so the sequence AGT, TCG would be mirror-imaged in the other strand of the helix with the sequence TCA, AGC.

This mirror-imaging also occurs when an RNA copy is made of a single strand of DNA. In film-making, when a positive copy is made from an original film negative, black is exchanged for white, red for blue, green for yellow, etc. When a copy is made in genetics, A is exchanged for T, C for G, and vice versa. The spliceosome then works on this 'positive' RNA copy, purging it of junk (introns), rearranging the remaining valid information (exons) and splicing it together into a considerably shortened 'film strip' called *messenger RNA*.

When this edited 'positive film strip' of messenger RNA is subsequently taken up by a ribosome, a further 'negative' copy is made, flipping the letters back to what they were in the DNA original (although now cleaned up and 'de-junked' by the spliceosome). It is from this final version, called *transfer RNA*, that proteins are finally constructed. In film-making terms, this would be a final theatrical print (the protein) made from an internegative (the transfer RNA).

Dov Seidman to Tom Friedman

14: HANA AND HARVEY

Canine Ketamine

Hana came into our lives as a puppy in the spring of 1996, a couple of months after our son Walter, then aged twenty-seven, had been diagnosed with a brain tumour. I was editing *The English Patient* at the time, and after Walter's operation had taken place and he was recovering at home in Bolinas, my wife Aggie felt that a furry companion would be a help for all concerned. And Hana – named after the nurse played by Juliette Binoche in *The English Patient* – certainly filled the bill.[1]

From 2001 on, Aggie had been living mostly in England, caring for her eighty-three-year-old mother Bobby, who was suffering from congestive heart problems. Fortunately, in 2002 I got the job of editing Anthony Minghella's *Cold Mountain*, and although the filming was mostly done in Romania, post-production would take place in London.

So, in the summer of 2003, Aggie brought Hana from California to London. She was one of the first dogs to come to England after the 1897 rabies quarantine laws had been relaxed. She had been given a bill of good health by an American vet seventy-two hours prior to departure from Los Angeles and 'chipped' to establish her identity, so she was exempt from the draconian rule of six months' quarantine.

Hana was a Border terrier, a breed native to Great Britain, from the Cheviot Hills on the border between England and Scotland, so in a sense she was coming home, but she had been born just outside San Francisco. She was a happy dog who loved nothing better than chasing rats, gophers and occasionally raccoons – and getting covered in mud along the way – but, in London, she had to be a bit more civilised (although she would get excited by the scent trails of water rats down by Regent's Canal).

1. More detail about this period can be found in *In the Blink of an Eye*, pp. 97–107, and will also be found in the 'English and Half-English Patients' chapter of the subsequent volume of this book.

Things will arrive simultaneously from a thousand directions, but through some mysterious magnetism they will all find their right places

After getting over her jet lag, Hana settled into a routine: she would be with Aggie and Bobby on odd-numbered days and come to work with me on the evens. Old Chapel Studios, where I was editing *Cold Mountain*, were a refreshing mile-and-a-quarter walk from where Aggie and I lived in Primrose Hill.

Cold Mountain, a film about the American Civil War, was based on the book of the same name by Charles Frazier, and the Old Chapel was a nineteenth-century church that had been abandoned by the Baptists sometime in the 1950s and converted into a photography studio by Gered Mankowitz in the 1970s.[2] After *The Talented Mr. Ripley*, producer/director Sydney Pollack had invited Anthony Minghella to become a partner in his production company, Mirage, and they had bought the chapel in the early 2000s as the company's London HQ. The editing rooms were upstairs in a kind of loft conversion where only angels had previously flown.

Old Chapel Studios

The walk there and back was the high point of Hana's day with me. The rest of the time she would curl up on her pillow in a corner of the editing room and endure the monotonous repetition of fragments of dialogue, explosions and music from the editing machine, her rival for attention. My son Walter was working as an assistant on the film, and he would take her out for midday walks.

2. Mankowitz would photograph many stars of the rock world, including the Rolling Stones, Jimi Hendrix, Marianne Faithfull and Elton John. He shot the famous cover of the Stones' album *Between the Buttons* (1967) on Primrose Hill: https://en.wikipedia.org/wiki/Between_the_ Buttons#Artwork.

Jean Cocteau

Romanian locations had been used on *Cold Mountain* in order to reduce the budget from the supposed $120 million it would have cost to shoot in North Carolina – the Carpathian mountains standing in for the Appalachians – and Eurozone tax breaks helped to shrink the budget even further, to just over $80 million. Miramax, Harvey Weinstein's company, had become *Cold Mountain*'s sole financing studio when MGM pulled out of a fifty–fifty arrangement shortly after filming started.

Once that happened, the only alternatives were to either find another partner (and the timing of MGM's withdrawal made this almost impossible), cancel the film (which would have been a huge write-down) or proceed anyway. With these cards in his hand, Harvey decided to go all in. The difficulty underlying that decision was Miramax's purchase by Disney in 1993. Part of that deal was that the Weinstein brothers, Harvey and Bob, could exercise their own judgement in terms of what movies to finance, provided no single film's budget was over $45 million. This put *Cold Mountain* in decidedly dangerous territory: a failure would threaten Miramax's relations with Disney, which were already strained because of cost overruns on Scorsese's *Gangs of New York* (2002) and the Miramax release of Michael Moore's *Fahrenheit 9/11* (2004), of which Disney had disapproved.

For producers like Harvey, a shorter film was always a better one, with an improved chance of box-office success, so when he flew to London in early August 2003, after our first preview in July, the atmosphere at the Old Chapel was slightly febrile. His visit was scheduled for Friday 8 August, by which time Anthony and I had reduced the running time of *Cold Mountain* from an initial five hours and ten minutes down to two hours and fifty-four minutes.

Sadly, Aggie's mother had died on 3 August, and the funeral was set for the 11th. Our son Walter was already in London, but the three girls – Beatrice, Carrie and Connie – were flying in from California. Things got very complicated: within the next month we were scheduled to fly out for a preview in Edgewater, New Jersey, return to London for changes, go back to the US for another preview in Charleston, South Carolina, and in early September to begin music recording at Abbey Road and final dialogue premixing at De Lane Lea Studios in London. How feasible this schedule was would depend on Harvey's reaction to the 8 August screening in the editing rooms at the Old Chapel.

Cold Mountain was the third film I had edited for Anthony Minghella, and Miramax had been the producing studio on each one, so this was not unfamiliar territory to

You will not know till much later if your film is worth the mountain
range of efforts it is costing you

me. Harvey was notorious for taking versions of the films he was financing back to his editing room in Connecticut to see how he could 'improve' them.

On *The English Patient*, a couple of weeks after a copy had been made and sent to him, there had still been no comment from Harvey. When Anthony finally asked him if he had any insights, Harvey only said, 'It's a very complicated film,' and that was the last we heard on the subject. On *The Talented Mr. Ripley*, however, a Connecticut version emerged that I thankfully never saw. Anthony, who was exposed to it, was so outraged that he 'fired' Harvey, and for weeks it looked like an irrevocable split had occurred between them. As far as I understood it, the central issue was the final twenty minutes: Ripley's murder of his lover Peter, and whether or not he would get away with it. A reshoot was even considered in which Ripley would arrive in Istanbul and be arrested by the police. In the end, the solution Anthony and I came up with was to fracture the time sequence so that the audience never saw the murder take place, hearing instead its delayed soundtrack, while Ripley, stone-faced and alone in his cabin, was multiply reflected in the slowly swinging mirrored doors of his closet. This solution was enough to restore semi-cordial relations with Harvey, and reshoots were cancelled.

> A peace offering from Harvey to Anthony was a Cartier watch – and one for me, too, even though I was not personally involved in the quarrel. It was one of those chunky producer-watches that I would never wear, so I stashed it away in the editing room and forgot all about it, until Aggie heard the 'Cartier' rumour from someone else. She got the idea of trading it in for cash – our house needed repainting – but Cartier said that it had been bought at a considerable discount from a jewellery shop in Westwood, Los Angeles, and would have to be exchanged there. That shop said they wouldn't refund the money, but we could exchange it for another watch. Which we subsequently did, getting two very nice but simple watches, one for Aggie and one for me. The salesman taking care of the swap confided discreetly that Mr Minghella had exchanged his watch the previous day.

When Anthony and I (and Hana, since 8 August was an even-numbered day) heard Harvey coming upstairs to the editing room, he was bringing along a considerable amount of emotional baggage and trailing clouds of cigarette smoke. Whether we would meet the deadlines of the next four weeks would depend on his reaction.

Robert Bresson

As soon as Harvey sat down, Hana ran over, jumped up on the sofa and snuggled down on his lap. I was astonished. Neither of them had seen each other before, but both acted as if this were perfectly normal. Harvey took Hana's friendship as his due and began to pet her without breaking stride as he harangued us about the urgent need for the film to be much shorter. But within five minutes his personality transformed, as if he had been slipped a dose of ketamine. All the changes that we had made to the film were now 'wonderful' and we were 'geniuses'. I looked at Anthony, and Anthony looked at me. Harvey smoked and drank coffee as the film ran. Hana sighed contentedly, Harvey continued petting her, the minutes raced by, and we were suddenly finished with the screening.

'See you in Edgewater,' were Harvey's parting words, as he drowned his final cigarette in the coffee cup and floated downstairs to his waiting car.

Harvey's 8 August coffee and cigarettes.

There was a minute of stunned silence as Anthony and I absorbed the implications: the film had escaped Harvey's scissor hands – at least for the moment – and we were now going to be able to meet the deadlines of the coming month.

Hana stared at us from the warm spot on the sofa where Harvey had been sitting.

'Hana, you now have an executive position at Mirage,' said Anthony. 'My people will talk to your people. Let's get your deal wrapped up over the weekend!'

Hana wagged her tail.

Isn't it a hell of a thing, that the fate of a great country can depend on camera angles?

Coda . . .

But, of course, Hana's ketamine effect wore off. The two August previews went well, but not well enough, and despite the ongoing music recording and final premixing, big changes to the film were back on the agenda. Harvey returned to London in early September, demanding significant reductions in its length – 'and not just five minutes'.

By mid-September we had cut out ten. When we showed Harvey this version (it was an odd-numbered day, without Hana), he asked for more: 'Now that you have done the heavy lifting, there are some trims that are even more obviously to be made.'

I should mention that Anthony had final cut: contractually, he could have refused to consider any further reductions in length. But this would have created a stand-off with Harvey, who could have then refused to put sufficient money into promotion and distribution. This is the reality of the prerogative of final cut, a medal for past victories won, but whose effect is largely illusory.

So, jumping back and forth from De Lane Lea Studios in Soho, where Mike Prestwood-Smith and I were mixing during the day, to the Old Chapel at night to make more cuts to the film, we managed to get the length down to two hours and thirty-four minutes – twenty minutes shorter than it had been at the 'Hana' screening in August. On 15 October Hana once again made a beeline for Harvey's lap as he declared, 'Let's lock this picture!' and they sat there together as we went through the film reel by reel.

From my journal, 17 October 2003:

> 2 a.m. Locked the film: Congratulations!! It seemed (it always seems) anticlimactic, a kind of wobbling to a stop. But there it is. We will check-screen it tomorrow morning and then release the reels to the various departments for changes.

At the end-of-film party, prizes were handed out to those who had contributed to getting *Cold Mountain* across the finish line:

> 23 November 2003: Party for Mirage at Landsdowne pub • very good – they ran Tom's spoof trailer of *Cold Mountain*, with Bruna as Ada, Cassius as Teague, Caroline as Ruby, Walter and Dei as Stobrod and Pangle • I won 'most promising newcomer' award • Hana won the Achievement award, particularly cited for bravery in sitting on Harvey's lap.

Cold Mountain was a solid but not runaway financial success and received seven Academy Award nominations, winning one for Renée Zellweger's performance as Ruby. But none of that was enough to repair the Disney/Miramax relationship. In March 2005 Disney and the Weinstein brothers parted ways, and Disney took over the management of Miramax, eventually selling the name and library of films to an investment group, Filmyard Holdings, in 2010.

Snatch your story out of thin air. And if fate is against you, fight back: cheat it with some card trick

15: ELEMENTS OF STYLE

Use with Caution!

Often I will ask my assistants to assemble a few scenes from the dailies, both to help us get to a first cut as quickly as possible and also to enliven their work, because assisting can get monotonous. Being able to have multiple editors working simultaneously is one of the great advantages of digital editing, where the cost of the media and workstation is negligible compared to what it was in the analogue days of Moviola or KEM editing.

Thirty years ago, I wrote the following to help everyone on The English Patient *get up to speed with my workflow, methodology and aesthetic approach to editing, and I have continued to distribute these pages whenever there are multiple editors working under my supervision. The goal each time was to create a first assembly that was as stylistically integrated as possible, despite being the product of many hands.*

Every film will have its own stylistic language, and it is part of our job to discover that unique language and learn how to 'speak' it and, even more importantly, how to 'listen' to it. As a result, the pages that follow might be dangerous because they detail a particular editorial approach that may not be right for every editor, nor for every film.

So read these notes with caution, simply as an example of one editor's approach.

First of all, remember you are telling a story, taking advantage of and amplifying the appropriate emotional colours, keeping all of the characters in the scene alive to the degree that is necessary.

Take notes to reveal the hidden architecture of the scene. Make detailed notes on a selected take for each set-up. What happens from moment to moment? This will help you to 'see into' the shot and discover its hidden structure. Painters study anatomy for the same reason: what is bone and what is flesh, where are the ligaments and tendons.

Include the time code (MM:SS – minutes and seconds) to identify the location of each of your notes. That way, you can easily get back to a specific moment. It will also streamline your note-taking because you won't have to describe where a moment happens in the shot.

Then take notes on the other takes, referring to my original dailies notes to find variations and improvements in performance and camera. This can give you an insight into the process the crew were going through when they were shooting.

If you describe something as being *NG* (no good), always write down *why* it is no good. Something that seems NG in dailies may be exactly what you will be looking for three months later.

Any association, no matter how silly it seems, will help you to recall a moment or a feeling. *She looks like a banana*, for instance.

Print out notes and review them once they are printed.

Highlight the good material with orange markers.

Tick with red the really good.

Green highlights for NG material.

Don't try to digest more than three–four hours of dailies at a time.

It usually take about three times as long to take notes as it would to run the material straight through. So schedule in nine hours of note-taking for every three hours of dailies.

Find the opening image. Usually it is fairly obvious from the way the material is shot: a move up or into, or a crane shot, or dolly, etc.

Then swing from good (orange) moment to good (orange) moment.

Try to get as many of the highlighted moments in the first cut as possible. But not too many!

Metaphor of the animator who draws key frames (A, B, C), and it is the task of the animation 'tweeners' to fill in the action from point A to point B.

The film editor is both animator and 'tweener'.

The ballet of focus of attention. Follow the eyes of the actors. Look INTO their eyes, not at them.

Editing can be thought of as a complex, patterned dance of eyes: the eyes of the characters and the eyes of the spectators following them.

Always be aware of the *tension and release* of contact or broken contact in looks between characters. WHO is NOT looking at whom is as significant as the opposite.

The audience is almost, but not always, looking at the eyes of the speaking character. If they are not looking at the eyes, they are looking at the lips. See https://vimeo.com/19788132 (QR code on left) for a fascinating video clip from *There Will Be Blood*, showing how the audience's focus of attention shifts from moment to moment. That focus of attention on the screen has *speed, direction and inertia*. Think of it as a ball

The best thing about the future is that it arrives one day at a time

being tossed around the field of the screen. Consequently, it is also the job of the subsequent shot to 'receive' energy from the previous one and do something creative with it: swing with it, hit it back, dissipate it, freeze it, etc.

Your job as editor is to make the motion of this 'ball' of attention interesting and sometimes thrilling.

Leading edges of light against dark are magnetically attractive to the attention of the spectator.

Choose the last frame of a shot by marking 'on the fly'. This is the most significant thing that you can do to sharpen your cutting edge.

Get approximately close to the end frame when you select the clip, then go into trim mode and hit the space bar (the stop command) when you feel the urge to cut – it is a musical thing, and has the same exactitude as the moment when a new instrument joins the melody.

Read the time code of your out point, and then try it again and again until you are reading the rhythmic patterns of the shot accurately enough to hit the exact same frame, several times in a row.

When you have identified the end frame of your shot, scan the photobook (the library of still frames, which I have captured from dailies), which acts as a kind of thesaurus, to suggest an appropriate next image.

Then fit the incoming image to the outgoing in a poetic way that makes a comparison or a contrast to further bring out the images (light vs dark, large vs small, left vs right). Try not to cut medium or full shots together.

Register where the spectator's eye is at the moment of the cut.

Try turning the sound off when first assembling the scene. This concentrates your perceptions on the body language of the actors and the images. Also, you will find you become able to 'hear' the final sound, in all its fullness, in your imagination. The as-yet-unwritten music.

You can always turn the sound on if you really need to.

Light and dark. Explore the idea of compressible space as objects or people move within the frame, building up pressure against the 'walls' of the frame as they move towards the edges, and then releasing that pressure as they go 'through' the edge, exiting the frame.

Abraham Lincoln

Someone is exiting frame. Cut at the point of maximum pressure, when it is clear that they must leave, but have not yet left. It is like the moment when an airplane must take off.

However, there are times when you may want to make a specific point by emptying the frame and returning the spectator's attention to the centre, depending on the shot and the context.

Maintain variations in the size of the image, variations that are harmonic with the story and its emotional points. Except when cutting dialogue scenes: there, too much variation in size can be distracting.

A few extra frames (one or two) are often needed at the head of the incoming shot for the eye to 'catch' its point of interest. More or fewer, depending on the violence of the cutting and the receptivity of the incoming shot.

Remember that the image is 'really' thirty to fifty feet wide, which increases the 'momentum' of the spectators' gaze.

Identical return. When cutting back to a character after a point-of-view (POV – what the character is looking at), their head should be in the same position, with the same expression as we left them with. This applies even after a double POV (character – POV #1 – POV #2 – character).

If it is impossible to do this for some reason, then mask the mismatch by cutting back to the character's head position at the beginning of a movement.

If there are three POVs in sequence, you have the freedom to cut back to the character in a different position. This is because the triad forms a new conceptual unity unto itself, weakening the chemical–temporal bond between the object and the character. This encourages the spectator to think about the relations between the three objects themselves, rather than just the relation of each object to the character, which is what happens in an ABA or ABBA structure. But not ABBBA structure.

Avoid action match cutting. 'Cutting on action' is where an action is initiated in the outgoing shot (someone turns their head) and is completed in the incoming shot (the head turns and then stops). This is conventional 'Hollywood' editing, and should mostly be avoided.

The blink – the cut – is a null point of attention, when thoughts are shifting gears. Take advantage of this. But never cut *when* someone is blinking. Almost always right

If you have a problem in the third act, the real problem is in the first act before. Occasionally right after, if the character has been startled by something.

Shots should open up from their first frame: find the beginning of some unfolding movement and make that the first frame of the incoming shot.

Edit points are like branching nodes in a tree. There are a number of them, in a certain pattern, for each shot. But not every frame can be an edit point, just like a branch cannot form at every point along a trunk.

Dialogue cutting: the fricative consonant. Dialogue is normally best when NOT cut at the end of the phrase, so that it has an impact when it IS cut that way.

A line of free-verse poetry is over when the secret architecture of the line is at the correct tension. This rarely coincides with the grammatical punctuation of the sentence. Poetry whose line breaks always coincided with the grammatical punctuation of the sentence would be predictable, boring and incapable of deeper insight.

Cutting from one shot to another while someone is speaking most often works best on or immediately around a fricative consonant: 's', 'sh', 'z', 'th', 'f', 'v', etc.

Not coincidentally, people often blink when they are pronouncing a fricative consonant. Watch for this in the footage (or in life), and you will notice that it is mostly true.

Cutting on the off-beat (upbeat – downbeat). Comparison with walking: right step – shift weight – left step – shift weight – right step, etc.

When cutting someone who is walking, almost always cut on the upbeat (shift of weight) rather than the hit of the step. Unless you are making a point (usually about them stopping or turning or making a noise – something that intentionally breaks the rhythm).

Parallels with conducting music: the music starts when the conductor lifts the baton, not when the baton hits the bottom of its arc.

A four-second pre-roll is good for getting the rhythm of the shot. Two and a half seconds for a post-roll.

Good luck! Make discoveries!

Billy Wilder

16: COOK TING
BY ZHUANGZI

'At First, I Could See Nothing That Was Not Ox'

*The following story/poem/meditation was written around 2,500 years ago by the
Chinese Daoist master Zhuangzi (sometimes spelled Chuang Tsu). He gives voice to the
thoughts and skills of Ting, the cook for a certain Lord Wen-hui.
The action described is the carving up of the carcass of an ox, but we film editors
will find parallels with our state of mind when the work is challenging, and especially
when it is going well.*

Cook Ting was slicing up an ox for Lord Wen-hui. At every push of his hand, every
angle of his shoulder, every step with his feet, every bend of his knee, he slithered the
knife along, and all was in perfect rhythm, as though he were dancing.

'Ah, this is marvellous!' said Lord Wen-hui. 'Imagine skill reaching such heights!'

Cook Ting laid down his knife and replied, 'When I began cutting up oxen, at
first I could see nothing that was not ox. After three years, I no longer saw the ox,
but only the joints. Now I go at the work with spirit alone and do not look with my
eyes. Knowledge has stopped and my spirit wills the performance. I depend on the
natural make-up to cut through the creases, guide the knife through the fissures.
I depend on things as they are. So I never touch the smallest ligament or tendon,
much less bone.

'A good cook changes his knife once a year because he cuts. A mediocre cook,
once a month because he hacks. I have had my knife for nineteen years and I have cut
up thousands of oxen with it, yet the blade is as good as if it had just come from the
grindstone . . .'

> The joints have openings,
> and the knife's blade has no thickness.
> Insert this lack of thickness into the openings,
> and the moving blade slides through,
> with room to spare.

Hide the ideas, but so that people will find them. The most
important will be the most hidden

Despite all this,
I often come across the unexpected.
Then it is hard to continue on the usual path.
I become alert.
My gaze comes to rest.

I move the knife very slightly,
whump! It has already separated.
The ox doesn't even know it is dead,
and falls to the ground like mud.

I stand holding the knife,
and look all around.
The work gives me much satisfaction.
I clean the knife and put it away.

I can think of no better ending for this section on film editing than those final four lines.

Robert Bresson

Every good idea begins as a movement, becomes a business,
and winds up as a racket

PART TWO
SOUND DESIGN

Mixing *Cold Mountain* (2003)

These chapters on film sound follow the same approach as those on film editing: theory mixes with experience, and practical tips jostle between metaphysics and neurology.

One of the great things about working in film is the ability we have to push at the limits of human perception and study what effect that has on audiences, but in a setting where there are real-world (which is to say, economic) consequences to our experiments.

But I never expected to be tear-gassed while doing it.

Eric Hoffer

Shot by shot you must win the match

17: FRANCIS COPPOLA'S SPECIAL BALLPOINT PEN

A 3 a.m. Crisis in the Mixing Studio

We had seven days to mix the soundtrack of Francis Coppola's *The Rain People*. It was the first week of June 1969, and the film had to be on a plane at 8 a.m. the following Monday in time to get to the San Sebastián Film Festival in Spain.

The KEM mixing equipment Francis had bought in Germany arrived the previous month, and we had assembled the eight film transports and a mixing desk, but there were still unresolved issues with differing electrical voltages, cycles per second and other mysteries, so we were in constant communication with KEM Hamburg via telex. On top of that, the remodelling of the Zoetrope studios, in a former warehouse on San Francisco's Folsom Street, South of Market (today's SOMA district), was months from being finished and there were clouds of plaster dust, wet cement, tools and unfinished carpentry lying around.

Our temporary mixing theatre was a 12 × 20-foot basement storage room, fitted with panels of exposed fibreglass insulation for sound absorption. There was no projector as such; we threaded the reels of 35 mm black-and-white duplicates of the colour workprint on one of the film transports, which had a video camera connected to a television set that was perched just in front of the mixing desk. The 35 mm black-and-white copy of the workprint was a contrasty, low-quality image to begin with, and the NTSC video didn't improve things. Plus, it was upside down. There was only one way of orienting the camera, so we tried various semi-sophisticated electronic solutions, flipping image polarity and so on, but nothing worked, until Francis found the obvious solution: just turn the television set upside down. I am confident that *Rain People* is the only film ever to be mixed while watched on an upside-down television set.

After six eighteen-hour days – coping with various electrical and mechanical problems, installing new capacitors (by Francis!), blowing plaster dust away, eating takeaway sushi delivered by Francis's wife Ellie – it had come down to two o'clock in the morning of the day we were supposed to deliver, and we had two reels still to finish. There were five of us: Francis, stretched out on the jumbled cardboard packing boxes in which the KEM had been shipped; me at the mixing desk; the composer,

Ronnie Stein, who would help mix if needed; Bill Neil, who had supervised putting the KEM together; and Dave MacMillan, who was Bill's assistant.[1]

Suddenly, at 2.30 a.m., all of us exploded in fits of violent coughing. The hit was instant and unexpected: one moment we were mixing the film, the next we were out in the corridor, gasping for air. We were already disoriented from working those long hours. It felt like there had been a jump cut in the fabric of reality.

After a few minutes spent recovering, Dave ventured back into the mix room. He stood in front of the mixing desk for a few seconds and then was struck with another coughing fit. We grabbed a large ventilation fan the builders had been using and hoped it would recirculate the air. Every couple of minutes one of us would try standing at the mixing desk but then be forced back out, coughing. Was it fragments of the fibreglass insulation or something else from the warehouse construction? But then why did it hit us only on the last day of the mix?

Finally, after about twenty-five minutes, I was able to go in, take a deep breath and give the all-clear. We still had no idea what the problem had been, but whatever it was, we just had to keep mixing. After about half an hour of work, there was a small voice from the pile of cardboard boxes:

'It was me.'

The voice was Francis's.

'What? What do you mean, "It was me"?'

'I caused the problem.'

'What!?'

'With the coughing. I went to a store yesterday . . .'

Francis had been doing research for his script of *The Conversation* and had come across a store in downtown San Francisco that sold quasi-legal spy, security and eavesdropping equipment. On an impulse, he had bought a ballpoint pen filled with mace. And while he was listening to the mix, he had absent-mindedly taken the pen out of his pocket and, as you do with ballpoints when you are nervous, was clicking

1. Dave would go on to be the location sound recordist on over ninety films, winning three Oscars along the way (*The Right Stuff* (1983), *Speed* (1994) and *Apollo 13* (1995)), as well as the Cinema Audio Society's career achievement award in 2013.

Your film might be explained later, but nothing can prevent it from having been gloriously inexplicable to you as you were making it

the plunger repeatedly. Each click would release a little puff of mace, and the puffs eventually built up to a toxic level.

All we could do was burst out laughing at the absurdity of it all: the director had just maced his crew at 2.30 a.m. on the day we had to deliver the mix. It was an interesting preview, on my first feature film, of the sometimes surreal relationships between a director and his crew.

It was also my first encounter with the themes of *The Conversation.*

Luckily, that was the last of our problems, and four and a half hours later, Francis boarded a plane with the finished magnetic soundtrack, heading to the lab in Los Angeles where the release print would be made. From there, release print in his luggage, he went on to the San Sebastián Film Festival, where *The Rain People* won first prize.

American Zoetrope film-makers in 1969, shortly after finishing *The Rain People*.
From left to right: Barry Beckerman, Robert Dalva, Walter Murch (wielding a pitchfork),
Steve Wax (prominent in foreground), George Lucas (wearing a dark hat and
sunglasses and partially hidden by a strip of film hanging from my pitchfork),
Jim McBride, John Milius (with sombrero), Carroll Ballard (on ladder with camera),
Francis Coppola (with zoetrope), Larry Sturhan, Denis Jakob (holding up the 1000 mm
lens), Tim Huntley and John Korty (with camera)

Jean-Paul Sartre (adapted by Walter Murch)

18: THE DANCING SHADOW

From King to Queen

I wrote the following essay in 1995 for Projections, *a book-format periodical in which film-makers wrote about their work that was edited by John Boorman and Walter Donohue and published by Faber & Faber.*

The Window

It disappeared long ago, but in 1972 the Window was still there, peering through milky cataracts of dust, ten metres above the floor of Samuel Goldwyn's old Stage 7. I never would have noticed it if Richard hadn't suddenly stopped in his tracks as we were taking a shortcut on our way back from lunch.

'That! Was when Sound! Was King!' he said, gesturing dramatically into the upper darkness of Stage 7.

It took me a moment, but I finally saw what he was pointing at: something near the ceiling that resembled the observation window of a 1930s Zeppelin, nosing its way into the stage. Goldwyn Studios, where Richard Portman and I were working on the mix of *The Godfather*, had originally been the studio lot of United Artists, built for Pickford, Chaplin, Fairbanks and Griffith in 1922.

By 1972 Stage 7 was functioning as an attic – stuffed with the mysterious lumbering shapes of disused equipment – but it was there that Samuel Goldwyn produced one of the earliest of his many musicals: *Whoopee!* (1930), starring Eddie Cantor and choreographed by Busby Berkeley. And it was there that Goldwyn's director of sound, Gordon Sawyer, sat at the controls behind the Window, hands gliding across three Bakelite knobs, piloting his Zeppelin of Sound into a new world . . . a world in which Sound Was King!

Down below, Eddie Cantor and the All-Singing, All-Dancing Goldwyn Girls had lived in terror of the distinguished Man Behind the Window. And not just the actors: Gregg Toland, the cameraman, Thornton Freedland, the director, Florenz Ziegfeld, the producer – even Sam Goldwyn himself. No one could contradict it if Mr Sawyer, dissatisfied with the quality of the sound, leaned into his microphone and pronounced dispassionately, but irrevocably, the word 'Cut!'

By 1972, forty-five years after his exhilarating coronation, King Sound seemed to be living in considerably reduced circumstances. No longer did the Man Behind the

Blessed is the actor who, in spite of himself and of you, frees the real character from the fictitious one you had imagined

Window survey the scene from on high. Instead, the sound recordist was usually stuck in some dark corner with his equipment cart. The very idea of his demanding 'Cut!' was inconceivable: not only did none of the other crew fear his opinion, they hardly consulted him and were frequently impatient when he did voice his concerns. The situation today, more than fifty years further along, has not changed: the century since 1926 seems to have turned Sound from King to footman.

Was Richard's nostalgia misplaced? What had befallen the Window? And most importantly, were Sound's misfortunes all they appeared to be?

Sound + Biology

There is something about the liquidity and all-encompassing embrace of Sound that might make it more accurate to speak of her as a Queen rather than a King. But was she perhaps a Queen for whom the crown was a burden, who preferred to slip on a handmaiden's bonnet and scurry incognito through the back passageways of the palace, accomplishing her tasks anonymously?

There is a similar mystery hidden in our own biology: four and a half months after conception we begin to hear, and by six months we can be seen by sonogram (and felt by our mother!) to be reacting to sounds.[1] And for the final three months, Sound reigns as a solitary Queen of the Senses: the close and liquid world of the womb makes sight and smell impossible, taste and touch a dim and slippery hint of what is to come. Instead, we luxuriate in a continuous bath of sounds: the song of our mother's voice, the swash of her breathing, the piping of her intestines, the timpani of her heart. The almost industrial intensity of this womb sound is emphasised by its loudness in our ears, equivalent to the 75 decibels in the cabin of a cruising passenger jet, with some occasional sounds reaching well over 100 decibels.[2]

Birth, however, brings with it the sudden and simultaneous ignition of the other four senses, and an intense jostling for the throne that Sound had claimed as hers alone. The most notable pretender is the darting and insistent Sight, who crowns himself King and ascends the throne as if it had been standing vacant, waiting for him.

Surprisingly, Sound pulls a veil of oblivion across her reign and withdraws into the shadows.

1. https://www.healthline.com/health/pregnancy/when-can-a-fetus-hear.
2. C. V. Smith, B. Satt, J. P. Phelan and R. H. Paul, 'Intrauterine Sound Levels: Intrapartum Assessment with an Intrauterine Microphone', *American Journal of Perinatology*, vol. 7, no. 4, 1990, pp. 312–15: https://www.ncbi.nlm.nih.gov/pubmed/2222618.

Robert Bresson

So we all begin as hearing beings – our four-and-a-half-month baptism in a sea of sound must have a profound and everlasting effect on us – but from the moment of birth onwards, hearing seems to recede into the background of our consciousness and function more as an accompaniment to what we see. Why this should be, rather than the reverse, is still somewhat of a mystery: why does the first of our senses to be activated not retain a lifelong dominance over all the others?[3]

Something of this same situation marks the relationship between what we see and hear in the cinema. Film sound is rarely consciously appreciated for itself alone but functions largely as an enhancement of the visuals: by means of some perceptual alchemy, whatever virtues sound brings to film are largely perceived and appreciated by the audience in visual terms. The better the sound, the better the image.

What had given film sound its brief reign over the film image was a temporary and uncharacteristic inflexibility. In those first few years after the commercialisation of film sound, in 1926, everything had to be recorded simultaneously – music, dialogue, sound effects – onto a 33⅓ rpm Vitaphone disc, and once recorded, nothing could be changed. The joke in Mel Brooks's *Blazing Saddles* about panning the camera and revealing the off-stage orchestra was not far from the truth.

Clem Portman (Richard's father), Gordon Sawyer, Murray Spivack and the other founders of film sound had the responsibility for recording the singer's voice, and the orchestra accompanying him, and his tap-dancing all at the same time, in as good a balance as they could manage. There was no possibility of fixing it later in the mix, because this was the mix. It had to be right the first time, or you called 'Cut!' and began again.

Power and Flexibility

Power on a film tends to gravitate towards those who control a bottleneck of some kind. Movie stars wield this kind of power, extras do not; the director of photography usually has more of it than the production designer. Film sound in its first few years was one of these bottlenecks, and so the Man Behind the Window held sway, temporarily, with a kingly power he has never had since.

3. Neurons devoted to visual processing take up about 30 per cent of the cortex, compared with 8 per cent for touch and just 3 per cent for hearing. Each of the two optic nerves, which carry signals from the retina to the brain, consists of a million fibres; each auditory nerve carries only 30,000. Denise Grady, 'The Vision Thing: Mainly in the Brain', *Discover*, 1 June 1993: https://www.discovermagazine.com/mind/the-vision-thing-mainly-in-the-brain (QR code on left).

If you bring forth what is within you, what you have done will save you. If you do not bring forth what is within you, it will kill you

The true nature and power of sound, though – its feminine fluidity and malleability, its yin to the yang of the image – was not revealed until the perfection of the sprocketed 35 mm optical soundtrack (1929), which could be edited, rearranged and put in different synchronous relationships with the image, opening up the bottleneck of the early days of sound recording. This opening was further enlarged by the revolutionary art of re-recording (1929–30), where multiple tracks of sound could be separately controlled and then recombined in multiple ways to yield more than the sum of their parts.

These developments took some time to work their way into the creative bloodstream: as late as 1936, films were being produced that added only seventeen additional sound effects for the whole film (instead of the tens of thousands that we might have today). But the possibilities were richly indicated by the imaginative sound work in Disney's animated film *Steamboat Willie* (1928) and DeMille's live-action prison film *Dynamite* (1929). Certainly, they were well established by the time of Murray Spivack and Clem Portman's ground-breaking work on *King Kong* (1933).

In fact, animation – of both the *Steamboat Willie* and the *King Kong* varieties – has probably played a more significant role in the evolution of creative sound than has been acknowledged. In the beginning of the sound era, it was so astonishing to hear people speak and move and sing and shoot one another in sync that almost any sound was more than acceptable. But with animated characters this did not work: they are two-dimensional creatures who make no sound at all unless the illusion is created through sound out of context – sound from one reality transposed onto another. The most famous of these is the thin falsetto that Walt Disney himself gave to the voice of Mickey Mouse, but a close second is the roar that Murray Spivack and Clem Portman provided King Kong.

The Dancing Shadow

There is a symbiotic relationship between the techniques that we use to represent the world and the vision that we attempt to represent with those same techniques: a change in one eventually results in a change in the other. The sudden availability of cheap pigments in flexible metal tubes in the mid-nineteenth century, for instance, allowed the Impressionists to paint quickly out of doors in fleeting light. And face to face with nature, they realised that shadows come in many other colours than shades of grey, which is what the paintings of the previous 'indoor' generations had taught us to see.

Similarly, humble sounds had always been considered the inevitable (and, there-fore, mostly ignored) accompaniment of the visual – stuck like an insubstantial, submissive shadow to the object that caused them. And like a shadow, they appeared to be explained by reference to the objects that gave them birth: a metallic clang was always 'cast' by the hammer, just as the village steeple cast its shape upon the ground.

Prior to Edison's astonishing invention of the phonograph in 1877, it was impossible to imagine that sound could be captured and played back later. In fact, sound was often the prime example of impermanence: a rose that wilted and died right after blooming.

Magically, Edison's discovery loosened the bonds of causality and lifted the shadow away from the object, standing it on its own and giving it a miraculous and some-times frightening autonomy. According to an account in *Ota Benga*, a 1992 book by P. V. Bradford, King Ndombe of the Congo consented to have his voice recorded in 1904 but immediately regretted it when the cylinder was played back: the 'shadow' danced on its own, and he heard his people cry in dismay, 'The King sits still, his lips are sealed, while the white man forces his soul to sing!'

Moore's Law

Neither Richard Portman nor I had any inkling, on that afternoon when he showed me the Window, that the record-breaking success of *The Godfather* several months later would trigger a revival in the fortunes of the film industry in general and of sound in particular.

Three years earlier, in 1969, Francis Coppola had hired me to create the sound effects for, and mix, *The Rain People*. Francis was a recent film-school graduate, as was I, and we were both eager to make films professionally, the way we had made them at school. He had felt that the sound on his previous film (*Finian's Rainbow*) had strug-gled against the bureaucratic and technical inertia at Warner Brothers, and he didn't want to repeat the experience.

He also felt that if he stayed in Los Angeles, he wouldn't be able to produce the inexpensive, independent films he had in mind. So he and a fellow film student, George Lucas, and I, and our families, moved up to San Francisco to start American Zoetrope studios, all tied together with several shoestrings. The first item on the agenda was the mix of *The Rain People* in the unfinished basement of an old ware-house at 827 Folsom Street.

Ten years earlier, this would have been unthinkable, but the invention of the tran-sistor had changed things, technically and economically, to such an extent that it

An old thing becomes new if you detach it from its usual surroundings

seemed natural for the twenty-nine-year-old Francis to go to Germany and buy – almost off the shelf – mixing and editing equipment from KEM in Hamburg and hire me, a twenty-five-year-old, to use them.

Technically, the equipment was state of the art, and yet it cost a fourth of what comparable equipment would have cost ten years earlier. This quartering of price and doubling of quality is familiar to everyone now, after fifty-five years of Moore's Law, but at the time it was astonishing. The frontier between professional and consumer electronics was beginning to fade away. In fact, it faded to the extent that it now became economically and technically possible for one person to do what several had done before, and that other frontier – between sound effects creation and mixing – also began to disappear.

From Zoetrope's beginning, the idea was to try to avoid the divisions that were the byproduct of sound's technical complexity, and that tended too often to set mixers, who came mostly from engineering – direct descendants of the Man Behind the Window – against the editors who created, selected and organised the sounds. It was as if there were two directors of photography on a film, one who lit the scene and another who photographed it, and neither could do much to countermand the other.

We felt that there was now no reason – given the equipment that was becoming available in 1969 – why the person who designed and built the soundtrack shouldn't also be able to mix it, and the director would then be able to talk to one person, the sound designer, about the sound of the film the way he was able to talk to the director of photography about the look of it.

At any rate, it was against this background that the success of *The Godfather* led directly to the green-lighting of two Zoetrope productions: George Lucas's *American Graffiti* and Francis Coppola's *The Conversation*, both with very different but equally adventuresome soundtracks where we were able to put our ideas to work.

Steven Spielberg's *Jaws* (1975) soon topped the box office of *The Godfather* and introduced the world at large to the music of John Williams. The success of *Graffiti* led to *Star Wars* (with music by the same John Williams), which in turn topped *Jaws*. The 70 mm Dolby release format of *Star Wars* revived and reinvented magnetic six-track sound and helped Dolby Cinema Sound increase its influence on film post-production and exhibition. The success of the two *Godfather* films would allow Francis to make *Apocalypse Now*, which broke further ground in originating, at the end of the 1970s, what has now become the standard 5.1 film sound format: three channels of sound behind the screen (left, centre and right), and then left and right surrounds behind

Robert Bresson

the audience, and a separate channel of infrasound low-frequency enhancement. This infrasound is the 0.1 channel in the term '5.1', because it only reproduces a tenth of the frequency range of the other channels.

Metaphorical Audio

Almost all of the technical advances in sound recording, manipulation and exhibition since 1980 can be summed up in one word: digitisation. The effect of digitisation on the techniques and aesthetics of film sound is worth a book in itself, but it is enough to say at this point that it has continued forcefully in the direction of earlier techniques to liberate the shadow of sound and break up bottlenecks whenever they begin to form.

The Window is long gone, and will never return, but the autocratic power that disappeared with it has been repaid a hundred – a thousand – times in creative power: the ability to freely reassociate image and sound in different contexts and combinations.

This reassociation of image and sound is the fundamental pillar upon which the creative use of sound rests, and without which it would collapse. Sometimes it is done simply for convenience (walking on cornstarch, for instance, happens to record as a better footstep-in-snow than snow itself); or for necessity (the window that Gary Cooper broke in *High Noon* (1952) was made not of real glass but from sheets of crystallised sugar; the boulder that chased Indiana Jones was made not of real stone but of plastic foam); or for reasons of morality (crushing a watermelon is ethically preferable to crushing a human head). In each case, our multimillion-year reflex of thinking of sound as a submissive causal shadow now works in the film-maker's favour, and the audience is disposed to accept, within certain limits, these new juxtapositions as the truth.

But beyond any practical considerations, I believe this reassociation should stretch the relationship of sound to image wherever possible. It should strive to create a purposeful and fruitful tension between what is on the screen and what is kindled in the mind of the audience. The danger of present-day cinema is that it can suffocate its subjects by its very ability to represent them; it doesn't possess the built-in escape valves of ambiguity that painting, music, literature, radio drama and black-and-white silent film automatically have simply by virtue of their sensory incompleteness – an incompleteness that engages the imagination of the viewer as compensation for what is only evoked by the artist.

By comparison, film seems to be 'all there' (it isn't, but it seems to be), and thus the responsibility of film-makers is to find ways within that completeness to refrain

---

Accomplish the exceptional. Struggle against that Inquisition which tortures anything that is out of the ordinary

from achieving it. To that end, the metaphorical use of sound is one of the most fruitful, flexible and inexpensive means: by choosing carefully what to eliminate, and then adding back sounds that seem at first hearing to be somewhat at odds with the accompanying image, the film-maker can open up a perceptual vacuum into which the minds of the audience must inevitably rush.

Every successful reassociation is a kind of metaphor, and every metaphor is seen momentarily as a mistake, but then suddenly as a deeper truth about the thing named and our relationship to it. The greater the stretch between the 'thing' and the 'name', the deeper the potential truth.

The tension produced by the metaphorical distance between sound and image serves somewhat the same purpose as the perceptual tension generated by the similar but slightly different images sent by our two eyes to the brain. The brain, not content with this duality, adds its own purely mental version of three-dimensionality to the two flat images, unifying them into a single image with depth added.

There really is, of course, a third dimension out there in the world; the depth we perceive is not a complete hallucination. But the way we perceive it – its particular flavour – is uniquely our own, not only unique to us as a species but, in its finer details, unique to each of us individually, dependent as it is on the variable distance between human eyes. And in that sense it is a kind of hallucination, because the brain does not alert us to what is actually going on. Instead, the dimensionality is fused into the image and made to seem as if it is coming from 'out there' rather than 'in here'.

In much the same way, the mental effort of fusing image and sound produces a dimensionality that the mind projects back onto the screen as if it had come from the image in the first place. The result is that we actually see something on screen that exists only in our minds and is, in its finer details, unique to each member of the audience. We do not see and hear a film, we hear/see/hear/see it.

This metaphorical distance between the images of a film and the accompanying sounds is – and should be – continuously changing and flexible, and it often takes a fraction of a second (sometimes even several seconds) to make the right connections. The image of a light being turned on, for instance, accompanied by a simple click: this basic association is fused almost instantly and produces a relatively flat mental image.

Still fairly flat, but a level up in dimensionality: the image of a door closing accompanied by the right slam can indicate not only the material of the door and the space around it but also the emotional state of the person closing it. The sound of the door in the final shot of *The Godfather*, for instance, needed to give the audience more than the correct physical cues about the door; it was even more important to get a firm, irrevocable closure that resonated with and underscored Michael's final line: 'Never ask me about my business, Kay.'

That door sound was related to a specific image, and it was fused by the audience fairly quickly. Sounds, however, that do not relate to the visuals in a direct way function at an even higher level of dimensionality, and take proportionately longer to resolve. The rumbling and piercing metallic scream just before Michael Corleone kills Sollozzo and McCluskey in *The Godfather* is not linked directly to anything seen on screen, and so the audience is made to wonder at least momentarily, if perhaps only subconsciously, 'What is this?' The screech is from an elevated train rounding a sharp turn, so it is presumably coming from somewhere in the neighbourhood of the restaurant where the murder takes place.

But precisely because it is so detached from the image, the metallic scream works as a clue to the state of Michael's mind at that moment – the critical moment before he commits his first murder and his life turns an irrevocable corner. It is all the more effective because Michael's face appears so calm and the sound is played so abnormally loud. This broadening tension between what we see and what we hear is brought to an abrupt end with the pistol shots that kill Sollozzo and McCluskey: the distance between what we see and what we hear is suddenly collapsed at the moment that Michael's destiny is fixed.

This moment is mirrored and inverted at the end of *Godfather III* (1990). Instead of a calm face with a scream, we see a screaming face in silence. When Michael realises that his daughter Mary has been shot, he tries several times to scream – but no sound comes out. In fact, Al Pacino was actually screaming at the time of filming, but on a whim I removed the sound in the editing and was astonished at the effect. We are dealing here with an absence of sound, yet a fertile tension is created between what we see and what we would expect to hear, allowing the moment to be sustained over many seconds. Finally, the scream that was suppressed when Michael killed Sollozzo, simultaneously killing his dream of a life apart from the family, is let loose after forty years, and the film – as well as *The Godfather* trilogy – is over.

The elevated train in *The Godfather* was at least somewhere in the vicinity of the restaurant, even though it could not be seen. In the opening reel of *Apocalypse Now*, the jungle sounds that fill Willard's hotel room come from nowhere on screen or in the 'neighbourhood', and the only way to resolve the great disparity between what we are seeing and hearing is to imagine that these sounds are in Willard's

When you finish your film you will think, *Now I know how it should have been made.* But you will be wrong

mind: that his body is in a hotel room in Saigon, but his mind is off in the jungle, where he dreams of returning. If the audience can be brought to a point where each member will bridge with their own imagination such an extreme distance between picture and sound, they will be rewarded with a correspondingly greater dimensionality of experience.

The risk, of course, is that the conceptual threads that connect image and sound can be stretched too far, and the dimensionality will collapse.[4] But without risk there is no discovery: the moment of greatest dimension is always the moment of greatest tension.

The question remains: why do we generally perceive the product of the fusion of image and sound in terms of the image? Why does sound usually enhance the image, and not the other way around? In other words, why does King Sight still sit on his throne and Queen Sound patrol the hidden stairways of the palace?

The *Acousmêtre*

In his book *AudioVision*, French film theorist Michel Chion describes an effect that he calls the *acousmêtre*,[5] which depends on delaying the fusion of sound and image to the extreme by supplying only the sound – most frequently, a voice – and withholding the revelation of the sound's true source until nearly the end of the film. Only then, when the audience has used its imagination to the fullest, is the identity of the source revealed. The wizard in *The Wizard of Oz* (1939) is one of a number of examples, along with the mother in *Psycho* (1960) and Hal in *2001*, Wolfman Jack in *American Graffiti* and Colonel Kurtz in *Apocalypse Now*. The *acousmêtre* is – for various reasons having to do with our perceptions – a uniquely cinematic device: the disembodied voice seems to come from everywhere and, therefore, to have no clearly defined limits to its power. And yet . . .

And yet there is an echo here of our earliest experience of the world: the revelation at birth that the song that sang to us from the very dawn of our consciousness in the womb – a song that seemed to come from everywhere and to be part of us before we had any conception of what 'us' meant – that this song is the voice of our mother and that she is now separate from us, and we from her. We regret the loss of former unity – some say that our lives are a ceaseless quest to retrieve it – and yet we delight in seeing the face of our mother; the lost unity is the price paid for the delight.

---

4. Cross your eyes for a quick demonstration of this kind of collapse.

5. *Acousmêtre* could be translated as 'acoustic being' or 'sound creature'.

Walter Murch

This earliest, most powerful and fundamental fusion of sound and image sets the tone for all that is to come.

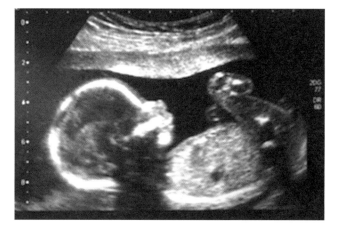

Womb tone with mother's song: https://vimeo.com/911439798 (QR code on left)

19: ODE TO SPO

The Road to *Apocalypse*

Optical Follies

In the late 1960s and early '70s the sound quality of most films, as experienced in the theatre, was virtually identical to how they would have sounded thirty years earlier. *The Godfather* in 1972 was essentially the same as *Gone with the Wind* in 1939. The culprit was the optical soundtrack, the wiggly waveforms running just inside the sprockets on every 35 mm film print.

By 1939 great leaps had been made since the beginning of optical film sound a dozen years earlier, but when World War II broke out, development slowed down, and the Paramount Decree of 1948, divorcing studios from theatre ownership, stifled innovation even further. It also appeared to many engineers that the technical limits of the so-called 'Academy' optical track had just about been reached.[1]

A decade later, in 1948, there was an almost mystical confluence of personalities

---

1. The frequency response of the motion picture optical soundtrack was standardised in 1938 by the Academy of Motion Picture Arts and Sciences (AMPAS).

Jean Cocteau

and technology in the San Francisco Bay Area, with Ray Dolby – a teenager interning with the Ampex Corporation in Redwood City – meeting Major Jack Mullin, who had brought back from Germany, as war booty, a prized Magnetophon tape recorder and fifty reels of IG Farben (BASF) magnetic tape. Their collaboration, along with a $50,000 investment from Bing Crosby, resulted in the birth of the first American tape recorder in 1948, giving an order-of-magnitude improvement in sound quality and flexibility over the existing standards of disc and optical recording. People who experienced tape-recorded sound for the first time were flabbergasted to not be able to tell the difference between the sound of a live event and a tape recording of it. (During World War II, German radio had used this almost holographic clarity to convince the Allies that Hitler was in one city giving a speech, when he was in fact somewhere else entirely.)

Magnetic sound recording revolutionised the behind-the-scenes mixing of cinema sound, giving full fidelity, greater dynamic range and relatively noiseless quality to location recording, editing and mixing. Magnetic stripes could be applied to 35 mm and 70 mm prints for the 1 per cent of films distributed for special roadshow engagements, with three or five channels of sound behind the screen and one of surrounds enveloping the audience in . . .

> . . . amorous Cinemascope, stretching Vistavision and startling Stereophonic Sound, with all your heavenly dimensions, reverberations and iconoclasms![2]

But the humble optical track had to suffice for the other 99 per cent. Despite the backstage improvements in microphones and speakers and newly invented portable Nagra tape recorders, the magnetic soundtrack mix would be embalmed, at the final stage, into the optical format. The frequency range of optical was limited – 60 to 8,000 Hz – giving a range of seven octaves instead of the ten (20 to 20,000 Hz) of magnetic sound and human hearing, and latent system noise or dirt – electronic hiss, crackle and pop – would reveal itself in any quiet scene. As the film print got older, the noise would increase.

I remember bracing myself, in the early 1970s, for the moment when the answer print would come back from the laboratory. We had been straining against the limitations of optical sound, doing what we could in the magnetic 'kitchen', so to speak. But when our films were delivered to the dining room of the optical-track theatres, it was

2. Frank O'Hara, 'To the Film Industry in Crisis' (1957). See https://tinyurl.com/4yfn4kmb (QR code on left).

We rage against materialism, forgetting that there has been no material improvement that has not also spiritualised the world

as if the sound had been shrink-wrapped in plastic packaging, losing texture, 'aroma' and sizzle. It was disappointing, but this was apparently the price that had to be paid to get a film into the theatres. Why was this tolerated?

The great virtue of the optical track for the film industry was its low cost and high speed of manufacture. Thousands of prints could be made automatically in a few days, whereas hi-fi stereo magnetic soundtracks required painstaking 'bespoke' treatment: four to six tracks of liquid magnetic emulsion had to be slowly and carefully applied (striped) onto the print, which then had to dry and cure for a couple of days before the sound could be recorded onto it in real time. Much could go wrong, and when it did, a whole 70 mm reel would have to be scrapped at a cost of a thousand mid-century dollars.

This was a frustrating situation for us in the early 1970s. The culture of the time was saturated with 33⅓ rpm stereophonic long-playing albums of great creativity, dynamism and a full 40–16,000 Hz frequency range, and it was frustrating to have to hitch our soundtrack wagons to the old grey mare of pre-war optical technology. So, as young people will, we Zoetroopers tried to hot-rod as much quality into the old optical track as possible.

By carefully emphasising more of the higher frequencies, we could eke out a bit more clarity in the muffled top end. Dynamic range was another matter: the loudest sounds in the film could be only twice as loud as normal dialogue. The reason for this lay in the architecture of the optical track: the wider the wiggles, the louder the sound, but there was a limit to that width, thanks simply to the real estate allocated to the soundtrack. In a 35 mm release print, picture and sound were crammed into a one-inch (25.4 mm) aperture (leaving 4.8 mm for the sprockets on either side), with optical sound granted a width of 2.8 mm, an eighth of that allocated to picture. Engineers back in the 1920s had determined this was the best compromise, and that was what we were still working with fifty years later.

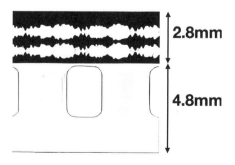

One way around this situation, ironically, stemmed from an unintended consequence of the sorry state of theatre maintenance. Quality control had shifted from
the studios to the individual theatre owners, and even though there were nominal
standards for setting the level of sound in projection, by the early 1970s the decision
was usually left to the judgement of the projectionist. It was a Wild West situation.

Aware of this, we would attempt to outsmart the system by setting the level of the
opening music in our films just a few notches *lower* than full volume, which would
encourage the projectionist to turn the volume control slightly *higher* than normal.
This meant that for those sounds later in the film that we wanted to be as powerful as
possible, there were a few extra notches of amplitude available. This allowed the car
crashes, explosions and other loud sounds in *THX 1138*, *American Graffiti* and *The
Conversation* to have the impact that they did. The price to pay was a proportionate
(slight) increase in the hiss of surface noise, but we felt that it was worth paying. Dick
Portman, the re-recording mixer of *The Godfather*, was complimentary and also a bit
mystified about how we had pulled this off.

Those 'notches' were measured in *decibels* (abbreviated as dB), which are a measure of
sound intensity; a one-decibel shift in loudness is the smallest increment that human
beings can perceive. A sound 6 dB greater than another has twice the sound-pressure
level. The scale starts at zero – the limit of human hearing – and proceeds upwards
from there. Theoretically, there is no upper threshold to the decibel scale, although
death awaits when 200 dB is exceeded. Sperm whales can apparently produce a sound
loud enough to kill a human scuba diver.[3]

The Krakatoa volcano explosion of 1883 produced a sound that was loud enough
to be heard 3,000 miles away. At the weather station in Batavia, 100 miles distant
from Krakatoa, the sound produced a severe 2.5-inch drop in barometric pressure,
which could be translated as the equivalent of 172 dB. 200 dB is powerful enough to
liquefy your brain. Estimates of the level of sound at Krakatoa itself are in the region
of 250–300 dB. Turning the noise down to more familiar levels, as I sit here in London
with the window open on a quiet afternoon of coronavirus self-isolation, the average
decibel level is 45.[4]

3. See https://roaring.earth/sperm-whales-can-vibrate-humans-to-death (QR code on left).

4. This is using the C-weighted scale, which, unlike the A-weighted scale, does not ignore super-
low frequencies.

A physicist is an atom's way of looking at itself

32 dB – very quiet, perceived as almost silence

45 dB – quiet interior

55 dB – refrigerator compressor 1 m distant

65 dB – quiet conversation

75 dB – average sound in the womb; interior of cruising passenger jet

72–8 dB – normal film dialogue, measured from centre of theatre

85 dB – talking forcefully

95 dB – electric drill; shouted dialogue

104 dB – aboard a London Northern Line train coming into Euston Station as its steel wheels rake against a sharp curve in the rails

120 dB – a loud rock concert; can hit the pain level and beyond, depending on how close the listener is to the speakers

160 dB – ruptured ear drums; death after medium to long exposure

200 dB – instant death[5]

By fortuitous coincidence, there is a close alignment between the subjective experience of loudness in decibels and the temperature scale in degrees Fahrenheit:[6]

32°F – freezing

45°F – cold

55°F – beginning to be chilly

65°F – pleasant, but cooler

75°F – the comfort zone

85°F – warm, but can be pleasant under the right circumstances

95°F – hot, but can be sustained for longer

105°F – endurable for brief periods

125°F – painful and damaging

160°F – death after medium to long exposure

200°F – instant death

(I should say that there is no scientific reason for this alignment between the scales of two such very different properties; it is simply an interesting analogy that helps to give a feel for the numbers.)

5. Excruciatingly loud sound is the murder weapon in *The Nine Tailors*, a detective novel by Dorothy L. Sayers.

6. Apologies to readers who are familiar only with the Celsius scale.

Niels Bohr

I had managed to create an expanded dynamic range for both *American Graffiti* and *The Conversation*, and I pushed my luck further with *The Godfather: Part II*, expanding it another couple of decibels, which I thought was appropriate, given the scope of the film, with the violent, noisy Cuban Revolution the set piece at the centre of the story. My monitor setting was turned clockwise 4 dB above normal.

I should have stuck with my *Graffiti* solution.

The mix of *Godfather II* at Zoetrope's Folsom Street studio in San Francisco took six weeks – from October to mid-November 1974 – and went smoothly, although at times it was a twenty-four-hour operation, since the film was three hours and twenty minutes long. We previewed around Thanksgiving and made substantial picture changes, before a second preview in early December. Robert Evans, the head of Paramount, saw the second showing and mentioned how good he thought the film sounded. Everything looked promising for the premiere on 20 December.

Mark Berger, Francis Coppola and Walter Murch during
the mix of *The Godfather: Part II*

Trouble arose after the optical tracks were made. Francis called me at home a week after the mix and said that the dynamic range was proving to be too great. The optical track couldn't take it, nor could some of the hundreds of theatres where the film would be playing. If the theatre monitor was set for dialogue level, the loud sections were deafening, and vice versa, if the loud sections were at the correct level, the dialogue was too low and couldn't be understood.

Character is plot . . . and casting is character

I felt terrible, burning all over with a kind of caustic shame that was made worse because I didn't know exactly what had happened: the previews had been in large theatres with a full audience and had gone well. But we had previewed with the magnetic master, not an optical track.

The next day I took the three-track magnetic master and flew down to Goldwyn Studios in LA, where Dick Portman had mixed *The Godfather* in 1972. We ran *Godfather II* in mixing theatre 'A', and Dick felt that the dynamics were indeed too great. The range between the loudest sounds and the dialogue had to be compressed by 3–4 dB. So we rebalanced the mix at Goldwyn, copying the master and making a whole new magnetic soundtrack, with the dialogue selectively nudged up. Hundreds of prints that had already been made had to be destroyed: it seemed I had driven the Academy optical track beyond what it and the theatres of the time could handle; like hot-rodding a 1939 Buick, black smoke was pouring out of the tailpipe!

The automobile analogy is not entirely specious, because there was another factor in play: the size of the mixing room itself. Re-recording in a small room is like driving a nimble sports car that can accelerate quickly and take corners easily. Mixing in a large one is, acoustically, like driving a family saloon with slightly squishy suspension. The squishiness comes from the greater volume of air: molecules of air are springy things, pushing and rolling against each other like ping-pong balls, and that springiness, in a large room, dampens the ability of the massive volume of air to respond quickly to small signals.

The Zoetrope theatre on Folsom Street was about a third of the size of the mixing theatre at Goldwyn, and to rouse the volume of air there did not take as much acoustic energy at it did at Goldwyn. Dialogue is spoken across the relatively restricted frequency range of the human voice. Music and sound effects, on the other hand – particularly when they are loud – operate continuously across a wide range of frequencies. This energy, like a huge blast from a church organ, can energise and resonate a large volume of air much more easily than the intermittent Morse code-like signals of the human voice. So a small room, thanks to its acoustic nimbleness, can handle a wide dynamic range more easily than a large one; whispers can still be clearly audible. In a large space, the whisper – or any low-level sound – will struggle against the massive volume of air that it has to push against. And not only that: the air-conditioning systems and the physical presence of hundreds of people have to be taken into account. Low-level sounds, therefore, have to be mixed at a higher level than they would be in a small mixing room to overcome a higher noise floor and energise all those cubic feet of air.

F. Scott Fitzgerald

In the end, there is still a lingering mystery about what actually happened on *Godfather II*, but it was probably a four-car collision between the limits of the optical tracks of the time, the size of the mixing room at Zoetrope, the technical state of motion-picture theatres in the pre-Dolby days of the early 1970s and my own hubris. A few years later I was to discover that Stanley Kubrick had experienced a similar Waterloo.

In February 1977, while we were premixing some soundtracks for Fred Zinnemann's *Julia* at EMI-Elstree, I noticed a chinagraph mark on the master monitor-level knob, lower than the louder level of our premix.

'What's that?' I asked Bill Rowe, the lead mixer at EMI-Elstree.

'That's Stanley's mark,' he replied – meaning Stanley Kubrick, who mixed his films with Bill at Elstree. 'Stanley wants his films monitored at a lower level to encourage us to boost the dialogue and keep the loud sounds compressed, reducing the headroom. It's a psychological thing. He was burned by a too-dynamic mix on *Spartacus*, and that mark keeps us in check.' Naturally, it sank in that Kubrick had encountered the same problem in 1960 that had tripped me up on *Godfather II* in 1974. Les Hodgson, who was a sound editor on *Julia* (and later on *Apocalypse Now*), had also worked on Kubrick's *Dr. Strangelove* (1964), and he confirmed that the machine guns in that film – at 88 dB – were only 3 dB (50 per cent) louder than George C. Scott's shouted dialogue.

But did this mean that all films had to be mixed in large rooms, with such compressed dynamics? I was to face this question again, even more pointedly, on *Apocalypse Now*.

Enter the *Apocalypse*

Just as I was pondering these issues regarding dynamics, I received a call from Francis Coppola, asking if I could fly from London to the Philippines for a weekend in early March, as he had some ideas he wanted to discuss about the music and sound format for *Apocalypse Now*. He had also asked editor Richie Marks and sound recordist Richard Beggs to fly in from San Francisco for a meeting with electronic-music composer Isao Tomita, who would be coming from Tokyo.

On 20 March 1977 *Apocalypse* was due to celebrate the first anniversary of the start of principal photography.[7] There had been two month-long breaks in 1976 – one due to the damage caused by Typhoon Olga in May/June, and then a vacation for everybody at Christmas – but Francis thought shooting might be finished in April. At that point, the target release date was Christmas 1977.

7. George Lucas started shooting *Star Wars* on 22 March 1976, two days after *Apocalypse*.

Bring together things that have as yet never been brought together and
did not seem predisposed to be so

I made arrangements to leave London on Thursday 10 March and return on the following Tuesday, but on the 5th Marty Sheen, the star of the film, had a heart attack. Under the circumstances, I thought the last thing on Francis's mind would be a meeting about the sound mix, but he wanted to keep to the plan. So I flew out to the Philippines and was on location in the jungle on Friday the 11th.

Marty was recovering in hospital, but his return was not certain. Shooting continued, with Marty's brother standing in as Willard. The mood was one of white-knuckled gallows humour: this was *the* existential crisis that every film-maker fears, made worse because *Apocalypse* was already over schedule and budget, and Francis had staked his personal fortune as collateral to make up the difference.

Richie and Richard were already there, and once Tomita arrived on the Saturday, we gathered for the meeting. Francis explained that he had heard some beautiful compositions by Tomita in quadraphonic sound and he wanted him to write the music for the film; he also wanted the release format of *Apocalypse* to be quadraphonic. He was excited about the potential of hearing helicopters flying around the theatre in 360°. 'Vietnam is the helicopter war!' he concluded. 'The helicopter is its sound signature.'

It was an astonishing thing to hear under the circumstances: the star of the film was in hospital with a heart attack, the production was facing an existential crisis, and Francis was in the middle of the jungle pursuing a revolutionary idea for the multi-track release of the film, talking to people (me, Richard Beggs, Richard Marks) who had only ever worked with monophonic film.

After the initial excitement, disorientation and terror, my first thought was that four channels was not enough. Quadraphonic meant a speaker in each corner of the theatre; that might be all right for Tomita's music, but dialogue needs its own dedicated speaker in the centre of the screen, not a phantom-centre blend of left and right.[8] So we needed five channels.

'Fine,' Francis said. 'Five channels. Quintaphonic.'

Tomita nodded his approval.

'Where are we going to mix this?' I asked.

Serendipitously, there was one re-recording mixer in the world who had already worked in quintaphonic: Bill Rowe at EMI-Elstree, where I was currently editing *Julia*. He had mixed *Tommy*, directed by Ken Russell, for The Who in 1975, using a Sansui

8. A phantom centre is an audio illusion: the same signal equally balanced from left and right speakers will appear to originate in the midpoint between them. The problem in a large theatrical setting is that the phantom centre will 'pull' to the left or the right, depending on where a spectator is sitting.

Robert Bresson

quadraphonic system modified to quintaphonic by audio engineer John Mosely. I said that I would consult with Bill and talk to Mosely as soon as I returned to London.

'And one more thing . . .' Francis added.

He wanted explosions to be felt as well as heard, to have the frequencies go so low – below the limits of normal human hearing – that they would resonate within the body of the listener, 'so your guts and your lungs would vibrate, even though you might not hear that sound with your ears'.

```
CHEF
Hey, what's that?

WILLARD
Arc light. B-52 strike.

CHEF
Every time I hear that, something terrible happens.

CLEAN
Charlie don't never see 'em or hear 'em. Concussion suck the air outta your
damn lungs.
```

Now I was really excited and doubly terrified, because this meant we had to add yet another track – bringing the total to six – to carry these infrasounds to speakers that hadn't been designed yet; and, once they were built, they would have to be specially installed in every theatre where the film would be playing.

I asked Francis again where we were going to mix.

Coppola and Murch (in background) in the Philippines, March 1977

Keep hold of the threads controlling this enormous and delicate mechanism; suppress all the dust, independent wills, ingenious disorder, then call for action, interrupt suddenly (because of a broken thread) start again and never lose sight of the big picture

'There's a space that used to be a Chinese sweatshop, next to the Little Fox Theatre on Pacific. We can turn that into a mixing room.'

I did a mental calculation: this was the middle of March 1977; Marty Sheen was still in hospital, his condition unknown; there were probably eight weeks of shooting left; Francis was talking about building a beyond-the-state-of-the-art re-recording studio in a former Chinese sweatshop in San Francisco; and the release date was a little over nine months away.

'How big is this sweatshop?' I asked.

A floor plan was unfurled. The space was 20 × 40 × 9 feet, smaller than the studio we had at the old Zoetrope mixing studio on Folsom Street.

I looked over at Richard Beggs, who had seen this space.

'Work has already begun,' he said, with his characteristic deadpan delivery.

To escape the chaos of production, Francis had a little cabin built in the jungle where he could go and work on the script, surrounded by silent trees and squawking birds. After we had all said goodbye to the smiling Tomita and the meeting had dispersed, Francis and I strolled along the quarter-mile path to the cabin. I was overwhelmed by all the ideas that had exploded into reality during this meeting. But I had also learned by now that when life proposes to push you out of your comfort zone, it is usually a good idea to take up the offer. But there was no way that I could supervise any of this preparatory work until I had finished editing and mixing *Julia*, which would be some-time in August. By the time I returned to San Francisco from London, many Rubicons would have been crossed.

Francis and I sat on the porch of his cabin and mulled over these things, staring into the dense foliage enveloping us. From time to time we could hear the saws of set construction singing through the trees. I explained my theories about squishy ping-pong balls of air, the problem of a too-small re-recording studio and what had happened with the mix of *Godfather II*. Francis listened patiently and said that they had asked Massachusetts Institute of Technology-trained architect and acoustician Jeff Cooper to design the room,[9] and I should write to him with my concerns. He thought everything would work out – somehow.

I suddenly recalled the Northpoint Theatre, where we had previewed *American Graffiti* and many other films. It was a classic 1960s single-screen theatre, ten blocks

9. See https://tinyurl.com/399fxue8 (QR code on right).

Jean Cocteau

from Zoetrope, that seated 900 people. I suggested that if we outfitted the Northpoint with the six-track system, we could use it as a real-life laboratory: as soon as we finished mixing a reel, we could walk over and check it at the Northpoint. Francis thought this was a good idea – and it gave him another: 'We could build our own IMAX-type theatre in the centre of the United States, somewhere in Kansas, and the film could play there for ten years. It would have a giant screen and this fabulous sound system. Families would gather from all over to see *Apocalypse*, like they go to Mount Rushmore. The screening would start in the afternoon, play for two hours, break for dinner and discussion, and then everyone back into the theatre for the final three hours.'

Coppola and Murch on location in the Philippines, March 1977

As I was mulling over the prospect of a five-hour *Apocalypse* somewhere on the Kansas–Nebraska border, I noticed a figure walking towards us through the jungle. As it got closer, we could see it was a man dressed in a business suit, carrying a briefcase.

Finally, the suit got close enough that we could recognise the face, and Francis shouted out a greeting:

'Hello, Mike . . .'

It was Mike Medavoy, at that time the head of production at United Artists, the studio that was part-financing *Apocalypse*.

'. . . I guess I'm worth more to you dead than alive.'

Mike continued for a few steps without answering, and then, after a slightly hollow laugh, said:

'Don't be silly, Francis. We're going to get through this.'

An expert is someone who has made all the mistakes that can be made in a very narrow field

Mike was right: Marty did recover, and sooner than expected. I flew back to London on 15 March and had lunch with Bill Rowe the next day. Tomita cabled that he could not write the music for the film because of prior commitments. Marty's first day back on set was 19 April, and filming continued for another four weeks, finally wrapping on 21 May 1977, for a total of 238 days of production. Each day, on average, a mile of film had been shot.

Bill was not encouraging about quintaphonic sound, even though the mix of *Tommy* had gone well under the controlled conditions at Elstree. It was a concert film, so once the general approach to the music had been worked out, things were fairly straightforward. The songs were different, but each reel, sonically, was pretty much like the others. The problems began out in the real world. The idea was to release *Tommy* on 35 mm, with four channels of magnetic sound. Normally, these would be assigned as Left, Centre, Right, Surround (LCRS). Mosely had reconfigured things so that the left track, with Sansui encoding, would supply two channels, sent to the left front and left back speakers. The right track would do the same for right front and right back. Centre would remain centre. The very thin monophonic surround track, barely half a millimetre wide, would stay unused.

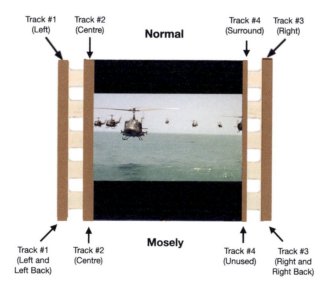

If applying those magnetic stripes and then transferring sound to them was problematic for 70 mm, it was even more so for 35 mm. And out in the field, the maintenance and alignment of magnetic-capable projectors had become increasingly lax in the 1960s and '70s. When The Who tried to get *Tommy* into theatres in 1975, they found that there were logistical problems installing the Sansui decoders, as well as the left back and right back speakers, but even more serious was the condition of the projectors. Much maintenance had been deferred, and there were difficulties in locating spare parts. In the end, on its release only a few theatres were able to play *Tommy* quintaphonically.[10]

Within a couple of years, right around the time of our meeting in the Philippines, the final axe for 35 mm magnetic was about to fall in the form of Dolby four-track optical, which was used by *Star Wars* on its general release on 25 May 1977. And for his 70 mm prints, George Lucas had modified the conventional arrangement by converting two of the five speaker channels behind the screen to so-called 'baby boom', supplying low frequencies only. This gave extra oomph to the explosions and kettledrums, but at the expense of some orchestral definition. One monophonic channel was sent to the surround speakers at the back of the theatre.

These two innovations from the mid-1970s – Dolby four-track optical and 'baby boom' – had already been used on other films, but they were given a rocket boost by the unprecedented success of *Star Wars*, and this changed cinema's sound landscape forever. The public's appetite for innovative sound in theatres was obviously there, and now we had to decide: what system were we going to use on *Apocalypse Now*?

While I was in London, Mark Berger, my co-mixer on *Godfather II*, was hired to work with Jeff Cooper on the design and construction of the Pacific Avenue mix room, and I would check in with him from time to time. The 20 × 40 × 9-foot room was indeed smaller in volume than the Folsom Street studio, but plans were under way to create sound traps and angles that would make it seem acoustically bigger than it was. We hoped. The Northpoint was equipped with film transports and speaker arrays that would duplicate our hoped-for installations out in the real world.

As small as the Pacific mix room was, the machine room was smaller. Under normal circumstances, we would have needed dozens of film transports, but there was room for only seven, including the two six-track film recorders. We decided to take a leap of faith and install two twenty-four-track tape machines and keep them in sync with the film using MiniMag time code.[11] This meant that all the 35 mm magnetic

10. There was a mono release, a conventional unencoded (LCRS) four-track magnetic release and, ultimately, a Dolby LCRS optical release.

11. MiniMag time code was an early 'electronic sprocket' system for synchronisation and editing of audio and videotape (see https://tinyurl.com/38suw4js). The more sophisticated SMPTE time-code system had already been invented, but for some reason we did not use it.

Literature is the only art form in which the audience performs the score

sound would have to be transferred, seven tracks at a time, to the twenty-four-track tape in what we called 'regroupings', using the dbx noise reduction system. There were so many sound elements for the film that a fader-automated twenty-eight-input MCI music mix board was installed and converted to film use. This would be an industry first: so far no film in Hollywood or New York had used, and depended upon, an automated board so extensively. The variables were building up at an astonishing speed.

Tom Scott (right) and Murch in the Pacific Avenue machine room

When *Julia* was completed and I returned to Bolinas in August (Aggie and the four kids had gone back in June), there was an interlude of a couple of weeks. Aggie and I took a vacation into the Sierra mountains, north-east of San Francisco, a break that was marked by the death of Elvis Presley. A week later I joined *Apocalypse* for post-production. Richie Marks, Jerry Greenberg and Dennis Jakob were editing picture, and Richard Cirincione was putting together a sound-editing team. The mixing room was still under construction. I screened what had been assembled – around four hours, minus the final Kurtz compound sequences – and it was clear to me that the December 1977 release date was a mirage. But I had signed aboard the good ship *Apocalypse*. It was a circumnavigation that was to last over two years.

Jerry Greenberg had been working on the Kilgore/'Valkyries' section: a whole film in itself, with fifty hours of material, one and a half times the amount of film shot for the whole of *Julia*. Dennis Jakob was grappling with the Kurtz compound, and Richie Marks was editing everything else. Altogether, the workprint for *Apocalypse* totalled over 230 hours. Around the beginning of September a new release date was set: June 1978. To celebrate this realignment, Francis invited all the editors to lunch at a local Chinese restaurant.

'My goal for the film is that it starts out normal and gets progressively weirder as the boat goes upriver. Anyone who works on this film goes crazy, and the longer they work, the crazier they get. By that logic, I am the craziest, Richie is next, then Jerry. Walter is the most normal because he has only been on the film for a couple of weeks. So I want Walter to edit everything up to Kilgore, then Jerry takes Kilgore, and Richie does the rest up to Kurtz.'

'What about Dennis?' I asked.

'Oh, Dennis has always been crazy, that's why he's working on Kurtz.'

We were each in our own way proud of Francis's evaluation of us and took it all in our stride, although the opening seven and a half minutes, arguably the craziest part of the whole film, kind of defeated the logic of Francis's triage. Or rather, quatrage.

I edited picture for a year, from September 1977 to September 1978. We had two unsuccessful previews during that time. The mirage of a June 1978 release date vanished as we approached it. Jerry left in the spring of that year to work on *Kramer vs. Kramer*, and Dennis departed around the same time. At that point I took on the first half of the film up to the Sampan massacre scene, Lisa Fruchtman started recutting the Hau Phat concert scene, and Richie shouldered everything from Do Lung Bridge to the end.

Dissolve to September 1978, when I dedicated myself to the sound.

There is much (very much) to say about the picture editing of *Apocalypse Now*: the restoration of the idea of Willard's interior voice; Michael Herr joining the team to write that voice; the struggle with the French plantation scene, culminating with it being completely removed; the writing and reshooting (three times) of the CIA's dossier material on Kurtz; the changing of the name of Brando's character from Kurtz to Leighley and back again to Kurtz; and a myriad of other things, small and large – above all, how to compress a five-and-a-half-hour first cut down to a releasable length. But the focus of this chapter has been sound, with a particular focus on dynamics. This will lead to the appearance of Spo, to whom this chapter is dedicated.

Your film: it is born in your head, it dies on the page; it is brought to life during shooting, where it is killed on film; and then resurrected in the editing, where it opens up like paper flowers in water

We gave John Mosely some of our premixes to experiment with, and on his recommendation (as well as that of Richard Beggs) all the equipment at Pacific Avenue was equipped with dbx noise reduction. Some kind of noise suppression was absolutely necessary in those primeval, pre-digital, analogue days, when sounds were copied many times – from tape to film, film to tape, tape back to film, film to film – and if there were no noise suppression, background hiss would accumulate with every copy, building up to a distracting level.[12] Dbx was capable of suppressing 30 dB of tape hiss, an astonishing amount compared to Dolby's multi-band 'A' system at the time, which could suppress 7 dB.[13] (Because of the logarithmic nature of decibels, 30 dB is over fourteen times greater than 7 dB.[14])

Spo

In the end, we were never completely satisfied with Mosely's demonstrations – something always seemed to go wrong – and we were concerned about the dilapidated state of the 35 mm four-track magnetic projectors out there in the world, as well as the problems of installing and maintaining Sansui decoders in every theatre. On the other hand, Dolby processors were installed in many of the top theatres, and the company's offices were just three blocks from Zoetrope. So, in the summer of 1978, we decided to go with Ioan Allen at Dolby and release *Apocalypse* on 70 mm six-track Dolby magnetic prints.

In retrospect, the decision was inevitable, but that we were even considering the Mosely system gives some flavour of the uncertainty of the times. A lingering benefit of that period, however, was that we stayed with dbx noise suppression for all of our internal transfers and premixes, switching over to Dolby only at the final stage of creating the master track for 70 mm. Without question, the clarity of the sound on *Apocalypse* is due to the dbx encoding and noise suppression for

12. See https://en.wikipedia.org/wiki/Tape_hiss (QR code on right).

13. Dolby's 'A' system was a four-band process, more sophisticated than dbx, that could selectively suppress noise in any of four frequency bands, eliminating the 'pumping' of sound in unaffected bands. But it could suppress only 7 dB of noise. Dbx used a sledgehammer single-band approach to suppress 30 dB, but the downside was occasional pumping. We opted for the sledgehammer and dealt with the pumping on an ad hoc basis, when and if it occurred (rarely).

14. Every 6 dB represents a doubling of sound-pressure level, so 30 dB is just under five doublings, since $2^5 = 32$. 7 dB is just over one doubling, $2^{1.16}$, which $= 2.25$. Thus, $32/2.25 = 14.25$.

the many generations of sound transfers and copying that were necessary in those analogue days.[15]

How we were going to get the final soundtrack out into the world was one question. More pressing, when I returned to sound full-time in September 1978, was how to organise the hundreds of sound and music tracks that were being built; how to get a creative handle on this six-track, split-surround format; and how to cope with the hugely increased dynamic possibilities of this format, in a room where the screen was only 15 feet from the mixing desk. My experience with the dynamics on *Godfather II* was still vivid, and I didn't want a repeat.

Enter Spo . . .

Spo

. . . also known by his official name, the Radio Shack SPL (Sound Pressure Level) Meter. Spo is an inexpensive, handheld 'light meter for sound' that was manufactured in the many tens of thousands in the mid-1970s, during the Carter administration, to help enforce workplace sound levels for the Occupational Safety and Health Administration (OSHA). They cost around $25 back then and can still be found on eBay for the same price.[16]

When mixing rooms are lined up technically, a more sensitive and expensive meter is used, positioned at 'ground zero', where the re-recording mixers will be sitting, to confirm that the electronic meters on the mixing board are aligned with the sound levels from the speakers. Lining up is a ritual that happens at least weekly, sometimes daily, to prevent electronic drift. It is a critical process that takes a certain amount of time. No mixing can proceed while this is happening.

Spo first joined our team when we started taking our test mixes from Zoetrope to the Northpoint, which had been modified to duplicate the set-up of our mixing room at Zoetrope: three channels of sound from speakers behind the screen (left, centre, right), two channels of surround sound (left back and right back) and a sixth channel for low-frequency enhancement (LFE). Crucially, we had engaged Meyer Sound

---

15. After *Apocalypse*, Dolby made it a policy that if a film's release used their system, then all of the mixes, premixes and transfers had to use Dolby as well. *Apocalypse* remains the only film ever to combine both systems, dbx and Dolby.

16. Now you can get an app for your smartphone that does the same thing, but without as much character.

If you like this kind of thing, this is the kind of thing you will like

Laboratories in Berkeley[17] to construct custom LFE speakers that would take sound down beyond human hearing into the region of 20 Hz. The Zoetrope mix room and the Northpoint were, at that time, the only cinema facilities in the world equipped with these speakers.

But the Northpoint was still a commercial theatre, of course, and we were only able to rent it for a couple of hours in the morning. It did not have audio metering, so Tom Scott went to Radio Shack one day and came back with the first Spo I had ever seen. It was love at first sight: a small handheld sound meter that was accurate, inexpensive and indestructible – 'Cheap and best', as advertisements in India say. Equipped with Spo, we could play a mix at the Northpoint at a level we felt was right in that big room, which had perhaps sixty times the volume of our mixing theatre, and then check Spo for the decibel reading. Say, for instance, a particular line of dialogue hit a maximum of 81 dB; now, back at Zoetrope, I could sit at the mixing desk (ground zero) and adjust that same line so that Spo also read 81 dB. Now, how did that line of dialogue sound, at that level, in this completely different room? To make it work at the Northpoint, and by extension every big venue, it would need to be at this level. Keep in mind that the mixing desk at Zoetrope was only 15 feet from the screen, whereas I might be sitting 50 or 60 feet away at the Northpoint.

There would be many trips back and forth from Zoetrope to the Northpoint as our premixes began to accumulate. Each time we ran a mix at the Northpoint we would be tuning our ears a little more, acclimatising to the differences between the two rooms, so that eventually, as we mixed in Zoetrope's small room, we could imagine how a certain sound would play (or not) in the real world of theatrical exhibition. Spo was an essential tool in helping us fine-tune that acclimatisation.

Mark Berger, Richard Beggs and I would be working twenty-four-hour days sometimes, constantly exposed to sound levels that OSHA would not approve of, and our ears would become less sensitive as the day (and night) wore on. We would often believe a sound was less loud than it really was, and Spo would offer a corrective opinion.

One noticeable difference between the two rooms arose when we panned (moved) a sound from one of the rear channels to the other, without reference to anything on the screen: a Huey helicopter flyover, for instance, or a mortar shell flying overhead.

17. See https://tinyurl.com/ybnoxkpp (QR code on right).

Abraham Lincoln

The speed of the flyover might sound correct at Zoetrope, but when we heard it at the Northpoint, the sound would simply jump from the left back channel to the right back, without spending any time in the middle. At first we thought something technical had gone wrong, but eventually we realised that it was because the Zoetrope mix room was 20 feet wide, and the Northpoint four times that. We subsequently had to gear down and 'pour molasses' into the panning of certain sounds from one back channel to the other, letting the joystick hover for a while, imagining how it all might sound in a much bigger space.

'Our Friend Algebra'

At three o'clock in the morning mixing a film becomes an otherworldly experience. You are tired but intensely concentrated; there are few distractions, and time simultaneously dilates and contracts; there is a great deal of repetition; you are 'in the moment' and surprised when someone mutters that it is time for breakfast.

Your struggle with destiny continues

It was while in one of these slightly hypnotic states, as I waited twenty minutes for all the elements of a new reel to be loaded, that I began to focus on a cartoon, 'Our Friend Algebra', which Richard Beggs had recently taped to the mix console. It was an early work by a young Roz Chast that had just been published in the *San Francisco Bay Guardian*. It took longer than it should have, given my hypnotised state, but I finally made the connection between that alien creature in the fourth 'D' panel and the Radio Shack SPL meter that was resting a few feet away. That was the moment SPL became Spo, and the name has stuck.

Its inexpensive utility (*Cheap and Best!*) was convincing, and many Spos have found themselves in the hands of re-recording mixers around the world in the decades since *Apocalypse Now*. In 2012 we invited Roz to the annual meeting of us Sound Nerds (official title!) in New York, and Presiding Nerd Larry Blake (sound designer and re-recording mixer for Steven Soderbergh) presented her with honorary membership, thirty-four years after the publication of 'Our Friend Algebra'.

These days every smartphone can download a decibel-meter app that duplicates the attributes of Spo in many ways (but not all!). But you would have to travel back to 1978 – before smartphones, before personal computers even – to understand the love at first sight we felt for Spo. It was portable, indestructible, inexpensive. It did the job that was required, and in ways we didn't understand but definitely felt, it pointed towards the future. A future that in many ways has come to pass.

Dynamic Range

If you imagine a person standing in a room whose ceiling height is, let's say, 8 feet, then the top of that person's head might be 6 feet from the floor and 2 feet from the ceiling. That 2-foot distance is accordingly named *headroom*.

Headroom gives one of the most immediate and visceral impressions when you enter a space. The lower the headroom, the more intimate the room will feel, but if it is *too* low, it will feel oppressive and uncomfortable. And vice versa: with generous headroom it will feel open and expansive, but if it is *too* high, it will feel remote and overbearing, oppressive in a different way. The exact amount of headroom is something that architects spend considerable time pondering. Ultimately, it is determined by the purpose of the room and how intimate or expansive it needs to feel.

When designing a soundtrack, there are close parallels to these architectural issues. The acoustic space of a film – its *dynamic range* – can be designed to feel intimate, oppressive, welcoming, expansive, remote and so on. The dynamic range of a

Jean Cocteau

soundtrack is the equivalent of the total height of the room, from the *noise floor* to the *distortion ceiling*. Every sound system – in fact, every system of whatever kind – has a latent level of system noise, and the floor is the point where information (a signal of some kind) cannot be distinguished from noise. Early sound recorders had a very high level of noise – think of Leon Scott's scratchy carbon-paper recordings from 1860[18] – and over the last 165 years technology has been relentlessly pushing that level down, to the point now where, with digital recording, it is hard to imagine it going much lower.

At the opposite end is the distortion ceiling, where the signal's amplitude is so great that it overwhelms the system's ability to record it accurately. Like the lowering of the noise floor, the distortion ceiling has been progressively raised over the years.

Dynamic range is measured, as you might expect, in decibels. The early optical film soundtracks of the 1920s and '30s had a narrow dynamic range of around 45 dB, which had risen to 58 dB by 1939. Vinyl LP recordings of the 1950s pushed it to 65 dB, which was roughly what was reached by cassette tapes with Dolby 'B' processing in the 1980s. A sixteen-bit digital recording today can attain 95 dB; twenty-four-bit, 192 Hz digital recordings might be capable of 110 dB.

Human hearing itself has a dynamic range of 120 dB, from the perception of absolute silence at 0 dB, where the noise of blood flow is louder than any external sound, to the threshold of pain (distortion of the eardrums) at 120 dB. Just as the introduction of a human figure into an architectural space helps us to evaluate and define that space, the introduction of the human voice into a soundtrack helps to establish the proportions and scale of that acoustic space.

Which returns us to the concept of headroom. The 'sweet spot' or 'comfort zone' for dialogue in a film hovers at around 75–77 dB, with excursions up into the low 80s and down into the high 60s (notice, again, how closely this mimics the comfort zone for temperature in degrees Fahrenheit). In a theatre, this level is comfortable, without the listener having to strain (if it is too low) or feel pressured (if it is too high). Perhaps not coincidentally, the average sound level in the womb, to which the developing foetus is sensitised, is 75 dB. We re-recording mixers are constantly nudging whispers up and compressing loud yelling down into this zone. You will happily listen to an explosion at 100 dB, but a voice at that level is intolerable.

Because of the narrowness of this sweet spot, the dialogue in a movie provides

18. Leon Scott's recordings from 1860: https://www.youtube.com/watch?v=-0H8Q4QD-cM (QR code on left) .

How do you know what you know until you see what you say?

the reference 'spirit level' for the rest of the film's sound. It is somewhat similar to the role that skin tone plays in image colour correction. If skin tone, on the one hand, and dialogue level, on the other, are correctly rendered, then it is likely that everything else will fall into place around them. This is why the first premix that we re-recordists make is the dialogue. It is the spine on which everything else in the mix depends.

Scalar headroom is the term I am going to propose to describe the range from this 'spirit level' of average dialogue to the distortion ceiling of the medium in question.[19] Using this definition, Academy optical had a scalar headroom of about 13 dB (from 75 to 88 dB). This was a frustratingly low ceiling for us at Zoetrope back in the early 1970s, and I kept trying to break through it, until I blundered too far with the initial mix of *The Godfather: Part II*.

In addition, the noise floor of a theatre, with air conditioning and an audience in the hundreds, is greater than that of a piece of film analysed in the laboratory – or, in fact, the noise floor of a mixing studio, which is an abnormally quiet place. To give us a reality check, we took Spo and a recorder to the Northpoint and captured the sound when the theatre was full of people sitting in the air-conditioned space, waiting patiently for a film to begin. We called this our 'popcorn loop', and we had it available to play into the monitors of the mix when there was a question about whether a sound was too low to register out in the real world.

The fairy-tale, watch-out-what-you-wish-for situation with *Apocalypse Now* arose thanks to the powers of six-track 70 mm magnetic sound, Meyer LFE speakers, dbx and then Dolby noise suppression, which granted us a scalar headroom of 37 dB. This amount of headroom and frequency range enabled the very loudest of our sounds (at 112 dB) to have more than sixteen times the sound-pressure level allowed with Academy optical tracks (88 dB). Spo was getting a workout.

For the loudest sounds, like the napalm explosion, much of that energy was in the ultra-low infrasound region around 20 Hz, which was carried by the Meyer speakers. Experiencing this was extremely exciting for all of us – it was the first time this frequency range, in a tuneable speaker, had been available for a film – and we

---

19. I am deviating from the technical orthodoxy about headroom. It is defined as the distance in decibels from the *nominal level* of an operating system, its most efficient operating level, to the point where distortion becomes unacceptable. The nominal level would usually be 7–10 dB above the average dialogue level.

Graham Wallas (paraphrased)

were immediately aware of its revolutionary potential.[20] Having the ability to steer sounds 360° around a theatre was thrilling, but being able to extend the frequency range down another octave and a half was perhaps even more impressive in its impact on music and sound. The problem was that we had to figure out how to use this dynamic range judiciously, to hint at its existence occasionally, like the presence of a bear lurking in a cave, and then, at certain places, let it loose.

Quintaphenia

The amount of work needed to supply *Apocalypse* with the sound effects and atmospheres required to fill out the entire five-channel acoustic space of the film was overwhelming. This situation was particularly intense because the quality of 95 per cent of the dialogue recorded in the Philippines was compromised by pervasive motor sounds, to the extent that it was not suitable for the final mix.[21] But it was usable as a guide track for the eight weeks of ADR[22] dialogue we recorded with the actors in studio, supervised by Leslie Schatz. This meant that almost every sound in the film had to be recorded separately, from footsteps to lines of dialogue to napalm explosions and everything in between. This all had to be transferred to 35 mm magnetic film, edited by an army of sound editors, led by Richard Cirincione, Les Hodgson, Les Wiggins and Pat Jackson, into hundreds of reels – Dennie Thorpe drawing out acres of beautiful cue sheets for all of this – before regrouping the magnetic film to twenty-four-track tape and then premixing before the final mix could get under way.

Not only was it overwhelming, I also felt it would be counterproductive. We would do all this work, and the audience would acclimatise to it and accept it as 'normal', when it was anything but. We humans (and other animals as well) come to accept almost any new situation as normal relatively quickly, but once we are acclimatised,

20. There had been Sensurround in the early 1970s, but this was a fixed on/off low-frequency 'buzzer' signal that would kick in for earthquakes, explosions and other similar events.

21. The reason for the problem with location recording on *Apocalypse* did not have anything to do with the professionalism of Nat Boxer, who had worked with Francis on many previous films. It was Francis's decision to place his actors in real helicopters and in the patrol boat with its exposed diesel engine. The only two major scenes in which location recording predominated were the Nha Trang briefing, where Willard is given his mission, and large parts of Kurtz's monologue at the end.

22. Automated Dialogue Recording, also known in an earlier incarnation as 'looping'. It involves asking the actors to come to a studio and re-record their lines of dialogue in sync with the film of their original performance. See Chapter 24, 'Duality of the Soul', for an in-depth analysis of this process.

we become particularly sensitive to a change from that new normal. AM and FM radio, for example, have very different 'sound envelopes'. AM is mostly monophonic and has a highly compressed dynamic range and reduced frequency response (it actually resembles the Academy optical response fairly closely). FM radio, by contrast, is in stereo, is less compressed and has an extended frequency response. If you listen to an AM station for a certain length of time, your perceptions adjust to that reality; you normalise it, mentally filling in for its deficiencies. But when you switch from AM to FM, you suddenly appreciate the differences; there is an opening up because there is more information, and the subconscious filling-in no longer needs to occur. We tend to be most alert at moments of transition.

What I proposed for *Apocalypse*, and what we carried out, was to vary the sonic envelope of the film according to the flow and content of the sequences, and consequently to emphasise the transitions. Some sequences would be monophonic, some would be three-track (LCR) stereo and some would be full quintaphonic. In each case, there would be a full frequency response, with engagement of the LFE channel where appropriate, but the spatial engagement and the dynamic range would shift as the story moved from one 'room' of the film to the next. I drew diagrams for each reel to illustrate the variance, with music and sound effects not necessarily operating in sync with each other.

I hoped this would have two positive effects. On a practical level, it would reduce the workload for the sound editors because they could now concentrate on what was needed most. If a proposed sequence was in mono, they would not have to prepare stereo tracks for it, let alone quintaphonic. The second benefit was aesthetic: the audience would have the feeling, largely felt subconsciously, of moving from one sonic 'room' to another, like moving through the chambers, corridors and halls of a complex architectural space. My goal was to align these sonic environments to the dramatic content of each sequence, so that the contrast between these spaces would be most strongly felt at the moments of transition. For example, Willard alone in the cabin of the boat, at night, studying the Kurtz dossier by flashlight, would be monophonic. As the boat approached the Hau Phat amphitheatre and loading dock, the sonic envelope would expand to stereo, and then as the *Playboy* helicopter came in to land, the envelope would further expand to quintaphonic with the flyovers of the two escort helicopters.[23]

23. That sequence can be viewed at https://vimeo.com/426194328 (QR code on right).

Kim Stanley Robinson

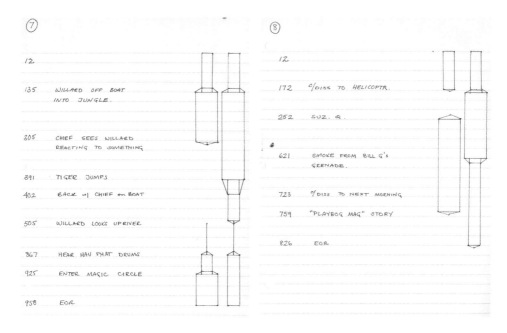

⑦

12	
135	WILLARD OFF BOAT INTO JUNGLE.
305	CHEF SEES WILLARD REACTING TO SOMETHING
391	TIGER JUMPS
402	BACK w/ CHIEF on BOAT
505	WILLARD LOOKS UPRIVER
867	HEAR HAU PHAT DRUMS
925	ENTER MAGIC CIRCLE
958	EOR

⑧

12	
172	c/DISS TO HELICOPTR.
252	SUZ. Q.
621	SMOKE FROM BILL G's GRENADE.
723	c/DISS TO NEXT MORNING
759	"PLAYBOG MAG" STORY
826	EOR

Above are two of those diagrams, covering reels 7 and 8 (Willard and Chef in the 'tiger' jungle through to leaving Hau Phat the next morning). I distributed this 'road map' for all sixteen reels to the post-production sound crew in the autumn of 1978. The numbers on the left are 35 mm feet, the vertical diagrams on the right are for music (left) and sound effects (right). The widest rectangle represents quintaphonic, the narrower rectangle is stereo and the single line is monophonic.

Did we stick religiously to these diagrams? No. These were drawn speculatively two months before we started the mix, and they didn't take into account some of the discoveries we would make along the way about the new format we were working with; in addition, there were changes to the picture between September 1978 and the film's premiere in August 1979. But if we may not have adhered to every single diagram, we did follow their outlines, and more often than not these fluctuating shapes do reflect the shifting sonic envelopes of the finished film.

One significant change to *Apocalypse* between these diagrams and the final mix was the elimination of a two-minute sound-only overture. Work was started on this but, in pursuit of a shorter running length, the idea was abandoned sometime between September and December 1978. What does survive, however, is the handwritten initial treatment I wrote for it, which is reproduced on the next page.

Some sound ideas from this overture also survived, but they were telescoped into the opening seven-and-a-half-minute sequence of Willard wrestling with his demons

When a sound can replace an image, cut the image, or neutralise it

in his Saigon hotel room. The 'bat-like' sound turned into what we called the 'ghost helicopter', which was created by Richard Beggs. Those quadraphonic jungle sounds appeared in the second, 'darker' section of the opening, where Willard muses about waking up back in the jungle.

As we neared the completion of the film, Francis asked me what I thought my credit should be. I was not the sound effects supervisor; that was Richard Cirincione's job. I was the lead re-recording mixer and one of the picture editors. But the strategical planning for the design of this new system, and then how to shape the sounds for it, seemed to me to resemble the work of production designers, who create three-dimensional spaces and then fill them with interesting and colourful detail. I had been given the three-dimensional shape of the theatre and was then charged with filling it with interesting and colourful sound shapes.

So I proposed *sound design* to Francis, and that is what it became.

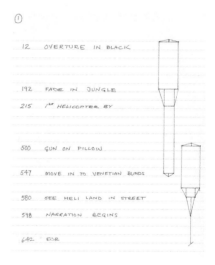

Opening –

Begin with Quad air – slowly open up the sounds of the jungle one by one, locating them in various positions around the room. Emerging out of this, is one particular sound that then moves around – flying around the room – as it flies it starts to change character, becoming more nightmarish and the other sounds of the jungle start to fade and melt away. All we are left with is this one sound flying around the room, becoming more and more bat-like in the dark: it disappears – the picture fades on – silence – then we hear it again, o.s., and finally it concretizes in the form of one of the dream helicopters.

The *sound* picks up the essence of the jungle – flying jungle that turns into helicopter!

throbbing element in the dark that becomes the fan.

Quintaphonic diagram for reel 1, *Apocalypse Now*. All ten quintaphonic diagrams for the first half of the film can be found at https://vimeo.com/426513852 (QR code on right)

This Throbbing Element

Like helicopters and steam trains, certain objects generate a rich spectrum of different sounds as they move through space. A diesel train or a car, not so much. A steam train in the distance might only be audible through its whistle and a distant chuffing, but as it gets closer, you begin to hear the clanking of the metal, joined by the plunging pistons, the hiss of steam and the grinding of wheels on rails. When it passes, there is a lovely lowering of frequency – the Doppler effect – and as it chuffs away into the distance a completely different spectrum is revealed, sometimes accompanied by an incongruous tinkling as the tracks reset themselves.

The sound components of helicopters, similarly, are revealed one by one: first, the distant thump of the blades, then the whine of the turbines, the nervous high-frequency 'skeeting' of the rotors, increased thumping, the vertical tail blades with their own harmonic whine, the Doppler shift, and finally the unravelling of a different spectrum as they all recede. To create the ghost helicopter sound, Richard Beggs ana-lysed those sounds, referencing *Apocalypse*'s extensive recordings of Huey helicopters, and then approximated each of these elements electronically on a Moog synthesiser. The goal was to assemble a kind of audio Lego kit, a virtual helicopter made up of nothing but electronic signals that would sound real when we fitted them all together, but which we could then disassemble into their 'ghostly' components. The first sound in the film is one of those: *whop, whop, whop* – an abstraction of the blade.

When it comes to moving sounds from one channel to another – panning from left to right, for example – I believe that it is good to start in the neutral zone of the centre speaker when a sound first becomes audible and, as it gets louder, move to the theoretical location of the source, then pan with the object (a car, a helicopter) at peak volume as it moves across the screen, hold at its vanishing point as the level begins to drop, and then just before it disappears completely return to the neutral centre zone as it fades away.

I had all this in mind as we were mixing the opening with that first synthesised ghost helicopter, but at the last minute I decided to reject my own advice and start the ghost helicopter in the right rear channel. It was a way of demonstrating, from the very beginning, the capabilities of this new sound system we were debuting with *Apocalypse Now* – a system, since dubbed 5.1, which has now become the standard for all film sound mixes.

Ziegfeld Follies

At the beginning of August 1979 we were mixing around the clock to meet the dead-line of 15 August, when *Apocalypse* was set to premiere at the Ziegfeld Theatre in New York. The film was spread out over sixteen ten-minute reels, and as we completed each

We are double-edged blades, and every time we whet our virtue,
the return stroke sharpens our vice

one we would send it down to Los Angeles, to what was then Goldwyn Studios, to be 'sounded' (transferred) onto the corresponding 70 mm reel of picture, which had already been colour-corrected, printed and striped with magnetic oxide.

When the last reel was finally sent on its way to Goldwyn, I had been awake for thirty-six hours. I blundered into a small office at Zoetrope that was equipped with mattresses and fell onto one of them. I slept for twenty-four hours – the longest sleep I have ever 'enjoyed' – and on waking was told that the last 70 mm reel had been shipped to the Ziegfeld to join the others. It was the afternoon of 14 August.

Twenty-four hours later, I was in New York, clutching my trusty Spo and sitting alone in the Ziegfeld for a test run of the entire film. The theatre's layout was very different from the Northpoint's. It was narrow and long; the Northpoint was wide and shallow; both held approximately the same number of spectators. How was this going to affect the sound? It was 3.30 p.m., and the premiere was at seven that evening. The film was two hours and thirty-five minutes long. Or so I thought.

The lights went down. The jungle faded up. The opening *whop, whop, whop* of the helicopter was in the right back channel, where it should be. According to Spo, it was playing at the correct level. I relaxed slightly. It was an emotional moment, to be sitting there, watching the film that we had all worked on for many years unspooling in 70 mm in New York. It looked great. Jim Morrison began to sing 'This is the end . . .', and I felt a tingling, which was not entirely pleasant.

This is the end, my friend . . .

Willard woke up from his nightmare and looked at the ceiling fan. He went to the window and stared out at the street. 'Saigon . . .' he said. My tingling suddenly turned into a three-alarm version. 'Shit . . . I'm still only in Saigon,' Willard continued. Except his voice had a Donald Duck quality to it. There was something wrong . . .

Or was there? These reels had been checked at Goldwyn before being sent to New York. Was I going crazy? I had flown in on a red-eye from San Francisco. Was it the lack of sleep? Willard continued his meditations. There was definitely something wrong. And then it hit me: the film was running too fast.

I burst into the projection booth. The two projectionists smiled at me. 'Is this projector running at the correct speed?'

'Yes, this is how it always runs,' one of them said.

I went back down to the theatre and listened again. Willard was complaining that 'Every minute I stay in this room I get weaker,' and he was still using his Donald Duck voice.

Henry David Thoreau

'This projector is not running at twenty-four frames a second, is it?'

The chief projectionist shook his head, slowly.

'No, it's running at twenty-five frames a second.'

I felt great relief that I wasn't going crazy and that the problem was with the Ziegfeld projector, not the film. But then there was a resurgence of that three-alarm tingling, with the lines already beginning to form outside the theatre.

'Why is it running at twenty-five frames a second?'

'These are Zeiss projectors – European projectors we imported through Montreal. Europe runs at twenty-five frames a second.'

'Well, change it! This is America! Turn the switch. Make it twenty-four frames.'

'There is no switch.'

Fred Roos, the producer of *Apocalypse*, poked his head in.

'How's it going?'

Willard was echoing my thoughts: 'I was going to the worst place in the world, and I didn't even know it yet.' Fred didn't notice that Willard's voice had a Donald Duck edge to it.

'We're adjusting the speed of the projectors,' I said.

The chief projectionist took out a screwdriver and waved it at the projector like a magic wand.

Fred smiled. 'There are already two hundred people outside,' he said, and he went downstairs to see if even more had gathered.

The fiddling with screwdrivers continued, and I went back down to watch the film, as Colonel Kurtz's voice assured me, 'That's my dream. That's my nightmare. Crawling, slithering, along the edge of a straight razor. And surviving.'

A couple of Ziegfeld employees were standing at the back of the theatre to watch. Could they tell there was something wrong? Did they know about the twenty-five frames a second?

Tom Sternberg, another producer, sat down next to me. 'It looks great!' he said. I waited for him to ask about the sound. 'And it sounds great, too!' was his unprompted evaluation. No one except me seemed bothered by the 4 per cent increase in speed.

I went back upstairs to the booth. The screwdrivers had been put away, and both projectionists were glued to their windows, watching Willard as he was being told to 'terminate with extreme prejudice'.

'How's it going?' I asked, knowing the answer.

'There's nothing we can do. It's always been this way.'

It is sometimes the flattest and dullest parts that have in the end the most life

Fred reappeared. 'We have to start letting people in.'

This was one of those moments when it was clear what was going to happen, and what was going to happen was something that in my wildest nightmares I would never have anticipated: *we are going to premiere this film, the end product of years of work by hundreds of people, at twenty-five frames per second.*

'Let them in,' I said.

The projectionist turned off the projector and unthreaded the reel to rewind it. I went down and watched as the crowd took their seats, buzzing. I was despondent.

Francis was suddenly alongside me, watching them. 'How was the check screening?'

'It's going to run at twenty-five frames per second.'

'Oh, like in Europe,' he said, unflustered. I found some solace in his composure at a time like this. We took our seats.

The lights went down. The jungle faded up. *Whop, whop, whop* from the right back channel. Spo's needle fluttered to the correct setting. The film was launched. I sat there, listening to the dialogue and the music, which had been pitched up 4 per cent by the Zeiss projectors. It was excruciating. Until it wasn't. To my amazement and shame, I *acclimatised* to this new and inevitable reality. Spo's needle danced; the dialogue was at the sweet spot, the sound effects also. The napalm explosion hit 112 dB. The Meyer speakers were working. Spo was happy, stretching his three legs as he ran around this new track, so I guess I had to be happy, too.

And two hours, twenty-one minutes and twenty seconds later it was over. Five minutes and forty seconds had been squeezed out of the running time by the muscles of those Zeiss projectors.

The 70 mm prints had no titles or credits, either at the beginning or the end. Francis had designed the 70 mm experience to be like live theatre – an echo of the pipe dream of that single IMAX-like 'Mount Rushmore' theatre in Kansas – so programmes had been printed and distributed to the audience. There was a silence at the final fade-out as the Ziegfeld was drowned in quintaphonic rain. I can't remember if there was applause or not. I was in a daze.

Robert Bresson

There was a cast and crew party afterwards. Everyone was happy. No one mentioned the six minutes or the Donald Duck voices.

Two days later, *Apocalypse* opened in Los Angeles at the Cinerama Dome, where it ran at twenty-four frames per second. Some people who attended that screening said it was a life-changing experience. Chalk that up to those extra six minutes and twelve seconds.

The Ziegfeld had opened for business in 1969 with those same Zeiss projectors, and they ran reliably at twenty-five frames per second for thirty years, until they were retired in 1999. Every film that was shown at the Ziegfeld had 4 per cent shaved off its running time, and its music and voices pitched up by the same amount. The management saved over 3,000 hours during those three decades, time that could now be spent selling popcorn.

There is an old saying in Hollywood that the projectionist has the final cut. At the Ziegfeld, he had the final mix as well.

The Ziegfeld Theatre

The real sound is always false. It must be reinvented, translated into another sound more precise than the original

20: BECAUSE YOU DON'T LISTEN!

Thoughts on the Sound of *Barton Fink*

I wrote the following essay on the Coen brothers' Barton Fink *for Stephen Deutsch and Larry Sider's book* The New Soundtrack. *I include it here, with permission, as an example of a close appreciation of sound design by someone (me), a sound designer himself, who admires not only Skip Lievsay's work but also the leading role, and the space, sound is granted in the screenplay.*

It is curious – even mysterious – that the evocative nouns *glance, stare, gaze, peek, glimpse,* etc. have no equivalent in sound: the *act of gazing* is *a gaze*, the *act of staring* is a *stare*, but the *act of listening* is . . . well, there isn't a word for it in English, let alone a couple of dozen.

And yet we pause and listen attentively to the world around us dozens, sometimes many dozens, of times a day – often with greatly heightened emotion. Our lives may even depend on it: *What was that?* and we are on pins and needles. Relief: *It was only the wind!* Or ecstasy: *The lover's key in the lock!* Or dread: *Someone is laughing mirthlessly in the next room . . .*

As in language, so in film. Every motion picture is full of looks, glances, stares, gazes, glimpses – cinema would be inconceivable without them – but there are many films, full of sound, in which the characters *do not listen.* More precisely: in which we do not see the characters listening.

And then there is Joel and Ethan Coen's *Barton Fink.*

BARTON hits a small silver bell next to the register. Its ring-out goes on and on without losing volume.

After a long beat there is the dull scuffle of shoes on stairs. Barton, puzzled, looks around the empty lobby, then down at the floor behind the front desk.

A TRAP DOOR
It swings open and a young man in a faded maroon uniform holding a shoe-brush and a shoe – not one of his own – climbs up from the basement.

Jean Cocteau

He closes the trap door, steps up to the desk, and sticks his finger out to touch
the small silver bell, finally muting it.

The lobby is now silent again.

This delicately surreal moment, ten minutes into the film, is followed a minute
later by another gentle dislocation of sound: the cheap lithograph of a bathing beauty
on the wall of Barton's room is accompanied by its 'soundtrack' of surf and seagulls.
Barton (and the audience) have been put on alert: pay attention to the sounds – here
at the Hotel Earle (*A Day or a Lifetime*) the usual laws do not apply.

Judging by the crowded ranks of shoes left out in the hallway for shining, Barton's
621 appears to be the only room available. But we meet only one of these other guests:
the affable (and affably named) Charlie Meadows, and our first 'glimpse' of him is that
muffled mirthless laughter:

A PILLOW
As Barton's head drops down into frame against it.

He reaches over and turns off the bedside light.

He lies back and closes his eyes.

A long beat.

We hear a faint hum, growing louder.

Barton opens his eyes.

HIS POV
A naked peeling ceiling.

Laugh at a bad reputation. Fear a good one that you could not sustain

The hum – a mosquito perhaps – stops.

BARTON
His eyes move this way and that.

After another silent beat we hear – muffled, probably from an adjacent room – a brief dying laugh. It is sighing and weary, like the end of a laughing fit, almost a sob.

Silence again.

We hear the rising mosquito hum.

FADE OUT.

The tense, mosquito'ed mystery of Barton's first night at the Earle is reprised and intensified in the days and nights that follow: the isolation of his seedy room makes Barton (and the audience) hyper-sensitive to those sounds that filter through the walls on either side – energetic lovemaking from room 619, mirthless laughing/sobbing from 623, repetitive thudding from 721 directly above (*is* there a seventh floor to the Hotel Earle?) – as well as tiny sounds within the room itself – the hum of mosquitoes; the gurgling of the drains; the suck of the hallway wind; the sticky, adhesive-giving-way *gaak* of peeling wallpaper.

Barton's only defence is the occasional fusillade from his Underwood: the *smack–smack–smack* of the typewriter keys obliterates all other sounds. But these outbursts are pathetically intermittent (writer's block) and the silence quickly floods back, bearing the spume of those muffled room-next-door sounds so distracting to the life of the mind.

These episodes of intense, wordless listening – Barton alone in his room at the Earle, head cocked, eyes darting – alternate with scenes of volcanic, lop-sided loquacity – Barton's meetings with executives Lipnik and Geisler at Capitol Studios; his encounters with the Faulkneresque writer/souse W. P. Mayhew (whom we first meet through the *gurgling rush* of his vomit); and the visits Charlie Meadows pays to room 621.

Charlie, Barton's next-door neighbour from 623, not only looks and acts like a blood-relative of Wallace Beery – the mooted star of Barton's barely begun 'wrestling' screenplay – but as it turns out is an expert wrestler himself. *I could tell you some stories*, he eagerly proffers, three times; but Barton is oblivious, even dismissive:

Robert Bresson

Thanks, Charlie, you can help by just being yourself. Later, Charlie demonstrates some wrestling moves, but Barton – flattened in a half-second by Charlie's swift bulk – says he is not interested in *the act itself.* Finally, Charlie thumps his chest and overtly proposes: *Make* me *your wrestler. Then you'll lick that story of yours!* If Barton had his wits about him, he would have simply picked up his pencil, let Charlie tell those stories, and his troubles with the screenplay would be over.

While the film's sound effects – created by sound supervisor Skip Lievsay – have been expertly priming Barton (and us, the audience) to listen to everything with microscopic and paranoid intensity, at these crucial moments Barton *does not listen*; locked in his intellectual hot-house reverie of a theatre for the common man (*the hopes and dreams of the common man are as noble as those of any king!* he tells Charlie) Barton remains oblivious to the hopes and dreams of the common man whom fate has obligingly set down right in front of him.

These are serious but not yet fatal mistakes: Charlie doggedly keeps up his offers of condolence and help after each of Barton's increasingly catastrophic meetings with Lipnik and Geisler.

Things take a murderous turn, though, when Barton reaches the breaking-point with his screenplay and finally calls out for help – not to Charlie but to Audrey Taylor, the mistress/secretary of creatively spent *littérateur* Bill Mayhew (*I just like making things up*). Audrey comes to Barton's room, takes him in hand, one thing leads to another and the breath and bed-springs of their lovemaking are suctioned down the washbasin drain into the resonant plumbing of the Hotel Earle (*Seems like I hear everything that goes on in this dump*, Charlie had mentioned to Barton earlier. *It's the pipes or something.*)

Barton, woken next morning by the hum of a mosquito, discovers that Audrey has been ripped apart sometime during the night: her corpse, lying beside him, is wrapped in blood-soaked sheets.

From this seemingly inexplicable moment, Barton's story careens into its death spiral, crashing through several metaphysical sound-barriers along the way, until he is left metaphorically and literally beached, watching with stunned fascination the cheap bathing-beauty lithograph come to life, while beside him sits a box wrapped in brown paper containing (most likely) the head of Audrey Taylor.

On our way down the spiral, we are treated to the sound/images of Barton shaking the paper-wrapped box Charlie had given him and hearing clearly – thanks to a brief *luftpause* in Carter Burwell's music – the dull *thuddle* of a roundish object weighing perhaps slightly more than nine pounds . . .

You must live in another world, where time and place are all yours: without newspapers, letters, telephone – without any contact with the outside world

. . . of Barton finally speed-typing his screenplay (*Burlyman*) with cotton stuffed in his ears, now truly oblivious to any sound or influence from the outside world (*This is my uniform!* he later yells at a crowd of servicemen at a dance, pointing at his head) . . . of little involuntary peepings coming from Barton's throat as he sits beside Audrey's corpse, the music again obliging with several well-timed *luftpausen*.

There is only one theme in Burwell's beautiful and creepy music for *Barton Fink*: it is stated over the opening credits, but not heard again, except in judiciously parceled-out fragments (usually at scene transitions) until the extended sequence of Barton writing the first draft of *Burlyman* three quarters of the way through the film. Prior to that, most scenes play without music. Which has the effect of making us (and Barton) listen more intently. Lievsay's carefully designed sound effects, heard without the safety-net of emotional colour that music inevitably brings, have a vivid clarity that rubs up against the image like static electricity.

The musical theme returns again for the murderous standoff between Charlie (in his 'Madman Mundt' mode) and the two LAPD detectives Mastrionotti and Deutch. Set against a hellish background of flames which burn but do not consume, Charlie dispatches the two detectives with blasts from his shotgun, and then liberates Barton, whom Deutch had handcuffed to his bloody bed-frame. Sobbing with relief and fear, at his wit's end, Barton pleads the existential question: *But Charlie, why? Why me?* and Charlie, world-weary at the foibles of humanity, gives the existential response:

```
CHARLIE
Because you DON'T LISTEN!
```

Jean Cocteau

And if he had? What if Barton had listened to Charlie's stories with the same focused attention he paid to the thumping from room 721 or the lovemaking from 619? In a film about listening and the creative process, which shouts: *LOOK UPON ME! I'LL SHOW YOU THE LIFE OF THE MIND!* and yet is metaphysically agile enough to surround its characters with flames and have them only complain about the heat – it has to be asked: Was it inevitable that Charlie would turn out to be Madman Mundt?

Maybe not. If Barton had let Charlie tell his stories, perhaps he would have remained Mr. Meadows after all; and perhaps Barton, inspired by those stories, would have written his screenplay; and then the move from New York to Hollywood would have kept Barton connected to *the wellspring of the common man*; and Lipnik would have green-lit *Burlyman*; and Barton would have been the Toast of a New Town.

But of course Barton *didn't listen*, and we have instead a parable of the terrible revenge exacted by the ignored and enraged Idea, who arrives fortuitously to help us in the midst of our creative struggles and to which our sense of self-importance often makes us deaf; and the betrayal felt by that Idea; and the consequently horrendous price to be paid, both by us, by those around us, and strangely enough by the disappointed Idea itself, returning dejected to its pathetic home (*A Day or a Lifetime!*) in the midst of eternal flame and torment.

21: DENSE CLARITY/CLEAR DENSITY

Encoded and Embodied Sound and the Rule of Two and a Half

Simple and Complex

One of the deepest impressions made on someone who happens to wander into a film sound-mixing studio is that there is no necessary connection between ends and means. Sometimes, to create the natural simplicity of an ordinary scene between two people, dozens and dozens of soundtracks have to be created and seamlessly blended into one; at other times an apparently complex 'action' soundtrack can be created with just a few carefully selected elements. In other words, what it took to get the final result is not always obvious. It can be simple to be complex, and complicated to be simple.

The general level of complexity, though, has been steadily rising over the nine decades since film sound was invented. And, starting with Dolby Stereo in the 1970s, and continuing with computerised mixing in the 1980s and the various digital formats in the 1990s and 2000s, that increase has accelerated even further. In the 1930s, for instance, it would not be unusual for an entire film to need only fifteen to twenty sound effects. Today that number could be thousands of times greater.

Well, the film business is not unique: compare the single-take, single-track 78 rpm discs of the 1930s to the multiple-take, multitrack surround-sound downloads of today. Or look at what has happened with visual effects: compare the *King Kong* of 1933 to the four films of the *Planet of the Apes* franchise (2011–24). The general level of detail, fidelity and what might be called the 'hormonal level' of sound and image has been vastly increased, but at the price of much greater complexity in preparation. The consequence of this, for sound, is that during the final recording of almost every film there are moments when the balance of dialogue, music and sound effects will suddenly (and sometimes unpredictably) turn into a logjam so extreme that even the most experienced of directors, editors and mixers can be overwhelmed by the choices they have to make.

So what I'd like to focus on are these 'logjam' moments: how they come about, and how to deal with them when they do. How to choose which sounds should predominate when they can't all be included? Which sounds should play second fiddle? And which sounds, if any, should be eliminated? As difficult as these questions are, and as

Arthur Koestler

vulnerable as such choices are to the politics of the film-making process, I'd like to suggest some conceptual and practical guidelines for threading your way through and perhaps even disentangling these logjams.

Or – better yet – not permitting them to occur in the first place.

Code and Body

To begin to get a handle on this, I'd like you to think about sound in terms of light. White light, for instance, which looks so simple, is in fact a tangled superimposition of every wavelength (that is to say, every colour) of light simultaneously. You can observe this in reverse when you shine a flashlight through a prism and see the white beam fan out into the familiar rainbow of colours, from violet (the shortest wavelength of visible light), through indigo, blue, green, yellow and orange, to red (the longest wavelength).

Keeping this in mind, I'd now like you to imagine *white sound* – every imaginable sound heard together at the same time. The sound of New York City, for instance: cries and whispers, sirens and shrieks, motors, subways, jackhammers, street music, the Grand Opera and Shea Stadium. Now imagine that you could 'shine' this white sound through some kind of magical prism that would reveal to us its hidden conceptual spectrum. Just as the 'rainbow' spectrum of colours is bracketed by violet and red, this conceptual sound spectrum will have its own brackets, or limits. Usually, we would now start talking about the lowest (20 Hz) and highest (20,000 Hz) audible frequencies of sound, but I am going to ask you to imagine limits of a completely different conceptual order: something I'll call *encoded* sound, and something I'll call *embodied* sound.

The clearest example of encoded sound is *speech*.

The clearest example of embodied sound is *music*.

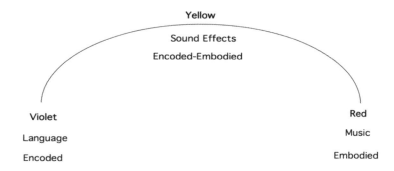

When you think about it, every language is a code, with its own particular set of rules. You have to understand those rules in order to break open the husk of language and extract the nut of meaning inside. Just because we usually do this automatically, without realising it, doesn't mean it isn't happening. If I were speaking, the meaning would be encoded in the words. Sound, in this case, would be acting simply as a vehicle by which to deliver the code, just as text delivers the code in words. Music, however, is completely different: it is sound experienced directly, without any intervening code, naked. Whatever meaning there is in a piece of music is 'embodied' in the sound itself. This is why music is sometimes called the *universal language*.

What lies between these outer limits? Just as every audible sound falls somewhere between the lower and upper limits of 20 and 20,000 Hz, so they will be found somewhere on this conceptual spectrum from speech to music. Most sound effects, for instance, fall midway: like 'sound centaurs', they are half language, half music. Since a sound effect usually refers to something specific – the steam engine of a train, the knocking at a door, the chirping of birds, the firing of a gun – it is not as 'pure' a sound as music. But, on the other hand, the language of sound effects, if I may call it that, is more universally and immediately understood than any spoken language.

Green and Orange

But now I'm going to throw a curveball (you expected this, I'm sure) and say that in practice, things are not quite as simple as I have just made them out to be. There are musical elements that make their way into almost all speech; think of how someone says something as a kind of music. For instance, even if you don't understand what they are saying, you can usually tell if someone is angry or happy just by listening to the tone (the music) of their voice. We understand R2-D2 entirely through the music of his beeps and boops, not from his 'words' (only C-3PO and Luke Skywalker can understand R2-D2's speech). Stephen Hawking's computerised speech, on the other hand, was perfectly understandable but monotonously even – it had very little musical content – and so we had to listen carefully to what he said, not how he said it. To the degree that speech has music in it, its 'colour' will drift towards the warmer (musical) end of the spectrum. In this regard, R2-D2 is warmer than Stephen Hawking, and Mr Spock is cooler than Rambo.

By the same token, there are elements of code that underlie every piece of music. Just think of the difficulty of listening to Chinese opera (unless you are Chinese!). If oriental music seems strange to you, it is because you do not understand its code, its underlying assumptions. In fact, much of your taste in music is dependent on how many musical languages you have become familiar with, and how difficult those languages are. Rock and roll has a simple underlying code (and a huge audience); modern European classical music has a complicated one (and a smaller audience). To the extent that this underlying code is an important element in the music, the 'colour' of the music will drift towards the cooler (linguistic) end of the spectrum. Schoenberg is cooler than Santana.

And sound effects can mercurially slip away from their home base of yellow towards either end of the spectrum, tinting themselves warmer and more 'musical' or cooler and more 'linguistic' in the process. Sometimes a sound effect can be almost pure music. It doesn't declare itself openly as such because it is not melodic, but it can have a musical effect on you nonetheless: think of Alan Splet's dense (orange) background sounds in David Lynch's *Eraserhead* (1977). And sometimes a sound effect can deliver discrete packets of meaning that are almost like words. A door knock, for instance, might be a 'blue' micro-language that says, 'Someone's here!' And certain kinds of footsteps say, simply, 'Step! Step! Step!'

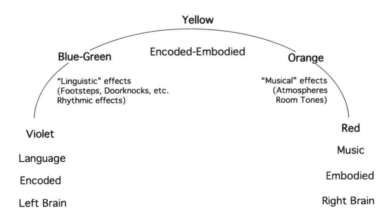

The reasonable man adapts himself to the world. All progress, therefore, depends on the unreasonable man

Such distinctions have a basic function in helping you to classify – conceptually – the sounds for your film. Just as a well-balanced painting will have an interesting and proportioned spread of colours from complementary parts of the spectrum, so the soundtrack of a film will appear balanced and interesting if it is made up of a well-proportioned spread of elements across our spectrum of 'sound colours'. I would like to emphasise, however, that these colours are completely independent of any emotional tone associated with 'warmth' or 'coolness'. Although I have put music at the red (warm) end of the spectrum, a piece can be emotionally cool, just as a line of dialogue – at the cool end of the spectrum – can be emotionally hot, even if given a flat delivery.

In addition, there is a practical consideration to take into account when it comes to the final mix. It seems that the combination of certain sounds will take on a correspondingly different character depending on which part of the spectrum they come from: some will superimpose transparently and effectively, whereas others will tend to interfere destructively with each other and 'block up', creating a muddy, unintelligible mix.

Before we get into the specifics of this, though, let me say a few words about the differences in superimposing images and sounds.

Harmonic and Non-Harmonic

When you look at a painting or a photograph, or the view outside your window, you see distinct areas of colour: a yellow dress on a washing line, for instance, outlined against a blue sky. The dress and the sky occupy separate areas of the image. If they didn't – if the foreground dress was semi-transparent – the wavelengths of yellow and blue would add together and create a new colour – green in this case. This is just the nature of the way we perceive light.

You can superimpose sounds, though, and they still retain their original identity. The notes C, E and G sounding together create something new – a harmonic C-major chord – but, if you listen carefully, you can still hear the original notes. It is as if, looking at that green dress, you could still see the blue and the yellow that went into making it. And it is a good thing that it works this way, because a film's soundtrack (as well as music itself) is utterly dependent on the ability of different sounds ('notes') to superimpose transparently upon each other, creating new 'chords' without themselves being transformed into something totally different.

Are there limits to how much superimposition can be achieved?

Well, it depends on what we mean by superimposition. Every note played by every instrument is actually a superimposition of a series of tones. A cello playing the note

A, for instance, will vibrate strongly at that string's fundamental frequency – 110 Hz, say. But the string also vibrates at exact multiples of that fundamental: 220, 330, 440, 550, 660, 770, 880 Hz, etc. These are called the harmonic overtones of the fundamental frequency, and their loudness, relative to the fundamental, decreases inversely to their frequency.

Harmonics, as the name indicates, are sounds whose waveforms are tightly linked – literally 'nested' together. In the example above, 220, 440 and 880 Hz are all higher octaves of the fundamental note A (110 Hz). And the other harmonics – 330, 550, 660 and 770 Hz – correspond to the notes E, Db, E and G, which, along with A, are the four notes of the A-major chord (A–Db–E–G–A). So when the note A is played on the violin (or piano or any other instrument), what you actually hear is a chord. But because the harmonic linkage is so tight, and because the fundamental (110 Hz in this case) is almost twice as loud as all of its overtones put together, we perceive the A as a single note, albeit one with 'character'. This character – or timbre, the exact proportions of the overtones to each other – is slightly different for each instrument, and that difference is what allows us to distinguish not only between types of instrument – clarinets from violins, for example – but also sometimes between individual instruments of the same type, such as a Stradivarius violin from a Guarneri.

This kind of harmonic superimposition has no practical limits to speak of. As long as the sounds are harmonically linked, you can superimpose as many elements as you want. Imagine an orchestra, with all the instruments playing octaves of the same note. Add an organ, playing more octaves. Then a chorus of two hundred, singing yet more octaves. Although we are superimposing hundreds and hundreds of individual instruments and voices, it will all still sound unified. If everyone started playing and singing whatever they felt like, however, that unity would immediately turn into chaos.

To give an example of non-musical harmonic superimposition: for *Apocalypse Now* we wanted to create the sound of a field full of crickets for one of the early scenes (Willard alone in his hotel room at night), but for story reasons we wanted the sound to have a hallucinatory degree of precision and focus. So rather than going out and simply recording a field of crickets, we decided to build the sound up layer by layer out of individually recorded crickets. We brought a few of them into Richard Beggs's basement studio, recorded them one by one on a multitrack machine, and then kept adding track after track, recombining them and then recording even more, until finally we had many thousands of chirps superimposed. The end result sounded unified – a field full of crickets – even though it had been built up out of many individual recordings, because the basic unit (the cricket's chirp) is so similar – each chirp sounds pretty much like any other. This was not music, but it would still qualify, in my mind, as an example of harmonic superimposition. (Incidentally, you'll be happy to know that the crickets escaped and lived happily behind the walls of Richard's studio for the next few years, chirping at the most inappropriate moments.)

Dagwood and Blondie

What happens, though, when the superimposition is *not* harmonic?

Technically, of course, you can superimpose as much as you want: you can create huge 'Dagwood sandwiches' of sound[1] – a layer of dialogue, two layers of traffic, a layer of automobile horns, of seagulls, of crowd hubbub, of footsteps, waves hitting the beach, foghorns, outboard motors, distant thunder, fireworks, and on and on, all playing together at the same time. (For the purposes of this discussion, let's define a layer as a conceptually unified series of sounds that run more or less continuously, without any large gaps. A single seagull cry, for instance, does not make a layer.)

The problem, of course, is that sooner or later (mostly sooner) this kind of intense layering winds up sounding like the rush of sound between broadcast radio stations – white noise – which is where we began our discussion. The trouble with white noise is that, like white light, there is not a lot of information to be extracted from it; or rather, there is so much information tangled together that it is impossible for the mind to separate it out. It is as indigestible as one of those gigantic Dagwood sandwiches. You still hear everything, technically speaking, but it is impossible to listen to it, to appreciate or even truly distinguish any single element. So the film-makers would have done all that work, put all those sounds together, for nothing. They could have just tuned between radio stations and achieved the same result.

To illustrate this, I would like to link you to a short section from *Apocalypse Now*. You will be seeing the same piece of film six times over, but you will be hearing different things each time: one separate layer of sound after another, which should

1. Dagwood Bumstead was a twentieth-century comic-strip character in American newspapers. He was notorious for constructing inedible foot-high sandwiches composed of everything in the refrigerator. His wife was named Blondie, and she did everything she could to keep Dagwood's appetites under control.

Robert Bresson

give an almost geological feel to the sound landscape of this film. This particular scene runs for a minute or so, from Kilgore's helicopters landing on the beach to the explosion of the storage jars and the medics trying to save the wounded soldier, ending with Kilgore saying, 'I want my men out!' But it is part of a much longer action sequence.

Originally, back in 1978, we organised the sound this way because we didn't have enough playback machines. There were over 175 separate soundtracks for this section of film alone. It was my very own Subway sandwich, so I had to break the sound down into smaller, more manageable groups – premixes – of about thirty tracks each. I still do the same thing today, even though I may have many more faders than I had back then.

The six premix layers were:

1. Dialogue
2. Helicopters
3. Music ('The Ride of the Valkyries')
4. Small arms (AK47s and M16s)
5. Explosions (mortars, grenades, heavy artillery)
6. Footsteps and other miscellaneous sounds

These layers are listed in order of importance, in somewhat the same way that you might arrange the instrumental groups in an orchestra. Mural painters do something similar when they grid a wall into squares and deal with just one square at a time. What murals, mixing and music all have in common is that in each of them, the details have to be in exact proportion to the immense scale of the work, so much so that it is easy to go wrong: either the details will overwhelm the eye (or ear) but give no sense of the whole, or the whole will be complete but without convincing details.

The human voice must be understood clearly in almost all circumstances, whether it is singing in an opera or dialogue in a film, so the first thing I did was mix the dialogue for this scene, isolated from any competing elements. With two exceptions, all the dialogue for this sequence was recorded long after shooting, as either wild lines (the soldiers exiting the helicopters) or in sync with the picture as ADR (the medics treating the wounded soldier).[2] The only lines of original dialogue are the young soldier screaming, 'I'm not going!' and Colonel Kilgore yelling, 'I want my men out!'

2. See Chapter 24 for more detail on the ADR process.

Poets do not go mad; but chess players do. Mathematicians go mad, and accountants; but artists very seldom

Then, what is the next most dominant sound in the scene? In this case, it was the helicopters, so we mixed all the helicopter tracks together onto a separate six-track roll of 35 mm film, while listening to playback of the dialogue to make sure we didn't do anything with the helicopters that would obscure it.

Then we progressed to the third most dominant sound, which was 'Ride of the Valkyries', as played through the speakers of Kilgore's helicopters. We mixed this to a third six-track roll of film, while monitoring the two previous premixes of helicopters and dialogue.

And so on to premix number four, small-arms fire, and then explosions, and finally miscellaneous sounds – footsteps and some extra explosion elements, fire, telemetry, wind, etc.

In the end, I had six premixes, each one a six-channel master (three channels behind the screen, left, centre and right; two surround channels in the rear of the theatre, left and right; and one channel for low frequency enhancement). Each premix was balanced against the others, so that – theoretically, anyway – the final mix should simply have been a question of playing everything together at one set level.[3]

These examples have a grainy black-and-white picture, what we called a 'dirty dupe', which is what we were using to guide us in editing the sound back in 1978. It was not until the final mix that we had the luxury of hearing the sound with a colour picture. Also, the sound in these examples is in mono, but we made our premixes in what is now called the 5.1 format: quintaphonic with LFE.

What I found to my dismay, however, was that in the first rehearsal of the final mix everything seemed to collapse into that big ball of noise I mentioned earlier. Each of the sound groups we had premixed was justified by what was happening on screen, but by some devilish alchemy they all melted into an unimpressive racket when they were played together. The challenge was to somehow find a balance point where there were enough interesting sounds to add meaning and help tell the story, but not so many that they overwhelmed each other – and to do it quickly.

The question was: where was that balance point?

Thankfully, I recalled my experience eight years earlier with robot footsteps, and my first encounter with what I came to call the rule of two and a half.

3. You can find these six premixes, one after the other, on Vimeo: https://vimeo.com/437642198 (QR code on right).

G. K. Chesterton

Robots and Grapes

This had happened in 1969, on one of the first feature films I worked on: George Lucas's *THX 1138*. It was a low-budget film, but it was also science fiction, so my job was to produce an otherworldly soundtrack on a shoestring. The shoestring bit was easy, because that was the only way I had worked up till then. The otherworldly part, though, meant that most of the sounds that automatically 'came with' the image (the sync sound) had to be replaced. A case in point: the footsteps of the policemen in the film, who were supposed to be robots made out of 600 pounds of steel and chrome. During filming, of course, these robots were actors in costume who made the same sound that anyone would make when they walked. But in the film we wanted them to sound massive, so I built some special metal shoes, fitted with springs and iron plates, went to the Museum of Natural History in San Francisco at 2 a.m., put them on and recorded lots of separate 'walk-bys' in different sonic environments, stalking around like some kind of Frankenstein's monster.

They sounded great, but I now had to put all these footsteps in sync. We would do this differently today: they would be recorded on what is called a Foley stage, in sync with the picture right from the beginning. But I was young and idealistic – I wanted it to sound right! – and besides, we didn't have the money to go to Los Angeles and rent a Foley stage.

So there I was with my overflowing basket of footsteps, sewing them into the film one step at a time like embroidery. It was going well, but too slowly, and I was afraid I wouldn't finish in time for the mix. Luckily, at 2 a.m. one morning a good fairy came to my rescue in the form of a sudden realisation: that if there was one robot, his footsteps had to be in sync; if there were two, their footsteps also had to be in sync; but if there were three, nothing had to be in sync – or rather, any sync point was as good as any other!

This discovery broke the logjam, and I was able to finish editing the footsteps in time for the mix. But why did this random sync phenomenon happen when there were more than two robots?

Somehow, it seems that our minds can keep track of one person's footsteps, or even those of two people, but with three or more, our minds give up – there are too many steps happening too quickly. As a result, each footstep is no longer evaluated individually, but rather the *group* of steps is evaluated as a single entity, like a musical chord. If their pace is roughly correct and it seems as if they are on the right surface, this is apparently enough. In effect, the mind says, 'Yes, I see a group of people walking down

---

It is not enough, sometimes, to do our very best. Sometimes, we have to do what we must

a concrete corridor, and what I hear sounds like a group of people walking down a concrete corridor. But I can't afford to pay attention to the individual steps.'

Sometime during the mid-nineteenth century, one of Édouard Manet's students was painting a bunch of grapes, diligently outlining every single one, when Manet suddenly knocked the brush out of her hand and shouted, 'Not like that! I don't give a damn about Every Single Grape! I want you to get the feel of the grapes, how they taste, their colour, how the dust shapes them and softens them at the same time.'

Similarly, if I had got Every Single Footstep in sync but failed to capture the energy of the group, the space through which they are moving, the surface on which they are walking and so on, I would have made the same kind of mistake as Manet's student. I would have paid too much attention to details that the audience is incapable of assimilating anyway, even if they wanted to.

One of the clearest examples of this grouping effect can be seen in the Chinese symbols for 'tree' and 'forest'. In Chinese, the character for the word 'tree' actually looks like a tree – like a pine with drooping limbs – while the word for 'forest' is three trees:

木 tree (mu)

林 grove (lin)

森 forest (sen)

Now it was clearly up to the ancient Chinese how many trees were needed to convey the idea of 'forest', but two didn't seem to be enough – that would describe a small grove – and sixteen, say, was far too many – it would have taken too long to write and just blotted up the paper. But three trees somehow seems to be just right. So, in evolving their writing system, the Chinese came across the same fact that I happened upon with my robot footsteps: three is the frontier where 'individual things' become a 'group'.

It turns out Bach also had something to say about this phenomenon in relation to music: he felt that three was the maximum number of polyphonic lines a listener can appreciate simultaneously. Even in religion you can detect its influence, when you compare Zoroastrian duality to the mysterious 'multiple singularity' of the Christian Trinity. And the counting systems of a large number of primitive tribes (and quite a few animals as well) end at three, beyond which more is simply 'many'. And I think it is the reason that large circuses have three rings, not five or two.

Winston Churchill

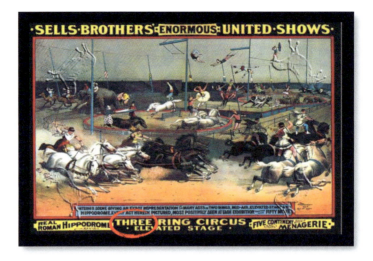

> The impresarios of the circus world knew that the audience could enjoy the spectacle and appreciate the details of a trapeze act in one ring and a high-wire act in another, but they made sure that the third ring would be occupied with the dismantling of the previous apparatus and maybe a bit of business from the clown. To have all three rings going full tilt would have diminished the overall effect – the whole would have been less than the sum of its parts. Except for a dramatic, overwhelming flourish at the end!

Similarly, it is just about possible to follow two conversations simultaneously, but not three. Listen to the scene in *The Godfather* where the family is sitting around, wondering what to do if Vito dies. Sonny is talking to Tom, and Clemenza is talking to Tessio. You can follow both conversations and also pay attention to Michael trying to contact Luca Brasi on the phone (Michael is the 'half' of the two and a half), but only because the scene was carefully written, performed and recorded. If Michael had started talking to Luca, the audience would have found it hard to understand any of the three conversations.

Or think about two pieces of music playing simultaneously: a background radio and a thematic score. This superimposure can be pulled off, but it has to be done carefully. If characters started having a conversation while the two pieces of music were playing, it would become difficult to concentrate on any of the three elements. This was behind editor Verna Fields's unease about the wall-to-wall use of music in *American Graffiti*. She felt that the audience would eventually become frustrated with it, and she asked me to help convince George to reduce the amount 'so as not to spoil such a wonderful story'. In the end, we didn't reduce the *amount* of music, but George and I did apply the technique of worldising, which selectively – when there was dialogue – reduced its presence to half or even less by blurring its outlines with location-appropriate reverberation.[4] So, in a scene between two characters, there would be their dialogue, the sound effects of the car they are riding in and blurred music coming from the car radio and/or reflecting off the roadside buildings. As soon as the dialogue ended, however, we would peel away the reverberation and play the music at full resolution, to be enjoyed for itself, with all of its internal harmonic layering clearly revealed.

So my problem on *Apocalypse* appeared to be caused by having six layers of sound, and six layers, especially at the loudness we were playing them, are essentially the same as sixteen or sixty. I had passed that threshold of two and a half, beyond which sounds congeal into a new singularity: dense noise in which a fragment or two can perhaps be distinguished, but not the developmental lines of the layers themselves. With six, I had achieved density, but at the expense of clarity.

Applying this rule of two and a half, I attempted to mix a fluid series of five-second moments, each with two to three layers of sound. If I wanted to add a new layer in the next moment, I had to take something else away, like a fast-moving game of three-card monte.

Here is that section of *Apocalypse* as it is heard in the final version:

Final mix of helicopters landing: https://vimeo.com/433278840
(QR code on right)

Listen, for example, to the moment when the young soldier repeatedly says, 'I'm not going!' where I removed the music. Logically, that didn't make sense, because he is actually *in* the helicopter that is producing the music, so it should be louder there than anywhere else. But, for story reasons, we needed to hear his dialogue, and we also wanted to emphasise the chaos outside – the AK-47 fire that he was frightened of – and the helicopter sound that represented 'safety'.

Under the circumstances, music and explosions were the sacrificial victims. The miraculous thing is that you do not hear the music go away; you believe that it is still

---

4. A detailed explanation of worldising can be found on pp. 330–2.

Robert Bresson

playing, even though, as I mentioned earlier, it should be louder here than anywhere else. And, in fact, as soon as this line of dialogue was over, we brought the music back in and sacrificed something else. Every moment in this section is similarly fluid, a kind of shell game where layers are disappearing and reappearing according to the dramatic focus of the moment.

> What I am suggesting is that, at any one moment (for practical purposes, let's say that a 'moment' is any five-second section of film), two and a half conceptual layers, spread across the spectrum, are the maximum that can be tolerated by an audience if – emphasising *if* – you also want them to maintain a clear sense of the individual elements that are contributing to the mix; to appreciate the scope of the forest and the detail of the trees. In other words, if you want the experience to be simultaneously dense and clear.

But should things *never* go above two and a half layers? You can certainly create really dense, almost opaque moments as a kind of end-of-circus flourish, but my suggestion is that two and a half is a kind of 'speed limit' that should not be surpassed without acknowledging the dangers.

The right thing to do is whatever serves the storytelling, in the broadest sense. My hope for this scene from *Apocalypse* was the impression of everything happening at once – density – yet everything heard distinctly – clarity. In fact, as you can see, simultaneous density and clarity can often only be achieved by a kind of subterfuge. As I said at the beginning, it can be complicated to be simple and simple to be complicated.

But sometimes it is just complicated to be complicated.

First, conquer the scoundrel who lies within

22: DENSE CLARITY: FURTHER THOUGHTS

Dramatic Polyphony

Glass study (Walter Tandy Murch)

Although this dense–clear rule of two and a half first occurred to me when I was working with sound, it seems from some of the other examples I have given that it may be a phenomenon with extensive roots elsewhere. So let me now say a bit more about what I believe is the broader appeal of dense clarity and explain why I am so attracted to it as a general principle.

In the concert hall, moments of dense clarity are those that permit us to appreciate the totality of the symphony's sound but also to clearly hear and appreciate the individual harmonic lines.

In the kitchen, it would be a preference for getting the sauce to the right degree of thickness (density), where the ingredients can be appreciated for their individual flavours (clarity), but also for those flavours and textures to collaborate to produce a balanced result that is greater than the sum of the ingredients.

In nature, it is those transcendental moments when we can simultaneously marvel at the vastness of the forest but also wonder at the detail of the individual trees.

Baron von Richthofen

In physics, this precarious state is called a *phase shift* – ice at the point of melting or water at the point of boiling, for example. It is a moment when we are able to observe both states simultaneously.[1]

I made an analogy with music, and I believe dense clarity – or clear density, if you prefer – can be found in all the arts. But cinema is an art of arts, a language of languages concocted from many divergent idioms and dialects: the script, the interpretation of that script by the actors, the staging of the scene by the director, the lighting, the framing of the photography, the music, production design, editing, sound, costumes and so on. Each of these disciplines is an art unto itself and has a distinct voice that can contribute a harmonic layer to the film, reinforcing or subtly (or *not* so subtly!) contradicting the other voices. And it is out of these reinforcements and contradictions that the most interesting and vibrant dramatic colours arise. A line in a script might be 'I love you,' but the actor can deliver that line as if to say, 'But I don't, actually.' And the director can arrange the staging to say, 'But he really does, even though he doesn't know it yet.' This is a kind of dramatic polyphony.

The degree of contradiction, its subtlety or overtness, will depend on the filmmaker. The director Mike Nichols was impressed 'by the fact that on entering a room full of people, you find them saying one thing, doing another, and wishing they were doing a third'. And Francis Coppola, a master at encouraging and corralling divergent voices, once described his job as being the 'ringmaster of a circus that is inventing itself'.

The risk of this multilayer approach is that it dances along a tightrope strung over an abyss of chaos, as I encountered when mixing *Apocalypse*. But the danger of that slippery rope is what makes things interesting and exciting, both for the people involved in the creation of the film and, hopefully, the audience who will be watching it. *Apocalypse*'s Colonel Kurtz ('his mind is clear but his soul is mad') vividly expressed this existential state:

COL. KURTZ
I watched a snail crawl along the edge of a straight razor. That's my dream.
That's my nightmare. Crawling, slithering, along the edge of a straight razor.
And surviving.

---

1. The physicist George Gamow wrote a popular book on physics, *One, Two, Three, Infinity* (1947), which I read with fascination as a teenager.

A new race of men will soon appear . . . Their language will be the cinema

How would dense clarity be achieved in a screenplay?

The author Steven Johnson has analysed an episode of *The Sopranos* in which there were nine separate story threads (which is to say, *layers*) interwoven, but done in such a way that over the fifty-five scenes, the average density was 2.13 (see illustration below).[2] Twelve of the scenes were single-layer, twenty-six were double-layer, thirteen were triple-layer, three were quadruple-layer and one was quintuple-layer.

"THE SOPRANOS" (EPISODE 6)

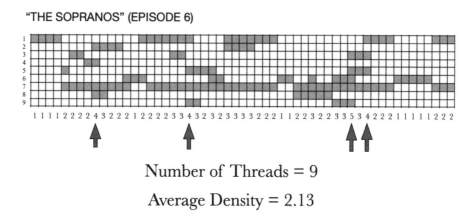

Number of Threads = 9

Average Density = 2.13

2.13 is not 2.5, but it is reasonably close.

Johnson contrasts this density with the simple (too simple?) clarity of earlier, more primitive television shows of the 1970s, such as *Starsky & Hutch*, where there are only two story threads and they never overlap, yielding an average density of 1.0.

"STARSKY AND HUTCH" (ANY EPISODE)

Number of Threads = 2
Average Density = 1

Even *Hill Street Blues*, which was considered advanced for television in the 1980s, had an average density of only 1.05 across its nine story layers. Only three scenes in the particular episode examined have two layers, as you can see in the illustration below.

Johnson could have just as easily analysed the opening wedding sequence of *The Godfather*, which has numerous story layers to it: Vito and Tom dispensing favours to

---

2. Steven Johnson, *Everything Bad Is Good for You.* Riverhead Books, 2005.

Attributed to Blaise Cendrars

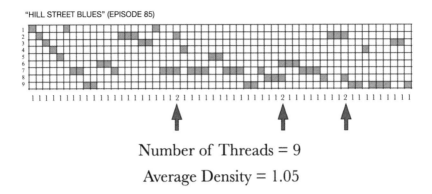

"HILL STREET BLUES" (EPISODE 85)

Number of Threads = 9
Average Density = 1.05

multiple supplicants; Kay (who is meeting the Corleone family for the first time) and Michael; newlyweds Connie and Carlo; Sonny and the FBI; Fredo, already unsteady on his feet; Sonny and Lucy Mancini; Johnny Fontane singing; Johnny with his special request for Vito; and finally a raft of minor supporting characters. It is a dense sequence of great clarity, particularly challenging to pull off since it is the opening of the film and we are meeting these characters for the first time. But how many of those story threads are on screen at the same time?

If all the different 'voices' of a film – all the contributing arts of this meta-art – were to be strictly aligned in agreement, all reinforcing each other, there would be no problem with superimposition, as I mentioned earlier. Everything would just become progressively more massive, like the instruments of an orchestra all playing the same notes. But that monolithic unity tends eventually to a flatness that is less interesting than harmonic polyphony, where each cinematic 'voice' is contributing a slightly different perspective on the characters and the situation, and it is finally up to the audience to resolve those differences.

Should every individual scene in a film attempt to achieve this razor-edge state? Absolutely not – and for the same reason that the soundtrack of *Apocalypse Now* is not continually in 5.1 sound or many scenes in that episode of *The Sopranos* have only one layer. In order to appreciate those moments of clear density when they occur, the audience needs relieving moments of simple clarity and even others of pure density; there are times when overwhelming, slightly confusing density is a virtue, like a cymbal clash or the finale of the circus, when all three rings are filled with acrobatic fireworks, or that five-layer scene three-quarters of the way through *The Sopranos*.

Shooting: put yourself into a state of intense ignorance and curiosity . . .
and yet see things in advance

In film editing, as well as writing, achieving clarity is sometimes simply a question of reducing a too-dense structure by judiciously eliminating scenes, such as lifting the lawn-party scene from the beginning of *Julia* or reducing to seven the scripted fourteen time transitions of *Godfather II*. On the other hand, Anthony Minghella and I thickened up the middle 'monastery' section of *The English Patient* by interleaving flashbacks from the Sahara desert sections of the film. And the density of the climactic scene, where Almásy confesses to Caravaggio the reasons for his failure to rescue Katharine, was increased by including Hana eavesdropping on the confession through a hole in the floor of her room. These images were stolen from a deleted 'break-up' scene between her and Kip; Kip was even digitally erased from one of the shots to allow for a wide angle of Hana alone. So, rather than having two climactic two-character scenes one after the other, this section of the film was simplified by eliminating one of the scenes – the Hana–Kip break-up – but then the density of the remaining confession scene was increased by including Hana as a silent witness.[3]

Soot and Diamonds

Pure carbon can take many forms, depending on how the atoms are arranged. In one of its states, soot, carbon is black, powdery and silky soft. Mix soot with some wax and you have shoe polish.

The polar opposite of soot is the most compressed and atomically rigid form of carbon: a diamond, crystalline, transparent, the hardest mineral, capable of scratching anything and being scratched by nothing – except another diamond.

Soot is amorphous and opaque, a diamond is dense and clear. Both are made of pure carbon.

Carbon is transformed into a diamond by the geological forces of intense heat and pressure. Our goal in film-making is to somehow 'diamondise' amorphous cinematic carbon through the heat of creativity and the relentless pressure of the schedule.

There is, theoretically, an optimal structure to the organisation of every film, just as there is an optimal atomic structure for every grouping of atoms – what is referred to in physics as a *ground state*. The most efficient packing of carbon atoms is the triangular tetrahedral pattern that gives the diamond its density, clarity and strength.

---

3. Hana's eavesdropping was particularly significant, because she now knows the guilt that Almásy feels, and when he asks her to kill him with extra doses of morphine, she has a reason to comply. This added layer was not in the screenplay or the novel, but was an invention during the previews, and it added density and clarity to the resolution of the film.

Robert Bresson

But there are many intermediate states between amorphous soot and tetrahedral diamond – shelves, so to speak, along the slope down to the valley floor of the diamond's ground state. In physics these shelves are called *metastable states*, and films, like carbon, can often get stuck on one of these metastable shelves, like a tumbling rock interrupted on its way downhill.

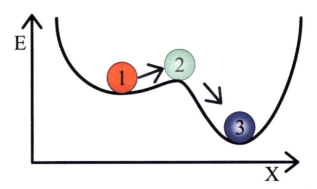

A metastable state of weaker bonding (1), a
transitional 'saddle' configuration (2) and a stable
ground state of strongest bonding (3)

How – and whether – we get a film to its optimal structure is the struggle during post-production. I would suggest that the 'ground state' of a movie can be recognised by its balanced proportion of density and clarity, a balance appropriate to that particular film. But evaluating this is a judgement, a feeling, rather than a scientific fact like freezing or boiling point temperatures. And in the harsh world of business realities, many films find themselves stuck on one of those metastable shelves: they simply run out of money, time and patience before ever attaining their ideal state.

Also, the diamond analogy, while colourful, is imprecise because films are heterogenous 'living' things, made of many elements, with some inevitable amount of impurities (mistakes!) woven in. Diamonds are minerals made of just one thing: carbon. So, even with adequate time and money, it is rarely absolutely certain when the film has hit its balance point between density and clarity.[4]

The director's cut of *The Godfather* was close to three hours long, but Francis had the contractual obligation to show the studio a version that was under two hours and

4. For more about the preview process, see the 'Pandemic of Desire' chapter in the subsequent volume of this book.

twenty minutes. So editors Bill Reynolds and Peter Zinner, supervised by Francis, cut the film down to that length, and I did the corresponding sound mix. We screened this version for Robert Evans, the head of Paramount at the time, and to his credit, he decided, 'This is a long, bad trailer for a good movie. Put everything back.' Which we did. And, with only a couple of small changes, that restoration was the final version of the film. Evans's other decision, which also took courage, was to ask for the removal of the intermission planned for just after the assassination of Sollozzo and McCluskey. His reasoning? 'We don't want to let the audience off the hook.'

Given the thematic density of that particular film, the shorter version was flimsy, unclear and seemed longer than its running time. But the longer version did achieve that ideal balance – or as close to it as can be imagined – of density and clarity, where the temporal length is not felt to be an issue.

For the record, *Godfather* was the first long Hollywood film not to have an intermission. This drove the exhibitors crazy – how were they going to sell enough popcorn? – but when it started making huge amounts of money, the popcorn didn't seem so important. Evans's decision set a pattern which persists to this day. Even Scorsese's *Killers of the Flower Moon* (2023), at three hours and twenty-six minutes – the length of two feature films – has no intermission.

The density and clarity of a diamond are due to the nature of carbon and the heat and pressure of forces deep within the Earth, but its sparkle and fire come from the carefully calculated angles of the facets that have been cut and polished by human hands, in ways that enhance its brilliance. Light – a stream of photons – enters the diamond through one or several of the facets and then bounces around internally, refracting into different colours of the spectrum (diamonds have one of the highest

Jean Cocteau

refractive indexes of all gemstones), splitting into multiple beams, until it finally escapes its brilliant prism and hits our delighted eyes.

What are the equivalent of the diamond's facets in cinema? I would suggest they come from the tolerance of the director for the different 'refractive indices' of the multiple arts that cinema is made of, their degree of what I have called dramatic polyphony – those subtle and not-so-subtle contradictions and reinforcements: 'I love you.' (*But I don't, actually.*) (*But I really do, even though I don't know it yet.*) Or Mike Nichols's fascination with the three layers of speech, action and aspiration: what the actor says, which is contradicted by how he says it and belied by his costume, but then reinforced by the camera angle and lighting, and further modulated by the music.

If all this can be organised – a very big *if*, hence Coppola's 'ringmaster of a circus that is inventing itself' – then the film has a chance of achieving a spectral brilliance and fire arising from the interaction of all the different minds that gathered collaboratively to make it, and this carefully organised spectrality will have a possibility of appealing to a wide audience, which is itself a multifaceted entity in search of cohesion.

So I would add to density and clarity the *faceting* of cinema, which I believe is fundamental to the kind of medium that it is: a work of art made up of multiple arts through the collaboration of dozens, often hundreds of people, and which will be viewed by millions, tens of millions, maybe – if we're lucky – hundreds of millions of people, who will in turn become the film's final collaborators in its creation.

Be just as ignorant about what you are going to shoot as a fisherman is about what is on the end of his line

23: YOU'LL NEVER WORK IN THIS TOWN AGAIN

And Other Studio Follies

Responding to producer Al Ruddy's call, I walked over to his office for a discussion about the mixing schedule for *The Godfather*. It was October 1971, and the film had just moved from Zoetrope in San Francisco to the Paramount lot in Hollywood for final completion: lab work at Technicolor, voice replacement with some of the actors, music recording and the final sound mix at Goldwyn Studios.

Ruddy had a modest office on the lot, but Robert Evans, the head of production at Paramount, hung out instead at swankier suites in Beverly Hills. I had never worked behind the gates of a Hollywood studio before, so every day was a revelation. Expecting glamour, what I saw as I walked around was a cross between a down-at-heel factory and a half-abandoned prison.[1] Of the nine studios in Los Angeles at the time, Paramount ranked ninth in terms of revenue. There was a rumour that Charles Bluhdorn, who had bought Paramount five years earlier, was angling to sell off the studio's real estate, following 20th Century-Fox's 1961 decision to sell part of their lot to the developers of luxurious Century City. On the other side of Paramount's north wall was Hollywood Forever, the crematorium and cemetery where, among many others, Rudolph Valentino, Judy Garland and Fay Wray lay waiting for their next casting call.

Meeting over, as soon as I stepped back into the sound effects library, Howard 'Baldy' Beals pulled me into his office with urgent words of advice:

'Whenever you leave this building, make sure you're carrying something in your hand.'

Baldy was the head of the sound effects department. He was responsible for three sounds that had affected me deeply: the death ray in Byron Haskin's *War of the Worlds* (1953), the drill at the end of John Frankenheimer's *Seconds* (1966) and the cavernous room tone of New York's Grand Central station in that same film. I explained to Baldy that I had only gone to hear what Ruddy had to say about the schedule.

---

1. The physical upgrades that would come during Sherry Lansing's administration were many years in the future.

'It doesn't matter. No empty hands. Take anything . . . A box. Take an empty box.'

I was mystified. 'An empty box?'

Baldy jabbed out of the window at what looked like a prison watchtower. 'If it doesn't look like you're on an errand, that son-of-a-bitch . . .' – and he made sure I noticed the silhouetted figure sitting at a desk in the watchtower – '. . . will rip you up and down for wasting Paramount's money.'

The man in the tower with an eagle eye for boxes in hands was forty-three-year-old drill sergeant Paul Haggar, head of the studio's post-production. As far as he was concerned, the only excuse for an editor leaving his bench was to run an errand.

Baldy laughed and handed me an empty film box.

'There's your ticket. Don't lose it.'

My position at Paramount was looked upon with suspicion. I was in the San Francisco, not the Los Angeles, film union, and it was only at Francis's insistence that the rules were bent to allow me to pass through the Paramount gates. My job on *The Godfather* was what would be called sound effects supervisor. I had done all of the custom sound effects recording (period cars, etc.) and some premixing at Zoetrope, but that meant I had displaced a Los Angeles-based editor. As a result, my credit on the film is 'Post-Production Consultant', a title that did not step on any sensitive toes.

How any job gets done in a collaborative medium like film is, of course, dependent on the artistic vision of the director and all the various department heads, but it can also be fatally vulnerable to the unpredictable interpersonal relationships and rivalries of the people involved, and as I discovered, to the long-simmering politics endemic to the studio. Think of the palace intrigues in *Wolf Hall* or *House of Cards*. Your artistic success may be hostage to how you can play, or sidestep, the political games that you will inevitably experience.

> The *auteur* theory has its roots in this conflict between vision and politics. The original idea, as formulated by André Bazin, Jean-Luc Godard and François Truffaut in the 1950s, was that certain film-makers had the ability to put their recognisable artistic stamp on a film *despite* the interference of studio politics, *not* that they were auteurs in complete control of their film, which is how the theory is interpreted today.

The truth told cleverly is the greatest lie

Baldy and I quickly developed a good working relationship thanks to my love for that death-ray sound from *War of the Worlds*, and we would work together again on *The Conversation* and *The Godfather: Part II*.[2] But Baldy and Paul Haggar had a contentious relationship that went back decades to when Paul first started working at Paramount in the early 1950s, in the mail room. Baldy, ten years older, had been at the studio since 1943. Now, Paul, expertly swinging through the jungle-gym of studio politics, was head of post-production and had become Baldy's superior. I didn't know any of this at the time, nor any of the other forces at work under the surface, but I was soon to encounter them.

One of the limitations in those pre-digital days was our inability to routinely monitor sound effects in relation to each other as we were weaving them into a film. You might build six or sixteen tracks of sound effects, but you had to use your imagination to 'hear' how their interaction would play out. Of course, you would experience the reality of this in the final mix, but by then the hands of re-recording mixers would be controlling the balance and it would be too late to make many changes. As a result, editors understandably tended to play things safe and by the book. It was also the reason behind Paramount's decision to assign a single sound editor per reel, thinking that this would give a better chance of the selected sounds working with each other.

This one-editor, one-reel approach was different to the system in the UK, where editors would build sound effects thematically: one editor would prepare atmospheres and background sounds, another would take on weaponry, a third would do footsteps, and so on. The British approach was influenced by the analogy with instrumental groupings in music: strings, brass, woodwinds, percussion, etc.[3]

There are advantages and drawbacks to each system, so the choice finally comes down to the nature of the particular film and the organising guidelines of the producing studio. Temperamentally, I prefer the British system.

There was one small screening room in the Paramount sound library offices where up to five tracks of sound could be auditioned simultaneously, and it was here that six of us – Paul, Baldy, me and the three sound effects editors whose reels would be

2. I learned from Baldy that the death-ray sound was a distorted, reversed and repeat-looped fragment of three electric guitars: https://www.youtube.com/watch?v=w36lXrwz2sY (QR code on right).

3. Influenced by the British sound editors Les Hodgson and Les Wiggins, this was the approach that we took for the sound effects on *Apocalypse Now*.

Thomas Hardy

evaluated – assembled one evening to check the effects a week before the start of pre-mixing on *The Godfather*. By 9 p.m. we had got halfway through the film, and we were intent on finishing by midnight. There were the expected notes about adjusting sync and choosing possible alternative sounds, but nothing that couldn't be dealt with in the time available before the mix. The next reel began with Don Corleone being released from hospital and heading home in an ambulance, accompanied by a police convoy.

Suddenly, the side door burst open and Jack Ballard careened into the room. He glanced at us without saying anything and collapsed onto the sofa between the mix console and the screen. Ballard was the vice president in charge of production, but was generally known, and feared, as Robert Evans's hatchet man. He was around fifty, with a pixie-ish, oddly menacing demeanour: completely bald, upturned collar, fastidious in an LA kind of way. As Francis would later describe him:

> The studio had a man named Jack Ballard who was there to make sure I didn't veer whatsoever from the agreed-upon schedule and things I had agreed to cut from the script. He had a lot of authority. He was there on set – a striking guy with a bald head – and he didn't like me.[4]

According to Paramount executive Peter Bart, in his book *Infamous Players*, Ballard was one of the executives angling to have Francis fired and replaced by editor Aram Avakian:

> To my astonishment, Ballard announced on a conference call that Coppola 'wasn't up to the job,' that he wanted to designate Aram Avakian, the editor, as the new director. Al Ruddy had warned me that Avakian had been hovering around Ballard in a conspiratorial manner and that something dire was afoot.[5]

The mood in the room, which had been business-like but fairly relaxed, changed to one of an icy tension. What was Ballard's agenda? Why was he here at nine o'clock at night?

On screen, the Corleone ambulance pulled away from the hospital, while journalists and police ran to their cars in pursuit, accompanied by a siren, the clatter of sparse

4. Scott Foundas, 'On Its Centennial, Paramount Pictures Celebrates Its Peak: The 1970s', *LA Weekly*, 7 June 2012: https://www.laweekly.com/on-its-centennial-paramount-pictures-celebrates-its-peak-the-1970s.

5. Nate Rawlings and Gilbert Cruz, 'The Anniversary You Can't Refuse: 40 Things You Didn't Know About *The Godfather*', *Time* magazine, 14 March 2012: https://entertainment.time.com/2012/03/15/the-anniversary-you-cant-refuse-40-things-you-didnt-know-about-the-godfather/slide/a-palace-coup.

Art produces ugly things which often become more beautiful with time. Fashion produces beautiful things which often become ugly with time

footsteps and a few shouted lines from the crowd of reporters. Because of the room's technical limit of five tracks, we were not playing the sync sound recorded at the time of filming, nor the four other atmosphere tracks that had been prepared.

After a few minutes, Ballard's head popped up into the glare of the projector. He fixed us with his gaze and let loose:

'If this is how the film is going to sound, none of you will ever work in this town again.'

There was a suspended moment, punctuated only by the siren of Don Corleone's ambulance. Baldy hit the stop button, the projector went dark, and there was only silence. It seemed that this ridiculously clichéd line had been spoken in earnest.

Ballard stood up and continued: 'These are the worst sound effects I've ever heard.'

Had he been sent by Evans? Or was this a solo venture? Everyone except me was an employee of Paramount Pictures. I waited for Paul to say something, but the silence just got thicker and thicker. I was aware of the risk of speaking up, but the urge got the better of me.

'Jack, this room can only run five tracks at a time, so we couldn't put up the production track, which carries most of the sound for this scene. These are supplementary tracks, and we're just checking sync. You don't know what you're talking about.

'And you're drunk.'

There was another suspended moment. Was this the end of my career in film? Ballard looked from me to Paul to Baldy, and back to me again. Finally, he spoke, waving his hands in front of his face:

'You're right. I am drunk. And I don't know what the hell I'm talking about.'

He spun on his heels and left the room.

Another suspended moment, with barely perceptible exhalations of breath. Paul looked at me with a blank expression and then slowly nodded his head. 'Let's get back to work.'

Of course, it could have gone very differently. Confrontations like these are unpredictable, and it was impossible for me to weigh all the unknown consequences in the seconds after Ballard's threat. I generally avoid getting involved with studio politics, preferring to keep my head down and do the work. So I wouldn't always recommend speaking out the way I did. I do know that in my case, in those circumstances, it was impossible for me *not* to speak out.

Francis, of course, was brutally exposed to the headwinds of studio politics as writer/director of *The Godfather*. But he is the *maestro* of bulldozing, dodging,

Jean Cocteau

tunnelling and spellbinding his way through seemingly insurmountable mountains of studio politics. Knowing that Francis had my back was certainly one of the things that gave me the confidence to challenge someone like Ballard.[6]

What I didn't know at the time was that Ballard and Haggar hated each other. Ballard apparently enjoyed yanking Paul's chain at the slightest excuse, so the fact that an outsider from San Francisco had called him out in front of Paul, with witnesses, raised my standing in Paul's eyes. He still made things difficult for me, as he did for all editors – it was in his drill-sergeant nature – but probably less difficult than it would otherwise have been. He and I would work together on another four Paramount films: *The Conversation*, *Godfather II*, *Ghost* and *Godfather III*.

The question was what would happen the next time I met Ballard. It was answered several weeks later, when we crossed paths after the *Godfather* mix was under way. He was remarkably friendly and greeted me as 'the Gordy Willis of sound'. I smiled and nodded: 'You're being far too generous, Jack. But thank you.'

Paul worked at Paramount until he retired in 2005, after more than fifty years at the studio. Jack Ballard was gone by 1975.

Studio politics

6. For an excellent summary of the balance of politics and creativity in making *The Godfather*, see Michael Sragow's 1997 article 'Godfatherhood' in *The New Yorker*: https://www.newyorker.com/magazine/1997/03/24/godfatherhood.

24: DUALITY OF THE SOUL

Mysteries of Narration and Dialogue Replacement

I regard dubbing, that is to say, the addition of sound after the picture has been shot, as an outrage. If we were living in the twelfth century, a period of lofty civilization, the practitioners of dubbing would be burnt in the market-place for heresy. Dubbing is equivalent to a belief in the duality of the soul.

– Jean Renoir

'People say I mumble.'

The voice was Marlon Brando's. He and I were alone in the dark, in late 1971, waiting for the next loop of dialogue from *The Godfather* to be threaded up. We were recording replacements for a couple of dozen lines and had got about three-quarters of the way through the list.

A slight pause as I considered how best to respond.

'That's right. People do say you mumble.'

Brando was forty-seven at the time. I was twenty years younger. There was a long pause.

Francis, Brando and I had been working our way through the film, changing Brando's inflections and increasing clarity, when Francis suddenly looked at his watch and realised he had to make an important phone call. 'This has been going great. The rest of the lines are pretty simple. I'll be back in twenty minutes.' And he was gone.

Brando and I got through the next couple of lines and were now waiting in the dark while some technical problem with the projection was sorted out.

Finally, Brando spoke: 'They're right. I *do* mumble. And I'll tell you why. When we shoot these things' – he gestured at the screen – 'we do everything out of order. I have no idea how it's all going to go together, what takes they're going to use, what will be cut out. You see what I'm saying?'

I nodded in agreement, but I doubt he saw me in the darkness.

'So I don't move my lips very much during shooting. That way, when I find out how they put it all together, I can change what I say and how I say it, depending on what they've done to the film.'

Graffiti on the side of a moving van

We film-makers do have this magical ability to erase an actor's voice and replace it, either with a different reading, sometimes different words or even someone else's voice entirely. And if we have this ability, why not use it to refine a performance once the film is locked – a movie that may now be very different from the one the actor signed on for at the beginning? So Brando had a point.

But Jean Renoir is also right. The human voice is expressive of the inner soul, and to tamper with it is to practise a kind of sorcery. If the twelfth century returned, film-makers – me, especially – *would* be burnt at the stake, following Renoir's *fatwa* against us.

Renoir's hatred of dubbing has to be understood in the context of the 1930s. Audio techniques then were basic – the equivalent of sketchy 1930s back-projection in cinematography. Did that looped voice really come from that mouth? No, not in any realistic sense. But audiences, especially in Italy, Hong Kong and similar places, took crude post-production dialogue in their stride: the voices were only 'associated with' the image, like speech bubbles in the popular Italian *fotoromanzo* comic books.[1] In other countries, there was the opposite aesthetic, and the Italian practice was frowned upon. In France, the reality of the sound captured at the time of shooting was sacred, with all of its subtleties of performance, acoustic atmosphere and occasional imperfections.

The aesthetic now, with our greater control of the recording medium, is to make all dialogue naturalistic, or at least appear so. The voices we record in post-production are (mostly) carefully massaged to sound as if they were captured at the time of

1. Actress Sophia Loren got her start as a model in *fotoromanzi*. And Federico Fellini's first film as solo director was *The White Sheik* (1951), a comedy based on characters from *fotoromanzi* that starred Leopoldo Trieste, who played Signor Roberto in *The Godfather: Part II*.

Your dream possesses you. It is a snow-white tablecloth spread in your heart

shooting. In the early days of this sorcery, the process was called *looping*, because we literally made buckled loops of 35 mm film for each line of dialogue (and the picture that went with it). These would be threaded one by one on a projector and the line repeated over and over for as long as necessary until the actor got his new performance in sync with the old one. It was time-consuming for the editors but relatively easy for the actors because of the quick repeat cycle of each loop.

Aside from the tedious editorial work involved, the real disadvantage of looping was the structural inability to play back all the selected takes in context at the end of a session, to check the work before the actor took off. This problem was not solved until the invention of computer-assisted ADR (Automated Dialogue Replacement), starting in the late 1960s.[2] When we were looping *The Godfather* in 1971, ADR technology had not yet percolated to Goldwyn Studios, so we were still struggling with those physical loops of film.[3]

Photo from *American Cinematographer* magazine, October 1978

Even though magnetic-film ADR has now been replaced by digital technology, which combines the quick repeat cycle of looping with the playback abilities of ADR, we film-makers still call the process ADR, and I will use that acronym for all methods of dialogue replacement.

There are five reasons for dialogue replacement: (1) to improve clarity because of noisy backgrounds or other technical problems at the time of filming; (2) to change the dialogue because of changes to the story (and this would include narration); (3) to change the accent, inflection or interpretation of a line of dialogue; (4) to add supplementary vocalisations – cries and whispers, moans and groans, breaths and laughter, etc.; (5) to change from one language to another. All of these can be crucial, but the most important is ADR that helps to change the story.

2. One of the inventors of ADR was Carlos Rivas, an Argentine immigrant who became chief engineer at MGM. He also invented the Rivas film splicer, named after him. Rivas won three technical Oscars in the early 1950s.

3. ADR did not become universally accepted until the late 1970s.

Jean Cocteau

Story: *The Conversation*

Large structural changes were made to *The Conversation* during editing, and ADR helped to make those changes appear to have been the original intention.

In the original script, professional eavesdropper Harry Caul mixed down three tapes of a secretly recorded Union Square conversation in one continuous session. In that long, thirteen-page (eleven-minute) scene, the audience had to: (1) understand Harry's complex sound-mixing process, as he selected the clearest phrases from the conversation between Mark and Ann; (2) grapple with the personal tensions between Harry and his assistant Stan; (3) follow the decoding and uncovering of the previously obscured line 'He'd kill us if he had the chance'; and (4) understand Caul's motivation in obscuring it again. As filmed and cut together, eleven minutes was just too long; there was too much information for audiences to take on board. So we made the decision, quite late in the editing, to split the scene into two sections (four and seven minutes in length). The first part would now simply show Harry at work: what he does and how he does it, as he mixes the three Union Square tape recordings to get the best out of each. After finishing, Harry calls from an anonymous payphone and makes arrangements to hand over the master tape and collect his $15,000 fee ($80,000 in 2024!). But the voice on the other end of the phone puts him off until the next day.

That evening Harry pays a difficult visit to his girlfriend Amy. And the next morning he takes the tape to the corporate offices of the executive who hired him to do

the recording, Mr C. But Mr C is not there, and his assistant Martin takes the tapes and gives Harry the $15,000 in cash. Harry's suspicions are raised by Mr C's absence, and he hands back the money and grabs the tapes. His misgivings are increased by new ADR dialogue from Martin (in italics): 'Those tapes are dangerous. *You've heard them. You know what I mean. Someone may get hurt.*'

But Harry has *not* heard anything dangerous (nor have we). The tapes were frustratingly innocuous. On the way to the elevator, he accidentally discovers that Mark and Ann work at Mr C's company, increasing his suspicions still further. He hurries back to his office, and the second section of the assembly scene begins.

The motivation, now urgent, is to find out what was so dangerous in the recording.

What did Harry miss in his first assembly? As he scans through the tapes, his assistant Stan becomes curious, and after Harry refuses to go to lunch ('I want to finish this'), Stan asks (in ADR), '*I thought you turned those tapes in.*' Harry replies (also ADR), '*Stan, be quiet, will you?*' And Stan answers (ADR), '*All right, all right.*'

These additions were simple, particularly since all of them were delivered over reaction shots, except for Stan's last line. But they did the job in pivoting this major shift in the structure of the film.

Once Stan leaves for lunch, Harry doubles down on his search and, after a few blind alleys, zeroes in on an overlooked fragment of distorted voice that is partially covered by music. He plugs in a self-made device that magically cancels out the music and clearly reveals Mark's words: 'He'd kill us if he got the chance.' This line proves crucial to the unfolding of the plot.[4]

The recording of the line itself was a 'location' ADR. When the scene was originally shot, Fred Forrest and Cindy Williams (playing Mark and Ann) were wearing wireless microphones, but San Francisco's Union Square was a hotbed of microwaves that would randomly hijack our wireless channel and spoil the audio of many takes. As back-up, while the film was still being shot, I went with Cindy and Fred to quiet Lafayette Park and, with a portable Nagra, recorded four clean takes of their Union Square conversation as we all walked together around the park. On three of the takes Fred put the emphasis (as in the original performance) on 'kill' ('He'd *kill* us if he got the chance'). But for some reason, on the fourth he shifted the emphasis to 'us' ('He'd kill *us* if he got the chance').

> Under certain circumstances, such as this, if you can get actors to a quiet environment as quickly as possible after a noisy location shoot, 90 per cent of their dialogue will be perfectly in sync with what was shot, or can easily be made so. The 'muscle memory' of the performance is still vividly intact in the actors' minds. This is often not the case when doing ADR six months after a shoot.

4. In theory, this erasure of music is possible through the digital manipulation of self-cancelling waveforms, but there was no device capable of something like this in 1973. Fifty years later, in 2023, something similar was achieved through AI, when John Lennon's voice was isolated from a musical background. See Greg Evans, 'Paul McCartney on Upcoming AI-Assisted Beatles Record: "It's All Real and We All Play on It"', *Deadline*, 22 June 2023: https://deadline.com/2023/06/paul-mccartney-john-lennon-beatles-now-and-then-new-record-1235422760.

Robert Bresson

Throughout the editing, I used the reading with the emphasis on 'kill', but during the mix I wondered what would happen if I switched out the final reading of that line and replaced it with the fourth 'Lafayette Park' take, which had the emphasis on 'us'. The last recitation of the line occurs as a voice-over near the end of the film, when we (and Harry) have discovered that Mark and Ann are alive, and it is Mr C who has been killed instead.

This substitution was an attempt to solve a persistent problem with the film: our small preview audiences had been confused about who did what to whom, and because the film is told solely from Harry's point of view, there was no way to get information across other than through his understanding of it. I thought this different inflection might help the penny to drop, as the saying goes. 'He'd kill *us* if he got the chance' implies that 'We should kill him first.'

This was a risky intervention in the premise of the movie, which was to repeat the Union Square conversation, unchanged, at various places in the film, discovering different things in it from the shift in context. This new line was a subtle shift in the conversation itself. It was justified, I hoped, because we're in Harry's head, and he's now realising the truth, and that is influencing how he hears the line. Or was the line this way all along, and Harry 'chose' to hear it the other way because he wanted to think Mark and Ann were victims? The reality of the film becomes subjective.

Another 'story ADR' occurs in the scene immediately following that seven-minute

tape-assembly section, when Harry – a practising Catholic – goes to confession. This scene was moved here from its original location near the end of the screenplay.[5] After confessing to taking the Lord's name in vain and several other minor sins, new dialogue was added to underline Harry's past history, paranoia and guilt (ADR lines in *italics*):

. . . On a number of occasions I've taken newspapers from the racks without paying for them . . . I've taken pleasure in impure thoughts . . . *I've been involved in some work . . . that I think will be used to hurt these two young people . . . It's happened to me before. People were . . . mm . . . hurt because of*

5. In the script, the confession scene originally followed Harry receiving his $15,000 fee from Martin and Mr C (p. 125 of the 159-page screenplay).

Only kings, presidents, editors, and people with tapeworms have the right to use the editorial 'we'

*my work. I'm afraid it could happen again . . . I was in no way responsible. I'm
not responsible . . . For these and all the sins of my past life I'm heartily sorry.*

In the scene as it was written and shot, Harry confesses only to trivial sins, but by
the time the camera had moved in close on the priest's ear, throwing Harry's profile
out of focus, there was no problem with these new lines appearing to be out of sync.

Two other uses of 'story ADR' occur when Harry receives phone calls in his apartment. In both cases, Francis rewrote the dialogue from the caller (Martin) to account
for editorial changes in the story and structure of the film. In the first, it was because
of the change involving Meredith, Harry's one-night stand, whom we had turned into
a secret agent of Mr C's, sent to steal Harry's tapes.

*Mr Caul? We have the tapes, they're perfectly safe. The Director was very
anxious to hear them as soon as possible and you were acting . . . I don't
know . . . disturbed. I couldn't take
the chance that you might destroy
our tapes. You understand, don't you,
Mr Caul? Our tapes have nothing to
do with you. Why don't you come over
now and bring the photographs? The
Director is here and prepared to pay
you in full.*

This call was also, like the confession scene, moved from its original position much
later in the film. It was helpful for the ADR that Francis shot the scene entirely from
behind Hackman's head. Most of the original scripted dialogue was from Mark, warning Harry not to get involved any further.

A few lines of Mark's dialogue from that call were given to Martin's character in the
second call, where it was made clear that Harry's apartment has been bugged. Before
Martin speaks, we hear a recording of the saxophone music that Harry has just been
playing. Then . . .

*We know that you know, Mr Caul. For your own sake, don't get involved any
further. We'll be listening to you.*

This was slightly more complicated to pull off, as Hackman was facing the camera,
and the call as originally shot was not long enough for the ADR. I optically stretched
the shot by repeating (scanning forwards and back) a four-second section three times,

which gave enough length for the dialogue and the playing of the sax recording. By today's standards, the optical stretching is crude, but it does the job.

Francis was in New York directing *Godfather II* when I was mixing *The Conversation*. When the mix was finished, my wife Aggie and I flew to New York and played it for Francis, and he approved, including this shift in emphasis of the new 'kill *us*' line, which he liked.[6] The original motivation for ADR-ing that line was to improve audio quality, but a chance shift of emphasis by Fred Forrest turned out to be helpful in resolving the story. As Jean-Luc Godard observed: 'Editing is the transformation of chance into destiny.'

All things considered, there was very little ADR in *The Conversation*, and most of it was placed over reaction shots and telephone calls, where there was no concern about lip sync. The dialogue in the Union Square conversation was, in the finished film, split about fifty–fifty between the production and the recording made in Lafayette Park. The motivation for the ADR in *The Conversation* was almost always to help with the story changes that had taken place during editing. There were no technical problems with the excellent production sound recording (by Art Rochester), other than the microwaves that spoiled a certain amount of the Union Square recordings.

This was certainly not the case for *Apocalypse Now*. Eighty-five per cent of the dialogue in *Apocalypse* is ADR. Unfortunately, much of the sound recorded on location by Nat Boxer was fatally compromised by the real-life noises of helicopters and the diesel engine of the patrol boat ferrying Captain Willard upriver.

Apocalypse also has narration, which *The Conversation* did not.

Narration: *Apocalypse Now*

I had joined the picture editorial team in August 1977 as the junior partner. Richie Marks and Jerry Greenberg were already splicing their way through the jungle of workprint: 236 hours' worth, eight times the amount I had on Fred Zinnemann's *Julia*.

The deeper I got into the editing, the more I realised that *Apocalypse* needed the narrative voice that had structured the original screenplay, but I was told that Francis

6. Francis has recently said that he now thinks it was a mistake to change the reading.

There is no problem, however complicated, which – when you look at it in just the right way – will not become even more complicated

had abandoned this idea during shooting. I fought for its restoration. Willard is an observer – he is our eyes and ears in this diabolical landscape – and for most of the journey, until he gets to the Kurtz compound, he is a mostly silent passenger on a boat heading up the Nung River, studying a CIA dossier on Kurtz. The audience judges character by comparing words spoken with actions taken, but if there are few words and fewer actions, the character has to emerge from somewhere else: out of an interior, quasi-novelistic voice.

So I dug out the old script and recorded myself reading Willard's narration, placing it selectively over the first half-hour of the film. I called everyone together – Francis, Richie, Jerry and the rest of the team – and made my pitch about character, silent observer, interior voice and so on. The verdict was: bring Willard's narration back into the film!

Francis then hired Michael Herr, author of the Vietnam memoir *Dispatches*, to write a whole new narration, geared to the evolving structure of the film. Every four weeks or so, Marty Sheen would come up from LA to record the new material, and we editors would fit this into the film. The narration would in turn change how the film told itself, which would then give us new ideas, which would lead to revised narration, and so on. Eight drafts of narration were eventually written and recorded.

Of course, it would be a further fifteen months before *Apocalypse* was finally released, in August 1979.

Shakespeare in the Doughnut Shop

Marty Sheen had flown up to San Francisco the evening before one of these recording sessions, in late spring 1978. On my way home that evening, I stopped by the

We recorded Marty in Richard Beggs's basement sound studio in Zoetrope's Columbus Tower building, sometimes to picture and sometimes not. In the spirit of *film noir*, I suggested we experiment with using the classic RCA 44-BX ribbon microphone (left) that had been used in films of the 1940s and '50s. But memory and reality are often different: the sound of the RCA mic was hard-edged and 'barking' when we set it against our images. It was definitely too *noir* for *Apocalypse*. Instead, we used the Neumann U 87 (right), a beautiful voice microphone that is still very much in use today

Poul Anderson

Albatross, a pub across Kearny Street, where I joined a group of Zoetroopers – Tony Dingman, Doug Claybourne and a couple of others – for a coffee.

'Where's Marty?' I asked Doug, who was the post-production co-ordinator.

'He went to the bathroom.'

As I drank my coffee, I caught up on things with Tony and Doug. We were aiming for a preview in May, and I asked about preparations for an ADR session with Robert Duvall, down in LA. After five minutes, Marty had not returned to the table, so Doug went to check on him. Marty's personal life was turbulent at the time.

'He's gone. He climbed out the window.'

The four of us went off to search in four different directions. As I rounded the corner of Kearny and Columbus, heading south, the customers at Winchell's Donuts – usually randomly scattered in their solitary reveries – were all aligned in the same direction, aiming their gaze at something I could not yet see.

I heard it before I could see it: Shakespeare – I think the St Crispin's Day speech from *Henry V*. A few steps further revealed the source: Marty, sitting on the stairs of the side entrance, with his back to the street, declaiming and gesticulating. I pushed

the door open, and Marty gradually became aware that someone was standing behind him. He turned around slowly, still declaiming. When he saw who it was, he paused. His face was a drunken blur. He pointed at me and his watery eyes widened. It was the same face as in the opening scene of *Apocalypse*.

'The Avenging Angel!' he stage-whispered, loud enough that the doughnut audience could hear it.

'Come on, Marty, let's go back to the Albatross.'

He stood up, turned and bowed to his audience, who applauded enthusiastically. He took a second bow, whirled around, and we were out on the street. I delivered Marty to Doug and Tony and then headed home after a long day.

But the night went on longer for those three. They moved from the Albatross on Columbus to Enrico's on Broadway, and then Vesuvio's next door. Tony stayed with Marty after Doug left for home, and they went on to Specs' bar, where chairs were thrown, the bar was jumped upon and the police were called, and Marty wound up in jail at 2 a.m., booked under his birth name: Ramón Estévez.

Truth is inimitable, the false, untransformable

> It all culminated in an arrest in San Francisco. I tried to beat up a couple of
> cops. I got rolled, lost all my money. Francis had to bail me out. It was terrible,
> horrible. I had to publicly confess my sins to the judge. It was the worst day of
> my whole life.[7]

Marty recovered somewhat after a few hours' sleep, feeling ashamed for what had happened, but he wanted to record the narration anyway. We were doubtful but thought maybe it might be worth experimenting. Willard was, in fact, drunk and hungover in the film's opening reels, so the voice of a hungover Marty might be interesting. It was also worth it just to soothe his feelings of guilt.[8]

But, no surprise, this version of the narration didn't work. The hangover quality certainly came through strongly, but Herr's narration required a voice that speaks to us more philosophically, long after a disaster, from a future time and place. Captain Willard, like Ishmael in *Moby-Dick*, is the survivor of a catastrophic 'shipwreck': the upriver mission to kill the white whale of Colonel Kurtz. 'I only am escaped alone to tell thee,' as Herman Melville wrote.

The influence of *Moby Dick*

When director John Huston was in London recording Richard Basehart's narration for *Moby Dick* (1956), they spent a morning trying various approaches. Basehart was isolated in a recording booth; Huston was in the main studio, listening over a monitor speaker. Nothing satisfied him. Finally, Basehart, who had played Ishmael, leaned forward, tired and frustrated, and pleaded, 'John, I think it's time for lunch!' Huston sat up in his chair, electrified: 'That's it! That's what we want!'

Basehart's forward lean-in to ask for lunch had put him closer to the microphone than engineers recommended, and this – combined with his fatigue – had produced a warmer and more intimate tone, which was what Huston had been searching for, without knowing it. The engineers were horrified because this close proximity of lips to mic was forbidden by the instruction manuals, but Huston insisted, and that was how *Moby Dick*'s narration was finally performed and recorded.

---

7. Jean Vallely, 'Martin Sheen: Heart of Darkness Heart of Gold', *Rolling Stone*, 1 November 1979: https://www.rollingstone.com/tv-movies/tv-movie-news/martin-sheen-heart-of-darkness-heart-of-gold-80879.

8. After this crisis, Marty successfully refocused his life, and things improved. By 1999, twenty years after *Apocalypse*, he had gone from being Willard in *Apocalypse* to Jed Bartlet, the President of the United States, in *The West Wing*.

Robert Bresson

Sound editor Les Hodgson had heard this story from his friend Russ Lloyd, the editor of *Moby Dick*, and he relayed the story to me when we were working together on *Julia*, twenty years later. This close-in 'Basehart' microphone technique was how we recorded Jane Fonda's narration for that film, and two years further on, we used the same approach for Marty Sheen's narration on *Apocalypse*.[9]

In the final mix of *Apocalypse*, I put Marty's narration at equal volume across all three front speakers – left, centre, right. This was also usually forbidden, but the intimate warmth of his voice was now all-embracing and further distinguished from the 'normal' dialogue in the film, which was heard only through the centre speaker.

Noisy Dialogue: *Apocalypse Now*

As on *The Conversation*, I was a film editor as well as sound designer and lead mixer on *Apocalypse*, so I was able to make certain structural decisions in picture editing that would help make the sound be as effective as possible. But it was obvious from the beginning that there would be a tremendous amount of ADR – much more than on any film I have ever worked on, before or since.

The underlying reasons for so much ADR were similar to those on any war or fantasy film: too much noisy equipment (helicopters, tanks, etc.) and frequently the wrong kind of noise (guns that fired blanks, for example). But Francis had further increased the problems for sound by making courageous decisions about visual authenticity: he put himself, cinematographer Vittorio Storaro and the actors in harm's way aboard real helicopters flying complex and dangerous manoeuvres, while Albert Hall, who played Chief, was actually piloting the noisy diesel patrol boat ferrying Willard upriver. Clear dialogue recording in those environments was impossible.

I was terrified. The menacing danger was that the film would sound 'loopy', zombie voices killing the electric atmosphere that Francis and Vittorio had created in the visuals. The question was: how could we ensure that this loopy zombification didn't occur?

Our approach to this challenge rode on two rails, one philosophical, one practical, and both based on the belief that we could achieve our goal: the ADR dialogue in *Apocalypse Now* would sound like it was all recorded on location!

---

9. The common thread here is Les Hodgson, who worked on all three of those films, as well as editing picture on my film *Return to Oz*.

The amazing thing about cinema is that it is an endless card trick performed in public without letting anyone glimpse the secret mechanism

The philosophical

The synchronisation of words with lips is only one of five kinds of sync: (1) the sync of space – the voice should sound like it is in the acoustic space implied by the visuals; (2) the sync of movement – if the actor is moving, the voice should give a sense of that movement; (3) the sync of tonal quality – the tone of the actor's voice should match their facial expression; (4) the sync of vocal projection – the actor's voice should have the strength required by the scene; and (5) the actor's lips should match the words being spoken.

The final result of an ADR recording, when successful, is the chemical interaction of these five elements. If the first four are correct, then the last, lip sync, can be slightly incorrect and yet still work, thanks to a psychological peculiarity called the *McGurk effect*: the listener will hear the 'correct' syllables, despite there being a technical mismatch between the sound and the visual. Our auditory cortex fills in what 'must be', despite the evidence of our eyes and ears.[10] We certainly would not carelessly ignore lip sync, but we knew that focusing exclusively on that and ignoring the other four 'synchronous' criteria would be a fatal mistake.

Sennheiser 'shotgun' microphone

The practical

(1) Microphones. Instead of studio microphones like the U 87, we chose the same ones used by Nat Boxer in the Philippines, mainly the Sennheiser 'shotgun' mic. The response of this microphone would better match the location recordings that *were* perfectly fine (around 15 per cent of the total), and using a shotgun mic in the studio would also encourage the actors to project their voices, since we would be placing the mic further away from them than was normal studio practice. Consequently, the ADR studio environments had to be carefully baffled with sound absorption panels to make this extra distance work.

(2) Movement. Using this microphone technique meant that we could get movement into the actor's voice when it was required, as the Sennheiser could easily be panned with the actor's movements. For some ADR sessions we hired a boom operator, just like on location.

10. The McGurk effect: https://www.youtube.com/watch?v=2k8fHR9jKVM (QR code on right).

(3) Exterior ADR. For certain scenes with group voices, we recorded ADR lines at an exterior location that allowed us to get the group moving relative to each other and the microphone. These dynamics – very convincing for characters in motion – are impossible to record authentically in the studio. A good example is the helicopter landing scene during the 'Valkyries' sequence.[11]

(4) ADR premixing. In premixing the ADR, I treated those lines to a kind of 'friendly distress', setting their filtering equalisation *as if* they had been difficult production tracks, mostly rolling off the lower frequencies. I would also dynamically adjust the higher frequencies in response to the actors' movements, increasing it when they were facing the camera and rolling it off if they were looking away.

On Chief's ADR to Willard ('You just going for a ride, Captain!'), you can hear the subtle variance in equalisation, depending on the position of Chief's head. After the motors were switched off, most – but not all – of the dialogue was recorded on location. The argument between Lance and Chief is ADR

(5) Worldising. It was also during the premix that I would add, onto tracks which could be separately adjusted later, acoustic reverberation to match the environment of the scene as photographed. Is it a shower stall or an amphitheatre? In those pre-digital days we did not have the plug-ins to achieve this with the click of a mouse, so we relied on a kitchen cabinet of analogue or very early digital rack-mounted devices – whatever would get us the results we were after: we had an early Eventide Clockworks digital delay, the 1745;[12] a spring-loaded metal-plate echo; an ordinary room (which doubled as an editing room) outfitted with a speaker and a microphone to give us 'room-ising' of ADR; a specially constructed, acoustically isolated 'coffin' that contained a microphone and a collection of things like bullhorns and walkie-talkies for special effects; we would also take certain recorded voices out into the world and play them through loudspeakers in real environments, capturing them on a second recorder to get 'worldised' reverb.

Worldising was pioneered by Orson Welles in his radio days during the 1930s (though he didn't use this not-yet-invented term) and he employed it extensively on

11. Available on Vimeo: https://vimeo.com/984419013.

12. For a very good history of Eventide digital delay devices, see https://www.perfectcircuit.com/signal/eventide-history-pt1.

It is easier to fool people than to convince them that they have been fooled

Touch of Evil in 1957. His pitch to Universal Studios to justify doing this ran as follows (available at the Internet Archive: https://tinyurl.com/25zcnpjr; QR code on right):

> It will not be enough in doing the final sound mixing to run this [music] track through an echo chamber with a certain amount of filter. To get the effect we're looking for it is absolutely vital that this music be played back through a cheap horn [i.e. speaker] in the alley outside the sound building. After this is recorded, it can be loused-up [i.e. distressed] even further in the basic process of re-recording. Since it does not represent very much in the way of money, I feel justified in insisting upon this, as the result will really be worth it.

I adapted and extended this technique on the mixes of *The Rain People*, *THX 1138*, *The Godfather*, *American Graffiti*, *Godfather II* and *Apocalypse Now*, and the practice of worldising later became widespread in post-production sound.[13]

Helicopter Pilot Chatter: Overcoming Self-Consciousness

We needed a supplementary track of helicopter-pilot radio chatter for the 'Valkyries' sequence, so we contacted four Air Cavalry pilots who had served in Vietnam and asked them to come in and improvise chatter as they watched the scene. We were recording, once again, in Richard Beggs's basement studio and outfitted the pilots with helmets that had live mics and headphones so that they could hear each other's cross-talk. Each pilot would be recorded on a separate track.

The first take was a disappointment. The second was no better: the pilots were self-conscious in this unfamiliar environment, hesitant and stilted, with little excitement in their voices. It would have been no encouragement to say, 'Don't be so self-conscious,' which would have just reinforced the obvious, like asking someone to not think of an elephant.

Richard and I put our heads together, and I asked him to conjure up the sound of Huey helicopters in flight and then feed that sound at maximum volume into the monitor speakers in the room where the pilots were. This would be exciting, giving them the sense that they were airborne, and they wouldn't be hearing each other or themselves so clearly, so the embarrassment factor would be less. But Richard, correctly, objected, asking, 'Why don't we just feed the sound into their headphones?'

---

13. Two links with more information about worldising: http://filmsound.org/terminology/worldizing. htm; https://www.youtube.com/watch?v=gAN9pBY7jHA.

Mark Twain

He had a point. If we put the helicopter loop on the monitor speakers, it would be 'in the air' and then recorded on the tracks of the pilots' voices. But I persisted: I wanted the pilots to feel the super-low-frequency *thudding* of the Huey blades with their bodies, not just with their ears. I knew that we could cut out the Huey effect when the pilots weren't speaking, and any leakage over their voices would be minimised because the helmet microphones were so close to their lips. Anyway, the leakage would be swamped in the final mix by the sound effects of the scene itself. So Richard quickly dug a Huey out of his effects library, threw a couple of switches, and we were recording again.

The effect was electric. The pilots' self-consciousness disappeared instantly, and the excitement in their voices boiled over. We recorded a couple of extra takes, and the job – at least the recording part of it – was done. There was still painstaking editorial work ahead to select the best moments, edit out the Hueys in between and place the chatter correctly with the picture, but in the end it all worked out.[14]

Aside from the unusual technical quirks, what I took away from this session was that there is no absolute 'by the book' way of doing ADR. The important thing is to evaluate the actors' needs, within reason, in order to give their best performance – and every actor is different. You cannot let them drive the session – it is much too technical and artificial for that – but if it means breaking some of the customary procedures to get a performance, then this is what you should do.

Colonel Kurtz becomes Colonel Leighley becomes Colonel Kurtz

When Marlon Brando first read the screenplay of *Apocalypse Now*, one of the things that bothered him was the short brutality of the name Kurtz (which *means* 'short' in German). He preferred a multisyllabic, 'flowery' name because, he said, many of the officers in the American military come from the southern states, where flowery, multisyllabic 'French' names are the norm. When Francis asked him for suggestions, Brando proposed *Leighley. Colonel Leighley.*

So Leighley it became, in the script and all of the on-screen documents. And it remained this way all through shooting, until Brando arrived in the Philippines. He

14. The results can be seen and heard on Vimeo: https://vimeo.com/984419013.

Analogies are imperfect, of course, but they make us feel at home

had promised to lose weight but had not done so, and perhaps his embarrassment led to disagreements about the screenplay, which called for him to be more active than his bulk would allow. These disagreements escalated to the point where filming stopped for a week while Francis and Brando hashed out the issues. The circularity of their arguments was finally broken when Brando appeared one morning with a shaved head and said he was ready to begin. He claimed to have reread *Heart of Darkness* overnight and was inspired to take this new direction.

'And change my name back to Kurtz, like in the book.'

Brando had been charging his full fee, even during the days when filming was suspended, so Francis was just happy that this nightmare was over. Vittorio had some ideas about how to deal with Brando's bulk (shadows were the answer), and filming began.

But the aftershocks of this switch continued to rumble on for almost two years. All of the documentation in the CIA dossier had to be reshot because of the change, and then there was the name Colonel Leighley, spoken six times in the briefing scene where Willard is given the order to kill Leighley *with extreme prejudice.*

I was well aware of the problem when I was editing that scene, so I used off-camera readings a few times, but there is a limit to such subterfuge. If no character ever spoke the name on camera, the audience would smell something fishy, even if they didn't know why. So, in the end, the lips of General Corman (G. D. Spradlin) and Colonel Lucas (Harrison Ford) both say the name Leighley on camera – twice for Spradlin and once for Ford.

We arranged for an ADR session to transform *Leighley* into *Kurtz*. Spradlin confronted the puzzle and solved it, twice (thanks in part to the McGurk effect!). But the challenge of saying it even once was a four-dimensional Rubik's cube for Harrison. This was early in his film career, and the idea that he had to look at an image of himself saying one thing and say something else instead caused him a perplexity that he could not overcome.

I got a call from Francis, who was directing the ADR sessions in LA, asking me to come up with a solution. 'Get Harrison to come up to San Francisco and we will sort it out,' I said, with as much confidence as I could muster. I figured that the problem had probably been a too-intense focus on getting lips and sound to match, which, of course, they never really would in this case.

In preparation for Harrison, I went back to a rough-and-ready technique we had used in film-school days: *speed looping*. This involved two tape recorders: one to play back a repeated loop of the dialogue to be replaced, and another to capture the actor's new performance. There is no projector – no image is involved; speed looping relied solely on the actor's ability to mimic himself from the rhythm of his original performance.

Harrison arrived in San Francisco a couple of days later, and we went to the basement screening room in Francis's Pacific Heights home – a comfortable, soothing environment. We had two Nagra recorders in place, one ready to play back a loop of the line 'Pick up Colonel Leighley's path at Nu Mung Ba,' and the other set to record Harrison saying, 'Pick up Colonel Kurtz's path at Nu Mung Ba.'

I explained the idea of speed looping to Harrison: 'We turn on both Nagras, one playing back and one recording. You listen to the loop as long as you need to in order to get into the rhythm of the line. When you are comfortable, press this button – it will kill the audio from the loop Nagra. Now speak the line several times. Press the button again, listen to the loop of the original line again and repeat until everyone is happy.'

Harrison did all this with a certain amount of wary enthusiasm. I took on the role of Willard, with Harrison looking at me as he delivered the line, much more like an actual in-character performance. In normal ADR, there is something absurdly Escher-like about an actor looking at an image of himself delivering lines *as* he delivers his new lines (talk about duality of the soul!).

The keys to the success of speed looping were: the absence of picture (picture can often confuse more than it helps); the quick, rhythmic repeat of the line to be replaced (ADR systems at that time had very slow repeat cycles); and, perhaps most importantly, granting control to the actor to deliver the line when they are ready to do so (in an ADR session, actors can feel like they are trapped in a relentless hamster wheel).

The disadvantage was that we couldn't check sync until we got back into the editing room, but the human auditory cortex is incredibly sophisticated at picking up rhythm, and we can easily tell if something is off by only a couple of frames, so we were 98 per cent certain that the new line would work.[15] And it did.

Of course, this was back in 1978, and the technology was primitive by today's standards: there was no digital recording, and even portable videotape was only just beginning to emerge out of its cocoon. There is no reason why the speed-looping approach cannot be adapted to ProTools, Final Cut, Premiere or any of today's digital editing programs.

15. The ADR of these 'Kurtz' lines can be seen on Vimeo: https://vimeo.com/1016324679 (QR code on left).

What you are looking for is what is looking

The Godfather: Part III: Family Relations and Duality of the Soul

Winona Ryder had been cast as Mary, Michael Corleone's daughter, in *The Godfather: Part III*, but the punishing schedule of her previous three films, shot one right after the other, caught up with her as soon as she arrived in Italy, and due to exhaustion and upper respiratory infections, she bowed out before any film was shot.

This crisis set off a search for her replacement, and after considering a number of other actresses, Francis cast his daughter, Sofia, aged eighteen, in the part. This was a risky, highly contentious decision, opposed by Paramount and many on the production team. Sofia had appeared in a number of Francis's previous films – in fact, as a baby she had played Michael Francis Rizzi, Connie's (Talia Shire's) baby, in the baptism scene of the first *Godfather* movie – but she was not a trained actress and had never taken on a major role. Sofia has recently gone on record saying that she never wanted to be an actress, but she did want to help her father:

> It seemed like he was under a lot of pressure and I was helping out. There was this panic and before I knew it, I was in a makeup chair in Cinecittà Studios in Rome having my hair dyed . . . I wasn't taking things super-seriously. I was at the age of trying anything. I just jumped into it without thinking much about it.[16]

There had been an earlier casting crisis with Robert Duvall (Tom Hagen in the two previous *Godfather*s), when Paramount refused to pay his fee (he had asked for the same deal as Al Pacino). The 1980s had taken a toll on Francis's finances and industry clout since the heady days of the 1970s, and he did what Paramount wanted, rewriting the screenplay without the crucial Hagen character.

> I was in much less of a strong position. Frankly, I needed the money, and I was coming out of a real financial doldrum where I had almost lost everything.[17]

The psychological toll of these two reversals, on a film that Francis has often said he didn't want to make in the first place, was immense. He probably reached out

---

16. Dave Itzkoff, 'How Francis Ford Coppola Got Pulled Back in to Make "The Godfather, Coda"', *New York Times*, 2 December 2020: https://www.nytimes.com/2020/12/02/movies/godfather-coda-francis-ford-coppola.html.

17. Itzkoff, 'How Francis Ford Coppola Got Pulled Back in to Make "The Godfather, Coda"'.

---

to his daughter Sofia as a kind of emotional lifejacket, as Francis's sister Talia Shire recently observed:

> It was a stressful time. [Sofia's] being in it and [Francis's] focus on sculpting her performance kept him connected to the piece. His passion for it returned.[18]

I joined the editorial team of *Godfather III* in August 1990, shortly after finishing Jerry Zucker's *Ghost*, to help the film meet its December release date. Barry Malkin and Lisa Fruchtman had been editing since the start of shooting and had already put together a first assembly. They were both using the VHS-based, computer-assisted Montage editing system. I stuck with the KEM flatbed machine that I had been using on *Ghost*.

It was clear to everyone, including Francis, that Sofia's performance needed help. She looked the part – half Italian, half Irish – and was the right age for Mary, but she was neither a trained nor an intuitive actress and her voice in the film was problematic: a Californian teenage drawl rather than Upper East Side New York, it lacked spark and was often hard to understand.

As we neared our preview in early December, Francis suggested ADR-ing Sofia's performance to improve the clarity of her diction and its emotional vibrance, but he realised that having Sofia listen to her own voice and then improve upon it was not going to work. So in the spirit of family values, he asked his forty-four-year-old sister Talia, who had played Connie in all three *Godfather* films, to ADR Sofia's lines.

Talia's ADR was astonishing. She is, of course, a trained actress, with a great range of experience, and she was able to pitch her voice convincingly to the teenage register. The underlying family tonalities of her voice were also a perfect match to Sofia, and yet it also had hints of maturity and depth: when Mary presents the Vatican with a cheque for $100 million, you believed that this girl, with that voice, somehow had the strength and intelligence to go with that amount of money. It also had articulation, along with youthful sexiness; the romantic scenes with Vincent Corleone, Mary's cousin, worked very well.

It was a surreal experience to watch the romantic involvement of two on-screen cousins, knowing that the voice of the girl cousin was actually that of her own aunt. I could feel Renoir's ghost shaking his chains at us for not only preaching but practising the duality of the soul. I also thought, heretically, that Talia's readings were so

---

18. Itzkoff, 'How Francis Ford Coppola Got Pulled Back in to Make "The Godfather, Coda"'.

Choose your actors well, so they lead you where you want to go

good they should replace Sofia's. But that would have been a momentous step, and not something I felt comfortable suggesting until we gave Sofia's ADR lines a chance. Renoir's fulmination still holds power: we film-makers hesitate before taking the irrevocable step of entirely replacing one actor's voice (their soul!) with another.

> Perhaps I was particularly susceptible to the idea of using Talia's voice because I had dabbled in this sorcery on my film *Return to Oz* six years earlier. The character of Ozma, played by Emma Ridley, was entirely revoiced by my eleven-year-old daughter Beatrice, using the speed-loop system (giving Ozma an American accent instead of a London one). And the actresses playing Mombi (Sophie Ward, Fiona Victory, Jean Marsh), with her different heads, all had Jean Marsh's voice – although Jean altered her tone slightly in each case.

When we recorded Sofia's ADR, guided by Talia's line readings and Francis's direction, it was a definite improvement but did not transform her performance the way Talia's readings had. And then, almost immediately, came the film's only public preview, in Seattle, three weeks before the theatrical release. That preview did not go particularly well, and Francis gave us editors and mixers a list of hundreds of picture and sound changes, which kept us fully occupied for the next ten days. It also turned out that the negative had already been cut – a pre-emptive move by Paul Haggar – so our picture changes had to take this into account. The slightest misstep would have been catastrophic.

We just barely succeeded in making all the changes on Francis's list, but in that period of controlled chaos, with the looming need to make thousands of release prints breathing down our necks, it seemed a bridge too far to bring up the idea of using Talia's ADR. If we'd had more time, if the release of the film had been a few months later – Easter, perhaps, as for the first *Godfather* movie – this heretical concept might have had the chance to get tested with an audience. But it was not to be. When *Godfather III* was released on Christmas Day 1990, the reviewers had honed their pens to stiletto sharpness. The film was praised for its beauty and the breadth of its story, as it took on the Mafia's complicated involvement with the Vatican's finances (the film eventually received seven Academy Award nominations). But when critics wanted to express disappointment with a sequel made sixteen years after two of the most-praised films in history, the easiest target was Sofia.

Robert Bresson

Thirty years later, Francis is resignedly philosophical about the matter:

> They wanted to attack the picture when, for some, it didn't live up to its
> promise. And they came after this 18-year-old girl, who had only done it for me.
> The daughter took the bullet for Michael Corleone – my daughter took the bullet
> for me.[19]

Francis's wife Ellie had mixed feelings, as she confessed in the diary she wrote for
Vogue magazine during shooting:

> Well-meaning people tell me I am permitting a form of child abuse . . . that she
> is not ready, not trained for what is being asked of her, and that in the end she
> will be fodder for critics' bad reviews that could scar her for years.[20]

For her part, Sofia bravely endured this storm and has since become an Oscar-
winning writer–director:

> It was embarrassing to be thrown out to the public in that kind of way. But it
> wasn't my dream to be an actress, so I wasn't crushed. I had other interests.
> It didn't destroy me . . . It taught me that as a creative person, you have to put
> your work out there. It toughens you up. I know it's a cliché, but it can make
> you stronger.[21]

Would Talia's voice have made a difference to the reception of the film? My sense
is that it might well have done, so powerful was the transformation of Mary's character. But could the voice change have been kept a secret? And what of the *soul-duality*
trauma of having your voice replaced?[22] Perhaps in the end, despite all the controversy,
it was better that things remained as they were.

As problematic as Sofia's casting proved to be, I believe it was the absence of the
Tom Hagen character that wounded the film more grievously. The presence of Hagen/
Duvall would have paired Al Pacino, the actor, with someone, a fictional brother,
who could also perform at his level. Pacino would have perhaps played Michael differently. Tom would have seen through Michael's lies and been able to challenge him

---

19. Itzkoff, 'How Francis Ford Coppola Got Pulled Back in to Make "The Godfather, Coda"'.

20. Melina Gerosa, 'Storm Over Sofia Coppola', *Entertainment Weekly*, 25 January 1991: https://
ew.com/article/1991/01/25/storm-over-sofia-coppola.

21. Itzkoff, 'How Francis Ford Coppola Got Pulled Back in to Make "The Godfather, Coda"'.

22. See Andie MacDowell on the pain of learning her voice was replaced by Glenn Close's in Hugh
Hudson's film *Greystoke* (1985): https://www.youtube.com/watch?v=6_wyHEXYAHc.

Don't try to force poetry. It will come of its own accord. Even whispering its name
will scare it away

in a way no other character in the film was capable of doing. As it was planned in Francis's original screenplay, this struggle between the brothers would have resulted in the death of Tom. And with that, the standing of the *Godfather* trilogy itself would have benefited: each of the three films would then have been about the death of a brother – Sonny, Fredo, Tom – leaving Michael, the youngest of the four, at his solipsistic summit of power. It would have had the shape of a myth: *Once upon a time, there was a king who had four sons . . .*

So the attacks on Sofia were, in part, probably a case of referred pain: the critics and a fair proportion of the public were disappointed by *Godfather III*, without fundamentally knowing why, and consequently they attacked the most visible and vulnerable target.

In December 2020 Francis issued a recut of the film entitled *The Godfather Coda: The Death of Michael Corleone*, which is four minutes shorter than the 1990 version.[23] The beginning now has the structure of the original screenplay, with a greying, crew-cut Michael making a deal with the Vatican. And the end is different: Michael does not die but is left sitting alone with his regrets at the final fade-out.

Soul-Duality Redux: Automatic Deepfake Replacement

Finally, the future may conjure up something that would make Jean Renoir's ghost apoplectic: *deepfake audio.*

For a number of years we have had the ability, with moving images, to use the metadata from a 'control' performance by one person to animate the database-stockpiled images of a second individual. In essence, the second person becomes the unwilling puppet of the first. We are further along with visuals than we are with audio, but astonishing progress is being made on both fronts.[24] Deepfake audio would take the stockpiled 'audio images' of one person's voice and 'animate' them with the performance of another. Humphrey Bogart, for instance, could be made to give a convincing lecture on particle physics. The implications for ADR are obvious: we could take the metadata from a noisy on-set performance by an actor and use it to 'pull the strings' of their stockpiled clean 'audio images' – ADR without the actor being present at all. Even more heretical, another actor could be called in to supply the metadata for an ADR-ed performance by the original performer.

23. I didn't know this recut was happening until it was finished and its release was announced.

24. As is usual, the pornographic industry is leading the charge into *deepfakery*, where celebrities can be made to give convincing X-rated performances, even from beyond the grave.

Jean Cocteau

The cultural and political implications of this are now beginning to be felt and will become increasingly evident in years to come. Barack Obama, for instance, was made to 'give' an interview that never happened, in a deepfake example put together by Jordan Peele.[25]

Interestingly, this 'metadata puppetry' is what happens spontaneously in the feedback between the neurons, vocal cords and facial expressions of talented mimics. Mimics use their mentally stored 'audio' and 'visual images' of another person, and then somehow (this is the real mystery) reconfigure their vocal cords and facial expressions to imitate the person to be mimicked.

We confronted exactly this situation for a scene in Anthony Minghella's *The Talented Mr. Ripley*. As written and performed, Ripley (Matt Damon) was required to do a 'perfect' imitation of Herbert Greenleaf, Dickie's father. At the time of filming, Matt did a workmanlike imitation, but it was not good enough to justify Dickie's amazed 'Uncanny!' reaction, so the line was slated to be perfected in ADR.

Mark Levinson, the ADR editor of *Ripley*, asked James Rebhorn, the actor who played Herbert Greenleaf, to ADR the lines spoken by Matt. These were in turn looped and fed into Matt's headset at the time of his ADR session (very similar to the set-up we had with Talia Shire, when her voice was fed into Sofia Coppola's headset). Matt – supremely talented actor and mimic that he is – was able to take those phrases and then convolute his own vocal cords into an astonishing imitation of Rebhorn's voice.

Mark took this ADR recording of Matt and proudly played it for Anthony. But Matt's imitation was so convincing that Anthony thought Mark had simply used Rebhorn's voice. Even when the trick was explained to him, he was reluctant to use Matt's ADR, because it was 'too good': he felt that audiences would react the same way as he did, believing that we had just used Rebhorn's voice. The painstaking solution was for Mark to go through the recording, syllable by syllable, and, using some of the earlier takes of Matt's ADR, make the imitation less convincing. In a paradoxical way, those imperfections made it *more* convincing.[26]

Coda: ADR – General Observations, Tips and Tricks

Despite Jean Renoir's objections, ADR sessions are necessary on almost every film. They are entirely artificial set-ups, conducted perhaps six months or more after the

25. This one was done in 2018 (https://www.youtube.com/watch?v=cQ54GDm1eL0; QR code on left). Since then, technical progress has vastly improved the 'quality' and reduced the cost of deepfakes.

26. This scene can be viewed on Vimeo: https://vimeo.com/1016426657.

Talent hits a target no one else can hit. Genius hits a target no one else can see

original performance. The actors might have acted in three other films by then, so the challenges are how to get back into character after so much time has passed and how to cope with the process of ADR recording, which is totally unlike the interpersonal, actor/actor give-and-take of the original production.

· One habit from the earliest days of ADR that is still often used is to feed the actor's previous reading into his headset and require him to say the new line *at the same time*. I would avoid doing this. It prevents the actor from hearing his own speaking voice and modulating his performance, and the result is often a sleepy or slightly 'drunken' reading. Instead, play the line to be replaced in a quick-repeat loop as many times as it takes for the actor to be comfortable with it, and then, just before the moment of recording, mute the playback of the old line and let the actor give the new reading.

· All actors confront the ADR problem differently, depending on their personality and abilities. There are supremely talented actors who are hopeless at ADR, and vice versa. Experience doesn't seem to count for much; it comes down to temperament and some peculiar innate ability, like being able to wiggle your ears. Fairuza Balk, who played Dorothy in *Return to Oz* when she was nine years old, was not only a supremely talented actress in front of the camera, she was preternaturally good at ADR, despite having never done it before. She would play around in the studio, hear the three ADR beeps, run up to the microphone, deliver her line and then scamper back to where she had been playing. Almost every one of her lines was a 'hole in one': one take, perfect in terms of sync and performance.

· On average – repeat, on *average* – you can expect to get eight to ten lines recorded in an hour. Harrison Ford, on Kathryn Bigelow's *K-19: The Widowmaker* (2002), recorded fifty lines in three hours, or one line every three and a half minutes.

· If you are ADR-ing a scene between two people and schedules permit, it is a good idea to have the two actors in the studio at the same time, bouncing off each other's interpretations, as they did in the original shoot. In fact, anything that reduces the artificial 'hamster wheel' aspect of an ADR session should be tried.

· Be wary of the actor who comes into the studio with bravado, claiming, 'I am great at ADR. We will have all thirty lines done in an hour.' Usually, these sessions will be problematic. Ideally, you want an actor who is slightly nervous but alert to the challenges; as Paul Newman's character said before the climactic pool game in *The Hustler* (1961), 'Tight but good.'

· An occupational hazard of ADR is the natural tendency of even experienced actors to speak too softly because of the dark, enclosed nature of the studio environment. They believe that they are projecting their voices correctly, but this is an illusion. A large microphone placed close to an actor is almost inevitably 'understood' to be another human head, and this will also result in softer projection. To have to keep reminding actors to elevate their projection becomes tedious after a while; using a more directional microphone placed further away (as we did on *Apocalypse*) can be a subtler encouragement.

· For ADR lines that require shouting, there is a natural tendency for actors to 'stage-shout' – the inverse of the 'stage whisper' – speaking loudly but holding back instead of going for full-throated shouting. Real volume is required. What seems like extreme loudness in the quiet studio will usually prove to be perfect once it is blended in with all the other sounds in the final mix.

· To record an ADR line that is supposed to be a distant exterior voice, it is best to record it outside, in the correct environment; if the shot is wide enough, lip sync will not be a problem. The speed-loop technique is good in these instances, or just recording the line 'wild', with no references. If exterior recording is impossible, then use a directional microphone in the studio and move it far enough away from the actor so that intimate vocal transients (lip smacks, etc.) are eliminated, but not so far away as to pick up room resonance. There are now fairly sophisticated digital plug-in filters that can 'deconvolute' resonance in a recording, but eliminating vocal transients is still very difficult, so make sure you do not record these.

· A distant exterior voice is characterised by four qualities:

(1) The correct amount of projection in the actor's voice.
(2) Very little low- or high-frequency information; a distant voice is heard primarily in the middle frequencies, 400–1,500 Hz.
(3) Very few dynamics; distance removes all intimate transients (lip smack, etc.).
(4) The level of spatial reverberation is often high relative to the voice itself, depending on the environment. On the other hand, if the location is the desert

or an open field, there will be no reverberation. Those previous three qualities (1–3) can be applied to the voice during the mix with filtering, compression and the appropriate reverb program, but you should always begin with a perfectly dry recording, without any room reverb or vocal transients, and with the right amount of projection in the line reading.

· Frequently, an actor's voice needs to be ADR-ed for intelligibility because some consonants were dropped in performance or recording. It is interesting that 'voice-less' consonants – the sounds of 'K', 'S', 'F', 'H', 'P', 'T', 'SH', 'CH', 'KS', 'TH', 'TS' – can be edited into a word that is missing them. Ask an actor to say the sentence 'Ten sleeping foxes should have cool charming peaceful thoughts' during production, and you have a library of these useful consonants, which can be inserted where these sounds might be missing. In fact, voiceless consonants from one actor can often be used in the performance of another; it is only the unique tonal vibrations of an actor's larynx and chest which give identity to a voice.[27]

---

27. The ten 'voiced' consonants are 'B', 'D', 'G', 'J', 'L', 'M', 'N', 'R', 'V', 'Z'. Speaking these sounds means engaging the voice box, which is not the case with the voiceless consonants.

Robert Bresson

25: THE MANY LIVES OF SOUND EFFECT 9413

A Hollywood Sound Effect Goes Back to Nebraska

This verbatim interview with sound effect 9413 was recorded a few years ago. It is a unique testimony, allowing us to understand things not from the point of view of sound editors or mixers, but from the sound effect herself. Like many young people who threw themselves on the altar of Hollywood in those years (late 1950s), 9413 was naive about the appeal of what she had to offer. But she had qualities that even she did not suspect, and I was happy to have played a small part in her resurrection. It just takes finding the right role for the inherent talent to shine through.

June 2015, the Corner Nook coffee shop, Red Cloud, Nebraska

INTERVIEWER: Thank you for taking the time. How would you like to be identified when this goes to print?

9413: They used to call me 9413. It's some kind of inside joke, but I'll go with that.[1]

INT.: OK. We are recording.

9413: I'm from Nebraska, born here in Red Cloud. Willa Cather grew up just a block over that way. But you know how young people are – I figured I had more to offer than Red Cloud could accommodate. So I went to Hollywood, following Nebraskans like Henry Fonda, Marlon Brando, Sandy Dennis, Alexander Payne, Hilary Swank. By the time Hilary came to Hollywood, though, I was long gone.

Here's my story.

I hung out on Barham Boulevard, where it crosses Route 101, over the Cahuenga Pass. I figured this was as good a place as any: lots of action and real close to Universal Studios. Anyone who goes into the Valley from Hollywood has to go under the Barham overpass. The idea was I would get noticed sooner or later – hopefully sooner, like those girls who hung out at Schwab's pharmacy, crossing their legs as they sat at

1. She is referring to the 1928 film by Robert Florey and Slavko Vorkapich, *The Life and Death of 9413: A Hollywood Extra*. Photographed by Gregg Toland, it was Toland's first film credit as DP (https://en.wikipedia.org/wiki/The_Life_and_Death_of_9413:_a_Hollywood_Extra).

Everyone would be happy to win a war. Not everyone is capable of losing one

the counter drinking cokes. Only a matter of time. This was back in the late 1950s, you see. With this set-up, I didn't think I needed an agent.

Well, nothing happened, even though thousands of film-makers drove past me every day. After a couple of years, I got an agent. They said it wasn't like the old days when Wilhelm Scream or Sonar Ping could just walk in off the street.[2] Too much competition now, especially for what I was offering: Freeway Traffic.

I stuck with it, though, and sent out flyers and résumés. I thought there would always be a need for freeway traffic – more and more, in fact – and my acoustics, because of the shape of the Cahuenga Pass, gave a lovely tonality. Much better than number 2962, the 405 traffic over the Sepulveda Pass, even if I do say so myself. More history; grittier also.

But, by the late 1960s, I'd only had a couple of callbacks. One of them was for a student film. I forget its name. *Passing* something.

INT.: *Passing Lane*?

9413: *Passing Lane*, yes. Young guys, enthusiastic. 1967, I think . . . 16 mm. Never saw it.

Anyway, by early 1969 I'd been at it for ten years, with almost nothing to show for it. Made a few friends, and we still keep in touch. I sent out one last flyer and started getting my bags ready to go back to Red Cloud in case that didn't connect. But my agent phoned at 3 a.m. on Valentine's Day. 'You've got a call, right now!' he said. 'I'm not at my best at 3 a.m.,' I said. He said, 'Doesn't matter. Beggars, choosers, you know?'

I knew. So I cleared my throat, getting ready for whatever.

At 3.15 a.m. a motorcycle shows up, pulls to a stop on the overpass. Guy gets off and unpacks a Nagra recorder from the saddlebag. 'Stupid way to carry an expensive recorder,' I thought. 'That's a professional piece of equipment, not some crummy cassette recorder' – the likes of which were starting to show up around that time.

The guy was young, too young. I expected someone in their forties or fifties – a studio type, you know? 'Is this another student film?' I thought. The guy looked familiar – maybe from *Passing Lane*? I'll see what I can come up with. He turned on the

2. For more about the Wilhelm Scream, see https://en.wikipedia.org/wiki/Wilhelm_scream.

Curzio Malaparte

Nagra. It took me a few minutes to get into the mood. He didn't say what he was looking for.

Anyway here it is, if you want to take a listen . . .

https://vimeo.com/777721733 (QR code on left)

> *Walter says:* Yes, I was the guy from *Passing Lane*, a USC student film from 1967. Matthew Robbins and I wrote it, Matthew directcd, Caleb Deschanel shot it, and I edited picture and mixed the sound. I remember recording the traffic over the Cahuenga Pass for some backgrounds for the film.
>
> Two years later, in 1969, aged twenty-five, I was doing sound montage and re-recording on Francis Coppola's *The Rain People*, starring Shirley Knight, James Caan and Robert Duvall. There was a love scene in a house trailer between Knight and Duvall, and I was wondering what would be the right atmosphere to evoke the huge nocturnal prairie space around the trailer, somewhere in Ogallala, Nebraska. Otherwise, it would just sound like something shot on a set. My first thought was crickets, but that wasn't original and wouldn't give a sense of space. Then it occurred to me to try to record the sound tractor trailers sometimes make, when the road surface is irregular and their eighteen wheels aren't balanced: a kind of high-pitched oscillating singing that carries for miles. Singing Semis.[3]
>
> For some reason, on Valentine's Day I woke suddenly at 3 a.m. and thought, 'Cahuenga Pass.'
>
> 'Where are you going at 3 a.m. on Valentine's Day?' said Aggie.

9413: Guy kept the tape rolling, I wasn't able to sustain much beyond three minutes. Exhausting to try and do that at 3 a.m. Then he switched off, packed the Nagra into his saddlebag, kick-started the BMW. I could tell from the sound it was an R50, 500cc, a few years old. And off he went, without saying what he thought. Typical . . . 'Don't call us, we'll call you.'

---

3. 'Semi' stands for 'semi-trailer truck', a vehicle in which the trailer lacks a front axle, relying on the tractor to support its front end.

The thing that matters is not what the actors show you, but what they hide from you and, above all, what they do not suspect is in them

Later on, I heard through the grapevine that I had been transferred to 35 mm magnetic – a good sign. I was afraid it was another 16 mm deal, like *Passing Lane*. But then the whole unit was moved out of Hollywood to San Francisco. They were going to mix the film there. Who mixes in San Francisco?! I started to pack for Red Cloud.

But the film got done – *The Rain People* – and, can you believe it, my aria from the Barham overpass was the atmosphere to a love scene set in . . . Ogallala, Nebraska! Ogallala's just 200 miles west of Red Cloud! I went all the way to Hollywood to make a sound I could have made just as easy if I had stayed at home here in Red Cloud!

But there was no crappy music to mess me up, and not much dialogue. Just me and the bedsprings. For three whole minutes. I thought, 'This could be my ticket!'

But the film came out and it bombed. I think twelve people saw it, total. Six of them were my relatives in Red Cloud. And some Spaniards – *Rain People* won a prize in Spain. Nebraska in Spain, go figure those odds! Of course, no callbacks. I let my agent go and moved back to Red Cloud. Ten years of my life. At least I had stories to tell.

Walter says: It was uncanny. Before I went to bed, I was thinking of the exact sound I needed, and I woke up sharply at 3 a.m. with clear instructions: 'Cahuenga Pass. Barham Boulevard. Now.'

I drove there on the BMW R50. Plugged the Sennheiser 415 mic into the Nagra III, set the tape going at 7.5 ips, and one minute later, I heard precisely the sound I had dreamed of recording. There was something perfect about the acoustics of Cahuenga Pass, how its shape focused the sound of the eighteen-wheeler as it barrelled down the hill, tyres singing, far off down into the Valley. With no other traffic to muddy things up.

I was back home by 4 a.m., and Aggie, Walter (five months old) and I had a lovely Valentine's Day breakfast when we woke up three hours later. I had to play the tape for Aggie to make sure I hadn't dreamed the whole thing.

'Very nice, dear,' she said. 'Now eat your grapefruit.'

9413: Then, a couple of years later, after I thought I had put Hollywood behind me, I heard somebody wanted to revive the Barham sound. I told them, 'Forget the semis.' I had lots of other stuff, great stuff – car crashes, you know, fire engines, tyre blowouts,

---

Robert Bresson

hubcaps coming off, squealing brakes – but they insisted on the Singing Semis. I figured it must be an inside job; there's no other explanation. Sure enough, it's the same *Passing Lane* kid, but now he's involved with a gangster movie set in New York, with a lot of Italian guys plotting in dark rooms – that kind of stuff.

But they want me for a funeral. Me (double take): 'A funeral? Will there be music?' 'No music,' they say. 'Almost no dialogue. Three minutes long. Some bells at the beginning. Footsteps. Car doors.'

'So why do you want me?' I ask. They tell me that way in the distance there is some traffic: an elevated highway leading to one of the bridges across New York's East River. I shrug. 'Doesn't make any sense. How about some birdsong? Sparrows?' No, they want what they want.

'*So let me get this straight*: a sound recorded at 3 a.m. in California, supposedly for a lonely/sad/romantic night in Ogallala, Nebraska, 1969, is now being used for a daytime scene in New York, the funeral of a mob boss, no less, in 1955? What a crazy business . . . Why would anyone go to see such a film?'

> *Walter says:* There were times when we also wondered. Even Francis was sometimes doubtful, saying, '*Godfather* is three hours long, and it's just a bunch of guys talking in dark rooms . . .' But we knew that the baptism/assassination scene was powerful, with great music and sounds, so for the funeral that immediately precedes it we wanted something different, hushed and sparse, no music, almost no dialogue. I grew up in New York and knew that location: Calvary Cemetery in Queens, 365 acres cut through by two elevated expressways – the Long Island and the Brooklyn–Queens. It's a weird place, so big and so close to Manhattan. Three million people are buried there – 50 per cent more than the population of Manhattan – including many real-life mob bosses. I thought about number 9413, that Barham overpass sound: lonely, with something strangely spiritual about it, like shimmering violins or, sometimes, buzzing bees. But urban at the same time, when placed in this context.
>
> And 9413 is right: very few people saw *The Rain People*, so I thought I could reuse this sound without it being noticed.
>
> Besides, it's all about context.

You can drive the bus wherever you want to go, but if it says 'HELL' on the front, you've got to remind people when they get on board

> *An image is transformed by contact with other images, as a colour is transformed by contact with other colours.*
>
> – Robert Bresson
>
> And you can say the same thing about sounds.

9413: Was I ever wrong . . . The film was a hit. Audiences loved it. Critics loved it. All over the world. *The Godfather*! It won Best Picture and even got nominated for Best Sound. And for the three minutes and fifty seconds of that funeral, I'm almost the only thing you hear. I was famous! And here I am, stuck in Red Cloud. Should I have gone back to Hollywood? (*She pauses to finish her coffee and light another cigarette.*)

Funeral scene from *The Godfather*: https://www.youtube.com/
watch?v=Ic6KR2CcUyA (QR code on right)

9413: No, I'm not going back. I'm 'famous' for something I did at 3 a.m., almost in my sleep. Not like number 7665, the elevated-train sound that went with the murder of that drug dealer and the cop. Besides, nobody wanted any of my other effects: rolling hubcaps, traffic jams, blowouts, crashes. I caught magic in a bottle once. What are the chances of doing it again? I'm happy here. Who knows, I could wind up being a card in Trivial Pursuit. It's a strange business, let me tell you. Thanks for looking me up.

INT.: You're welcome. It's been a privilege talking to you.

Walter says: Singing Semis, number 9413, can also be heard in a few other films. It's one of the sound elements for the Lake of Fire sequence in Matthew Robbins's *Dragonslayer* (1981), and it shows up for a moment in Peter Medak's *Romeo Is Bleeding* (1993) and Steven Soderbergh's *Erin Brockovich* (2000). And for all I know in some other films as well. There are certain sounds, and this is one of them, that have an uncanny ability to adapt themselves to a variety of situations. It is hard to predict in advance what makes that so.

The Corner Nook coffee shop, 345 North Webster
Street, Red Cloud, Nebraska

The mixture of true and false yields falsity. The false when it is
homogeneous can yield truth

26: 'VALKYRIES' IN CRISIS

Decca vs Zoetrope

I wrote the following essay for the science magazine Nautilus, *and it was published in the November 2015 issue. It is reprinted here with permission.*

In 1979, sometime during the barely controlled chaos of the last months of finishing *Apocalypse Now*, someone in legal affairs at Zoetrope had the presence of mind to ask if we had secured the rights to use the 1965 Georg Solti recording of 'Ride of the Valkyries', the music which accompanied Colonel Kilgore's attack on the Vietnamese village of Vin Drin Dop, otherwise known as Charlie's Point.

The idea of blasting music from Wagner's opera *Die Walküre* as a form of PsyWarOp (Psychological Warfare Operations) to terrify the Vietnamese had originated in the neuronal labyrinth of John Milius's mind in 1969, when he was writing the original screenplay for *Apocalypse*. The 'Ride of the Valkyries' was so deeply associated with the attack on Charlie's Point, and had been for so long – from birth, so to speak – that we who were working on the film, editing the picture and mixing the sound, could barely conceive of separating the two. How that particular Solti recording came to be chosen, I never found out – the decision predated my joining the film in the summer of 1977 – but there is a general consensus in musical circles that Solti's interpretation, conducting the Vienna Philharmonic, has never been surpassed.

So it came as an existential shock when Decca, the record company in question, refused to give us permission to use Solti's recording.

There was so little time left that we were forced to move forward along three fronts simultaneously, hoping that at least one would pay off: 1) to continue to petition Decca; 2) to make arrangements to record the 'Valkyries' with the San Francisco Symphony, trying to duplicate Solti's dynamics and meter; and 3) to comb through all the existing recordings with the hope of finding one that was close to Solti's interpretation and available to use in the film.

The last of these approaches fell to me, since I was responsible for the sound design of the film as a whole, as well as being, at that time, the picture editor for this section of the film. This was of course long before iTunes – the Apple II had only been recently released and the Macintosh was not yet gleaming in Steve Jobs's eye – so our database was the Schwann catalogue of recorded music.

It turned out that there were 19 stereo recordings of 'Valkyries' available in 1979, and I bought them all from Tower Records at the corner of Bay and Columbus in San Francisco. It was the musical equivalent of ransacking every bottle of burgundy – Gallo to Romanée-Conti – from the nearest wine shop. But as soon as I uncorked many of them, nestling the needle into the grooves of the LP, I knew that they wouldn't work: There was a vinegary tang to them – certainly in comparison to the Solti – that made my eyes water.

But a number of the others, perhaps half, deserved more serious consideration. How serious I was soon to discover.

There is always a complex rhythmic relationship between on-screen action and music, and during the editing process that relationship is constantly being adjusted and tightened, sometimes consciously, other times on a more intuitive basis. But that same kind of complex adjustment also takes place in the performance of the music itself, as the conductor balances the internal rhythmic signature of the score, adjusting it minutely, on a moment-by-moment basis, to his interpretation and the particular strengths of the orchestra he is leading.

The greatest conductors and orchestras – and Solti and the Vienna Philharmonic are certainly in that group – are able to shape these minute adjustments so that they are perceived as regular (although in reality they are not), thus enhancing the organic, living and breathing nature of the music itself – a conducting technique that musicians call *rubato*. The problem with many of the versions of 'Valkyries' that I rejected was that they were metronomically rigid, resulting in a robotic simulation of musical life rather than the real thing.

This is reflected in our intimate relationship with the rhythms of our own heartbeat. We may think that our heartbeat is regular most of the time, but in fact it is not. It is constantly adjusting, varying by small fractions of a second with each beat as it responds to the neurological feedback between the heart, the brain and the lungs. The medical term for this healthy but slightly irregular heart rhythm is *sinus arrhythmia*, and it is our largely unconscious awareness of this dynamic pulse that reminds us that we are alive. In certain cases of medical emergency, the feedback between the heart and the needs of the body is often weakened or severed, and a machine-like, robotic heartbeat appears. A perfectly regular rhythm may seem desirable, but in fact healthy systems rely on flexibility and variation as they respond to the body's requirements.

The law protects, but does not bind, the Rich. The law binds,
but does not protect, the Poor

Similarly, music that lacks this quicksilver pulse is perceived, consciously or not, as somehow lacking an essential spark of life.

Solti's *rubato* conducting of the 'Valkyries' was instead a sublime example of this dynamic flexibility – a musical sinus arrhythmia – and as such it was a powerful embodiment of the living, pulsing heart and breath of Wagner's composition.

When we had bound Solti's 'Valkyries' to that scene in *Apocalypse*, the DNA of both music and film had become inextricably linked on the largest thematic levels – remember that the Valkyries themselves are god-like female virgins riding winged horses carrying the bodies of battle-slaughtered soldiers to Valhalla – as well as the minuscule metrics of film-frame and semiquaver.

But as great as Wagner's music is, and as wonderful as Solti's recording is, we had taken a number of liberties. We had made a cut, after about 45 seconds, when the action suddenly shifts to the Vietnamese school and there is a shocking momentary silence, soon intruded upon by the distant sound of helicopters and the faint wafting of the music borne on the froth of whirring blades. This builds in intensity as the Air Cav gets closer, the teachers and students in the school begin to panic, and then the voices of the Valkyries are heard for the first time over a long shot of the helicopters, just specks on the horizon, with surf breaking in the foreground.

Whenever I watch the film, the chemistry of music and image in the next section always strikes me as particularly miraculous: the shot of the helicopters from behind as they approach the beach, the Vietnamese soldiers running along their elevated walkways, jumping into trenches, and then a remarkable series of moving shots of the helicopters, the singing Valkyrie accentuating each cut, building in intensity until the beach is crested and the first shots are finally fired.

There is a second cut in the music during a close shot of the muzzle of a mini-gun blasting its thousands of rounds a minute, and we reprise the previous section with the Valkyries vocal, although in a somewhat abbreviated form. We dropped the whole middle section of Wagner's original, where the Valkyries are calling out to each other: 'Here Helmwige, bring your horse here – Put your stallion next to Orlinde's mare, your bay will enjoy grazing with my gray – Who is hanging from your saddle?' and so on.

If we had included this, there would have been confusion along with a massive drop in energy. Instead, we take a break in the music for about 50 seconds to concentrate on dialogue between Kilgore and his men. Then as the helicopters begin to land on the beach, with the Marines jumping out under heavy Vietnamese fire, the

Frank Wilhoit

'Valkyries' starts up again, this time with the powerful final section. When some secondary ordnance explodes, knocking the legs out from under one of the marines, the music comes to an end.

So my task, desperately crucial given our dilemma, was to find another recording of the 'Valkyries' as close as possible to the rhythmic signatures of Solti's 1965 recording, that would also allow itself to be restructured in this way. I worked out a graph of the variations in Solti's rhythm, in 4-second increments, and with a stopwatch did the best I could to take the pulse of his music. It was a fantastic crash course in musicology, revealing like an X-ray the 'Valkyries'' hidden twists and turns, hesitations and accelerations.

I applied the same technique to the other recordings, hoping to find a rhythm as near as possible to Solti's. Recording after recording fell by the wayside, and in the end only one other 'Valkyries' came close: Erich Leinsdorf's 1978 Sheffield Lab recording with the Los Angeles Philharmonic.

I made a transfer from Leinsdorf's LP to 35 mm magnetic film (this was in the days when we were working with sprocketed film, unlike today's digital smorgasbord) and lined up the picture with the moment that Kilgore orders the PsyWarOp to begin, pushed the 'play' button on my KEM editing machine, and hoped for the best. As I watched the film, the images jostled together with this new music in their familiar way. The ectopic rhythms were holding, and perhaps this delicate organ transplant was going to work after all. I smiled along with Kilgore as the trumpets blared. Then suddenly . . .

I stopped the machine, disoriented. There was something wrong with the image. There had always been a peculiarly wonderful strength and acidity to the blue of the

What actors lose in apparent prominence during shooting, they gain in depth and in truth on the screen

ocean that had now disappeared. I asked my assistant, Steve Semel, if he had changed the print for some reason. No, he hadn't.

The problem turned out to be a classic case of synesthesia. At that point in the film – about 35 seconds from the start of the music – there is a series of shots featuring portraits of soldiers going into battle, the first one a down-angle shot of a rocket with the hand of marine caressing its breast, so to speak. In each of the shots the ocean is spread widely in the background.

Although Leinsdorf's performance of the 'Valkyries' was rhythmically in sync with Solti's, at this moment Leinsdorf had emphasized the strings in his orchestral balance, whereas at that same point Solti had chosen to emphasize the brasses, which – I realized now only in retrospect – were responsible for synergizing that wonderful acid blue of the ocean. In Leinsdorf's recording, the strings were soft and pillowy, and as a result the blue looked dead: The chemistry of the image and sound worked against each other to the detriment of both. I turned off the machine and abandoned the search, letting Francis know the sad result. He understood the problem.

As it turned out, Francis was able to get past Decca's gatekeepers and talk to Solti himself. Solti responded as one maestro to another, sympathizing with the artistic predicament Francis faced: 'Of course, dear boy, why didn't you talk to me in the first place?'

The permission to use Solti's 'Valkyries' came through so late in the process, however, that we were not able to get hold of the magnetic masters in time, and what you hear in the film is a tape transfer from the LP disk, spread in re-recording to six channels of sound as if it were coming from those military speaker-horns that you see sticking out of the side of the helicopters. But perhaps this contingency lends a certain serendipitous truth to the scene, since Kilgore himself, now revealed to be a connoisseur of music, would doubtless have also copied his tape directly, as we did, from Solti's Decca disk.

'Valkyries' attack on the village: https://vimeo.com/984419013 (QR code on left)

27: THE GODDESS ECHO

An Experiment in Acoustics

Echo by Alexandre Cabanel, 1874

Echo was a beautiful mountain nymph in the Greek pantheon who fell in love with Narcissus (the god who loved only his own reflection). She had previously been cursed by Zeus's wife, Hera, who correctly suspected Echo of distracting her with trivial gossip while Zeus was out having amorous adventures with other women.

Hera's curse removed Echo's own voice and condemned her to repeat only the words spoken by others. Rejected by Narcissus, Echo became a melancholy recluse, and to this day she haunts the hollow places of the Earth where, if you call out, her only answer will be a forlorn repetition of your own words.

It is a sad story, but for those of us who work with sound, Echo is one of our great loves, and I hope our devotion offers her some consolation.

So imagine our disappointment when we installed American Zoetrope's mixing equipment in 1969, and instead of an actual echo chamber, where we could worship that elusive nymph, all we could afford was a small AKG device equipped with a variable-tension spring. The AKG sounded metallic no matter what adjustment was made. Rather than Echo's 'hollow place', it was the twanging lair of Momus, a scurrilous god expelled in disgrace from Mount Olympus and relegated to mockery and satire.[1] The spring might be useful for comedy effects, but nothing else.

Today all sound designers have access to a vast array of digital echo and reverb plug-ins of great power and subtlety. But this was fifty-six years ago, long before the slightest glimmer of digital sound. At the time, I was simply grateful that I could get my hands on professional mixing equipment of any kind.

We call it an *echo chamber*, but really it should be a *reverb chamber*. An *echo* is, like the nymph's voice, a single, delayed repetition of a sound as it bounces off a distant surface and returns as a *clear repeat* of the original, the length of that delay depending on the distance to the reflecting surface. Sound travels roughly 1,100 feet per second, so a surface 550 feet distant would yield an echo with approximately a one-second delay.[2]

Reverb, on the other hand, is a complex tangle of many slightly different echoes all happening more or less at the same time. It is a diffusion of sounds rather than the return of a discrete, single sound. Singing in the shower is a classic example, your voice bouncing off the tile and glass in a complex, resonant pattern, smoothing out any slight irregularities of pitch.

Why would we be interested in the diffusion that takes place with reverb? Firstly, because it is the equivalent in sound of *sfumato*, Leonardo da Vinci's technique of shading tones and colours gradually into one another, producing softened outlines (see his *Mona Lisa*) which allowed his forms to merge with their surroundings.[3] Leonardo believed that the technique helped the artist to achieve a sense of depth, realism and atmospheric quality, capturing the subtleties and nuances of the natural world.

Secondly, because reverb helps to anchor the sound in the space we see on screen. Location recordists go to considerable lengths to get the optimal balance of direct sound to reverb in the dialogue of actors: too much reverb makes it hard to understand

1. Momus would later lend his name to 'mime' and 'mummery'.
2. In 1954, aged eleven, I went to a screening of Luis Buñuel's *Robinson Crusoe* at the Loews Olympia, one of the theatres in my neighbourhood of Manhattan. I remember being impressed by the use of echo in that film: Crusoe, lonely on his desert island, shouting out Psalm 23 and hearing his voice return to him two seconds later. It was the first time I became aware of echo being used in a film, but I had no idea how it was achieved. You can hear this moment on YouTube: https://youtu.be/b-YoBU0XT90?t=2418.
3. *Sfumato* on Wikipedia: https://en.wikipedia.org/wiki/Sfumato.

The point is not to direct someone else, but to direct yourself

the words; too little, and the actors' voices will seem to float, disconnected from the space they inhabit.

Thirdly, the sound of real life, if you pay attention to it, is full of different kinds of reverberation, and the ability to control reverb precisely makes the sound of cinema more realistic and colorful. And this was our goal for the soundtracks of the films I was mixing at the time: *The Rain People, THX 1138, The Godfather, American Graffiti, The Conversation, The Godfather: Part II* and *Apocalypse Now.*

Whether it is an actual physical reverb/echo chamber, a spring under tension or a digital algorithm, the procedure when using one of these reverb devices is the same: a certain proportion of the original sound on one fader is sent to the device in question. In the case of a physical echo chamber, the sound plays through a loudspeaker in the chamber, where there is also a microphone picking up all of the chamber's reverb. This reverbed signal returns to an adjacent fader on the mixing desk, and you then determine, by ear, what the correct balance should be between the original direct sound and the new reverb, adjusting the faders accordingly.

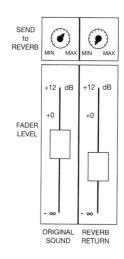

Controlling the amount of reverb also allows us to create a separate sonic foreground and background. A sound with added reverb diffusion will appear to be 'in the background' of the foreground sounds, which are crisp, with no (or minimal) diffusion. This ability to layer sound was particularly useful when films were monophonic, as was the case with our soundtrack mix of the original 1973 *American Graffiti.* In that movie, we were able to keep the dialogue in the foreground, where every consonant was articulated, in contrast to the diffuse reverbed music tracks in the background, where there were no 'hard edges' to attract and distract the ear from the dialogue (audio *sfumato*). When the scene's dialogue was finished, we would bring the music back into the sharply defined foreground by progressively increasing the volume of the original sound and reducing the amount of reverb.

This technique is the equivalent of manipulating depth of field in portrait photography, whereby the face is sharply defined and the background is thrown out of focus. As a result, the eye 'knows' instantly what it should be looking at. If the background were also in focus, there would be confusion. As it is for the eye, so it is for the ear.

Robert Bresson

Once we manage to get control of reverb diffusion, then it can be played with creatively, adding it where it may not be expected (a realistic scene that we may want to appear dream-like) or, vice versa, removing it where it might be expected (close-up dialogue when the actors are distant in a huge interior space). Or progressively adding or removing it during a scene. You can think of reverb as a perfume that gives the audience a feeling for a certain space, and this perfume can be intense (listen to David Lynch's *Eraserhead*) or it can lend just a slight suggestion.

Twenty years or so ago, I went to a performance of an adaptation of Jean Cocteau's play *Les Parents terribles* at the Marin Theatre Company, where the actors were equipped with microphones (well hidden). At the beginning of the play the sound designer gave their voices an acoustic reverb that sounded completely natural, to the extent that I (having never been to that theatre before) assumed it was how the theatre naturally sounded. Then, in the aftermath of the attempted suicide of one of the characters, the reverb was removed, and I suddenly realised how close the actors actually were to the audience, creating an instant intimacy that was appropriate to the new scene. It was achieved entirely through a shift in sound quality but had the emotional intensity of cutting to a close-up.

The possibilities are endless, and endlessly fascinating.

Every interior space has its own characteristic reverb, just as each musical instrument has its own characteristic tone – and for very much the same reasons. A living room sounds different to a bedroom, which sounds different to a bathroom. This has to do with the size of the room, the materials from which it is constructed and whatever rugs and furniture there may be. The size determines how quickly sound will bounce off the walls, ceilings and floors: the larger the room, the longer until the initial reflection. The material on the walls, ceilings and floors will determine how persistent the reverberation will be: how long it will continue to bounce back and forth – its decay time, in technical terms. The softer and more absorbent the materials, the shorter the decay time.

Sound in a bathroom has a quick initial bounce because bathrooms are generally small, and the hard surfaces (tile and glass) will sustain that reverberation, the sound bouncing from wall to wall, for a longer time. Sound in a living room will have a longer interval before the initial reflection because living rooms are generally large, while the softer materials (rugs, curtains, sofas, etc.) will dampen reverberation quickly. You can get the flavour of a room's reverberation – its perfume, so to speak – simply by clapping your hands and listening to the reverb of that clap.

Knowledge is a magic well: the more you draw from it, the more there is to draw

So, in perfuming an original sound with its reverb, there are three factors to consider:

(1) The size of the space, which will determine the interval to the initial reflection.
(2) The absorptive quality of the space's surfaces, which will determine the duration of the reverb (its decay time).
(3) The amount of reverb blended with the original sound.

Maximum reverb intensity would be achieved by having (1) a large space; (2) hard, reflective surfaces; and (3) a high proportion of reverb added to the original sound. It's also worth observing, as sound designer Randy Thom has pointed out, that there is a spiritual dimension to reverb, reinforced by . . .

> . . . the fact that almost all places of worship have been, since antiquity, highly reverberant spaces, giving everything that happened within, especially the leader's voice, a quality that the congregants were unlikely to hear anywhere else – except perhaps in a large cave, which could be where our fascination with reverb began.
>
> Lots of people in the modern world love to blow their car horns inside tunnels. Why? Do we somehow get affirmation of our existence via the feedback of reverb?[4]

But knowing these theories and fascinating speculations about reverb didn't solve our practical problems in 1969. There we were, stuck with that frustrating spring reverb device whose capabilities were so narrow – a simple *boing* sound – that they almost made us feel sorry for it.

A Solution . . .?

To modify the cliché: frustration is the mother of invention.

First, we temporarily repurposed one of the Zoetrope editing rooms and put it to use as a *room-iser* chamber. We equipped it with a loudspeaker and a microphone, so that any sound we wired from the mixing board to the room would be broadcast through the speaker and acquire a 'room' reverb, which was particularly useful for helping to match post-sync dialogue (ADR) to location dialogue. That reverbed sound would then return via the microphone to the mixing board, where it could be tweaked further by adjusting its level and equalisation, making it brighter and louder, if necessary, or softer and duller, if that was called for. But as good as it was,

---

4. Sound designer Randy Thom, personal correspondence with me, June 2023.

Karl von Frisch (adapted by Walter Murch)

it was just a room. We also needed bigger spaces, so if they wouldn't come to us, we decided to go to them.

This was the origin of what I called our *worldising* adventures: going out into the world, on location with two tape machines, one of them with a tape of the sounds that needed authentic echo/reverb and another ready to record that reverb. Our haunts were subway tunnels, the central hall of San Francisco's Natural History Museum at 2 a.m., high-school gymnasiums, suburban backyards, hilly landscapes, the tunnels of the Bay Area Rapid Transit system, and so on. Those 'reverb recordings' would be transferred to 35 mm magnetic sound film and edited in sync with the 35 mm magnetic of the original sound, and then, in the final mix, we would determine the correct balance between the two.

This worldising technique was used on all the films I mixed from the late 1960s until the mid-1990s, from *The Rain People* to *The English Patient*. Was this logistically involved and time-consuming? Absolutely. Was it worth it? Absolutely. Remember the limitations of analogue technologies during those years. And if authentic reverb was your goal, there was no alternative. Starting in the 1990s, digital reverb hardware devices (Eventide, etc.) and then software plug-ins began to appear, and the need for worldising began to recede. Nonetheless, it is still an excellent method of creating authentic reverb, if you have the time and the inclination.

The Experiment (First Conducted in 1970)

Inevitably, the logistics of worldising were challenging. It was not easy to secure permission to get into the main hall of the San Francisco Natural History Museum at 2 a.m. on short notice.

So, one evening, needing a reverb for a large space but unable to get access to one, I wondered if there was some method of increasing the reverb time of an ordinary living room by reducing the speed of the tape recording. If it took, say, 40 ms (one frame at 24 frames per second) for a sound to bounce back from a living-room wall 20 feet away, wouldn't 40 ms become 80 by slowing the tape by half? And then wouldn't slowing it by another half yield 160 ms, as if it were bouncing back from a 'virtual wall' 80 feet distant?

Slowing the tape down by that much, of course, would pitch the original sound down by many octaves, which was not what I wanted. *But . . .* if I sped it up by four times, played that version through a speaker in a living room and then recorded that sound on another recorder . . . Hmm . . . then . . .

That little gleam of light caught in the actor's eye gives meaning to his whole character

. . . then all I would have to do is slow this new recording down by the same amount that I had sped up the original and it might return to its original pitch. *But now with a much longer reverb time attached to it.*

In those days, the standard speeds of tape recorders were, in inches per second (ips), 3.75, 7.5 and 15 – the latter being four times faster than 3.75. The Nagra recorders I was working with had those three speeds, so I performed my experiment, taking my voice, recorded at 3.75 ips, and playing it back in the living room at 15 ips. Now it was just a little chirpy sound, and part of me thought, 'What am I doing? This is ridiculous.' But I recorded it anyway on a second Nagra at 15 ips.[5] Then I took that recording and slowed it down to 3.75 ips.

I was amazed. It sounded like it had been recorded in a cathedral. My voice had been restored to its correct pitch, but the *temporal length* of the reverb had been stretched to four times what it was in the living room. I had in effect quadrupled the linear dimensions of the space (height, width, length), making it sixty-four times (4 × 4 × 4) the volume of the living room. If I could get hold of a 30 ips recorder, I could make that space 512 times (8 × 8 × 8) the volume of the living room: 2,359,296 cubic feet, 70 per cent larger than the nave in Westminster Abbey!

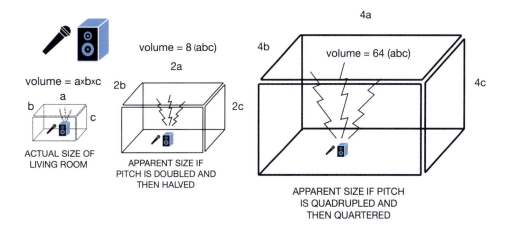

Did I do this? Of course I did . . . it was intoxicating. And it remains so to this day![6]

And you can perform this experiment yourself, using the twenty-first century's digital audio tools that, thankfully, we have at our disposal now.

5. By way of comparison, 35 mm film travels at 18 ips.

6. See and hear this effect at https://vimeo.com/837554429 (QR code on right).

Robert Bresson

Try This at Home!

Equipment you will need:

(1) A digital editing program (Apple's iMovie or Final Cut Pro, Pro Tools, Avid Media Composer, Adobe Premiere Pro, DaVinci Resolve, Hindenburg, etc.).

(2) A way of playing audio from your editing program through a fairly large speaker (not just the speakers on a laptop).

(3) A digital audio recorder. It can be very simple; a dictation-type recorder is fine.

Step by step:

(1) Record your voice (or any other sound).

(2) Import that soundtrack from the recorder into a timeline in your editing program.

(3) Using the appropriate command, *shrink* the audio clip of that sound to a fraction of its original length. If you shrink it by three-quarters, its pitch will rise four octaves higher.

(4) Play that sound through a loudspeaker in your living room and record it, placing your microphone as far as possible from the speaker.

(5) Import this new soundtrack into your editing program.

(6) Now, with the command you used previously, *stretch* the new audio clip to the length of the original recording. This will drop the pitch of the new recording and its reverb back to that of the original sound, but it will also increase the length of the reverberant field. If you have stretched the clip by a factor of four, the apparent volume of the acoustic space will be sixty-four times the size of your living room.

(7) Be amazed!

Religion is a way of making use of ideas whose time has not yet come

1.

WAVEFORMS OF ORIGINAL RECORDING

2.

ORIGINAL COMPRESSED 4 TIMES

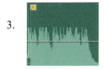

3.

REVERB RECORDED

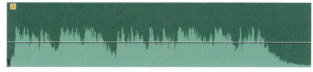

4.

REVERB EXPANDED 4 TIMES

(1) A picture of the original waveform. Notice the deep 'canyons' of silence between the individual words.

(2) That same waveform, but time-compressed (sped up) by a factor of four. The voice in the recording would sound like a super-squeaky Mickey Mouse.

(3) That time-compressed waveform re-recorded in a living room, now capturing the reverb of the room. Notice how the 'canyons' have disappeared, filled in by the reverb.

(4) The re-recorded waveform, now time-expanded by a factor of four, restoring the voice to its original frequency but stretching the reverb by that same multiple, lowering its pitch to match the voice and expanding the apparent size of the living room to that of a cathedral.

Attributed to Fred Hoyle

28: 'THAT'S MY SQUEAK!'

The First Sampling Lawsuit and a Long-Delayed Apology

It was a matter of pride and prudence in 1969 that I used hardly any library sound effects for *The Rain People* or *THX 1138*. Every sound effect in those films was a custom-recorded original, with two exceptions. There were a couple of reasons for this, the main one being that I was not yet a member of a film union and was terrified of opening a Pandora's box by going to the Warner Bros. sound library with a grocery list of sounds.

Another reason was the new KEM mixing machinery that Francis Coppola had just brought over from Germany to Zoetrope in San Francisco. It was state-of-the-art at the time, and it seemed disrespectful to use 'canned' sound effects on something so beautiful and modern. And, fifty years ago, most of those Hollywood library sound effects *were* canned: many of them had been recorded on optical cameras back in the 1930s and '40s, then transferred to magnetic film in the '50s, and their sell-by date was long past.

On *THX*, there was the additional requirement for the soundtrack to assist in creating the ambience of a strange underground future, which naturally required never-heard-before sounds. George Lucas and I made two exceptions, for film-historical reasons: a *fist punch* and a *thunder clap*, classic sounds that were surreptitiously smuggled out of the Warner Bros. library.

I also created a full temporary music score for *THX*, using 33⅓ rpm LPs of classical music as sources, transferring the recordings to quarter-inch tape and then slowing them down and/or running them backwards and layering them to obscure their origins, before transferring them to 35 mm magnetic film. When we engaged Lalo Schifrin to write the music – George had loved his theme for the *Mission: Impossible* TV series – he said that he loved our temp score and suggested simply transcribing everything I had done into musical notation and then recording it with a live orchestra. It was a surreal experience when we went to this session, knowing that the piece of music being played forwards in time by a symphony orchestra was actually Pergolesi's Stabat Mater slowed down by half and run backwards.

Probably intoxicated by this success, I decided to 'temp-track' a sound from *Variations for a Door and a Sigh* (1963), a composition by Pierre Henry. My intention was a tip-of-the-hat tribute to Henry, whose *First Panorama of Musique Concrète* I had heard in 1957, aged fourteen, and which had made a huge impression upon me – arguably setting in motion the decisions that would lead me to a career in film. The sound I had in mind was a door squeak from 'Gymnastique', Henry's sixteenth variation,[1] and my intention was to loop it and put it in the background of a scene between THX (Robert Duvall) and SRT (Don Pedro Colley), after they had become trapped in a so-called 'Reproduction Centre' stocked with jars of half-developed human embryos. A rotating device of some kind, unexplained, is seen in close-up during the scene, and I thought the looped squeak could seem to originate from it.

My audio and editing equipment was installed in a spare room (dubbed the 'Theatre of Noise') in George Lucas's rented house in Mill Valley: a 33⅓ rpm stereo turntable, a Nagra tape recorder with Sennheiser 404 microphone, a portable Omega 35 mm magnetic film recorder and a Moviola editing machine. This set-up allowed me to transfer Henry's squeaks from his record to 35 mm magnetic film on the Omega, select the 'best' squeak out of the many and then splice it into a six-second loop. I then ran that loop on the Moviola, sending the audio back to the Omega, where I recorded a continuous three-minute stretch of magnetic film, which became one of the background sounds for the 'Reproduction Centre' scene. Was this a tribute or was it theft? Aged twenty-six, I didn't think about the implications. I certainly didn't ask for permission.

THX was mixed and finished in January 1971 and released commercially in the US on 11 March to modest reviews and even more modest business. It was then shown (out of competition) during Directors' Fortnight at the Cannes Film Festival in May of that year. George, his wife Marcia, Aggie and I went to this screening – a heady experience for all of us first-time visitors to Cannes. The film was well received, and the soundtrack was particularly noted. To celebrate, Aggie and I ambitiously set off to bicycle the 280 miles up the Rhône Valley to Lyon.

We got as far as Avignon (130 miles) and hopped on a train, exhausted from battling against the mistral winds. On our return to England, where we had left our three-year-old son Walter with his grandmother, we learned that *THX* had secured European distribution. Hearing this was a lovely moment, capping two years of work

---

1. *Gymnastiques* can be heard at https://www.youtube.com/watch?v=aHgKZgNtsEk (QR code on right). The squeak that I selected occurs from 26.42 to 26.48. More information about Pierre Henry at: https://blog.wfmu.org/freeform/2011/12/on-pierre-henrys-84th-birthday-it-only-seemed-fitting-to-put-on-some-of-his-records-and-celebrate-the-man-who-most-revolutio.html.

Jean Cocteau

on *THX*, first writing the script with George and then designing, recording, editing and mixing the sound.

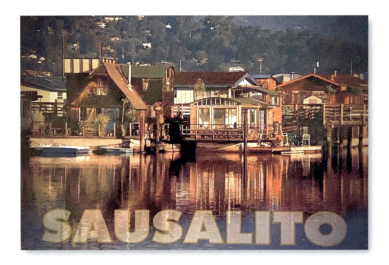

In summer 1971 Aggie and I, both twenty-eight, were living on our houseboat in Sausalito, just across the Golden Gate Bridge from San Francisco.[2] Aggie was working as a Lamaze childbirth instructor, and Francis had hired me to do the sound effects supervision and mix of *The Godfather*, which had finished shooting and was being edited by Bill Reynolds and Peter Zinner at Zoetrope's Folsom Street offices, to which I commuted on my BMW R50 motorcycle. *Godfather* would be mixed at Zoetrope later that year on our gleaming KEM equipment. Or so we hoped.

But, in September, Francis showed me a letter he had just received from Warner Bros, telling him that they had been sued by Philips Records for copyright infringement. It concerned a *grincement* – a squeak – used in *THX 1138*. *THX* had been playing for a couple of months at a theatre in Paris, and Pierre Henry had gone to see the film; someone had told him it had an interesting soundtrack. About halfway through the screening, however, Henry suddenly heard one of his musical 'children': the squeak from 'Gymnastique', kidnapped by one Walter Murch and forced to squeak repeatedly in the background of a scene. The composer complained to his record label that an outrage had been committed by an American film studio, and international legal gears were engaged: Philips Records vs Warner Bros.

As I read the letter I flushed with intense embarrassment. Yes, I was the guilty

2. Our houseboat (with the pointed roof) is on the left in the postcard above.

_____

A technician knows how to avoid accidents, an artist knows how to use them

party. Something that I thought might not be noticed at all or, alternatively, might bring a smile to my hero Pierre Henry's face was now the subject of a lawsuit between giant corporations. I could be labelled an audio sneak thief, outcast and unemployable. My burgeoning career would be over.

I confessed to Francis what I had done and why. He took it with greater equanimity than I had anticipated and responded to Warner's legal department, detailing the facts of the matter. I continued to work on the sound effects for *Godfather*, despite the imagined scarlet letter on my forehead. Weeks went by. I felt like a dead man walking.

When the response from Warner's legal team finally arrived, it was anticlimactic, certainly compared to my imagined fears. The suit had been dismissed because the loop of sound was so short. And furthermore, because of that repetitive looping, the sound had been, in legal terms, *transformed* from its original source.

I wouldn't be surprised if this was the first sampling lawsuit in history, a precursor to the legal decisions concerning the fair use of media in the 1980s and '90s. Sampling would proliferate in those decades, thanks to the arrival of digital technology, which allowed a sound to be snatched and looped with just a few mouse clicks. But, back in 1970, the technology was so cumbersome that few bothered with it. Except me.

My career survived this close brush with ignominy. But, to my shame, I never wrote to Monsieur Henry apologising for my theft of his squeak and the reasons for doing so. Unfortunately, he died in 2017, aged eighty-nine. I therefore dedicate this chapter to the memory of Pierre Henry, with a profuse posthumous apology and great appreciation.

Pierre Henry (1927–2017) at work

Randy Thom

29: MANHATTAN SYMPHONY

Redeem Us from the Chaos of Shapeless Noise

Manhattan: a remorseless grid of right-angled streets, rescued by a jumble sale of architectural styles thrown together by history and human willpower. Paris (or Prague or perhaps any other European city): an ancient broken crockery of random-angled streets, redeemed by architecture of great stylistic and cultural coherence.

Confronted with the classically American paradox of Manhattan's simultaneous rigidity and exuberance, the refined European sensibility discovers that . . .

> . . . beauty in the European sense has a premeditated quality. There was always an aesthetic intention and a long-range plan. That's what enabled Western man to spend decades building a Gothic cathedral or a Renaissance piazza. The beauty of New York rests on a completely different base. It's unintentional. It arose independent of human design, like a stalagmitic cavern. Forms which are in themselves quite ugly turn up fortuitously, without design, in such incredible surroundings that they sparkle with a sudden wondrous poetry.
>
> – Franz, from *The Unbearable Lightness of Being* by Milan Kundera

Growing up on Riverside Drive in Manhattan, I never questioned the stalagmites in which we lived. Our gang would roam across the rooftops, scrambling up and down the two or three storeys' difference in height between adjacent apartment buildings, all erected in the 1890s in different vernaculars of the Italianate Palazzo style. The cornices that capped taller buildings would jut perplexedly into thin air, while those of shorter ones would nuzzle up awkwardly against the window of someone's bathroom.

It was only years later, when I was living in Rome's Prati district – Rome's version of Manhattan's Upper West Side – that I saw cornices as they were intended: a continuous horizontal line atop several buildings, gathering them together in a single conceptual frame. When I returned to my old neighbourhood in Manhattan, it now looked wondrously stalagmitic.

Sometime after the success of his film *Blow-Up* (1966), the Italian director Michelangelo Antonioni visited Manhattan, thinking of setting his next project in New York. Confused and overwhelmed by the city's visual foreignness, he decided to listen rather than to look, to eavesdrop on the city's mutterings as it emerged into

---

Nothing is durable but what is caught up in rhythms. Bend context to form and sense to rhythms

consciousness from the previous night's sleep. Sitting in his room on the thirty-fourth floor of the Sherry-Netherland Hotel, Antonioni kept a journal of everything he heard between six and nine in the morning. Perhaps some inadvertent sound might provide the key to unlock the mysteries of this foreign world.

The first step towards understanding sound design is to learn to *listen* and become sensitive to the various layers of sound to which we are normally oblivious, and then make analogies: 'This sound is like that . . .'; 'That sound is like this . . .' And analogies are the next step towards the storytelling power of sound itself, as Béla Balázs wrote in his astonishingly perceptive 1930 essay on the potential of sound film:

> The sounds of our day-to-day life we hitherto perceived merely as a confused noise, as a formless mass of din, rather as an unmusical person may listen to a symphony; at best he may be able to distinguish the leading melody, the rest will fuse into a chaotic clamour.
>
> The sound film will teach us to analyze even chaotic noise with our ear and read the score of life's symphony. Our ear will hear the different voices in the general babble and distinguish their character as manifestations of individual life. It is an old maxim that art saves us from chaos. The arts differ from each other in the specific kind of chaos which they fight against. The vocation of the sound film is to redeem us from the chaos of shapeless noise by accepting it as expression, as significance, as meaning.
>
> – Béla Balázs, *The Spirit of Film* (1930)

Antonioni's New York film was never made, but the pages from his bed-side vigil survive and were published at a conference on film sound that I attended in Copenhagen in 1980. The organisers – composer Hans-Erik Philip and film-maker Vibeke Gad – have generously allowed me to reprint their translation of Antonioni's poetic soundscape of a long-vanished Manhattan, filtered through the sensibility of his acutely sensitive cinematic ear.

———————

New York from the 34th Floor Overlooking Central Park

The soundtrack for a film set in New York, circa 1970, by Michelangelo Antonioni

There is a constant murmur, hollow and deep: the traffic. And another sound, inter-mittent: the wind. It comes in gusts, and in the pauses I can hear it sighing, far away,

Robert Bresson

against other skyscrapers. Here, on the thirty-fourth floor, I can feel the vibration of every gust. It gives me a strange feeling as if, for a few moments, my brain freezes. A faint, short-lived siren comes and goes. The noise of two car horns. A rumble that approaches but is impatiently eclipsed by a sudden buffet of the wind. A tram car.

It is six o'clock in the morning. Another rumble blends with the first, then drowns it. A faint explosion, far, far away. The wind returns, rising from nothing, spreading, it seems to stretch in the still air, then dies. The hint of a tram, faint, remote. It is not a tram, after all, but another kind of sound I cannot recognize. A truck. A second one, accelerating. Two or three passing cars. The roads in Central Park twist and turn. A line of cars. Their exhausts a kind of organ playing a masterpiece.

A moment of absolute silence, eerie.

A huge truck passes. It seems so close that I feel I am on the second floor. But that sound, too, quickly fades. A squeal. A ship's siren, prolonged and melancholy. The wind has dropped. The siren again. The murmur of traffic beneath it. A bell, off key. From a country church. But perhaps it is the clang of iron and not a bell. It comes again. And still once more. A car engine races, furiously, with a sudden spurt of the accelerator. In a momentary hush, the siren again, far away. The metallic echo rises. A terribly noisy truck seems just outside the window. But it is an aircraft. All the sounds increase: car horns, the siren, trucks; and then they recede, gradually. But no, another rumble, another siren. Irritating, persistent, right across the horizon.

Quarter past six: the same series of sound in waves, each in turn, clearly defined. Brief intervals. A murmur continues. And, always, the siren. An abrupt car horn, very far away. Another muffled beneath it. Somewhere on a distant street, a car, very fast, perhaps European. The wind swirls against the wall outside. A single gust, immediately swallowed by a raucous truck and then a newer vehicle, steadier. The throb of the two different motors driving off, merging into one. But it is not a truck, it's an aircraft. No. Not an aircraft. A noise that rises and becomes deafening, only to fade unidentified. All that remains, obsessive, is the siren. And someone whistling (how can that be possible?) instantly drowned by an angry car horn.

Sounds of metal sheets thrown together. Clear and sharp, a winch. The sound of cogs. But it cannot be a winch, and this constant whine is not the siren. More sheets, more metallic. Then a hollow boom, barely audible, but lingering in the air. A faint hum suddenly stops. A car passes, another, then a third, fading, fading, fading. They mingle with other cars, other sounds. An aircraft seems to take off from right beside the building. And as suddenly as it appeared, it is gone. The very beautiful roar of a

The truth is rarely pure and never simple

car, completely appropriate for this moment. It speeds past and dies, distinct, satisfying. Two tones shimmer. A gust of wind.

Half past six: more gusts. A furious flurry of wind between the skyscrapers slides away and buffets across the park. Only a car horn interrupts, like a slap in the face. The wind drops. A peal of bells in the stillness. And always, the siren. A tone higher now. It wasn't bells. It is my Italian ear that hears it that way. The sheets of metal. A short clatter, like gunfire. A train passes, perhaps the elevated. A peal, prolonged, and then the siren, abrupt. Gone.

The sounds change in a moment, they arise and die again immediately. The hum reasserts itself, advancing like a camouflaged army, approaches, closes in, on the alert, ready to take over completely. It is very close. One can distinguish the wind, the cars, the aircraft, a clash of iron, and the siren. They advance, determined, against this skyscraper hotel. In the forefront, the sound of iron, but the aircraft closes in and takes over alone. And now – nothing. The struggle is over. A small revolution quelled by the authority of a car horn. The banging of wood. A pause. More banging. They must be moving tables. It sounds like a machine gun that is falling apart. The cars are under fire. They have to pull up and stop. Another siren, more real. The rumble of wheels, but it is not a car. It is the wind, which has risen again. Strong, but not strong enough to cover the aircraft.

Cars. A roar, as if from a cannon, echoless. Here and there, metallic sounds of various intensities. A roar of wind. The roar of a truck. The roar of the elevated railway. Two thuds in different tones. The noise grows and then stops suddenly, as if cut off by the thuds as they start again. Other sounds are born, clear yet unrecognizable. A long, startling car horn. A sound that does not die, that will never die. I cannot hear it any longer, but it has left me with this certainty. But the sound of the siren is dying. A gust of wind pushes it away, but a truck rises. Then diminishes in turn and mingles with the wind. Some kind of bell.

A voice is heard. The first voice.

Seven o'clock: A blast from the siren, as if to remind me of its existence. Now imperceptible, yet insistent. The squeal of tires. A thundering, a rumble, somewhere underground.

Half-past eight: And now the Sun has risen, but the sounds are still the same. With one exception. Drills. Nasty. Destroying a building. They are far away but occasionally, because of the wind, they are perfectly distinct. The other sounds remain. A whistle, shrill, anxious. It repeats – urgently. A noisy engine, I don't know what kind. And

Oscar Wilde

loud, yet distant, the drills. The only change is that it has all become stronger with the daylight. The wind, the cars, the siren. Only the car horns are less strident, more discreet, a reflection on the drivers who obey New York's traffic laws: they must use their horns only when absolutely necessary. They cannot afford the fines, and so they obey the law, which seems a little Teutonic. I imagine the drivers in this bewildering noise, melted together, inside their creeping cars: noise that hasn't the courage to explode, but hovers in the air, in the spring-like, clear, clean winter air.

At first glance: 'That's it!' or 'That's not it!' . . . Reasoning comes afterwards

30: THE SLOPE

Coming Back to Earth After a Long Project

As I bring this book to a close, four years of writing are coming to an end and a new phase of something*, as yet unknown, is about to begin. So I end with a chapter about transitions, which are a constant refrain in film-making because of the cyclical nature of our periodic cinematic voyages to previously unknown planets.*

I have been fired twice, both times by Disney.

The first occasion was after five weeks of directing *Return to Oz*, in March 1984. My crime was falling behind schedule, with dailies that did not please the Disney executives. I was rehired six days later, thanks to the personal interventions of George Lucas and Francis Coppola.[1]

The second firing was thirty years later, after fifteen months of editing Brad Bird's *Tomorrowland*. This time there was no intervention, and I stayed fired. Disney's ultimatum to Brad had been either move the editing from Marin County to Burbank, or replace me with an editor of their choosing. Brad chose the second option. I was out, Craig Wood was in, and the film was completed in Marin.

Being fired is an extreme example – very extreme! – of what happens at the end of every film, when you are suddenly thrust outside the 'pod-bay door' of the pressurised spaceship you have been travelling in and find yourself 'outside', where the gravitational forces and the atmospheric pressure are wildly different. There is relief, of course (even, in a weird way, when you are fired), but there is also the shock recoil from the daily work of making coherence out of all the disparate parts of the film. Now that you are back in normal life, you experience a kind of whiplash – the opposite of coherence – where everything seems to be flying off in all directions.

This whiplash phenomenon, or one very much like it, revealed itself to my astonished eyes on my first Macy's Thanksgiving Day Parade in 1947, when I was four. I left my mother and followed a slightly more experienced six-year-old friend through the tangle of adult legs and squatted down on the kerb of Central Park West to get a glorious kid's-eye view of the hour-long parade as it headed south to Herald Square.

---

1. Details can be found in the chapters on *Return to Oz* in the subsequent volume of this book.

Robert Bresson

Gigantic balloons of comic-book characters, marching bands, scantily clad drum majorettes (despite the November chill), caparisoned horses, more balloons, clowns throwing candy at us: what more could a four-year-old want?

But the best surprise was to come at the end, after the last giant balloon gave way to sweepers shovelling horse droppings into wheeled metal canisters.

'Look down!' my friend told me. 'The road is melting!'

And sure enough, the black asphalt of Central Park West had turned to molasses and was oozing to the left, northwards. If it was heading left, it must be coming from the right. But when I looked to the right, it was also oozing to the left.

'Touch it!' my friend said.

I hesitated but reached out and touched the asphalt. I couldn't feel any movement, but now my *hand* was oozing to the left. I yanked it away – no damage. The asphalt continued to ooze for a few more seconds and then slowly settled down to its normal asphaltic self.

It was too much for my four-year-old brain, but I repeated the trick at the next year's parade, and the next. It became a Macy's parade ritual, and I taught younger kids to do it, just as I had been. Who knows, it may be an ongoing ritual more than seventy-five years later.

I eventually figured out that it was an illusion caused by watching the parade go by, left to right, left to right, for an hour. When I looked down at the road afterwards, the asphalt would appear to be moving in the opposite direction, right to left. The scientific name for this is the *waterfall effect*, and you can see many examples of it

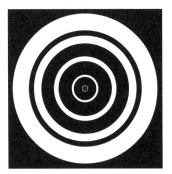

on the internet.[2] I have created my own version – converging circles rather than waterfalls or Macy's parades – which you can see on Vimeo (https://vimeo.com/561283539; QR code on left). If you stare fixedly for fifteen seconds at the circles converging 'inwards' to their central point, then when they dissolve to a still image, you should see this image bulging 'outwards' in the opposite direction to the circles. The illusion will last for around ten or fifteen seconds.

2. The Waterfall Illusion (aka Motion Aftereffect) at Michael Bach's excellent illusion website: https://michaelbach.de/ot/mot-adapt/index.html.

The key idea is that we humans – and probably other animals as well – will nor-malise an abnormal situation if it is sustained for long enough. A classic example is the pair of prismatic glasses that flip our vision upside down. After a couple of uncomfortable days, the visual cortex normalises the inversion and turns it right side up, the way it 'should' be. When we eventually take the glasses off, how-ever, the whiplash effect will show the world upside down again, even though we are now looking at it directly. A couple of days later, the world will flip back to normal again.[3]

The effect has philosophical implications in areas other than visual illusions, from Stockholm syndrome, whereby hostages come to sympathise with their captors, to religious or political cults, to domestic abuse, and so on . . .

. . . to film editing! Confinement in an enclosed space for long periods of time, under varying degrees of pressure, hearing the same things repeated over and over . . . This textbook definition of brainwashing pretty accurately describes the daily experience of a film editor. In a mostly benign sense, we become willing Stockholm syndrome hostages to every film we work on.

> My film, its face halfway between a brother and a blackmailer.
>
> – Federico Fellini

Those converging concentric circles are a schematic metaphor for our work as film editors, which is to take the rushes and slice them up into fragments, then fit those fragments into a compressed, coherent whole. And when that coherence-making suddenly stops, the whiplash waterfall effect occurs: the normal everyday world, rela-tively static compared to our just-completed work experience, will appear to bulge outwards, in a sense, becoming scattered, chaotic and confusing.

Of course, this situation is not unique to film editors. Anyone who is suddenly released from intense, prolonged situations will react similarly: the end of a marriage, sailors returning to shore after a long time at sea, the PTSD of soldiers like Captain Willard, returning from tours of duty:

> When I was home after my first tour, it was worse. I'd wake up and there'd be nothing . . . I hardly said a word to my wife until I said yes to a divorce. When

---

3. Of course, as is the case with every camera lens, the image of the world that reaches our retinas has already been turned upside down by the geometry of the lenses in our eyes, and it is our brain that flips it right side up. The prismatic glasses are simply telling our brain it doesn't need to do any flipping.

Jean-Luc Godard (paraphrased)

I was here, I wanted to be there. When I was there, all I could think of was
getting back into the jungle.

> – Captain Willard, in the opening scenes of *Apocalypse Now*

I don't want to compare the nightmares of soldiers returning from combat to the
relatively serene lives of film editors . . . although John Milius, author of *Apocalypse
Now*, has made the case for it:

Hollywood! The only thing I can think of remotely as horrible as war is
Hollywood. There are stories, things I have seen in that town that, believe me, I
would never tell anyone.[4]

At the end of a film, you have objectively achieved the goal that you set out to achieve
a year earlier: to scale a cinematic mountain. You imagined that at the summit there
would be a flat spot where you could sit down and admire the view.

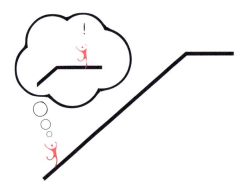

But on the way up the mountain a funny thing happens: the slope begins to flatten
out, to 'normalise' itself through the effect of long working hours and sheer repetition,
like the effect of those inverted glasses. But, in this case, an upwards slope gets, emotionally speaking, normalised into a horizontal one:

4. Lawrence Weschler, 'Valkyries Over Iraq', *Harper's Magazine*, November 2005, p. 73: https://
lawrenceweschler.com/static/images/uploads/Weschler_Valkyries_Harpers.pdf.

The bad: simplicity as starting point, sought too soon. The good: simplicity as end
product, recompense for years of effort

But then, when you reach the summit, you encounter the problem: by having flattened the slope, you have turned the formerly flat summit into a slope tilting in the opposite direction from the one you thought you were climbing!

Intellectually, you know that the summit is flat – you know that you are finished with the film – but, emotionally, the achievement is 'tilted' and disorienting. If you happen to screen your film during this state, you will see its faults, magnified. You will think everyone else can see them as well. Bad reviews (the inevitable bad reviews) will validate this feeling. What was it all about, anyway? Why did you give so much of yourself? You will never work again. What's happening to the world? Etc., etc.[5]

This parlous state of mind is similar to seasickness, when your senses send contradictory messages: your eyes are telling you one thing, and your sense of balance (via the Eustachian tubes in your ears) another. This conflict between brain and body suggests that something is wrong. Perhaps you have been poisoned! So you throw up, or attempt to. But since you haven't been poisoned, your body keeps trying to find and get rid of that 'poison'. People who have never been seasick before and suffer a bad case of it sometimes have to be prevented from committing suicide.

Knowing that the cause of seasickness is a sensory illusion doesn't make you feel any better, physically, but it does give you hope. And the same can be said of the period after the completion of a film. As disorienting as it may be, it is also an illusion that will pass with time, just like the asphalt of the Macy's parade. And then you will be ready to take on the next project!

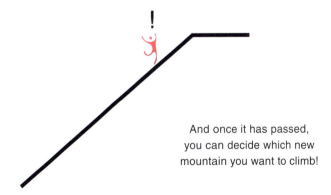

And once it has passed, you can decide which new mountain you want to climb!

5. An animated version of the little red film-maker's dilemma can be seen on Vimeo: https://vimeo. com/561449798 (QR code on right).

Robert Bresson

Just like seasickness, some lucky people don't suffer from this problem. For those who do, like me, the main corrective is to take it easy and avoid making any momentous decisions. It usually dissipates after two to four weeks – though sometimes much longer. I wish our teachers at film school had warned us about this phenomenon, but they didn't. Those of you who have been working in film for a while will know it from personal experience.

In a previous chapter, I mentioned language translation as a therapeutic activity that helps to get me through this awkward stage. I am privileged to be able to read French and Italian, and this led to the discovery that my mental activity during literary translation is very similar to the mental state I am in when editing film. So taking up this kind of 'embroidery' work at the end of a film, rather than going cold turkey, is my way of slowly withdrawing from the drug that film-making undoubtedly is. So, if you happen to have a second language, try putting it to use. If not, search out an activity that can be a substitute. Fred Zinnemann would go mountain climbing in the Alps, putting himself in life-or-death situations where he had to concentrate on his immediate predicament and yet think two or three steps ahead – and *not* think about the film. My son-in-law Peter, a camera operator, will go for thousand-mile motorcycle rides for similar reasons.

And there is always work around the house! Many of the chores that you were too busy to attend to during the film can now be tackled with a willing heart. Just before Christmas 2002, at the end of production on *Cold Mountain*, I was flying back to London from Romania with Anthony Minghella and his wife, Carolyn.

'What are you going to do over Christmas?' Anthony asked me.

'Change a light bulb or two.'

'Is that all?'

'It's a beginning,' I replied. 'It's the first step on the path back to normal life, and it will show Aggie that I can. And that I care.'

Film will only become an art when its materials are as inexpensive as pencil and paper

THE SHAPE OF THINGS TO COME

As noted in the Introduction, the present volume represents about 40 per cent of the manuscript of *Suddenly Something Clicked*. The topics that have been covered here – film editing and sound design – are without question vitally important. I hope to have shown that film editing (*montage!*) transformed motion photography into cinema, and that every film thrives with a well-recorded and inventively designed, composed and mixed soundtrack. But the truly fundamental components of a film's artistic and commercial success are the script, the casting and the vision of the director. These three pillars are the focus of the remaining 60 per cent of the manuscript, which is complete and awaiting the right moment for publication.

In that material, the reader will also find an analysis of the preview process (a kind of cinematic wind tunnel); a surprising discovery about the golden ratio's prevalence in cinematic framing, possibly explained by the anatomy of the human face; and chapters about my experiences of writing and directing *Return to Oz* (1985), how and why I was fired and then rehired a week later, and reflections on the director–producer dynamic. Additionally, there are a few chapters of a more personal nature: how Aggie and I met sixty-one years ago, before cinema had appeared on our radar, and how we have balanced intense film work with family life and (reasonably!) good physical and mental health. I also attempt to answer some fundamental questions: Why do we make films? What is cinema when pushed to its fullest potential?

In these early decades of the twenty-first century, the world appears to be hurtling towards multiple interlocked crises – environmental, cultural, religious, economic and political. Can cinema help resolve these existential challenges? The final sections of the subsequent volume will conclude with reasons to hope the answer is yes, exploring cinema's unparalleled ability to influence human behaviour and perception. But we must also acknowledge that cinema's potency, already being supercharged by artificial intelligence, can also be used to divide humanity and intensify these self-created problems.

Naturally, I hope for resolution, not division.

May it be so.

Jean Cocteau

ACKNOWLEDGEMENTS

Walter Donohue, editorial director at Faber & Faber, launched this book with a casual remark, when he enquired whether I would be interested in expanding on my previous book about cinema, *In the Blink of an Eye*, published thirty years previously. I started writing in the spring of 2020, and as the first draft of each chapter rolled out of the ink-jet printer, I would give it to my wife Aggie and then pass it along to Walter, for their essential evaluation and encouragement, and to keep my flights of fancy and digressions in check.

As the book began to take shape, I enlisted friends and family as additional readers and commenters. Each has been a collaborator in the creation of this book, and I kept their voices and presences in mind as the material continued to evolve. I would like to thank them all: (in alphabetical order) Taghi Amirani, Carroll Ballard, Hal Barwood, Howard Berry, Larry Blake, Dave Cerf, Doug Claybourne, Francis Coppola, Robert Dalva, Mark Danner, Caleb Deschanel, Dan Farrell, Andrew Feenberg, Anne-Marie Feenberg, Lisa Fruchtman, Vibeke Gad, Werner Herzog, Ana Hidalgo, Paul Hirsch, Pat Jackson, Steven Johnson, Nick Lane, Mark Levinson, George Lucas, Beatrice Murch, Walter Slater Murch, Hans-Erik Philip, Matthew Robbins, Tom Scott, Tim Smith, Rebecca Solnit, Randy Thom, Steve Wax, Lawrence Weschler and Tim Zinnemann.

I extend my particular thanks to copy-editor Ian Bahrami and project manager Kate Ward for their invaluable oversight, combining meticulous attention to detail with broad thematic insight. My gratitude also goes to Amanda Russell for her assistance in securing image rights; Rachel Thorne for securing textural rights; Dr Tim Smith, Professor of Cognitive Data Science, University of the Arts, London, for his insights on 'Saccadic Cinema'; Dr Nick Lane of University College London and Dr Denis Noble of Oxford University for their inspiration and guidance regarding 'The Spliceosome' and 'Saccadic Cinema'; Ali Musa for his friendship, technical expertise and assistance with all things computer-related; and the Internet Archive for its matchless resources.

One of the key revelations in writing *Suddenly Something Clicked* was discovering the extensive, detailed links between neurology, biology and the creative processes of film-making. In closing, I would like to share a mini-bibliography of six inspirational books that have greatly influenced my thinking:

Insight and Outlook (Macmillan, 1949) and *The Ghost in the Machine* (Hutchinson & Co., 1967) by Arthur Koestler

The Music of Life: Biology Beyond Genes by Denis Noble (Oxford University Press, 2006)

Subliminal: How Your Unconscious Rules Your Behavior by Leonard Mlodinow (Pantheon, 2012)

The Brain: The Story of You by David Eagleman (Canongate, 2015)

The Vital Question: Energy, Evolution, and the Origin of Complex Life by Nick Lane (Profile Books, 2015)

PHOTO CREDITS

All photos and illustrations courtesy of Walter Murch, with the following exceptions: pp. 1, 63, 95, 96, 102, 163, Wikimedia Commons, CC-BY-SA-3.0-RS; p. 11, Warner Bros. Discovery. All rights reserved; p. 13, courtesy of Goldberg Brothers Inc.; p. 20, Gjon Mili/The LIFE Picture Collection/Shutterstock; p. 35, Henk Bogaard/iStock; p. 58, Universal Studios/CC-BY-SA-3.0-RS; p. 65, public domain; pp. 65, 66, 75, 79, 115, 122, 123, 125, 127, 131, 134, 136, 137, 140, 221, 223, 290, 292–4, 296, 300, 302, 324–6 © American Zoetrope; p. 72 © 1962, renewed 1990 Columbia Pictures Industries, Inc. All rights reserved. Courtesy of Columbia Pictures; p. 81, photo by Zakaria Usluer (@zku); p. 82, generic clip art; p. 95, CC-BY-SA-3.0-RS; p. 95 © Andrew Dunn, 5 November 2004; http://www.andrewdunnphoto.com/; p. 97 © Association Marcel Duchamp/ADAGP, Paris and DACS, London 2024; p. 97, Wiki Art, CC-BY-SA-3.0-RS; pp. 100–1 © George V. Kelvin; p. 137 © Paramount Pictures. All rights reserved; p. 144 © USC School of Cinematic Arts; p. 145, *American Cinematographer*; p. 147, Courtesy of STUDIOCANAL; p. 151, public domain; p. 152, licensed by Warner Bros. Discovery. All rights reserved; p. 153, National Archives photo no. 80-G-311235; p. 154, Science Museum Group Collection © the Board of Trustees of the Science Museum; p. 155, Jonathan Silent Film Collection, MPE-003-02/Chapman University; pp. i, 156, 158–62, 173 © The Curators! Ltd; p. 163 © National Portrait Gallery, London; p. 164, Pictorial Press Ltd/Alamy; p. 168 © Greg Williams Photography; p. 177, copyright unknown; p. 188, public domain; p. 204 © 1947 Charles Addams, renewed 1973. With permission of Tee and Charles Addams foundation; p. 208, Defence Divas; p. 220, copyright unknown; pp. 230, 232, courtesy of Richard Beggs; pp. 240, 251 © Roz Chast; p. 252 © Joe Josephs; pp. 254, 257 © Circle Films/Coen Brothers; p. 260, CC SA 1.0 (http://creativecommons.org/licenses/sa/1.0/) via Wikimedia Commons; p. 265, Blondie © 2024 King Features Syndicate, Inc. World rights reserved; p. 270, public domain; pp. 275–6 © Stephen Johnson; p. 279, public domain; pp. 286, 319 © Paramount Pictures. All rights reserved; p. 288 *FotoRomanze*; p. 289, *American Cinematographer*; p. 295, AEA Ribbonmics; p. 299, Neumann GmbH; p. 327, The Metropolitan Museum of Art. Gift of Mary Phelps Smith, in memory of her husband, Howard Caswell Smith, 1965. Accession Number: 65.258.1; p. 338 © Bernard Andre; p. 339, Stephane De Sakutin/AFP via Getty Images; p. 346, Disney's Enterprises Inc.

TEXT CREDITS

We are grateful to the following for permission to reproduce copyright material: Dedication from *Pale Fire* by Vladimir Nabokov, copyright © Vladimir Nabokov, 1962. Renewed 1990 by the Estate of Vladimir Nabokov. Reproduced by permission of the Wylie Agency (UK) Limited and Vintage Books, an imprint of the Knopf Doubleday Publishing Group, a division of Penguin Random House LLC. All rights reserved; Quote from *The Big Brass Ring* by Orson Welles, 1987. Reproduced Courtesy of the Orson Welles Estate through Reeder Brand Management; Excerpt from *The Ghost in the Machine* by Arthur Koestler reprinted by permission of Peters Fraser & Dunlop (www.petersfraserdunlop.com) on behalf of the Estate of Arthur Koestler; Excerpt from *The River War* by Winston Churchill, Longmans, 1899, copyright © Winston S. Churchill / Portland Churchill Ltd. Reproduced with permission of Curtis Brown, London on behalf of Portland Churchill Ltd.

Extracts from *Notes on the Cinematograph*, NYRB, 2016 (*Notes sur le Cinematographe* by Robert Bresson, Gallimard, 1975). Reproduced by kind permission of Mme Bresson for the Estate of the author; and NYRB.

Extracts from *La Belle et la Bête: journal d'un Film* by Jean Cocteau, Éditions du Rocher, 1946. Translated by Walter Murch. Copyright © Éditions du Rocher, 1958; © Éditions du Rocher, 2003, pour la présente édition et la présente préface. Remerciements au Comité Jean Cocteau.

INDEX

Index compiled by Walter Murch